Jens Happe

**Predicting Software Performance in Symmetric
Multi-core and Multiprocessor Environments**

The Karlsruhe Series on Software Design and Quality

Volume 3

Chair Software Design and Quality
Faculty of Computer Science
Universität Karlsruhe (TH)

and

Software Engineering Division
Research Center for Information Technology (FZI), Karlsruhe

Editor: Prof. Dr. Ralf Reussner

Predicting Software Performance in Symmetric Multi-core and Multiprocessor Environments

by
Jens Happe

universitätsverlag karlsruhe

Dissertation, University of Oldenburg,
Department of Computer Science, 2008

Impressum

Universitätsverlag Karlsruhe
c/o Universitätsbibliothek
Straße am Forum 2
D-76131 Karlsruhe
www.uvka.de

Universitätsverlag Karlsruhe 2009
Print on Demand

ISSN: 1867-0067
ISBN: 978-3-86644-381-5

Contents

1. Introduction

Nowadays multi-core processor systems are becoming ubiquitous in the desktop market and in common server systems [Cre05]. Most of the main processor vendors, such as Intel and AMD, are adapting their product lines to the new technology. To exploit the available processor cores, software developers must design and implement applications with a high degree of concurrency. While the development of such applications is error prone and time consuming [Lee06], the possible benefit in software performance may be limited due to software bottlenecks or inherently sequential parts of the application (Amdahl's Law [Rod85]). Software architects and developers are thus confronted with the question of when the additional effort for introducing concurrency into their application pays off.

Performance predictions can support software architects in answering such questions early in the design phase. Predicted performance metrics like response time, throughput, and resource utilisation help to plan hard- and software capacities as well as to avoid design faults. Due to the counter-intuitive behaviour of concurrent software systems, such estimates are essential for their development [GPB+06]. Using performance prediction methods, software architects and developers can create software systems that confidently fulfil their performance requirements, such as being highly scalable and being able to serve several thousands of users simultaneously. In a business case for a medium sized project, Williams and Smith [WS03] estimate the possible financial benefit of software performance prediction to be several million US-dollars.

However, in order to be meaningful, prediction methods have to consider the influence of the underlying middleware, the operating system, and hardware on performance [LFG05, DPE04, Apa]. Especially for highly concurrent systems, like typical enterprise applications, the operating system and middleware have a major impact on performance (see, for example [CMZ02]). Some researchers even consider them to be the determining factors for the performance of enterprise applications (e.g., [LFG05, DPE04]). The influence of the infrastructure as well as the mutual dependencies between hardware, operating system, middleware, and software application pose new challenges for software performance prediction.

In this thesis, we address the problem of software performance prediction in symmetric multiprocessing (SMP) environments. Our work is focussed on the influence of **General**

Purpose Operating Systems (GPOS) schedulers, as implemented in the Windows and Linux operating system series. To capture their influence for software performance prediction, we introduce a performance modelling framework for GPOS schedulers. Furthermore, we propose a performance modelling technique for message-oriented middleware in order to analyse concurrent software systems in distributed settings. We validated the proposed models and methods by conducting a number of case studies based on real world applications. In the considered scenarios, our method increases the prediction accuracy up to several orders of magnitude compared to common methods.

1.1. Research Questions

In the scope of this thesis, we address research questions from the areas of (i) operating system schedulers, (ii) message-oriented middleware, and (iii) performance modelling methods which are discussed in the following.

General Purpose Operating System Schedulers   Operating system schedulers manage the concurrent access of multiple tasks to limited resources (e.g., processors). The chosen scheduling algorithm can affect software performance by several orders of magnitude [BSUK07]. In software performance engineering, common abstractions for operating system schedulers are processor sharing and first-come, first-served scheduling. However, real operating system schedulers are much more complex. They have to fulfil a broad range of different requirements for real-time, batch, and interactive systems.

When selecting tasks for execution, GPOS schedulers may take into account the previous behaviour of each task, e.g., the periods when it used different resources (e.g., network and hard drive). Other schedulers may prefer tasks which have just been granted access to some critical resource (e.g., protected by a semaphore). Such policies are meant to keep the overall utilisation of resources high while minimising response times [Tan01]. They lead to a strong mutual dependency between the behaviour of tasks and the GPOS scheduler which is usually not considered in performance prediction.

In multi-core and multiprocessor systems, schedulers must decide how the load is to be balanced among the available cores or processors. Balancing policies implemented in today's operating systems determine when load balancing is initiated, whether it dynamically intervenes with the system, and if it is adapted to different load conditions. During load balancing, schedulers have to identify processors that need to be balanced as well as tasks to be moved. In doing so, various constraints, such as processor and cache affinities of tasks, have to be considered.

Current operating systems employ a broad range of strategies for task scheduling and multiprocessor load balancing. For example, Windows keeps interference with the program execution as low as possible. By contrast, Linux constantly ensures a fair distribution of processing time among all competing tasks. Even though such behaviour is difficult to capture, performance prediction methods have to include its influences on software performance. Common scheduler abstractions can lead to prediction errors of several orders of magnitude for task response times and throughput (cf. Section 5.2). Therefore, modelling and prediction of GPOS schedulers require to answer the following questions:

1. What are the most relevant features of the behaviour of operating system schedulers with respect to software performance?

2. What are the important aspects for symmetric multiprocessing environments?

3. How can these aspects be identified?

4. How do task behaviour, scheduling policy, and workload influence software performance?

5. How can mutual influences task behaviour, scheduling policy, and workload on software performance be captured?

6. What level of abstraction of schedulers is adequate to provide good predictions?

7. What models and model solution techniques (analytical, simulation based, combined) are appropriate for modelling GPOS schedulers?

8. Is there a general method for modelling GPOS schedulers?

9. What prediction accuracy can be achieved using performance models for GPOS schedulers?

Message-oriented Middleware Enterprise applications mostly employ message-based communication (using, for example, Java Message Service, JMS [HBS+08, MHC02]) to process jobs asynchronously or to communicate in distributed systems. Hence, message passing is a major technology for implementing concurrent behaviour in enterprise applications. The performance of message passing depends on the vendor implementation and the execution environment. Furthermore, the usage of the message-oriented middleware (MOM) influences its resource demands. For example, the message size and the number of messages in a transaction significantly affect the delivery time of a message. Therefore, the following questions need to be answered before commencing performance model design:

1. How can message-oriented middleware be modelled independent of the vendor implementation?

2. What performance models are appropriate for MOM?

3. How can such performance models be integrated into existing software architecture models?

Derivation of Performance Models   The major challenge in the design of performance models for complex software systems is the *right level of abstraction*. Performance models need to include all relevant aspects of the system under study and, at the same time, provide an abstraction from its complexity in order to remain solvable. Hence, performance analysts are confronted with the question of what must be included into a performance model and what parts of the system under study can be simplified. Unfortunately, these questions cannot be answered from specifications, documentation, or source code, since, especially for concurrent systems, performance properties are often counter-intuitive even for experts [GPB⁺06]. In order to support performance analysts to find proper performance abstractions, we address the following questions in the scope of this thesis:

1. How can performance-relevant and -irrelevant features be distinguished?

2. How can degrees of freedom of the specification be fitted in?

3. How can performance models for accurate predictions be designed efficiently?

1.2. Existing Solutions

As discussed in the previous section, software architects and developers have to consider the influence of scheduling policies in order to accurately predict software performance. Several existing approaches address this problem. They (i) measure or model specific features of GPOS schedulers, simulate scheduling algorithms for (ii) high performance computing and (iii) real-time applications or stem from the area of (iv) queueing theory. In the following, we give a brief overview of the state-of-the-art for these areas.

Several *experimental evaluations* of the Linux scheduler [TCM06, KN07] give interesting insights into its interactivity and multiprocessor load-balancing properties. However, the results are not sufficient for the definition of scheduler performance models. Other authors use formal prediction methods (such as stochastic automata networks or continuous time Markov chains) to predict the influence of changes in the Linux scheduler on software performance (e.g., [CCF⁺06, CZS06, KGC⁺06]). The proposed performance models focus on one specific scheduler properties and, hence, employ strong simplifications. For this reason, the authors neglect most of the performance-relevant features of the Linux scheduler. Furthermore, they do not validate their predictions, i.e., they do not compare predictions with measurements.

In *high performance computing*, simulation models are used to evaluate the influence of different scheduling algorithms on the performance of highly concurrent applications [MEB88, LV90, GTU91, Maj92, AD96, RSSS98]. Interestingly, the authors come to different and often contradicting conclusions regarding the best and worst scheduling algorithms. Apart from different foci of the approaches, the varying assumptions of the simulation models are a major factor that leads to the diverging results. The considered scheduling policies are very specific to high performance computing and are usually not applied for enterprise applications.

Simulators for *real-time operating systems* are already widely used to assess the schedulability and timing behaviour of embedded software systems with soft and hard deadlines [SG06, MPC04, JLT85]. These simulators are very specific to the domain of real-time systems and reflect schedulers on a very detailed level. For example, the model includes the time for saving and restoring a task's context [MPC04]. While such aspects can be important for real-time systems, they are negligible for general-purpose operating systems. Furthermore, the scheduling algorithms which are modelled (e.g., round robin and earliest deadline first) as well as the performance metrics which are considered (e.g., the number of missed deadlines) are specific to real-time systems.

In *queueing theory* [Bos02], the implications of scheduling policies in single- and multi-server queueing systems are investigated from a more formal perspective (e.g., [BSUK07, SHB02, Oso05, HBOSWW05]). Several authors have demonstrated (and proven) that scheduling can have a major impact on software performance (e.g., [BSUK07, SHB02]). Furthermore, they have shown how load balancing (also called cycle stealing [Oso05]) and different routing policies for multi-server systems (e.g., [HBOSWW05]) influence mean response times. While these works give interesting insights into the nature of scheduling, they impose too strong abstractions for GPOS schedulers in most cases.

1.3. Contributions

In the scope of this work, we proposed a systematic method for the experiment-based derivation of performance models, conducted several experimental analyses of operating system schedulers, developed a performance modelling framework for GPOS schedulers, and designed a performance model for message-based communication. In the following, we discuss the contributions of this work in more detail.

A Method for the Experiment-Based Derivation of Performance Models Our novel method for the experiment-based derivation of performance models tightly couples performance model design with systematic experiments. The method is meant to identify features that are important for system performance and to quantify their effect. The modelling effort is focussed on the most crucial features and performance analysts are guided in finding appropriate performance abstractions. We extend the well known Goal-Question-Metrics approach [BCR94] for experiment design to fulfil the needs of software performance evaluation. For each experiment, performance analysts define specific questions about the performance properties of the system based on specification and documentation. The results of the experiments allow performance analysts to answer these questions as well as to fill in remaining degrees of freedom. With this information, they can design prediction models that capture the performance-relevant features of the system under study. Once a performance model is defined, its prediction accuracy is validated to ensure that the model is representative. In the scope of this thesis, we apply this method for the design of performance models of GPOS schedulers and of message-oriented middleware.

Experimental Analysis and Identification of Performance-relevant Features of Operating System Schedulers   In the scope of this thesis, we conducted a series of experiments to identify the performance-relevant features of GPOS schedulers. Each feature was evaluated extensively in order to quantify its effect on the performance of concurrently executing tasks. Furthermore, we classified the features considering the following dimensions: time sharing (e.g., priorities and timeslices); treatment of interactive and I/O-bound tasks; and different policies for multiprocessor load balancing. All features mentioned here exhibited significant influence on the performance of the considered experimental scenarios.

We structured the identified performance-relevant properties using feature diagrams and, additionally, used them for developing performance models of GPOS schedulers. The feature diagrams enable software architects to customise the performance model of GPOS schedulers to their execution environments.

Performance Modelling Framework for General Purpose Operating System Schedulers The main contribution of this thesis is a novel performance Model for general purpose Operating System Schedulers called MOSS. The model reflects the influence of time sharing, interactivity, and multiprocessor load balancing policies of GPOS schedulers on software performance. Software architects can provide their own configurations of the model based on feature diagrams [CE00] or choose among a set of standard configurations. MOSS supports the schedulers of the Linux 2.5 and 2.6 Kernel series (up to 2.6.22), Windows 2000, Windows XP, Windows Server 2003, and Windows Vista operating systems.

We use timed coloured Petri nets (CPNs) to model the behaviour of schedulers. The CPN models designed in the scope of this thesis can be customised using the configurations mentioned in the paragraph above. MOSS is structured hierarchically, so that different aspects of a scheduler can be modelled independently of one another. For performance evaluation, the CPNs are simulated in order to obtain the performance metrics of interest. For this purpose, existing simulation tools for CPNs can be used [JKW07]. Furthermore, as part part of this thesis, we implemented a discrete event simulation technique [LMV02, LB05] which is specialised for MOSS and was integrated with the Palladio Component Model (PCM [RBH+07, BKR08]). The PCM is an architectural modelling language that supports early design time performance predictions. The integration with the PCM hides the complexity of MOSS from software architects and performance analysts and enables them to consider realistic scheduling policies in their performance predictions without additional modelling effort.

MOSS was designed and validated applying the method for experiment-based model derivation introduced above. We conducted detailed experiments to identify the performance-relevant properties for each major scheduling feature (time sharing, interactivity, multiprocessor load balancing). We validated models iteratively to ensure a high prediction accuracy of MOSS.

Furthermore, we conducted a case study, demonstrating that MOSS can predict the influence of the Linux and Windows schedulers on software performance with an error less than 5% to 10% in most cases. Existing performance prediction techniques based on queueing models yield errors up to several orders of magnitude. The case study models a typical scenario for business intelligence reporting.

Performance Model for Message-based Communication Due to the importance of message-based communication for enterprise applications, we developed a performance model for message-oriented middleware (called messaging completion). The model is based on design patterns for message-based communication [HW03]. In combination with measurements, it allows a straightforward integration of enterprise messaging systems (like Java Message Service [MHC02]) into software performance models. To customise the model to new execution environments, software architects execute an automated test driver that collects the necessary performance data. A prediction model for a new execution environment is constructed by the injection of measurement results into the performance model.

Similarly to MOSS, we integrated the messaging completion with the PCM. Software architects can annotate connections between software components with configurations for messaging. The configuration reflects performance-relevant messaging patterns of the sender, receiver, and message channel, e.g., guaranteed delivery or transactional messages. A transformation generates the corresponding performance model. We defined the messaging completion in terms of the PCM, e.g., components, behavioural specifications of services, and connections.

To evaluate the prediction quality of the messaging completion, we conducted a case study using the SPECjms2007 Benchmark [SPE]. The benchmark models a typical supply chain management scenario of a supermarket. The scenario involves multiple parties, like supermarkets selling goods and headquarters responsible for administration and accounting. In the case study, we evaluated three design alternatives with varying pattern selections for message-based communication as well as with varying message sizes. The resulting predictions and measurements differ by less than 20%.

1.4. Overview

- **Chapter 2** describes the foundations necessary for this thesis. We introduce the basic terms and concepts of software performance engineering. We provide an overview of well established formal methods for performance prediction as well as of model-driven performance evaluation. A description of scheduling algorithms currently used in the operating systems Linux and Windows concludes the chapter.

- In **Chapter 3**, we introduce an iterative method for the experiment-based derivation of software performance models. We apply the method in Chapters 4, 5, and 6 to define customisable performance models of GPOS schedulers for single- and multiprocessor environments as well as for message-oriented middleware. The methodology provides a systematic approach to measurement, performance modelling and model evaluation. Additionally, Chapter 3 provides an overview of the hierarchical structure of MOSS. We demonstrate how different feature configurations can be realised in terms of CPNs and how MOSS is integrated with the Palladio Component Model. Finally, we summarise the performance-relevant features of GPOS schedulers that are evaluated in Chapters 4 and 5.

- In **Chapter 4**, we apply the method introduced in Chapter 3 to derive a performance model for GPOS schedulers in single processor systems. We systematically evaluate influences of different time sharing and interactivity policies on software performance. In addition to the extensive validation during model design, we evaluate the applicability and prediction accuracy of MOSS by means of a real world case study. The case study demonstrates that MOSS can increase prediction accuracy by several orders of magnitude.

- **Chapter 5** continues the evaluation and modelling of GPOS schedulers for symmetric multiprocessing environments. We evaluate the influence of different load balancing policies on software performance and include their performance-relevant behaviour into MOSS. Moreover, we extend the case study from Chapter 4 and demonstrate that the significant performance increase of multi-core processors for software performance can be accurately predicted by MOSS.

- In **Chapter 6**, we introduce a performance modelling technique for message-oriented middleware. The technique allows software architects to define relevant features of message-based communication. The available features were selected based on messaging patterns. Therefore, the technique is a general solution for a wide range of message-oriented middleware platforms. We validate the performance model by a comparison between measurements and predictions for the SPECjms2007 benchmark [SPE].

- In **Chapter 7**, we discuss the current state-of-the-art in software performance engineering with respect to modelling scheduling policies. The discussion includes work from the areas of queueing theory, operating systems research, real-time operating systems, and high performance computing. In addition, we summarise approaches that integrate details of the middleware platforms into performance prediction models.

- **Chapter 8** concludes this thesis. We summarise the most important scientific contributions of our work and discuss open questions. Finally, we discuss future directions of our research.

1.5. Executive Summary

Software performance engineering [Smi02] enables the reliable construction of software systems with high performance requirements. With today's rise of multi-core and multiprocessor systems, operating system schedulers can become a determining factor for software performance and, thus, must be considered in software performance prediction. In this thesis, we design and evaluate a performance model for **G**eneral **P**urpose **O**perating **S**ystems (GPOS) schedulers, such as implemented in the Windows and Linux operating system series.

In order to reach this aim, we propose a method that tightly couples systematic measurements with performance model design (Chapter 3). The method is inspired by the work of Jain [Jai91] and extends the Goal/Question/Metric approach of Basili, Caldiera, and Rombach [BCR94]. The tight coupling of measurements and performance model design is essential for the development of performance models of complex and highly concurrent systems, such as operating system schedulers and message-oriented middleware.

In Chapters 4 and 5, we apply the method to design a performance **M**odel for general purpose **O**perating **S**ystem **S**chedulers (MOSS). We describe a series of detailed performance evaluations of operating system schedulers. Based on the results, we construct a customisable performance model for operating system schedulers. Feature diagrams [CE00] enable the customisation of MOSS and specify its degrees of freedom. MOSS covers various features of run queues, of strategies to prefer I/O-bound and interactive tasks, and of static and dynamic multiprocessor load balancing. A case study demonstrates that MOSS can increase the prediction accuracy by several orders of magnitude.

In addition to MOSS, we develop a performance model for message-oriented middleware (Chapter 6) based on design patterns for message-based communication (called messaging completion). Messaging completions are an abstraction of details specific to vendor implementations. For this purpose, software architects inject measurements from the target platform into the messaging completion, adjusting the model to new execution environments. We use concepts and technologies of model-based (or model-driven) performance engineering [BMIS04] to hide the complexity of the messaging completion from software architects. In a case study based on the SPECjms2007 Benchmark [SPE], we predicted the influence of message-based communication with an error of less than 20%.

2. Foundations

In this chapter, we introduce the concepts and terms from the area of software performance engineering and operating system research relevant for this thesis. Section 2.1 describes the basic concepts of software performance engineering. It provides an overview of well-established prediction models and newly emerging approaches in model-driven performance engineering. In Section 2.2, we summarise the currently used scheduling policies in performance evaluation. Furthermore, we point out important aspects for the performance evaluation of scheduling policies. In Section 2.3, we describe the schedulers realised in today's operating systems: Windows XP, Windows Server 2003, Windows Vista, and Linux 2.5 – 2.6.22.

2.1. Software Performance Engineering

In 1980, Connie Smith introduced Software Performance Engineering (SPE) [Smi80] to provide a better integration of performance predictions in the software development process. Her approach was meant to enable performance evaluation of software systems on the basis of simple models during early development phases [Smi02, Smi90]. The predictions help software architects to identify and solve potential performance problems. For this purpose, she used well-established performance modelling techniques (Sections 2.1.1 and 2.1.2) and made them easily accessible for software architects and developers.

Later, model-based performance prediction approaches (Section 2.1.3) picked up SPE's core idea. They provide performance annotations for architecture description languages, such as UML [(OM04], to close the gap between performance models and domain-specific languages used by software architects and developers. The annotated software models are transformed to analytical models such as queueing networks, stochastic Petri nets, or stochastic process algebras.

In addition, newly emerging approaches exploit the capabilities of model-driven technologies to increase prediction accuracy. They inject low-level details of the target execution environment into high-level architecture models by means of so-called performance completions (Section 2.1.4). In the following, we give a brief overview of performance models, workload characterisation, model-driven performance engineering, and performance completions.

2.1.1. Performance Models

Numerous models for performance analysis emerged during the past decades (see [BH07] for an overview). In the following, we briefly discuss queueing network models, stochastic Petri nets, and stochastic process algebras.

Queueing network models are the central approach to performance evaluation [LZGS84, BGTdM98, RS95, DB78, Whi83, BCS07]. They provide a resource-centric view of the system under study. A system is modelled in terms of service centres (see Figure 2.1(a) and (b)) that embody a queue and one or multiple servers. Jobs (also called customers, users, or tasks) float through the system and request service from the service centre.

Jobs have to wait in the service centre's queue until the server is available. A server processes jobs according to some scheduling policy, e.g., first-come, first-served (cf. Section 2.2). Once the resource demand of a job has been processed, it leaves the service centre. Jobs can either circulate infinitely in the system (closed workload) or arrive at the system according to some arrival process and leave the system as soon as they finished processing (open workload).

Stochastic Petri Nets (SPN) [MBB$^+$89, CGL94, MBC$^+$95, BK96, ZFH01] and *Stochastic Process Algebras (SPA)* [Hil96, BBG97, HHK02, BDC02, BD04] provide a behaviour-centric view on the system under study. Both model the timing behaviour and interaction of multiple processes or tokens. Their expressiveness with respect to stochastic processes ranges from simple continuous-time Markov processes with exponentially distributed delays (e.g., [Hil96, HHK02]) to generalised semi-Markov processes with generally distributed delays (e.g., [BD04]). While the first can be solved analytically, the latter have to be simulated.

Queueing network models allow straightforward modelling of resources with different scheduling policies. However, the description of complex control flow, i.e., software behaviour, is challenging [Kou06]. For example, queueing networks cannot model the forking of new jobs or the synchronisation of multiple jobs in the system. By contrast, SPNs and SPAs can describe complex (software) behaviour but suffer from missing resource models.

Thus, several combined approaches have been proposed in literature (e.g., [Bau93, Fra99, KB06, Jen92]). These combined models integrate resource models from queueing theory with complex behavioural models. In this thesis, timed coloured Petri nets (Appendix B) are used to model the behaviour of general purpose operating system schedulers.

2.1.2. Open and Closed Workloads

For software performance evaluation, the workload of a system under study specifies the arrival of new jobs. In a closed system model, new job arrivals are only triggered by job completions followed by think time. By contrast, new jobs arrive independently of job completions in an open system model. In the scope of this thesis, the *workload type* refers to the available variants of workloads.

For open and closed systems, jobs request service from a particular service centre (queue and server) or system (one or more services centres). For a job t, the response time $RT(t)$ with mean $E[RT(t)]$ is the time from the moment the job submits a request until its request is processed, i.e., it leaves the service centre. Furthermore, the utilisation of a single server (denoted by u) is the fraction of time that the server is busy. In the following, we describe how requests are generated in closed and open systems.

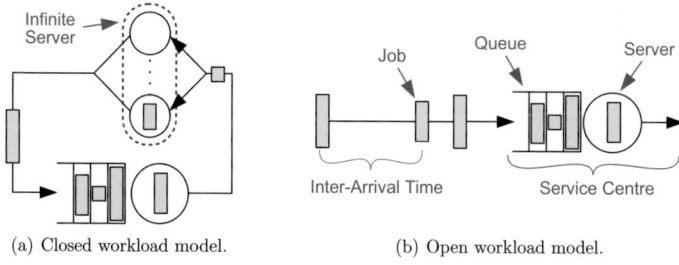

(a) Closed workload model.   (b) Open workload model.

Figure 2.1.: Open and closed workload models.

Closed Systems Figure 2.1(a) depicts a closed system, where a fixed number of jobs uses the system forever. This number of tasks is typically called the multiprogramming level (MPL) and denoted by N. Each of these N jobs submits a request, waits for the response, and, once the response is received, waits (or "thinks" in case of users or customers) for some amount of time. Thus, a new request is only triggered by the completion of a previous request.

In a closed system, N_{think} denotes the number of jobs, who are currently thinking, and N_{system} the number of users, who are either running or waiting in the queue. Since the the total number of jobs is N, both numbers must sum up to N, i.e., $N_{\text{think}} + N_{\text{system}} = N$. In closed systems, the utilisation of a single server is the product of its (mean) throughput (usually denoted by X) and the mean resource demand ($E[S]$).

Open System Figure 2.1(b) depicts an open system. Jobs arrive at the service centre as a constant stream with average arrival rate λ for a Poisson arrival process. Each job is assumed to submit one request to the system, wait to receive the response, and then leave the system. The number of tasks in the system (queued or running, N_{system}) may range from zero to infinity ($N_{system} \in \mathbb{N}$). Its mean value is denoted by $E[N_{system}]$. For an open system, the utilisation u is the product of the mean arrival rate of requests, λ, and the mean resource demand $E[S]$.

The above modelling formalisms and workload types allow well-trained performance analysts to model and evaluate software performance. For better integration of performance evaluation into the software development process, model-driven performance engineering employs transformations of architectural models to performance models. In the following section, we describe the envisioned approach in more detail.

2.1.3. Model-driven Performance Engineering

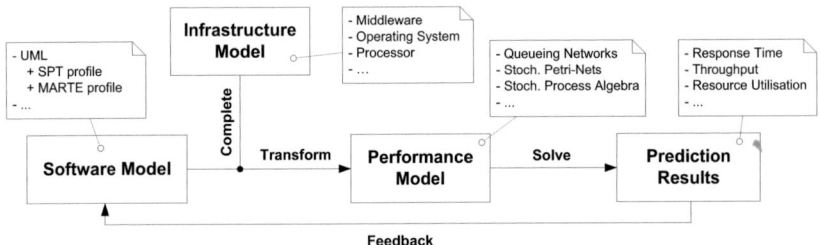

Figure 2.2.: Overview of the model-driven performance engineering process.

Model-driven performance prediction [BMIS04] allows software architects to design performance models in a language specific to their domain. This can be UML models [(OM07c] annotated with performance-relevant information (using for instance the UML-SPT profile [(OM05] or MARTE [(OM07b]) or architecture description languages specialised for performance evaluation like the Palladio Component Model (PCM, see Section A). To derive performance metrics from architectural models enriched with performance-relevant information, the software model is transformed into a performance model as shown in Figure 2.2. Typical models for performance analysis are queueing networks [LZGS84, Bos02], stochastic Petri nets [BK96, CGL94] or stochastic process algebras [HHK02, Hil96]. Thus, model-driven performance engineering closes the gap between formal performance model and architectural description languages. The solution of the performance models by analytical or simulation-based methods yields various performance metrics for the system under study, such as response times, throughput, and resource utilisation. Finally, the results are fed back into the software model. This enables software architects to interpret the effect of different design and allocation decisions on the system performance and plan capacities of the application's hard- and software environment. In practice, tools encapsulate the transformation and solution of the models and hide their complexity.

Often detailed information on the execution environment (middleware, database, operating system, processor architecture) is required to get meaningful predictions. Model-driven technologies can be exploited to add such performance-relevant information on the infrastructure to high-level architectural specifications.

2.1.4. Performance Completions

For performance predictions during early development phases, software architecture models have to be kept on a high level of abstraction since implementation details are not yet known. By contrast, detailed information on the system is necessary to determine the performance of the modelled architecture correctly [VDGD05, GMS06]. While such information is not available for the modelled system, the infrastructure of the system, e.g., the middleware platform used, might be known even during early development stages.

Based on technologies from model-driven software development [VS06], performance completions [WPS02, WW04] automatically refine design time software models with low-level infrastructure details to increase prediction accuracy. In the process shown in Figure 2.2, infrastructure models are used to complete the transformation from the software to the performance model. Performance completions hide the complexity of the underlying infrastructure from software architects, who only choose among the infrastructure's performance-relevant options.

For example, a transformation can insert the influence of Message-oriented Middleware (MOM) into the application's performance model (cf. Chapter 6). The result of the transformation reflects the influence of message-based communication (as implemented in the middleware) on the application's performance. Software architects can configure message channels in their software architecture based on a set of performance-relevant options.

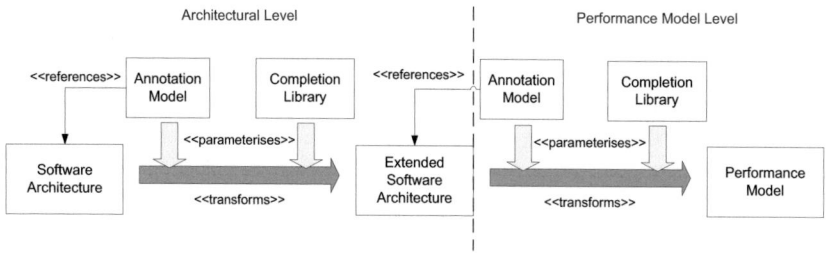

Figure 2.3.: Performance completions in the PCM.

Figure 2.3 shows how performance completions can be realised. Elements of a software architecture model, such as components or connectors, are referenced by elements of an *Annotation Model*. Annotations mark elements in the architecture model that are to be refined and provide configurations that are required. For example, if a connector is to be replaced by a remote procedure call, the annotation can provide information about the target infrastructure, e.g., SOAP or Java RMI. A transformation takes the necessary infrastructure models from a *Completion Library*, adjusts them according to the configuration, and generates a performance model that reflects the performance properties of the software model completed by the infrastructure model.

Performance completions can occur on the architectural level, on the performance model level, or on some intermediate level (e.g., if the transformation uses some intermediate performance model such as the core scenario model [PW02] or KLAPER [GMS05]). Which level is best suited for a specific performance completion depends on its modelling requirements (i.e., can it be expressed in terms of the architectural description language) as well as on the intended usage.

For example, the performance completion for GPOS schedulers proposed in this thesis (Chapter 3 to Chapter 5) is specified in terms of CPNs and, thus, placed on the performance model level. The advantage of an accurate prediction model that exploits the specific features of CPNs comes at the cost of the commitment to a single analysis formalism.

By contrast, the messaging completion (cf. Chapter 6) is defined on the architectural level. The result of the transformation is an expanded architectural model whose annotated elements have been replaced by detailed performance specifications. Keeping the model on the architectural level allows the use of all analytical and simulation-based solvers implemented for the architectural specification language. However, this approach has the drawback that the messaging completion cannot be used in other architectural languages.

In the next section, we describe how scheduling and routing policies are modelled in software performance prediction.

2.2. Scheduling in Software Performance Evaluation

In software performance evaluation, various policies have been introduced and studied to model the scheduling and routing in single-server systems and multi-server systems. In the following, we describe scheduling and routing policies available in approaches and tools that are commonly used in software performance evaluation, e.g., approaches from queueing theory [HSZT00, BCS06, BCS07, LZGS84, Bos02], Layered Queueing Networks (LQNs) [Fra99, FMW+07], Queueing Petri Nets (QPNs) [Bau93, KB06], and the standardised performance modelling notations

"UML Profile for Schedulability, Performance and Time" (UML-SPT) [(OM05] and "UML Profile for Modelling and Analysis of Real-Time and Embedded systems" (MARTE) [(OM07b].

2.2.1. Scheduling Policies

Scheduling policies determine the execution order of tasks at a single server. The policies assign the server to competing tasks in a non-preemptive or in a preemptive way. While non-preemptive policies wait until the currently running task is finished before they schedule a new task, pre-emptive policies can interrupt a currently running task to allocate the server to a new task. When a task is pre-empted, its already completed work can either be kept or neglected. This mainly depends on the analyses method that is used to solve the queueing network model. For example, mean value analysis is limited to FCFS, LCFS, PS, and IS scheduling [RL80]. The following list summarises scheduling policies used in queueing theory:

- **First Come, First Served (FCFS)** serves tasks in the order of their arrival.
- **Last Come, First Served (LCFS)** serves newly arriving tasks immediately, pre-empting the running task. The work of the interrupted task is not lost (preemptive-resume).
- **Round-Robin Scheduling (RR)** Round-Robin limits the time a task is allowed to use the processor to a fixed timeslice. When a task's timeslice expires, the scheduler preempts the task's execution and reinserts it at the end of the processor's queue.
- **Priority, Preemptive Resume (PPR)** Tasks with priorities higher than the task currently running on the server will preempt the running task. The work of the interrupted task is not lost. If multiple tasks with equal priorities exist, PPR schedules them with round-robin.
- **Head-of-Line priority (HoL)** Tasks with higher priorities will be served by the processor first. Tasks in the queue will not preempt a task running on the processor even though the running task may have a lower priority. HoL uses FCFS to schedule tasks of equal priority.
- **Processor Sharing (PS)** The processor runs all tasks "simultaneously". For performance predictions, PS approximates the behaviour of round-robin scheduling [LZGS84]. Processor sharing describes a round robin algorithm, whose time slice and context switch times converge to zero. So, if n tasks are in the system, each task receives approximately $1/n$ of the processor's power.
- **Random scheduling (Rand)** The processor selects a task at random. The execution of tasks is not preempted.

- **Infinite Server (IS)** An infinite number of servers is available so that each task can be processed within its service time.
- **Preemptive Expected Longest Job First (PELJF)** The task with the largest resource demand is given preemptive priority. PELJF is an example of a policy that performs badly and is included to understand the full range of possible response times.

2.2.2. Task Routing in Multi-Server Systems

If a task can be serviced by any of a set of servers, the system needs to decide on which of the servers the task is to be executed. Such situations are particularly important in symmetric multiprocessing environments where multiple processors can execute a single task. The distribution of tasks among the available processors strongly influences software performance. Determining the optimal assignment strategy for multiple service centres is one of today's major research questions in queueing theory [HBOSWW05]. In the following, we describe the central queue model and the immediate dispatching model as inherently different concepts for load distribution in multi-server systems. Furthermore, we summarise some of the most important routing strategies for the immediate dispatching model.

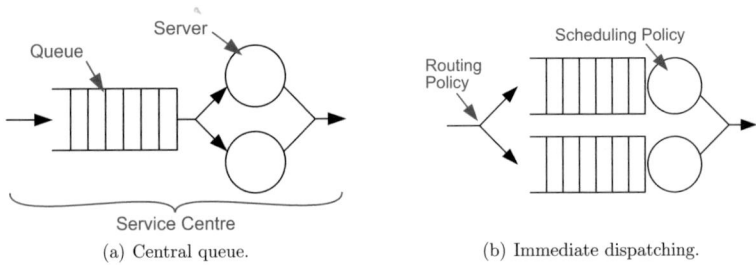

(a) Central queue.   (b) Immediate dispatching.

Figure 2.4.: Load distribution in multi-server queueing models.

Central Queue and Immediate Dispatching Figure 2.4 illustrates the central queue and immediate dispatching models for load distribution in multi-server systems. The central queue model (Figure 2.4(a)) holds all tasks that require service in a central queue. Whenever a server finishes a task, it fetches the first task waiting in the queue. The immediate dispatching model (Figure 2.4(b)) distributes tasks among the available servers at the moment of their arrival. Each server holds a separate queue of tasks and is scheduled according to the policy of the local server. A routing policy decides how the tasks are distributed among the available servers. The policy can distribute arriving tasks statically or dynamically. In the first case, the policy does not consider the state the system or properties of the task. In the second case, the policy may take into account the current state of the queues, the past performance of the server, or the resource demand of the task. The following list summarises typical routing policies for multi-server systems as depicted in Figure 2.4(b).

- **Round Robin (RR)** starts at the first service centre and assigns new tasks to successive service centres in a cyclic fashion.
- **Probabilistic Routing (PR)** assigns arriving tasks to a server with a specific probability (e.g., $1/k$ where k is the number of service centres).
- **Join Shortest Queue (JSQ)** assigns arriving tasks to the service centre with the least number of waiting tasks.
- **Join-Shortest-Response-Time (JSRT)** routes tasks to the service centre with the shortest average response time observed so far.
- **Join Least Utilisation (JLU)** assigns arriving tasks to the service centre with the smallest observed average utilisation.
- **Join Fastest Service (JFS)** routes tasks to the server with the shortest average service time for its class. This method is related to the dedicated policy [SHB04, HBCM99] which separates tasks according to their size.

2.2.3. The Performance Influence of Workload Types and Scheduling Policies

Open and closed workloads (cf. Section 2.1.2) are widely employed in all areas of software performance evaluation, e.g., performance benchmarking [SPE, ZBLG07], simulation-based evaluations [BCS07, Kou06], and analytical solution methods [BK92, DB78]. While widely used, the impact of different workload types on the resulting performance metrics has only been pointed out recently by Schroeder et al. [SWHB06].

In a series of implementation and simulation experiments, Schroeder et al. have observed vast differences in performance between open and closed workloads in real-world settings. Their results for both types of workload differ significantly even if resource utilisations and service time distributions are equal. For example, the mean response time for a system with an open workload (open system) can exceed that for a system with a closed workload (closed system) by several orders of magnitude. Furthermore, both workload types respond fundamentally differently to variance in service demands and of scheduling policies. For example, the variance in service demands (job sizes) has a huge impact on response times for open workloads but much less of an effect for closed workloads.

The Effect of Mean Response Times   *For a fixed utilisation of each server, mean response times are significantly lower in closed systems than in open systems* [SWHB06].
If the utilisation of a server becomes high, the response times for closed systems are orders of magnitude lower than those for open systems. Schatte [Sch84] has proven that, under FCFS, the open system will always serve as an upper bound for the response time of the closed system. The effect is a consequence of the fixed number of tasks, N, in closed systems, also called the multi-programming level (MPL). The MPL limits the queue length observed in closed systems even under very high load. By contrast, no such limit exists for an open system.

Approximating Open with Closed Systems   *As the MPL grows, closed systems become open, but convergence is slow for practical purposes* [SWHB06].
With an increasing MPL the mean response time of a closed system approaches the mean response time of a similar open system (equal resource demand and load). Schatte [Sch84] has proven that as N (i.e., the number of tasks) grows to infinity, a closed FCFS queue converges to an open FCFS queue. Even though the response times differ significantly for both systems, an open system can thus be a reasonable approximation for a closed system with a high MPL. However, the closed and open system models may still behave significantly differently if the service times are highly variable. Furthermore, convergence of closed systems is slow in practice [SWHB06].

Service Time Variability   *While variability has a large effect in open systems, the effect is much smaller in closed systems* [SWHB06].
The variability of service times directly affects the mean response time in open systems. For example, a service centre with an FCFS scheduling policy and high service time variability results in larger mean response times for short requests, which get stuck behind long requests.

   For closed systems, variability has comparatively little effect on mean response time. The number of requests in the system (N_{system}) is bounded by the overall number of tasks (N). Thus, only a limited number of short requests get stuck behind long requests. The influence of resource demand variability thereby depends on the MPL. With an increasing MPL, the influence of variability on mean response times can increase as well.

The Effect of Scheduling Policies   *While open systems benefit significantly from scheduling with respect to response time, closed systems improve much less. Scheduling only significantly improves response time in closed systems under very specific parameter settings: Moderate load (think times) and high MPL* [SWHB06].
The choice of scheduling policies yields fundamentally different behaviour of mean response time in the open and closed systems. In an open system, the discrepancy between the

response times of the scheduling policies grows with an increasing utilisation and eventually differs by orders of magnitude. By contrast, scheduling policies tend to perform similarly at both high and low resource utilisation in closed systems. Only for moderate resource utilisation, Schroeder et al. observed larger differences (factor of 2.5) between the considered policies (FCFS, PS, SRPT, PELJF).

The limited effects of scheduling in closed systems are a consequence of the closed feedback loop. Especially for closed systems with a think time of zero, the above scheduling policies yielded similar response times. Schroeder et al. explain this effect as follows.

For a closed system with N tasks, throughput X, and a mean response time $E[RT(t)]$ for task t, Little's Law states that $N = X\,E[RT(t)]$. Thus, the mean response time, $E[RT(t)]$, is constant if X and N are also constant across all work conserving scheduling policies. While performance analysts specify the number of tasks, N, the throughput is determined by the number of tasks, the think time, and the service time of the system. For systems with a think time of zero and a low service time variability, all work conserving scheduling policies will complete the same number of requests over a long period of time, since a new request is only created when a request is completed. The constant throughput across work conserving scheduling policies results in similar mean response times.

The argument above does not hold for open systems because for such systems Little's Law states that $E[N] = \lambda\,E[RT(u)]$ and $E[N]$ is not constant across scheduling policies. For closed systems, scheduling provides small improvement across all loads, but can only result in substantial improvement when load (think time) is moderate. In contrast, scheduling always provides substantial improvements for open systems.

However, the argument above does hold for the specific cases of closed workloads with low resource demand variability, a single class of tasks, and FCFS, PS, SRPT, or PELJF scheduling policies. If resource demand variability increases or different classes of tasks have to be considered, closed systems also yield larger differences in response times for different scheduling policies, as the results in Chapter 3 to Chapter 6 demonstrate.

Variability Reduction of Scheduling Policies *Scheduling can limit the effect of variability in both open and closed systems* [SWHB06].
For open and closed systems, scheduling policies such as PS and SRPT reduce the negative effect of increased variability on mean response times. For such policies, short requests cannot get stuck behind large ones. For PS, a request immediately gets a share of $1/N_{system}$'th of the server. For SRPT, a request receives service as soon as all shorter requests have been finished. The overall response time strongly benefits from the preference of short requests. However, the improvement is smaller for closed systems since variability has less of an effect in closed systems in general.

2.3. General Purpose Operating System Schedulers

In general purpose operating systems (GPOS), complex scheduling algorithms share the available processing power among competing tasks. These algorithms are based on multi-level feedback queues and exhibit a much higher complexity than the scheduling and routing policies currently used in software performance prediction. They prefer tasks according to resources used and past behaviour. Furthermore, they redistribute load dynamically during run time.

In this section, we describe fundamental scheduling concepts necessary to understand the influence of operating system schedulers on software performance. We introduce basic concepts and terminology (Section 2.3.1) including processes and threads (Section 2.3.2) and multilevel feedback queues (Section 2.3.3). Based on these concepts, we give a detailed description of the scheduling algorithms implemented in the operating system series of Windows (Section 2.3.4) and Linux (Section 2.3.5).

2.3.1. Basic Concepts and Terms

Schedulers manage the access of processes, threads, or tasks to limited resources. For example, if only one CPU is available, a scheduler chooses the process to run next according to a defined scheduling algorithm [Tan01, p.132]. In most cases, the GPOS schedulers use preemptive scheduling policies. They run a task for the maximum of some fixed time called *timeslice* (or quantum) and suspend it afterwards. To implement such a behaviour, a clock interrupt triggers the operating system scheduler, which can suspend the currently running task and assign another task to the resource. For the scope of this thesis, we define a scheduler as follows.

Definition 2.1 (Scheduler [SGG05]). If multiple processes share access to a limited resource, the scheduler selects one of the processes in the queue that are ready to be executed and allocates the resource to that process. The algorithm used is called *scheduling algorithm* or *scheduling policy*.

Scheduling policies mainly differ in their extra-functional properties, such as fairness and efficiency of the scheduler, and software performance. Thus, the choice of a good scheduling algorithm depends on the system's functional and performance requirements. The requirements can be classified into the three major categories of interactive, batch, and real-time systems.

Interactive Systems Interactive systems feature many interactions with users and with different resources in the systems. Therefore, interactive processes are I/O-bound, i.e., they wait long times for users or for I/O devices, followed by short bursts of computation. To keep response times short and all resources as busy as possible, schedulers have to process requests of interactive processes as quickly as possible [SGG05, Tan01]. Furthermore, the fulfilment of user expectations is especially important in interactive systems. The system must respond to requests quickly. For example, users are not meant to notice the time between a keystroke and the character appearing on the screen (key to glass response time). By contrast, processes with long execution times can be further deferred without beeing noticed by users. For example, longly running tasks, such as compiling a Kernel, can be delayed for a few seconds longer without being noticed. The different treatment of interactive and non-interactive processes requires the scheduler to automatically classify tasks according to their runtime behaviour.

Batch Systems   In batch systems, a series of jobs is processed without human interaction. The overall aims are to maximise the throughput of jobs while minimising turnaround times (i.e., the time necessary to process a job including its waiting time). To reach these conflicting goals, batch systems have to do as much real work (i.e., job processing) as possible. A reduction of the number of context switches may limit the scheduling overhead and grants more processing time to tasks. However, a high throughput can only be achieved if all resources are kept busy. To do so, multiple jobs have to be executed in parallel, leading to additional context switches.

Real-Time Systems   Real-time systems can be considered as mission critical in a given context. For example, the control system of a car's air bag has to react within a given time interval to protect passengers in case of an accident. Thus, the total correctness of real-time systems not only depends on the functional correctness of the system, but also on the time upon which an action is performed. To construct systems that meet hard and soft deadlines, a high predictability of the scheduling algorithm and of the software are required. Research on performance analysis of real-time systems deals with worst and best case execution times as well as with schedulability and feasibility analysis for periodic and aperiodic tasks under different scheduling algorithms [LM99, Hap05a, KH05].

Fairness and Efficiency   Furthermore, fairness and efficiency are important properties of schedulers for all kinds of systems. A fair scheduler assigns comparable service to comparable processes [Tan01, p.137]. Thus, each process receives a fair share of the resource, depending on its class. A scheduler is called efficient if it produces as little overhead as possible and lets the system do as much real work (e.g., execute processes) as possible [Tan01]. The overhead of a scheduler refers, for example, to the number and the time consumption of context switches. In order to achieve a high efficiency, schedulers may prefer *I/O-bound* processes over *compute-bound* processes, to keep all resources busy. I/O-bound processes are limited by the processing power of external resources, while compute-bound processes are limited by the processing power of the CPU. Each process issues a sequence of I/O bursts and CPU bursts. Depending on the duration and frequency of the bursts the scheduler can classify processes.

The different requirements are often contradictory. For example, an interactive scheduler needs relatively small timeslices, which introduce a lot of scheduling overhead contradicting the general goal of efficiency. However, widely used operating systems, such as Windows (2000, XP, Server 2003, and Vista, cf. Section 2.3.4) and Linux (Kernel 2.6 series, cf. Section 2.3.5), implement multipurpose schedulers which can handle real-time, interactive and batch processes.

2.3.2. Processes and Threads

In modern operating systems, processes, kernel-level threads, and user-level threads are different types of active entities. Informally, a process is a program in execution [SGG05, p.82]. A (heavyweight) process contains all information necessary for executing a program, including a program counter, code, data, file handlers, registers, and an execution stack. Threads belong to a process. They share code, data, and file handlers, but own separate program counters, registers and stack copies. Therefore, context switches between threads of the same process are faster than switches between separate processes in terms of clock cycles needed to complete the switch. Switching between threads of one process instead of switching between processes has further performance benefits. Since the threads of one process share data, the thread is likely to find its data in the processor cache.

Furthermore, threads are subdivided into kernel-level and user-level threads. While kernel-level threads are directly managed by the operating system, user-level threads are managed without direct support of the operating system [SGG05, p.129]. However, the user-level threads need to be mapped to kernel-level threads for execution. This mapping can yield a many-to-one, one-to-one, or many-to-many relationship between user-level and kernel-level threads.

In a *many-to-one* relationship, a thread library maps many user-level threads to one kernel-level thread. This will block the whole process if one of its threads issues a blocking system call. Furthermore, multiple threads cannot run in parallel on multiprocessors, since the Kernel can only access one kernel-level thread.

A *one-to-one* mapping of user-level threads to kernel-level threads allows more concurrency, but leads to additional overhead. Creating a kernel-level thread for each user-level thread can put a high load on the operating system. Therefore, operating systems limit the total number of threads in the system. In general, the Linux and Windows operating system series implement a one-to-one mapping [SGG05, p.130]. However, the actual type of mapping depends on the thread library used.

A *many-to-many* relationship multiplexes many user-level threads to a smaller or equal number of kernel-level threads. This strategy allows high concurrency and does not require a limit for the number of user-level threads in the system.

Definition 2.2 (Task). A *task* is an active and executable entity visible to the operating system scheduler.

For performance prediction, an explicit distinction between processes, kernel-level, and user-level threads is not necessary in most cases. Therefore, definition 2.2 introduces the term *task* for the general concept of processes, user-level and kernel-level threads, which are visible to the operating system scheduler. For the remainder of this thesis, we use the term task as an abstraction from processes or threads and apply the exact terms only if necessary.

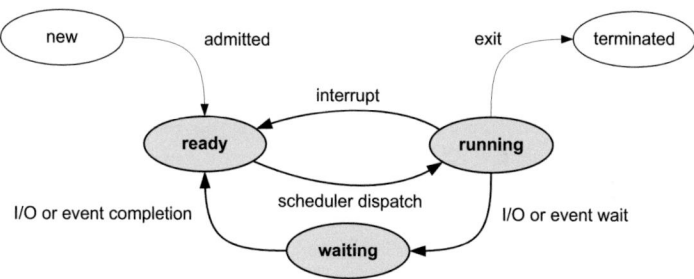

Figure 2.5.: Task states [SGG05, p.83].

From the scheduler's perspective, all tasks (no matter whether processes or threads) pass through different states during their life cycle. Figure 2.5 illustrates the states important to a scheduling algorithm [SGG05, p.83]. The states printed in dark gray are relevant for the performance model developed in Chapter 3 to Chapter 5.

The lifecycle of a task starts in state new when it is being created. If the scheduler accepts a task, it enters state ready where it is waiting to be assigned to a processor. Once the scheduler dispatches the tasks, it enters state running and can execute instructions on a processor. From there, the scheduler can either interrupt the task putting it back into state ready, the task can wait for the completion of an I/O operation or an external event entering state waiting, or it can finish execution going to state terminated. This overall behaviour of a task is independent of the actual scheduling algorithm.

2.3.3. Multilevel Feedback Queues

Multilevel Feedback Queues (MLFQ) classify tasks into different groups with similar properties and schedule each group separately. The tasks which belong to the same class can be
scheduled according to an arbitrary scheduling algorithm, e.g., FCFS or RR. MLFQs create
multimode systems [SGG05]. For example, a MLFQ can distinguish interactive and batch
tasks. Both types have different response time requirements and, thus, different scheduling
needs. Since interactive tasks have to respond quickly to user requests, they have priority
over batch tasks.

To be able to adopt separate scheduling algorithms for each class, MLFQs partition the
queue of tasks that request processing into several separate queues. All tasks are assigned to
a queue based on their properties, such as their memory size, priority, or type. Furthermore,
MLFQs realise scheduling among the queues, in order to decide which class is processed
next, if tasks of multiple classes are available. For example, priority preemptive scheduling
can be used to prefer tasks in the interactive queue over tasks in the batch queue.

In MLFQs, the classification of a task can change according to its behaviour. Thus, tasks
can move between queues. MLFQs usually distinguish tasks with respect to the characteristics of their CPU-bursts. For example, if a task uses too much CPU time, it will be
moved to a lower-priority queue. This scheme leaves I/O-bound and interactive tasks in the
higher-priority queues. Furthermore, if long waiting tasks in low-priority queues are moved
to higher-priority queues, starvation is prevented.

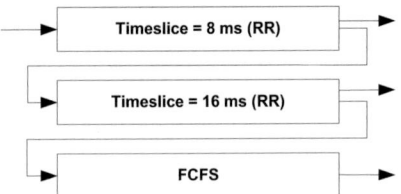

Figure 2.6.: Simple example of a multilevel feedback queue [SGG05, p.168].

Figure 2.6 shows a simple example of an MLFQ which distinguishes three classes of
tasks [SGG05]. The upper two classes manage foreground tasks while the bottom class
holds batch tasks. When a task arrives, it lines up at the end of the top-level queue. The
scheduler assigns a timeslice of 8 ms to each task in the queue. If a task does not finish
processing within its timeslice, the scheduler moves it to the end of the middle queue. Only if
the top-level queue is empty, the scheduler selects a task of the middle queue for processing.
If the task still requires processing time after 16 ms, the scheduler moves it to the bottom
queue, which processes all tasks with FCFS. This queue holds batch processes and is only

served if both other queues are empty. With this strategy, the scheduler prefers interactive tasks, which finish in less than 8 ms over tasks which require between 8 and 16 ms and batch processes.

MLFQ schedulers provide a high flexibility for the design of scheduling algorithms. They defined by the following parameters [SGG05]:

- The number of queues
- The scheduling algorithm for each queue
- The method to determine when to upgrade or degrade a process to a higher- or lower-priority queue
- The method used to determine which queue a process will enter, when that process needs service

In the operating systems Windows and Linux, MLFQ schedulers are implemented (cf. Sections 2.3.4 and 2.3.5). However, both implementations differ significantly in their concepts of time sharing, interactivity, and multiprocessor load balancing.

2.3.4. Windows

Today, the Windows operating system is available in many different versions and variants. At the time of writing Windows XP, Windows 2000, Windows Server 2003, and Windows Vista are the most relevant ones. For the scope of this thesis, we use the term *Windows* to refer to all Windows versions. The full operating system name is only used if the versions differ in the realisation of the described concepts. In the following, we explain the basic scheduling concepts of time sharing, interactivity handling, and multiprocessor load-balancing realised in the Windows operating system series.

Time Sharing

Priorities   Windows implements an MLFQ scheduling algorithm. It supports 32 different priority levels ranging from 0 (lowest priority) to 31 (highest priority) [SR05, p.329]. Each priority level represents a separate task class with its own run queue. Windows employs a priority preemptive scheduling algorithm between the queues, i.e. higher priority tasks preempt lower priority ones. A task on a certain priority level can only be executed if all queues on higher priority levels are empty. Furthermore, the priority levels are divided into the classes real-time (16 to 31), interactive (1 to 15), and idle (0). Depending on their behaviour, tasks can change the priority within their class, but cannot migrate between classes.

Windows categorises all user and business applications, like word processors, databases, and application servers, as interactive tasks. Since the scheduler performance model developed in Chapter 3 to Chapter 5) is targeted at such applications, the following explanation focusses on Windows' processing of interactive tasks.

Run Queues Windows uses a separate run queue (also called a ready queue) for each priority level to hold the tasks ready for execution (i.e., the tasks in the ready state, cf. Figure 2.5). The tasks in a queue on each priority level are executed using a round robin scheduling algorithm. The timeslice duration depends on the Windows operating system version as explained in the next paragraph.

Timeslices Windows defines the duration of a timeslice in terms of scheduling quanta. For example, on x86 systems, a scheduling quantum is 15.625ms. This value is mainly determined by the clock interrupt frequency of the underlying hardware. Windows distinguishes short (2 quanta, 31.5ms) and long (12 quanta, 187.5ms) timeslices. Short timeslices are generally used on client systems (Windows 2000/XP/Vista), as they lead to a higher responsiveness. On server systems (Windows Server 2003), long timeslices are preferred, since they reduce context switching overhead [SR05].

Interactivity and I/O Operations

Windows specifically "boosts" tasks which interact with the user or access I/O devices, in order to increase the responsiveness of the system. For this purpose, the scheduler increases a task's priority and timeslices (more specifically, grants more processing time to the task). The completion of an I/O operation, the occurrence of events or the access of semaphores triggers the boosting of a task's priority. Furthermore, tasks which did not receive any processing time for a long period get a top level priority for a full timeslice to prevent starvation (i.e., to not perpetually deny their access to the processor). Table 2.1 shows the priority boosts for different I/O devices and semaphores.

Resource	Boost
semaphore	+1
disk	+1
network	+2
keyboard or mouse	+6
sound	+8

Table 2.1.: Priority boosts after the acquisition of the named resources [SR05].

To realise changing priorities, Windows distinguishes dynamic and static priorities for each task. While the latter are explicitly given, for example, by a user or by another task, the former depend on a task's behaviour, e.g., its accesses to I/O devices and semaphores. When a task is boosted, Windows computes its new dynamic priority by adding the corresponding priority boost (cf. Table 2.1) to the task's static priority. This strategy prevents tasks from accumulating priority boosts. Furthermore, the dynamic priority of interactive tasks cannot exceed the highest priority for interactive tasks (15), no matter how large their boost is. When a task received a priority boost, Windows decreases its dynamic priority again over time. Whenever the task's timeslice expires, its dynamic priority is reduced by 1 until its static priority is reached. As a consequence, full boosts are only available to tasks until the end of their timeslices.

In addition to priority boosts, the timeslice of a task can be reset when it finishes a wait operation, e.g., for user input or an I/O device. Windows only resets the timeslice if the task's priority is increased at the same time (i.e., the task is not already boosted) or the task's static priority is equal to or above 14. Windows also employs a mechanism to ensure that task's timeslice will eventually expire (is used up). Each time a task accesses one of the resources listed in Table 2.1, Windows reduces its timeslice by one third of a scheduler quantum. Thus, tasks cannot access critical resources too often without using up their timeslice.

Multiprocessor Systems

Windows can handle systems with multiple processors and cores, including simultaneous multithreading (SMT), symmetric multiprocessing (SMP) and non-uniform memory access (NUMA) architectures. Scheduling tasks in such environments requires strategies to decide which task should run on which processor. This question can be examined from the perspective of a task or from the perspective of a processor. If a task becomes ready, schedulers for multiprocessing systems have to assign the task to a processor, where it can execute ("'task's perspective'"). By contrast, schedulers have to select the next runnable task for an idle processor ("'processor's perspective'"). Schedulers for multiprocessing systems need to implement strategies for both perspectives. For the Windows operating system series, the processor selection from a task's perspective is similar for all versions, but the task selection from a processor's perspective differs for Windows 2000/XP and Windows Server 2003/Vista.

While Windows 2000/XP provide a single run queue for all processors, Windows Server 2003/Vista hold a separate run queue for each processor. This difference leads to different process selection strategies and has a significant influence on scalability and performance (cf. Section 5.1). The following discussion first explains the processor selection from a task's perspective common to all Windows versions [SR05]. Then the processor selection from a task's perspective based on a single run queue realised in Windows 2000 and Windows XP is explained. Finally, the scheduling of run queues for each processor implemented in Windows Server 2003 and Windows Vista is described.

Windows restricts the selection of processors for a runnable task to a list of processors called *affinity mask*. The scheduler can only assign a task to processors listed in its affinity mask. This strategy allows the explicit distribution of tasks among the available processors by users of an application or by the applications themselves. Moreover, affinity masks can prevent undesirable processor switches by forcing a task to remain on one of the available processors.

To optimise a task's performance, Windows tries to always assign one task to the same processor. The assignment to the same processor increases the probability for a task to find its data in the processor caches, which is likely to improve the task's computation speed. On the other hand, Windows needs to keep all processors busy. To deal with these conflicting requirements, Windows identifies an appropriate processor for a task in multiple steps.

Each task receives an *ideal processor* during its creation following a simple round robin schema. Windows always tries to allocate a task to its ideal processor first. This might require the interruption of a running process or the task's insertion into the processor's run queue. Only if the ideal processor is busy and other processors are idle, Windows looks for an appropriate new processor. Its first choice is the *last processor* the task ran on (if not the same as the ideal processor). Next, it is checked whether the currently active processor (i.e., the one performing the scheduling operation) is in the list of idle processors. If none of the above processors is idle, the task is allocated to the first idle processor that is in the affinity mask of the task and not sleeping. For SMT and NUMA architectures, the processor selection has to consider various other conditions, e.g., shared internal resources of a processor and memory access times.

Windows XP and 2000 manage tasks that are ready for execution in a single run queue. To choose a runnable task for a processor, the scheduler looks at the highest priority non-empty queue. It chooses the first task fulfilling one of the following conditions in the given order: The task previously ran on the current processor; the current processor is its ideal processor; or the task is the first in its queue. The use of a single run queue ensures that the highest priority tasks always run first. Furthermore, the load is automatically balanced between different processors, since each processor selects its tasks from the same run queue. However, the run queue can become a bottleneck of the system, as system-wide locks are needed to access it. Especially on multiprocessor systems, global locks can be very expensive. This results in major scalability issues, which led to the development of per-processor run queues implemented in Windows Server 2003 and Vista.

To improve scalability, Windows Server 2003 and Vista use per-processor run queues. This limits the use of global locks to special cases, such as load balancing or priority changes of a task. To select a runnable task for a processor, the scheduler simply looks at the processor's run queue. It chooses the head of the highest priority non-empty queue for execution.

The use of per-processor run queues improves the scalability of the scheduler, but requires additional effort to balance the load among the available processors. If a processor is idle and its run queue is empty, it looks for another executable task and moves it to its run queue. This strategy avoids processors from idling while tasks for execution are available. Furthermore, it prevents additional overhead through intensive balancing attempts in an overloaded system. However, the system may not achieve a fully balanced state using this strategy.

Important Details for Performance Prediction

Some details of the Windows scheduler are especially important for performance prediction. In the following, we describe the most important aspects.

Fairness and Starvation In general, the Windows scheduler is not fair and only guarantees to run the single highest priority task on one of the available processors [SR05]. The unfairness is a result of the strict preference of high-priority tasks over low-priority ones. Thus, no statements about other tasks can be made. Especially for Windows versions with per-processor run queues (Server 2003 and Vista), this policy can lead to major imbalances. In a system with two processors, for example, multiple high priority tasks might share one processor, while the other processor is used by a single low priority task.

Windows implements a basic mechanism to prevent starvation. If a task cannot use the processor for more than 4 seconds, its dynamic priority is set to 15, the highest priority for interactive tasks. The task receives a timeslice of either 62.5ms (for systems with short timeslices) or 750ms (for systems with long timeslices). When the task has used up its timeslice, its dynamic priority is immediately reset to its static priority. This strategy differs from the usual resetting of timeslices, where the dynamic priority of a task decreases one by one with each timeslice until the static priority is reached.

Run Queue Management Windows' management of task interruptions can significantly influence software performance. When a higher priority task becomes ready, the currently running task is preempted and returned to the head of its priority queue. Windows stores the task's timeslice and priority. So, the task can finish its timeslice when the processor becomes available again. The keeping of the task's priority and timeslice needs to be modelled for performance predictions to be accurate.

Resetting Timeslices   When the priority of a task is boosted, Windows might also reset its timeslice. The amount of time granted to an interactive task can significantly influence its performance. It depends on the resources used and the task's remaining timeslice.

Windows manages timeslices as multiples of so-called scheduling quanta, which directly relate to the intervals of the timer interrupt. Thus, a quantum's exact duration is determined by the underlying hardware. For example, a quantum lasts 15.625 ms for x86 architectures. For internal computations, Windows stores a task's remaining timeslice as the number of remaining scheduling quanta multiplied by three. For short timeslices with 2 quanta this yields 6, for long timeslices with 12 quanta this yields 36.

The scaling of a task's remaining quanta allows Windows to stepwise degrade its remaining processing time. Thus, Windows can prevent tasks from blocking the processor without punishing them too hard. Such preventions become necessary when a task accesses the same resource multiple times and avoid that a tasks receives infinite processing time [SR05]. For this purpose, Windows reduces a task's remaining quanta each time the task accesses a resource. The reduction affects the reset of timeslices and differs for each type of resource. Depending on the considered system and its load conditions, this can have a major impact on software performance (cf. Section 4.2).

2.3.5. Linux

When the Linux 2.6 Kernel was introduced major changes were incorporated in the implementation of the scheduler. These changes were aimed at improving the Kernel's support for multiprocessor systems and at enhancing interactivity for desktop applications [Aas05, BC05, Mau03]. While the former 2.4 Kernel uses a single run queue for all processors, the 2.6 Kernel maintains a separate run queue for each processor. This separation increases the scalability of the scheduler for multiprocessors and offers better support for server systems with an increasing amount of processors. However, the strongly conflicting goals of scalability and interactivity had led to multiple revisions of the scheduler implementation. At the moment of writing, a new Completely Fair Scheduler (CFS) has just been introduced into the Kernel's main line [Tra]. The following sections describe the implementation of the Linux 2.6.22 scheduler which is a variant of the initial O(1) scheduler [Aas05].

Time Sharing

Priorities   Linux distinguishes 140 different priority levels ranging from 0 (highest) to 139 (lowest) [Aas05, BC05, Mau03]. For each priority level, a separate run queue manages the tasks with equal priorities. Furthermore, Linux divides the priorities into classes for real-time (0 – 99) and interactive or batch tasks (100 – 139). The latter directly map to so called nice levels, which represent the usual priorities of user and business applications. Nice levels range from the highest priority of -20 (= 100) to the lowest priority of 19 (= 139). The following description focusses on Linux' task processing within this range.

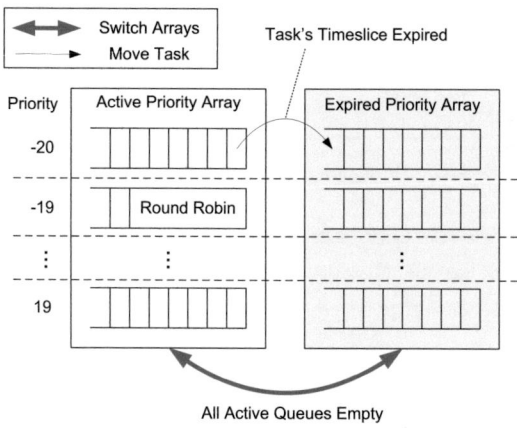

Figure 2.7.: Schematic overview of the run queue of Linux' O(1) scheduler.

Run Queues Linux keeps a separate queue for each priority level in a data structure called priority array. The tasks within the same priority level are executed using a RR scheduling algorithm. To ensure fairness between different priority levels and to minimise scheduling overhead, Linux uses an active and an expired priority array. Figure 2.7 illustrates the main concepts of Linux' run queue. The active priority array contains all tasks whose timeslice is not yet used up, while the expired priority array contains all tasks which have already finished their timeslice. The scheduler only executes tasks from the active priority array. It always selects tasks on higher priority levels first. If the timeslice of a task expires, it is moved from the active to the expired priority array. If the active priority array becomes empty, both arrays are switched making the expired array active again. This is called an epoch of the scheduler. The complete arrays are exchanged in this process. For Linux, different timeslice sizes are used to assign a larger share of processing time to tasks with higher priorities. The following paragraph explains the concept of timeslices used in Linux 2.6.22 in more detail.

Timeslices   Linux assigns different timeslices to tasks depending on their priority. The higher the priority of a task is, the larger is its timeslice. For example, tasks on the lowest priority level (nice level 19) receive a timeslice of 5ms, while tasks on the highest priority level (nice level -20) get 800ms.

Priority	-20	-19	-18	-17	-16	-15	-14	-13	-12	-11
Timeslice (ms)	800.0	780.0	760.0	740.0	720.0	700.0	680.0	660.0	640.0	620.0
Priority	-10	-9	-8	-7	-6	-5	-4	-3	-2	-1
Timeslice (ms)	600.0	580.0	560.0	540.0	520.0	500.0	480.0	460.0	440.0	420.0
Priority	0	1	2	3	4	5	6	7	8	9
Timeslice (ms)	100.0	95.0	90.0	85.0	80.0	75.0	70.0	65.0	60.0	55.0
Priority	10	11	12	13	14	15	16	17	18	19
Timeslice (ms)	50.0	45.0	40.0	35.0	30.0	25.0	20.0	15.0	10.0	5.0

Table 2.2.: Priority-dependent timeslices of the Linux scheduler.

Table 2.2 lists the timeslices in dependency of the process priority. The table is derived from the following formula implemented in the Linux scheduler [lin]. Let p_t be the priority of the current task, $p_{min} = 19$ which is the lowest priority, and

$$ts = \begin{cases} 100\,\mathrm{ms} & \text{, if } p_t \geq 0 \\ 400\,\mathrm{ms} & \text{, if } p_t < 0 \end{cases}$$

the basic timeslice from which all other timeslices are derived. Then

$$\frac{(|p_t - p_{min}| + 1) * ts}{20}$$

yields the exact timeslice assigned to each task by the Linux scheduler. Scaling the timeslices from 5 ms to 800 ms enables a fair scheduling between all tasks in all queues. During an epoch, all tasks in the active priority array receive a share of processing time according to their priority. The higher their priority, the larger is their share of computation time.

Interactivity and I/O Operations

Linux rewards I/O-bound tasks with an increased priority, while compute-bound tasks are punished with a priority decrease. This improves the interactive behaviour of the system and efficient use of I/O devices. Analogously to Windows, Linux assigns a dynamic priority to each task in addition to its static priority. The dynamic priority depends on the task's behaviour. Linux keeps track of the time a task is waiting, compared to the time it computes. This value is called *sleep average*. A task's priority bonus ranges from -5 to +5 and depends on its sleep average.

Furthermore, Linux classifies tasks as interactive and non-interactive. If the timeslice of an interactive task expires, the task's timeslice is reset and it is reinserted into the active priority array. Non-interactive tasks are moved to the expired priority array. This distinction ensures that interactive tasks remain reactive all the time. The exact realisation of Linux interactivity handling has a major impact on software performance (cf. Section 4.2 and [TCM06]). Therefore, the following paragraphs explain the sleep average, the computation of dynamic priorities, and the classification of interactive tasks.

Sleep Average   The Linux scheduler uses a so-called sleep average to determine a task's dynamic priority. The sleep average keeps track of a task's waiting and computation times. It thus monitors the task's past behaviour as it is relevant from the scheduler's perspective. In general, the scheduler assigns a larger priority bonus to tasks with relatively long waiting times and strongly penalises tasks with long periods of processing and short waiting times. Therefore, the scheduler adds the waiting time of a task to its sleep average and subtracts the scaled computation time from its sleep average.

A task can only accumulate $sa_{max} = 1000\,\text{ms}$ of sleeping time, which limits the maximum bonus. When a task finishes waiting for a resource, its new sleep average sa_{n+1} results from the last value sa_n and the waiting time t_{wait}:

$$sa_{n+1} = min(sa_{max}, sa_n + t_{wait}).$$

To account for the time a task is allocated to a processor, Linux subtracts its computation time from the sleep average. Since interactive tasks should not loose their status too quickly, Linux explicitly scales down the influence of the computation time by the last priority bonus it received. Let t_{comp} be a task's computation time, sa_n its last sleep average and b_n its last bonus (ranging from 0 to 10). Then the computation time accounted to its sleep average given by

$$t'_{comp} = \begin{cases} t_{comp}/b_n & \text{, if } b_n > 0 \\ t_{comp} & \text{, otherwise} \end{cases}$$

The new sleep average sa_{n+1} is further computed by

$$sa_{n+1} = max(0, sa_n - t'_{comp}).$$

where zero represents the sleep average's lower limit. The dynamic priority of a task directly results from its sleep average.

Dynamic Priorities   To compute the dynamic priority of a task, Linux linearly scales the sleep average to a priority bonus from 0 to $b_{max} = 10$. The new bonus b_{n+1} of a task results from

$$b_{n+1} = \frac{sa_{n+1}}{sa_{max}} * b_{max}.$$

The task t's dynamic priority dy_t is then derived by

$$dy_t = p_t - (b_{n+1} - \frac{b_{max}}{2})$$

where the actual bonus (or penalty) is first shifted into the range from -5 to +5 and then subtracted from t's static priority p_t. The dynamic priority is not the only determining factor of Linux' interactivity handling. The classification of interactive tasks described next can also have a major impact on software performance.

Interactivity Classification   The classification of tasks as interactive and non-interactive depends on their sleep averages and static priorities. For a maximum sleep average of $sa_{max} = 1000\,\mathrm{ms}$, Linux computes an interactivity threshold ranging from $290\,\mathrm{ms}$ for tasks with a priority of -20 to more than $1000\,\mathrm{ms}$ for tasks with a priority of 8 or less. In other words, tasks with low priorities never receive the interactivity status. The complex computations in [lin] for this threshold boil down to the following formula. Let $sa_{max} = 1000\,\mathrm{ms}$ be the maximum sleep average, $b_{max} = 10$ the maximum bonus, and p_t the tasks static priority, and $t_{sched} = 10\,\mathrm{ms}$ the time of a clock interval, then

$$\mathrm{int}(t) = sa_{max} * (\frac{3}{b_{max}} + \frac{20 + p_t}{40}) - t_{sched}$$

defines the interactivity threshold for a task t.

Since some interactive tasks might stay in the active priority array for a long period, other tasks, whose timeslices have expired, might not be able to access the processor for a long time. To prevent starvation, Linux moves interactive tasks only back into the active priority array until a task spend more then the maximum sleep average ($sa = 1000\,\mathrm{ms}$) in the expired priority array. Section 4.2 evaluates and predicts the large performance influences of Linux' dynamic priority bonuses and interactivity handling on software performance.

Multiprocessor Systems

The Linux scheduler balances the system's load among all available CPUs, in order to maximise system performance and to assign fair shares of processing time to each task. However, balancing the load in large multiprocessor systems can lead to large costs in terms of long delays. For example, load balancing has to take into account the cost of moving a task from one processor to another and the effect of different memory access times for different processors. For good load balancing decisions, Linux maintains a simplified model of the underlying hardware architecture. Based on this model that consists of hierarchically structured *scheduling domains* (more precisely, sched_domain [lin]), Linux' load balancer decides whether and where to move tasks.

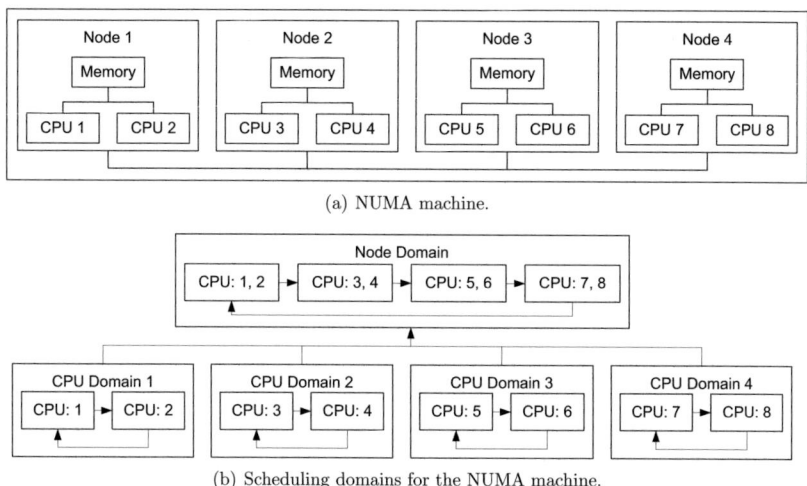

(a) NUMA machine.

(b) Scheduling domains for the NUMA machine.

Figure 2.8.: Example of multiple levels of scheduling domains [CCF+06].

Figure 2.8(a) shows an example for a NUMA machine with multiple nodes and processors and the hierarchy of scheduling domains maintained by the Linux scheduler [CCF+06]. The NUMA machine consists of four different nodes, each of which contains a memory unit and two CPUs. All nodes communicate via a bus. While all nodes can access all memory units, the access times of a node's local memory are much faster than the access times of distant memory. Linux has to take into account such facts when balancing the load among the available processors.

The structure of the scheduling domains resembles the physical hardware [BDHH04]. CPUs at the bottom of the hierarchy are most closely related in terms of memory access. For this reason, Linux performs load balancing most often at the lower domains that are closely related. Each scheduling domain contains one or more *CPU groups* among which the domain balances its load. The scheduling domain treats CPU groups as a single unit. So, it does not care about how the load is distributed within a group. The lower level scheduling domains balance the load within the CPU-groups.

Figure 2.8(b) shows the scheduling domains and CPU groups for the NUMA machine in Figure 2.8(a). The processors on each node form a separate scheduling domain called CPU Domain, which contains two CPU groups with one processor, respectively. The top level scheduling domain Node Domain balances the load among the four nodes. Each of its four CPU groups contains the processors of one node.

The balancing of each level involves different costs including, for example, the time needed to move a task from one processor to another. The scheduling domains thus need to employ different strategies for load balancing. A strategy determines how often the processors need to be balanced, how much the load must differ for balancing to be triggered, and how much time must pass until cache affinity of a task is lost (i.e., the time a task is likely to find valid data in a processor cache). The Linux scheduler uses different values depending on how the CPU groups in a domain are related to each other. In SMT systems, for example, processors share the same caches and moving a task cannot affect its cached data.

In each scheduling domain, load balancing can be triggered by an event (called *event balancing*) or periodically at regular intervals (called *active balancing*). Events are state changes of a processor's run queue, such as the creation of a new task, the awakening of a task, or the removal of the last task from queue (leaving the processor idle). While event balancing occurs locally, active balancing can affect all scheduling domains. Starting at the highest level, it is checked whether the CPUs in each domain require balancing. Active balancing ensures that processors with few events, which execute multiple CPU-intensive tasks, also participate in load balancing. The balancing interval determines how often balancing efforts occur. The interval grows if the system stays in balance. The scheduler moves up the domain hierarchy and checks if balancing is needed. If the load of the domain's CPU groups differs too much, it moves processes from the busiest CPU group to the most idle one. Factors such as cache affinity times, CPU-power, and the last time a domain was last balanced, influence the scheduler's load balancing decisions. In general, the scheduler performs less balancing at higher domains in the hierarchy.

Even though scheduling domains can represent nearly any combination of SMT, SMP, and NUMA systems, this section mainly focusses on the load balancing decisions for SMP systems. SMP systems contain a set of similar physical processors that have equal access times to memory and may also share a common memory bus. Furthermore, each processor provides its own caches and does not share any internal resources (i.e., parts of its processing logic) with other processors. The separate caches for each processor compel the scheduler to consider cache affinities before moving a task. To maximise performance, Linux always selects tasks with the least cache affinity for moving. Furthermore, it is assumed that caches do not contain any useful data for a task after a few seconds. Active balancing of SMP systems occurs in regular intervals, which are curtailed fairly sharply if the system as a whole is busy. Event balancing is triggered, when the system's load changes. In general, balancing attempts should occur only when necessary and useful. Therefore, the balancing threshold for SMP systems tolerates minor imbalances between the processors.

Important Details for Software Performance Prediction

Linux' classification of tasks into interactive and non-interactive has to be considered in software performance prediction. Since interactive tasks remain in the active priority array, the classification destroys the fundamental concept of differently sized timeslices. Linux' run queue (consisting of the active and expired priority arrays) are meant to avoid starvation and ensure fair scheduling. With the exception of interactive tasks, Linux loses these properties. The evaluations in Sections 4.1 and 4.2 demonstrate the this effect as well as the influence of the accuracy and the computation of the sleep average discussed in the following.

Being a part of Linux' interactivity handling, the computation of the sleep average mainly influences the performance of systems with interactivity and/or I/O operations. The computation of the sleep average is performed in terms of the number of scheduling interrupts that occurred (called jiffies). Therefore, its accuracy is limited by the scheduling interval. With a typical scheduling rate of 100 Hz, this leaves an accuracy of 10 ms for the sleep average. This inaccuracy can influence a task's dynamic priority as well as its interactivity classification.

Furthermore, the accounting of a task's waiting time affects the sleep average. For the Linux scheduler, a task is waiting from the moment it is put into the waiting state. The waiting period is terminated as soon as the task is executed on one of the processors. Thus, the waiting time that is accounted by the scheduler period includes the time a task is waiting for a resource as well as the time it is ready and waiting the run queue. The additional time that is added to the sleep average can influence the task's dynamic priority and, thus, its performance.

2.4. Summary

In this chapter, we have introduced fundamental concepts in the areas of (i) software performance engineering and (ii) scheduling theory that are necessary to understand the performance model for general purpose operating system schedulers developed in Chapters 3 to 5. The performance influence of scheduling policies is mainly determined by the following factors:

- The *workload type* determines the effect of scheduling policies on software performance mean response time. While scheduling policies can influence mean response time by orders of magnitudes for open systems, they have limited influence in closed systems.

- The performance influence of scheduling policies depends on the *variance* of resource demand distributions. "Good" scheduling policies help to minimize mean response times for all requests. For "bad" scheduling policies, mean response times suffer from disproportionally long delays.

The behaviour of the schedulers of the Linux and Windows operating system series follow entirely different philosophies. Windows interferes as little as possible with the running system and, thus, accepts major imbalances for the distribution of processing time among competing tasks. Linux assigns a "fair" share of processing time to all tasks. These different philosophies affect all parts of the scheduler behaviour:

- *Run queues*: Linux assigns timeslices to tasks according to their static priority. Since all tasks have to be processed before new timeslices are assigned, each task is guaranteed to receive a minimum share of processing time. Windows assigns equal time slices to all tasks. Furthermore, the Windows scheduler strictly prefers higher priority tasks over lower priority ones. Lower priority tasks may thus starve.

- *Dynamic priorities*: Linux keeps track of a task's behaviour to determine its dynamic priorities. By contrast, Windows uses the resources acquired by a task in order to assign dynamic priorities.

- *Load balancing*: While Linux constantly tries to keep the load balanced among the available processors, Windows moves tasks only if a processor becomes idle.

3. Basics of the Performance Modelling Framework for Operating System Schedulers

In this chapter, we introduce the basic concepts and terms of our novel performance Model for general purpose Operating System Schedulers called MOSS. This model is based on validated hypotheses about the performance properties of GPOS schedulers implemented in the Windows and the Linux operating system series. Using MOSS, software architects and developers can predict influences of different time sharing strategies, dynamic priorities for I/O bound and interactive tasks, and different multiprocessor load balancing strategies on software performance. Furthermore, we integrated MOSS with the Palladio Component Model (PCM, cf. Appendix A). Software architects can choose between different scheduler configurations, e.g., Windows Server 2003 and Linux 2.6.

We use feature diagrams [CE00] to capture the performance-relevant configurations for GPOS schedulers. Based on a specific configuration, transformations generate Coloured Petri Nets (CPN, cf. Appendix B), which model the behaviour of GPOS schedulers and formally define their performance-relevant features. The CPNs are hierarchically structured allowing the combination of different scheduling features. This structure enables a straightforward integration of new scheduling algorithms into the model.

We validated MOSS in two steps. In the first step, we focussed on specific features of the scheduler model and evaluated each feature in isolation. This strategy provides a high control over possible disturbing factors. In the second step, we compared predictions and measurements in a general scenario. A larger case study evaluates the combined effect of different scheduling features. The results show a prediction accuracy of 5 – 10% in most cases. The comparison with classical scheduler models for performance prediction emphasis the benefit of more detailed models. MOSS increases the prediction accuracy by several orders of magnitude.

This chapter is structured as follows. In Section 3.1, we present an iterative method for the experiment-based derivation of performance models. The method is employed in Chapters 4 and 5 to design MOSS. Section 3.2 provides a broader overview of MOSS, its scheduling features, and hierarchical structure.

3.1. Experiment-based Derivation of Software Performance-Models

Creating accurate performance models for complex software systems requires a systematic approach to (i) identify and quantify performance-relevant features of the system under study (e.g., which configurations of an application server influence software performance?), (ii) define accurate performance models of the identified features (e.g., model the application server's thread pool with CPNs), and (iii) validate the prediction accuracy of the proposed models (i.e., compare predictions to measurements). In this section, we propose a systematic approach for the definition of performance models of black box systems where only limited information on the system's internals are available. Inspired by the general ideas and rules proposed by Jain [Jai91], the method combines existing knowledge of the system under study with iterative, goal-oriented measurements. The measurements support performance analysts to identify valid assumptions for performance modelling and allow assessing the prediction accuracy of the model.

3.1.1. Motivation

Jain [Jai91] points out several common mistakes in software performance evaluation, which motivate the experiment-based derivation of software performance models proposed in this chapter. In the following, we list some of the most common mistakes in no specific order [Jai91]:

- No goals
- Unsystematic approach
- Analysis without understanding the problem
- Overlooking important parameters
- Ignoring significant factors
- Inappropriate experimental design
- Inappropriate level of detail

In software performance engineering, one of the most common mistakes is the absence of concrete goals. Performance analysts try to design models that answer all design questions that may arise. According to Jain [Jai91] such general purpose models do not exist, since a part of the system design varies from problem to problem. Most factors require different levels of modelling detail in different contexts.

For example, an enterprise application (such as used in the case studies in Sections 5.2 and 6.4) may suffer from very different performance problems. Lock contention in the database may cause long delays for one company using the application. For another client, the database works fine, but the communication delay between the involved parties takes too much time. While both clients use the same business application, their performance problems are very different (probably caused by customisations or the execution environment) and, thus, require detailed models of different parts of the system. While a general and detailed model of the complete software application is possible in theory, it cannot be realised in practice. Thus, performance analysts need to state their modelling goals to adhere to in advance.

Furthermore, unsystematic approaches and analyses without understanding the problem can lead to unnecessary high effort and inaccurate performance models. Relying on specifications and knowledge of the system alone does not suffice to design performance models. Such an approach may lead to overlooking important parameters and factors. The choice of modelled factors must be driven by the problem and their relevance, not the analyst's knowledge.

Moreover, the experimental design must follow certain standards in order to yield reliable results. Often inappropriate experimental designs can lead to wrong conclusions [Jai91]. Another risk of performance model design lies in the level of detail. Abstractions which are too strong may lead to erroneous predictions. For example, processor sharing is a common abstraction for round-robin scheduling in software performance evaluation. While it is a good abstraction in many cases, it can lead to large prediction errors in many others (cf. Section 4.1).

Similarly, too many details are likely to distract performance analysts from the important influences and can lead to overcomplicated models that are difficult to maintain. However, whether detailed modelling is necessary or not strongly depends on the system under study. For example, the performance properties of message-oriented middleware can be modelled with a high level of abstraction. For GPOS schedulers on the other hand, many details have to be included in the model in order to yield accurate predictions. These modelling risks as well as the varying level of abstraction emphasise the need for a tight coupling of experimental evaluation and performance modelling.

According to Jain [Jai91], a performance model has to be validated and verified. For validation, Jain proposes comparing predictions with expert intuition, real system measurements, or theoretical results. However, expert intuition can be misleading especially for highly complex and concurrent software systems [GPB+06]. Theoretical results can be as erroneous as the predictions. Therefore, real system measurements provide the only acceptable alternative for validation. In the context of this thesis, validation always refers to the comparison between predictions and measurements, i.e., performance observations.

Verification (in the sense of Jain) is mainly "model debugging", e.g., continuity tests and seed independence for simulations. While such tests are necessary, they are not sufficient. Performance analysts have to ensure that their models include all performance-relevant factors and lie on an appropriate level of abstraction. Due to the above differences and possible misunderstandings with formal verification, the following uses the terms *assumption validation* and *model validation*.

During performance model design, analysts must make assumptions about the system under test. To efficiently construct models that accurately reflect the performance properties of the system, *assumption validation* helps performance analysts to (i) identify the assumptions necessary and (ii) assess their validity. The early validation allows performance analysts to focus their design effort on the most influential factors of the system under study.

Furthermore, performance analysts need to examine the prediction accuracy of their performance models. Even if all assumptions stated by the analysts hold, the models may break others that have not yet been considered. Moreover, the models may not reflect the model assumptions correctly (caused by errors or oversimplification) or the assumption validation did not capture all necessary factors completely.

3.1.2. A Method for Experiment-based Performance Model Derivation

The design of reliable performance models that accurately predict the performance properties must be tightly coupled with goal-oriented measurements. The measurements narrow down the design space to the performance-relevant factors and allow a systematic model design based on validated assumptions. In this section, we introduce a method for experiment-based performance model derivation which has been employed in the context of this thesis.

The method supports performance analysts and software architect in evaluating the performance of complex software systems. Performance analysts can use the method to design customisable performance models, such as a performance model for operating system schedulers (MOSS, cf. Chapters 4 and 5) or a messaging completion (cf. Chapter 6).

Furthermore, software architects (who use the performance completions designed by performance analysts) can employ the method to create prediction models for existing parts of a system. The usage of measurements enables them to keep the model on an abstract level and to focus on the most relevant factors.

Performance model design is driven by a specific goal that directs the design effort to the factors of interest. Similar to the GQM-approach (cf. Section 3.1.3), the goal is defined by a specific purpose, issue, object, and viewpoint. For the proposed method, the *purpose* sets the general goal, for example, designing a configurable performance model or performance prediction in general. Furthermore, *issues* focus the goal on specific characteristics of the system under test, such as different configurations or a high load. *Objects* determine the system under test and direct the effort towards a specific part of the system, e.g., the messaging service of an application server. Finally, *viewpoints* define the perspective for which the performance predictions are to be made. The viewpoint can be a specific user group or another part of the system, e.g., the performance of the database from the perspective of the application layer.

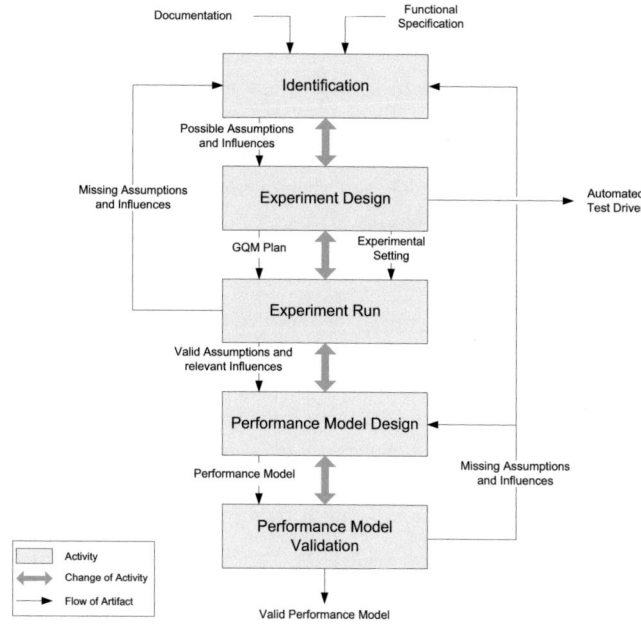

Figure 3.1.: Experimental derivation of performance models.

Driven by a concrete goal, performance analysts can design performance models for highly complex software systems following the process model shown in Figure 3.1. The steps listed there are executed iteratively. With each iteration, performance analysts and software architects successively refine the performance model and add further assumptions and performance-relevant factors. In the following, we describe the experimental derivation of software performance models in more detail.

Identification of Performance-relevant Factors and Degrees of Freedom   The first step of the experimental performance model derivation method aims for the identification of an initial set of possible performance-relevant factors and degrees of freedom of the system under study. Following the GQM schema, questions address these factors and degrees of freedom. For example, the configuration of a message channel may influence its performance (cf. Chapter 6). Thus, performance analysts may ask: "How does guaranteed delivery (storing messages persistently) influence the performance of a message channel?". Based on documentation and (functional) specifications, performance analysts formulate questions regarding the remaining degrees of freedom (with respect to performance) and performance-relevant factors. Since documentation and specification focus on the description of functional features, it may be difficult or even impossible to judge whether a specific factor influences software performance (e.g., does a selective consumer, i.e., a message filter, affect performance?). Moreover, interactions (with respect to performance) of multiple factors are difficult to assess (e.g., does the message size change affect performance similarly for messages with and without guaranteed delivery?). In the first step of the experiment-based performance model derivation, all possible performance-relevant factors (e.g., all configurations of a message channel) are listed if they are of interest with respect to the modelling goal. Then, the following steps systematically identify those features that influence performance.

Experiment Design   The experiment designed in this step systematically evaluates the performance influences of the factors and degrees of freedom, separating relevant ones from irrelevant ones. Furthermore, they provide information to fill in the degrees of freedom and the necessary parametrisation of performance models. The Goal-Question-Metric (GQM) method of Basili, Caldiera, and Rombach [BCR94] supports the definition of questions and performance metrics. Its extension for software performance evaluation adds specific scenarios and hypotheses leading to experiment results. However, the detailed introduction is deferred to Section 3.1.3.

To answer the question, whether guaranteed delivery influences the performance of a message channel, a concrete scenario has to be defined first. The scenario includes the experimental setting, e.g., the workload and execution environment. In the example, sender, receiver, and MOM are deployed on the same machine. Furthermore, the message size is fixed to 1000 bytes. Comparing the delivery time of messages (i.e., the time it takes from sending a message until it reaches its receiver) allows to compare both configurations. Performance analysts formulate hypotheses that define the expected outcome of the experiment to assess whether the performance of a messaging channel conforms to their expectation. For example, they may state that the mean delivery time of a message increases by 50% for a channel with guranteed delivery compared to a channel without guranteed delivery. After the experiments have been designed, the next step guides the conduction of experiments.

Experiment In this step, the previously defined experiments are executed and the required performance metrics are measured. The results directly relate to the previously formulated questions and hypotheses. If the results conform to the hypotheses, performance analysts may consider the underlying assumptions as valid for the construction of a performance model until proved otherwise. In case the measurements deviate from the hypotheses, the causes need to be examined and more detailed evaluations might be necessary.

For the above example, performance analysts need to set up the MOM and deploy a test driver which measures the delivery time for a message channel with and without guaranteed delivery. After the execution of the test driver, they can compare the results to their hypotheses. If the results show, for example, that guaranteed delivery delays the message transfer by 25% only, the hypothesis needs to be revised. Futhermore, the results raise the question if the factor is constant for different message sizes. Performance analysts need to evaluate such newly arising questions in an additional iteration.

If the experiment successfully validated the hypotheses, performance analysts can build a prediction model for the system under study. At this point, the model can already be considered as "assumption valid".

Performance Model Design Based on the experiments above, performance analysts can design a prediction model. In combination with the hypotheses, the experiment results provide the necessary answers to the questions of the GQM-plan. The results provide enough information to decide whether a specific feature needs to be included in the performance model or whether it can be neglected. Furthermore, the results should give direct hints on how degrees of freedom in the specification and documentation can be approximated and/or modelled. Finally, the experiment results quantify resource demands on a specific platform.

For the example above, performance analysts may decide to model the two messaging channels by a single resource demand to a processor, where channels with guaranteed delivery request 25% more processing time. At this stage, the models are strong abstractions of the system under study, focussing on the factors that have been evaluated. Therefore, the model may not reflect the system's performance correctly for all scenarios. For example, it may not scale correctly, since resources, such as network and hard drive, are not considered. An additional validation step is necessary to decide under which conditions a prediction model is a valid abstraction of a system.

Model Validation The model validation ensures that the model predicts the performance metrics of interest with the expected accuracy and reflects the influences of all performance-relevant factors. Creating abstract performance models for complex software systems carries several risks that can be minimised by this step. In the following, we briefly summarise the most important ones:

- The degrees of freedom of specifications and documentations are not filled in correctly, i.e., the chosen abstraction or model reflects their influence partially but cannot be generalised for other scenarios.

  Similarly, overfitted models accurately reflect the performance of a specific behaviour or scenario but cannot be generalised. Thus, such models are only valid for specific scenarios. However, these performance models can be adequate if they not used in more general scenarios. For the example above, the model of a message channel with guaranteed delivery does not issue resource demands to the hard drive and, thus, incorrectly reflects performance for high loads.

- Not all performance-relevant factors have been identified. There are influences that may not be directly observable from the measurements but shown by comparing predictions to measurements.

- Factors that are considered as independed on the first glance may influence each other's performance.

- The main cause of an observed effect is not included in the model. Since it is not always obvious what caused a specific performance observation, the performance model may not include the actual cause.

- Modelling errors. Model validation identifies modelling errors, which can be easily introduced in performance models of highly complex software systems.

The outcome of the validation may require the performance analyst to refine or adjust the model. These refinements can require further experiments to evaluate and quantify additional properties of the system under study. Similar to the initial experiments, the model validation employs the scenario-based GQM method to evaluate the prediction quality of the proposed model in a controlled environment. In this case, the hypotheses do not make statements about the expected performance of the system under study, but on the expected prediction accuracy of the model. While it is intuitive to minimise the prediction error of the model, it may be necessary and desirable to allow a certain degree of inaccuracy in particular scenarios. Thus, performance analysts (and software architects) can keep the performance model simple, while still achieving a moderate prediction accuracy. Model validations give insights into the expected error for such scenarios and may direct future modelling effort.

Prediction models may be used in more general scenarios than evaluated during their design. However, each model only reflects factors identified in preceding experiments. For all other scenarios and factors, the validation does not make any statement about the expected prediction accuracy of the model. The generalisation of the prediction model to other scenarios strongly depends on the broadness of the considered scenarios and the sensitivity of the system to changes. To ensure a good prediction accuracy, experiments must reflect a wide range of different scenarios and environments to give a higher confidence in the prediction model.

3.1.3. The Goal/Question/Metric-Approach for Experiment-based Performance Model Design

In this section, we summarise the Goal/Question/Metric (GQM) approach proposed by Basili, Caldiera, and Rombach [BCR94] and extend the GQM-approach for the experiment-based derivation of performance models.

The Goal/Question/Metric Appraoch

GQM is a process model for measurements targeting a particular set of issues (goals) and a set of rules for the interpretation of the measured data. In order to be meaningful, measurements must be goal-oriented and, thus, are defined in a top-down fashion. Basili, Caldiera, and Rombach argue that measurements, which are not performed in a goal-oriented way, are likely to be inefficient. The absence of concrete goals carries the risk of collecting large amounts of unnecessary data. Large amounts of data and missing goals may complicate the interpretation of measurements. For the scope of this thesis, GQM provides a structured approach for the evaluation of operating system schedulers with respect to software performance.

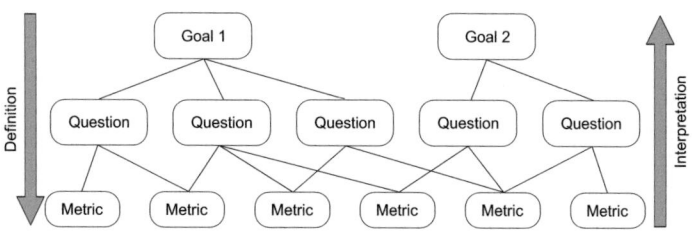

Figure 3.2.: Relations between goals, questions, and metrics [BCR94].

The GQM method starts with the explicit definition of a measurement goal. Several questions serve to refine the goal and to identify its major components that need to be answered by the measurements. Questions are further refined by metrics. Figure 3.2 depicts the relation between goals, questions, and metrics.

When the measurements for each metric have been taken, the resulting data is interpreted bottom up. Each metric is directed towards specific questions. The collected data answers the questions with respect to the goal. This evaluation allows deciding whether the goal has been attained or not. Figure 3.2 further indicates that the same metric can answer different questions.

Goals, Questions, Metrics, and Hypotheses   In GQM, *goals* are located on a conceptual level. They strongly depend on the context in which measurements take place. The context subsumes the objects, the reasons, the points of view, and the environment of the measurements, as well as the considered models of quality. Possible objects of measurements are products (artefacts, deliverables, or documents), processes (software related activities), or resources (e.g., personnel, hardware, or software). To correctly embed a goal into a given context, the GQM method requires the explicit definition of the goal's issue, object or process, viewpoint, and purpose.

Questions determine the assessment of a specific goal. They characterise the object of measurement (product, process, resource) with respect to selected quality attributes from the selected viewpoint.

On a quantitative level, *metrics* associate a set of data to each question. The data answer the questions in a quantitative way. In GQM, there exists a distinction between objective and subjective metrics. While objective metrics depend only on the object under measurement (e.g., lines of code), subjective metrics depend on the viewpoint from which the measurements are taken (e.g., readability of a text).

When selecting metrics, various factors have to be considered. Basili et al. [BCR94] summarise the most important ones as follows:

- **Amount and quality of existing data**: To minimise the effort during data collection, the use of existing data sources can be maximised.

- **Maturity of the objects of measurement**: Objective metrics are preferable for more mature measurement objects, while subjective evaluations are better suited for informal or unstable objects.

- **Learning process**: GQM plans need iterative refinement and adaptation. The defined metrics have to evaluate not only the object of measurement but also the reliability of the model in use.

Solingen and Berghout [SB99] extend the GQM approach by *hypotheses*, which define the expected outcome of the measurements for each question. Hypotheses initiate thinking about the system under study and stimulate a better understanding of the process and/or product. After measurement and during data interpretation, these hypotheses can be compared with actual measurements. Solingen and Berghout use hypotheses as (informal) descriptions of the expected outcome. The comparison between expectation and observation supports the identification and analysis of the underlying reasons for any possible deviation.

The experiment-based derivation of performance models heavily relies on hypotheses to define the expected outcome of an experiment and to stepwise evaluate modelling assumptions. However, the performance evaluations require the definition of concrete scenarios in order to be reproducible and in order to allow a clear formulation of hypotheses.

Introducing Scenarios to the GQM Approach

In the following, we extend the GQM approach for the area of software performance evaluation. The extensions add scenarios to the GQM method and make intensive use of hypotheses.

Scenarios A *scenario* determines the experimental setting for performance evaluation. The setting includes, for example, the workload (e.g., the arrival rate of messages), the execution environment, the deployment of the system under test, task behaviour, and resource demands. Scenarios operationalise the questions defined within a GQM-plan and fill in the degrees of freedom. For typical applications of the GQM approach (e.g., [FLM+98, SB99, SB01]), the scenario is fixed by external sources (e.g., the structure of company) and cannot be changed. In such cases, GQM-plans are designed for a single, specific scenario. In the context of software performance evaluation, such constraints are (usually) not given. Therefore, scenarios have to be defined explicitly. Analysts have to identify representative scenarios to evaluate the influence of specific factors on software performance.

For example, the question "How does guaranteed delivery influence the performance of a message channel?" does not provide enough information for measurement and data collection. Several degrees of freedom remain even if the performance metrics of interest (e.g., delivery time) are known. Without a specific scenario (e.g., an execution environment, the deployment of senders, receivers, and message-oriented middleware) the experiment is not reproducible and hypotheses cannot be formulated.

Scenarios fill the gaps and define the experimental setting that should answer the questions posed in the GQM-plan. The performance influences of a specific factor (e.g., guaranteed delivery) are likely to depend on the experimental setting (e.g., the message size and the distribution of senders, receivers, and MOM). Thus, a carelessly chosen scenario can lead to wrong conclusions from the measurements. Furthermore, the inclusion of scenarios into the GQM-plan ensures the reproducibility of experiments. The scenarios can be used to quantify platform dependent influences for different execution environments (cf. Section 3.1.4). In addition, scenarios define the scope of validity for the answers of the experiments. The assumptions and restrictions of the scenarios must also hold for the target environment. Therefore, the scenarios must be representative for the overall measurement goal. For example, if the delivery time of a message has only been measured on a single machine, then no statement about message transfer in distributed systems can be made.

Hypotheses Scenarios allow the definition of concrete hypotheses with respect to the expected outcomes. Based on the available specification and documentation of the system under study, hypotheses formulate the expected outcome of the experiments for each question. Similar to Solingen and Berghout [SB99], the term "hypothesis" is used in a general sense. Hypotheses help performance analysts to answer questions posed in the GQM-Plan. For this purpose, hypotheses must be revisable. They must be formulated in such a way that they can be rejected and/or revised based on the measured data.

For example, a simple hypothesis "Factor X affects performance" does not help in answering any specific question. By contrast, hypothesis "The mean response time without factor X is at least 30% below the mean response time with factor X. The mean processor utilisation for both cases deviates less than 5%" is a formulation which enables a comparsion between expectation and measured data.

3.1.4. Parametrisation of Performance Models

The performance-relevant factors and degrees of freedom that have been identified in the previous steps may depend on the execution environment of the system under study. For example, the delivery time of a message (i.e., the time from sending the message until it is processed) depends not only on the system's configuration, but also on the underlying hard- and software of the MOM as well as its implementation. While all available MOM platforms offer a similar set of features (defined in standards such as Java Message Services [HBS+08]), their implementation may vary significantly. Performance models should abstract from such implementation dependencies (if possible) and provide an abstract view on the system under study. In combination with measurements, the abstraction can be customised automatically for different vendor implementations and yield accurate predictions for a broad range of middleware platforms.

Filling in degrees of freedom by measurements allows parametrising over the underlying software and hardware layers. However, resource demands cannot be accurately determined in every case. For example, the message delivery time is measurable but the processing demands for hard drives, network connections, or processors cannot be determined with the accuracy necessary. A mapping of all resource demands to the same (possibly load depended) resource is a possible solution to this problem. Even though such an abstraction requires strong assumptions (e.g., no severe resource conflicts with other parts of the system), it can yield a simple but accurate performance model. For example, Section 6 demonstrates the applicability of this approach for messaging systems.

In the following, we describe how the scenarios of the GQM-plan can support the parametrisation of performance models. Furthermore, we introduce the process model for combining measurements with parametric performance models.

From Performance Model Design to Automated Parametrisation Many performance models require the specification of resource demands (e.g., processing time on the CPU), which strongly depend on the underlying hardware, operating system, and middleware. If the performance model has to be employed for numerous different environments, performance analysts may want to parametrise the resource demands and keep the general behaviour of the model constant.

For example, the delivery time of a message changes for different MOM implementations and different hardware while the general behaviour for each configuration is not affected (cf. Chapter 6). Thus, it is sufficient to determine the resource demands for a new environment in order to instantiate the performance model for that environment.

Performance analysts have designed experiments to evaluate the performance of a system under study and to answer questions related to its performance properties. Therefore, they have implemented a series of test drivers that collect the necessary data, which also includes demands to different resources. Thus, it is sufficient to re-execute the relevant test drivers and determine the new resource demands from the results.

The execution of the test driver and the computation of resource demands can be done in an automated fashion, transparent to the software architect. Therefore, performance analysts provide *automated test drivers* (based on their initial experiments) that collect necessary measurement data and determine resource demands for the system under study. For example, software architects can use such automated test drivers to automatically determine the resource demands of a MOM platform and, thus, to include the influence of message-based communication into their prediction model.

Parametrising Performance Models More generally, performance evaluations of a system under test yield a performance model that fills in several degrees of freedom with measurements. Parametrising over these degrees of freedom allows performance analysts to create platform independent models that can be refined with measurements of an automated test driver.

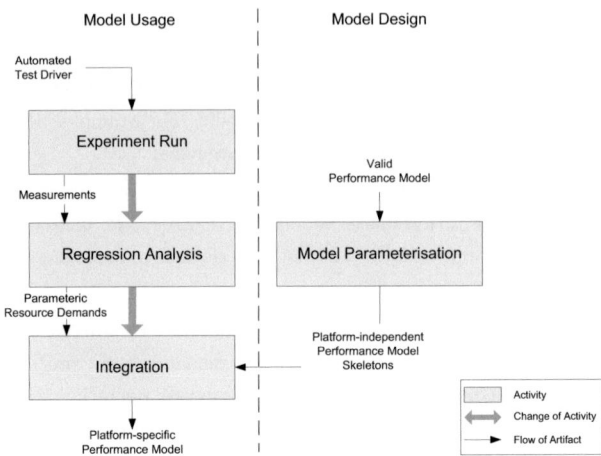

Figure 3.3.: Process of creating platform-specific completion components.

Figure 3.3 illustrates the process of creating a platform-specific performance model from a platform-independent performance model. The *automated test driver* runs on the selected target platform. The driver measures the performance of the infrastructure for all performance-relevant features identified during the experimentation phase.

For example, a performance analyst constructs a prediction model for MOM based on messaging patterns (cf. Chapter 6). The model without the platform-specific resource demands is called a *performance model skeleton*. Software architects then execute the automated test driver on their specific MOM platform (*Experiment Run*). The measurements provide the necessary information to determine the resource demands for the specific platform.

Furthermore, resource demands may depend on input parameters of the system under study (cf. Section A). Conducting *regression analyses* of measurement results identifies dependencies between input parameters and the resource demands. For example, the delivery time of a message may depend on its size. Regression analyses yields an (approximated) functional dependency between the message size and the corresponding resource demands. The resulting *parametric resource demands* are integrated with the *performance model skeletons* to define a *platform-specific performance model*. For example, executing the automated test driver for MOM on a system with Sun's Java System Message Queue 3.6 and an AMD X2 machine yields a performance model specific to this environment. The combination of model-based and measurement-based methods allows considering the infrastructure as a black-box, neglecting details specific to the implementation. In this thesis, we combine this concept with performance completions (cf. Section 2.1.4) to integrate performance-relevant factors of the infrastructure into high-level software performance models.

In the following section, we provide an overview of the performance modelling framework for GPOS schedulers developed in Chapters 4 and 5. During model design, we intensively employed the method for experiment-based derivation of performance models. Furthermore, in Chapter 6, we use the parametrisation of performance models to capture the various performance influences of MOM on different platforms.

3.2. Overview of the Performance Modelling Framework

In this section, we provide an overview of MOSS, a complex modelling and prediction framework for GPOS schedulers. During its design, we addressed various questions regarding the influence of GPOS schedulers on software performance (Section 3.2.1). Based on a series of experiments (cf. Chapters 4 and 5), we identified categories of performance-relevant factors of GPOS Schedulers (Section 3.2.2). These categories form the basic configuration options for GPOS schedulers whose performance influence can be evaluated using MOSS. For performance predictions, we defined a set of hierarchically structured CPNs (cf. Appendix B) that formally model the behaviour of the possible configurations of MOSS (Section 3.2.3.

3.2.1. Performance-related Questions for GPOS Schedulers

The mutual dependencies of task behaviour, underlying symmetric multiprocessing environments, and GPOS schedulers raise various questions regarding their influence on software performance. Our aim is to to create a performance model which captures these mutual influences and accurately predicts the performance from a user's perspective:

Goal:	*Purpose*	Predict
	Issue	mutual performance influences
	Object	of of task behaviour, GPOS schedulers
		in symmetric multiprocessing environments
	Viewpoint	from the user's point of view.

Table 3.1 refines the goal by three questions concerned with the performance modelling of different features of GPOS schedulers and their interaction with task behaviour and multiprocessing environments. In the following, we describe the rationale of these questions.

GPOS schedulers execute competing tasks pseudo-concurrently on a single processor. They employ different strategies to share the available processing time among all tasks. Thus, the first question asks how a performance model needs to reflect the influence of

Performance Model for Operating System Schedulers	
Question	Experiment / Section
How to model the influence of GPOS schedulers' time sharing features on software performance?	Time Sharing
How to model the influence of the interaction of GPOS schedulers with task behaviour on software performance?	Interactivity
How to model the influence of GPOS schedulers in symmetric multiprocessing environments on software performance?	Multiprocessor Load Balancing

Table 3.1.: How to model different scheduling features influencing software performance.

GPOS scheduler's time sharing features on software performance. In software performance evaluation, FCFS, PS, or preemptive priority are common approximations for time sharing policies of GPOS schedulers. However, these abstractions are not adequate for many scenarios. Consequently, we design a more realistic time sharing model for GPOS schedulers in Chapter 4 (Section 4.1).

For interactive and I/O-bound tasks, the current and past behaviour of tasks (i.e., how long a task used what resources) influences decisions of GPOS schedulers. Therefore, the second question asks for a valid performance model of schedulers with respect to task behaviour. In Chapter 4 (Section 4.2), we refine MOSS by adding the interactivity features necessary.

In (symmetric) multiprocessing environments, GPOS schedulers distribute competing tasks among the available processors. For accurate predictions, performance models need to reflect their load balancing and distribution policies. Thus, the third question asks for accurate performance models of GPOS schedulers in symmetric multiprocessing environments. In Chapter 5, we enhance MOSS by introducing multiprocessor load balancing capabilities.

3.2.2. Categorisation of Performance-relevant Factors of GPOS Schedulers

In this section, we introduce the categories of performance-relevant features for time sharing, interactivity, and multiprocessor load balancing. We use feature diagrams [CE00] to model the performance-relevant factors and variation points of MOSS.

Time Sharing

Time sharing addresses the management of tasks and the selection of the next task for execution. For this purpose, priority levels and run queues are used. The feature diagram in Figure 3.4 reflects the available *priorities*, the type of the *run queue*, and the *timeslices* of a

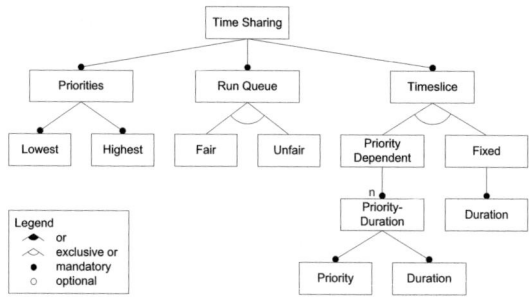

Figure 3.4.: Feature diagram of a scheduler's time sharing properties.

scheduler. A range from the *lowest* to the *highest* priority defines the available interactive priority levels. For example, the interactive priorities (also called nice-levels) of Linux range from 19 (lowest) to -20 (highest). *Run queues* can either be *fair* (e.g., Linux) or *unfair* (e.g., Windows). Fair run queues assign a fair share of processing time to each task. By contrast, unfair run queues always prefer the task with the highest priority over the tasks with lower priorities and, thus, accept the risk of starvation for the latter. Finally, *timeslices* can be of a *fixed* (Windows) or *priority-dependent* duration (Linux). The first option defines the timeslice's duration by a single value (*duration*), while the second specifies a different timeslice (*duration*) for each (*priority*) level.

Interactivity

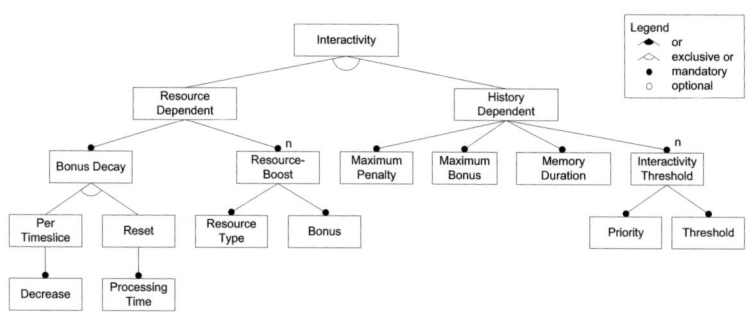

Figure 3.5.: Feature diagram of a scheduler's interactivity properties.

Interactivity refers to the different strategies used to prefer interactive and I/O-bound tasks over CPU-bound ones (for details see Section 2.3). Figure 3.5 shows a feature diagram of the performance-relevant properties of a scheduler's interactivity handling. The feature diagram distinguishes between *resource-dependent* and *history-dependent* policies. The first considers the type of resource used by a task to boost its dynamic priority (as implemented in Windows). The second policy observes a task's behaviour and determines its dynamic priority based on its past waiting and processing times (as implemented in Linux). A combination of both policies is not possible (exclusive or). The *resource-dependent* policy increases a task's priority depending on the resources it holds. Therefore, it contains a list associating a *bonus* with each type of *resource*. By contrast, the *history-dependent* policy maps the observed processing and waiting times to a range of dynamic priorities reaching from *maximum bonus* (e.g., +5 for Linux) to *maximum penalty* (e.g., -5 for Linux). Furthermore, the *memory period* determines the time, a scheduler remembers a task's behaviour (e.g., 1 second for Linux). Finally, the *interactivity threshold* determines how long a task must wait for a resource in order to be considered as interactive. This value depends on the task's static *priority* (e.g, 790 ms for a task with a nice-level of 0 under Linux on x86 systems).

Multiprocessor Load-Balancing

The multiprocessor load balancing is responsible for distributing the system's load among the available processors. In the following, we introduce a classification for multiprocessor load balancing strategies based on the work of Shivaratri et al. [SKS92], who categorise load balancing strategies of distributed systems. Even though multiprocessor systems differ in some important aspects (e.g., the communication is much faster than between distributed nodes) their classification provides a sound basis for multiprocessor systems. We extend the general features (Figure 3.6(a)) from Shivarati et al. with concrete characteristics for multiprocessor systems (Figures 3.6(b) to (e)). The latter directly relates to multiprocessor load balancing policies realised in GPOS schedulers, such as Windows and Linux. The next paragraphs systematically introduce the feature diagrams in Figure 3.6.

The first distinguishing feature for load balancing policies is their degree of centralisation. Load balancing policies can be centralised, hierarchical, fully decentralised, or in any combination of these. Policies with centralised components suffer from a potential bottleneck and a single point of failure. These limitations affect their scalability and reliability. Hierarchy can reduce these risks, but only fully decentralised systems, where all nodes function independently, can solve these problems. Centralisation mainly influences the location policy of the load balancing depicted in Figure 3.6(f).

Furthermore, load balancing policies can be characterised as static, dynamic, adaptive, or any combination of these. Figure 3.6(a) shows relevant features for multiprocessor systems, i.e., static and dynamic policies. Static policies use a priori knowledge on the system for balancing decisions. In Figure 3.6(a), the exclusive choice for static policies offers the features

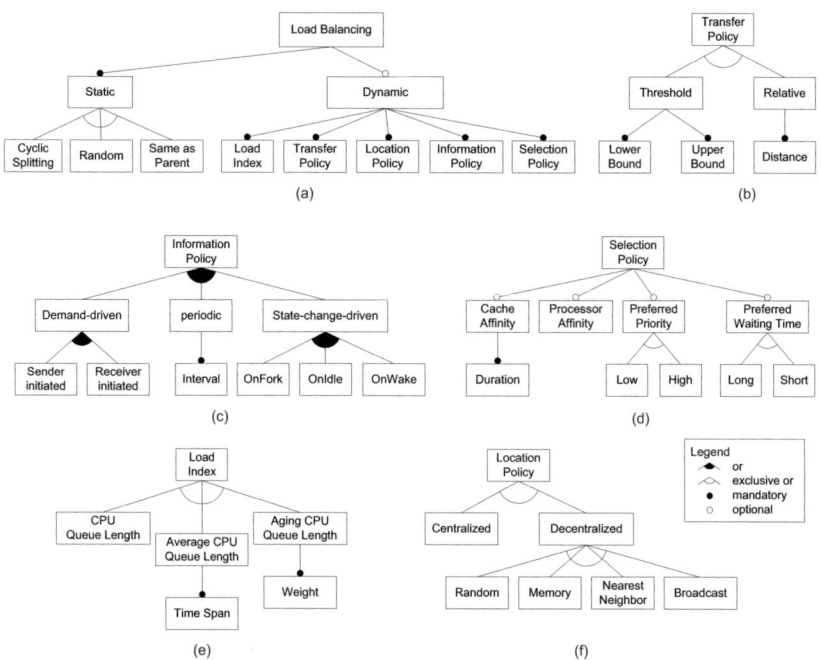

Figure 3.6.: Feature diagrams for classifying load balancing strategies.

cyclic splitting, same as parent, and *random.* Cyclic splitting assigns tasks to processors in a round robin fashion independently of the task and the processor's load. Following a similar philosophy, the random policy assigns tasks to each processor with a predefined probability. The probability can be equally distributed or varied for different CPUs, e.g, to consider the influence of differing processing power. Same as parent is specific to multiprocessor environments. It allocates a new task to the same processor as its creator. Thus, it leaves the actual load balancing to the dynamic policies, which use information on the system state for load balancing decisions. Dynamic load balancing policies consider, for example, the current load of each processor and assign a new task to the least loaded processor. A more detailed description of performance-relevant load balancing features follows in the next paragraphs. Finally, adaptive policies choose between different policies (static and dynamic) depending on the observed system state. These policies allow, for example, the reduction of load balancing activity when the load is balanced among all processors. However, adaptivity is a cross cutting concern with respect to static and dynamic load balancing policies and is thus not depicted in Figure 3.6.

The mandatory features of dynamic load balancing policies in Figure 3.6(a) determine when and where load balancing will take place. *Load indices* estimate the performance of a task on a particular processor (Figure 3.6(e)). Therefore, load indices reflect a processor's load during runtime. Multiple different measures have been proposed for this purpose. However, Kunz showed that the current *CPU queue length* represents the best indicator for a tasks performance on a particular node [Kun91]. For multiprocessor systems, various derivations of the CPU queue length have been used, such as the *average CPU queue length* over a predefined *time span* or an *ageing CPU queue length*.

Ageing variables are on-the-fly estimators for continuously changing variables. They take into account past valuations of the variable and level out brief peak conditions providing stable estimates of the CPU's queue length. The weighted sum of the processor's last and current load yields the ageing CPU queue length. The *weight* determines the influence of the last load on the estimator. To compute the ageing load index $\text{Load}_{n+1}(\text{CPU})$ at time $n+1$ for processor CPU, let $\text{Load}_{curr}(\text{CPU})$ be the processors current load (without ageing), $\text{Load}_n(\text{CPU})$ its previous load index (i.e., its ageing load at time n), and w the weight, then the new value of the load index is computed by [Tan01, p. 146]:

$$\text{Load}_{n+1}(\text{CPU}) = w\,\text{Load}_{curr}(\text{CPU}) + (1 - w)\,\text{Load}_n(\text{CPU})$$

Taking into account a CPU queue's history levels out disturbances of short peak loads and idle periods. It avoids unnecessary balancing attempts in systems with strongly fluctuating loads.

The *transfer policy* (Figure 3.6(b)) determines whether a processor can participate in a task transfer as a sender or as a receiver. *Threshold*-based policies define an upper and lower bound for a processor's load index. If a processor's load falls below the *lower bound*, it becomes a (potential) receiver. Otherwise, if a processor's load rises above the *upper bound* it becomes a (potential) sender. The processor does not participate in load balancing as it is assumed to be ideally loaded between these bounds. *Relative* policies consider a processor's load in relation to loads of other processors. Load balancing is initiated if the load of two processors differs more than a predefined value.

The *location policy* (Figure 3.6(f)) is responsible for the identification of a suitable transfer partner for processors which require load balancing. In a centralised system, this step is not an issue, as the coordinator can easily assign a transfer partner to a processor. In decentralised systems, the current processor cannot know the global system state. So, it can pick a node at *random*, *broadcast* its request to all nodes, choose the *nearest neighbour*, or use information collected during previous calls to find a transfer partner (*memory*). The different policies vary in chance and overhead for finding a transfer partner. However, for

SMP systems this is in general no issue as all processors and cores have equal access to the necessary data.

The *information policy* (Figure 3.6(c)) determines when information about the states of other processors in the system is to be collected and triggers load balancing. *Demand-driven* policies exchange information whenever a processor becomes a sender (*sender-initiated*) or receiver (*receiver-initiated*). If both cases are possible, the policy is called symmetrically initiated. When collecting data *periodically*, the *interval* determines the period length in which balancing efforts occur. Furthermore, *state-change-driven* policies pass information whenever a node's state changes. The most important events for multiprocessing systems are *OnFork*, which is activated whenever a new task is created, *OnIdle*, which is activated whenever a processor becomes idle, and *OnWake*, which signals that a process resumes execution after waiting.

If a processor becomes a sender, the *selection policy* (Figure 3.6(d)) chooses tasks for transfer. The policy can optimise load balancing by minimising transfer overhead. To achieve a good optimisation, the policy selects tasks which (presumably) have a long live-span and which have a minimum number of location dependencies. For example, newly originated tasks are preferable for transfer, since they do not need to be preempted and do not have any state that needs to be transferred. Moreover, they can be assumed to live relatively long and do not have any location dependencies. If the selection policy does not find a suitable task for transfer, it no longer considers the processor as a sender. All selection criteria in Figure 3.6(d) are optional and can be combined arbitrarily. Selection policies that take into account *cache affinities* migrate only tasks that did not run on the processor for at least *duration* milliseconds. The selection policy assumes that all other tasks still have useful data in the cache and, thus, avoids to move them. Additionally, *processor affinity* limits the shifting of tasks to a predefined set of processors. This option allows the load balancer to select only tasks whose affinity list contains the receiving processor. When multiple tasks are available for migration, the options *preferred priority* and *preferred waiting time* determine which one to select. If the preferred priority is *high* (*low*), higher (lower) priority tasks are migrated first. Furthermore, if the *preferred waiting time* is *short*, tasks at the end of a queue are preferred over tasks in the beginning of the queue and vice versa for *long* waiting times.

For multiprocessing systems, the choice of an optimal task for transfer mainly depends on the underlying hardware architecture. In SMT systems, for example, task transfers are cheap since the virtual processors share all necessary resources. Task transfers can thus happen quite often. For NUMA systems, the scheduler has to consider dependencies on the local memory and high costs for transfer. Task transfers on this level should happen only when necessary. Consequently, schedulers for multiprocessing systems employ different balancing policies for different architectural levels.

Feature Configurations for Windows and Linux

The Windows and Linux operating systems differ with respect to time sharing, interactivity, and multiprocessor load balancing. Table 3.2 summarises the feature configurations for both operating systems. In the following, we describe the different feature configurations in more detail.

As time sharing policy, Windows uses an unfair run queue with fixed timeslices. By contrast, Linux employs a fair run queue and priority-dependent timeslices to allow a fair distribution of processing time among competing tasks.

The operating systems further differ in their interaction with task behaviour. Linux keeps track of a task's history, to determine its bonus or penalty. For this purpose, Linux compares the time a task spend waiting (or sleeping) to the time it spend processing. Furthermore, tasks that spend a larger fraction waiting than processing are classified as interactive. In general, interactive tasks are privileged and, thus, can circumvent the fairness properties of Linux' run queue. The amount of waiting time necessary to be classified as interactive depends on a task's static priority. By contrast, Windows uses static priority boosts. Table 3.2 lists the bonuses for different resources. A task's bonus decreases slowly with each timeslice it receives.

For multiprocessor load balancing, both operating systems combine static and dynamic load balancing policies. While Windows balances as little as possible, Linux keeps the system's evenly balanced among the available processors. Windows' static balancing policy uses cyclic splitting to assign newly created tasks to processors. Its dynamic balancing policy realises a threshold-based transfer policy. Windows uses the CPU queue length (including the running task) as a load index. If the load of a CPU drops below one (the CPU becomes idle), the CPU becomes a receiver. All CPUs with a load greater than one are potential senders (threshold-based transfer policy). Once idle, a processor looks for executable tasks on other processors implementing a demand-driven, receiver initiated information policy. Windows' location policy chooses the processor with the highest load as sender. Its selection policy prefers tasks with high priorities, but also considers their processor and cache affinity. The latter directly relates to the time a task last ran. When more time elapses, a task's cache affinity decreases and it becomes more likely that it will be moved. Additionally, processor affinities restrict the selection of processors where a task can be moved. Windows employs a state-change-driven policy. Whenever a task becomes ready (e.g., after blocking or creation) and an idle CPU (receiver) is available, the scheduler tries to migrate the task to the idle CPU.

	Linux	Windows	
	2.6	**XP / 2000**	**Server 2003**
Time Sharing			
Highest Priority	-20	15	15
Lowest Priority	19	0	0
Run Queue	Fair	Unfair	Unfair
Timeslice	Priority Dependent 5 - 800 ms c.f. Table 2.2	Fixed 31,25 ms	Fixed 187,5 ms
Interactivity			
Priority Boost Values	Dynamic [-5, +5] Linearly scaled depending on the time waiting compared to the time computing Memory: 1 second	Static Semaphore +1 Disk +1 Network +2 Keyboard +6 Mouse +6 Sound +8	Static Semaphore +1 Disk +1 Network +2 Keyboard +6 Mouse +6 Sound +8
Priority Updates	When timeslice expired	After waiting When timeslice expired	After waiting When timeslice expired
Load Balancing			
Initial Processor Selection	Same as Parent	Cyclic Splitting	Cyclic Splitting
Load Index Transfer Policy Information Policy	Aging CPU Load Relative Symetrically initiated, periodic, OnFork, OnIdle, and OnWake	- - -	CPU Load Threshold Receiver Initiated
Selection Policy	Cache Affinity, Processor Affinity, Prefer High Priority, Prefer longer Waiting Times	-	Cache Affinity, Processor Affinity, Prefer High Priority, Prefer longer Waiting Times

Table 3.2.: Comparison between Linux and Windows schedulers.

In contrast to Windows, Linux uses an ageing CPU queue length as load index. Its relative transfer policy initiates load balancing only if the distance exceeds a threshold of 2. Furthermore, Linux uses a state-change-driven as well as periodic information policy. The state-change-driven policy reacts whenever a new task is created (OnFork), a task is about to be awakened (OnWake), or a CPU becomes idle (OnIdle). The periodic policy checks at regular intervals if the CPUs of a scheduling domain need to be balanced. If the load differs too much, it moves tasks from the busiest processor in the domain to the most idle one. The selection policy of the Linux scheduler considers factors like cache affinity time and processor affinities. Moreover, it prefers tasks with a low priority and a long waiting time for migration.

3.2.3. MOSS – Overview of the Prediction Model

In the following, we give an overview of the definition of MOSS in terms of timed Coloured Petri Nets (CPNs, cf. Appendix B). The hierarchical structure of CPNs allows the straight-forward integration of different feature configurations for schedulers. Due to the simulation and analysis capabilities of CPNs, they are well suited for performance evaluation of complex systems. The detailed models of MOSS follow in Chapters 4 and 5.

For performance prediction, we integrated MOSS with the Palladio Component Model (PCM, cf. Appendix A). Software architects can configure schedulers either using the available scheduler features or selecting from a set of predefined configurations, e.g., for Windows XP or Linux 2.6. In the following, we explain the basic concepts of the integration of MOSS and the PCM.

Relation to the PCM   The PCM describes the behaviour of a software system in an abstract fashion. It decomposes the system's behaviour into hierarchically structured components. Each component provides and requires a set of services grouped to interfaces. For performance prediction, so-called "resource demanding service effect specifications" (RD-SEFFs, cf. Section A) abstractly describe the behaviour of each service (cf. Figure 3.7). They model the order and extent of resource usages as well as calls to other components. The static architecture shown on the left-hand side of Figure 3.7 contains components (basic and composite) their connections and their deployment. Each (basic) component's service is associated with an abstract behavioural specification (RD-SEFF). Components, connections, RD-SEFFs, and deployment relations provide a full description of the overall system needed for performance prediction.

While the PCM provides a detailed model of the software system, MOSS describes the behaviour and performance influences of GPOS schedulers on performance. Figure 3.7 ab-

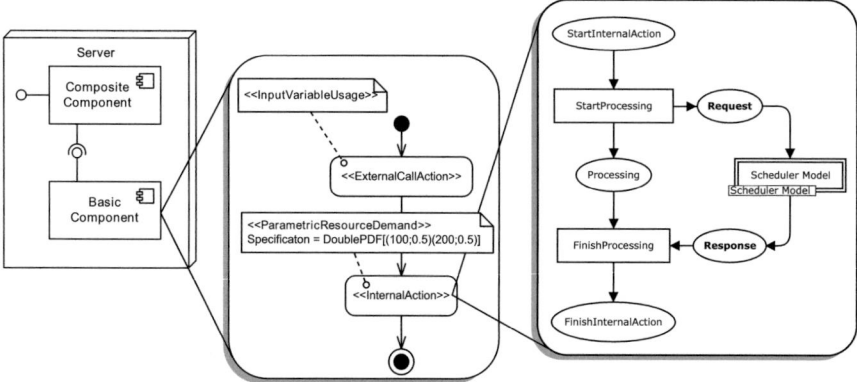

Figure 3.7.: Integration of the scheduler performance model (MOSS) into the PCM.

stractly illustrates the connection of MOSS to the PCM. For each service provided by a basic component, the PCM abstractly models the service's behaviour as an RD-SEFF. RD-SEFF's consist of a set of internal an external actions that are structured by control flow elements (e.g., loops, branches, and forks). For all internal actions that require processing time on a CPU, MOSS refines the behaviour of that action and decomposes it into multiple steps (right hand side of Figure 3.7).

When an internal action demands processing time on the CPU, it notifies MOSS by putting a token on place Request. The scheduler model processes the request (including possible contention in the system). Once the request has been processed, it notifies the internal action, whose demand has been processed, by putting a token on place Response. This token allows to continue the RD-SEFF's execution. Furthermore, the behavioural model informs MOSS whenever a task changes its state of processing, e.g., is waiting for a passive resource or is waking up.

MOSS – Hierarchical Structure In Figure 3.7, substitution transition Scheduler Model encapsulates MOSS' behaviour. The transition's interactions are limited to Requests and Responses. Figure 3.8 illustrates the hierarchical refinement of MOSS by multiple layers of substitution transitions. The hierarchical structure of CPNs encapsulates the behaviour of all feature configurations in separate subnets. The top level scheduler model contains several fusion places which enable the communication of the scheduler model with behavioural performance models, such as the PCM. Several substitution transitions serve to further refine the top level net. Figure 3.8 exemplarily shows the subnet for transition Schedule. Its subnet contains further fusion places and substitution transitions.

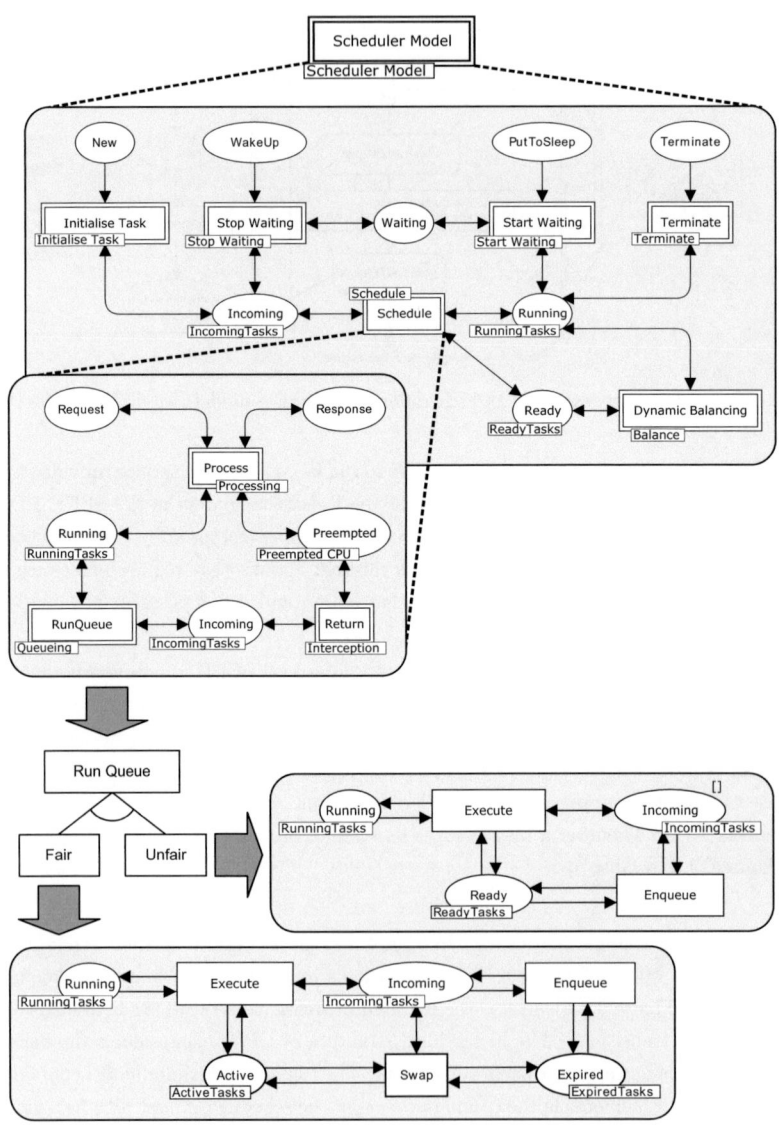

Figure 3.8.: Hierarchical structure of the scheduler performance model (MOSS).

MOSS' hierarchical structure integrates different time sharing, interactivity, and load balancing features into a single CPN. Each substitution transition resembles a possible variation point. Transformations select the subnets according to a given feature configuration. Each feature may be further subdivided into several smaller parts, which represent its independent variation points. Figure 3.8 illustrates exemplarily how a run queue's fairness property affects the subnet selection of substitution transition RunQueue. For unfair run queues, the transformation selects a different subnet than for its fair counterpart. While different features are defined independently in separate subnets, they strongly interact with each other. For this purpose, fusion places model interaction points which allow flexible communication between the separate scheduler features.

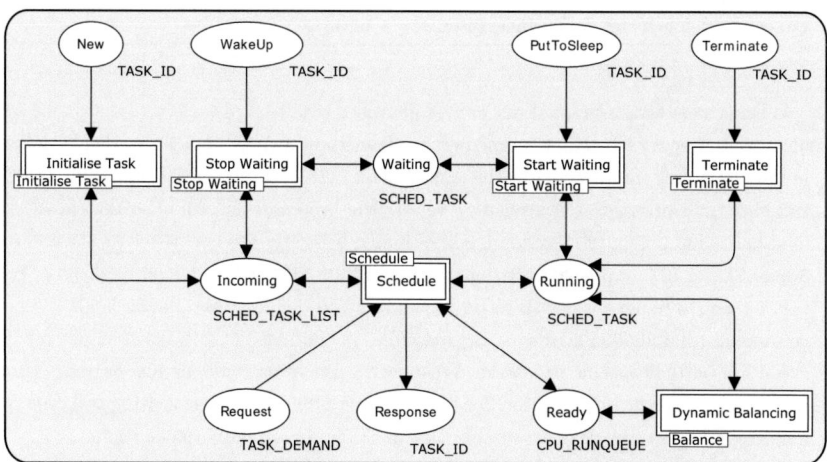

Figure 3.9.: Schematic overview of the scheduler performance model.

An abstract view of MOSS From an abstract point of view, MOSS behaves similarly for all feature configurations. It accepts requests, i.e., demands of processing time, notifies the calling behaviour when its request is finished, starts processing new tasks, terminates finished tasks, and puts tasks to sleep or wakes them up. Figure 3.9 gives a schematic overview of the CPN model realising this behaviour. The model's substitution transitions encapsulate the scheduler's time sharing, interactivity, and multiprocessor load balancing strategies. The boldly printed places represent interaction points of MOSS to task behaviour models (such as the PCM), which require access to scheduled resources. All other places are internal to MOSS. The communication between all subnets is based on fusion places. However, for reasons of readability, Figure 3.9 uses input/output places to denote communication. Figure 3.9 is only an abstract representation of the actual CPN.

All places accept tokens of colours printed in Listing 3.1. MOSS communicates with behavioural models of tasks based on a unique task identifier (TASK_ID). For each identifier, the scheduler model manages its internal information (e.g., timeslices and priorities) using colour SCHED_TASK.

Listing 3.1: Basic colour sets of the scheduler model.

```
colset TASK_ID = INT;p
colset DEMAND = INT;
colset TASK_DEMAND = (TASK_ID, DEMAND);

colset SCHED_TASK = product ID * CPU_ID * PRIORITY * TIMESLICE timed;
colset SCHED_TASK_LIST = list SCHED_TASK;
colset CPU_RUNQUEUE = product CPU_ID * TASKLIST;
```

When a new task is created, its unique identifier is put on place New to notify the scheduler, that a new task requires scheduling. Transition Initialise Task then creates the initial scheduling information for the task (SCHED_TASK), which contains its initial processor, timeslice, and priority. The transition selects the processor according to the chosen static load balancing policy (cf. Section 3.2.2). Finally, it inserts the new token at the end of list SCHED_TASK_LIST on place Incoming. Whenever, a SCHED_TASK is added to this list, transition Schedule assigns the task to its processor's run queue. Place Ready holds a separate run queue (CPU_RUNQUEUE) for each processor. It contains those tasks that are ready for execution on that specific processor. Whenever a processor is idle or the currently running task's timeslice expires, transition Schedule removes the currently executing task from place Running and puts the next executable task of the processor's run queue there.

When a task requests processing time, it puts a TASK_DEMAND token on place Request. The token contains the task's unique identifier (TASK_ID) as well as the demand which is required (DEMAND). As soon as the task is running (i.e., its SCHED_TASK token lies on place Running), it can reduce its demand according to the time it spend on place Running. As soon as a task's demand reaches zero, transition Schedule puts its TASK_ID on place Response to notify the task behavioural model that its request has been processed and that it can continue execution. Transition Dynamic Balancing levels the load between multiple processors according to the specified dynamic load balancing policy.

Furthermore, MOSS reflects the mutual performance influences of passive resources (i.e., semaphores) and the GPOS scheduler. It may be necessary to put a task to sleep until the resources that have been requested by a task become available. As soon as these resources are available, the scheduler needs to resume processing of that task. To notify the scheduler about such state changes, a task's unique identifier is put on places `PutToSleep` or `WakeUp`. Transition `Start Waiting` removes the task from the processor it is currently running on and puts its token on place `Waiting`. As soon as a passive resource notifies the scheduler to wake up that task, transition `Stop Waiting` removes the corresponding token from place `Waiting` and inserts it at the end of the `SCHED_TASK_LIST` on place `Incoming`.

Finally, when the execution of a task is finished, the behavioural model notifies MOSS by putting the task's unique identifier on place `Terminate`. Transition `Terminate` then removes the internal `SCHED_TASK` token of that task.

3.3. Summary

In this chapter, we have presented an iterative method for the design of performance models for complex systems. For the experiment-based derivation of performance models, performance analysts (i) start from existing documentation and specifications, (ii) systematically evaluate all candidates of performance-relevant features using the GQM approach, (iii) design performance models based on the measurements, and (iv) validate the resulting performance models. These steps are repeated iteratively until the desired degree of accuracy has been achieved.

Furthermore, we have provided an overview of MOSS' hierarchical structure which is defined in terms of CPNs. MOSS consists of multiple subnets that reflect the behaviour of different parts of operating system schedulers. For performance prediction, different subnets can be combined in order to consider the influence of different operating system schedulers on software performance.

In the following chapters, we refine MOSS' behavioural model systematically with time sharing and interactivity handling (Chapter 4) as well as multiprocessor load balancing (Chapter 5).

4. Single Processor Scheduling

In this chapter, we systematically evaluate the performance influence of operating system schedulers in single processor environments. Based on the results, we define a hierarchical CPN model called MOSS. The model captures the performance influence of different time sharing policies (Section 4.1) and of different interactivity policies (Section 4.2). In a case study (Section 4.3), we demonstrate MOSS' broader applicability using a real-world business information system. We discuss the benefits and drawbacks of MOSS (Section 4.4) and summarise our results (Section 4.5) to conclude this chapter.

4.1. Time Sharing

Time sharing can strongly influence the response time and throughput of a software system. Depending on the chosen policy, different tasks benefit (i.e., shorter response times) or suffer (i.e., longer response times). In this section, we evaluate and model the influence of time sharing on software performance. We focus on mutual dependencies of priorities, timeslices, run queues, and task behaviour (i.e., the type of workload and request sizes).

The structure of this section follows the experiment-based derivation of software performance models introduced in Section 3.1. In a series of experiments, we answer questions regarding the performance influence of different time sharing features (Section 4.1.1). Based on the results, we design a CPN model for time sharing (Section 4.1.3). The model refines the abstract CPN model introduced in Section 3.2.3. In a case study, we validate the prediction accuracy of the model (Section 4.1.4). The model predicts the influence of the time sharing policies for Windows and Linux with an error of less than 5% in the considered scenarios.

4.1.1. Experiments – Overview and Motivation

The experiments presented in this section were conducted to evaluate time sharing and to identify valid assumptions for MOSS. Based on documentation (cf. Section 2.3), hypotheses state preliminary assumptions regarding the influence of time sharing properties on software performance. For example, fair run queues might be expected to prevent starvation. While such statements can be found in literature (e.g., [Aas05]), it remains unclear under which conditions they hold. The combination with other scheduler properties (e.g., interactivity handling, cf. Section 4.2) might affect the behaviour and performance of fair run queues. In the following GQM plan, we formulate questions that address such mutual dependencies of task behaviour, time sharing and other scheduler properties.

The Goal

For the experiments, we applied the scenario-based GQM methodology introduced in Section 3.1.3. Like in the original GQM approach, goals are refined by a purpose, an issue, an object, and a view point. In the following, we describe the goal for the performance evaluation of different time sharing properties for GPOS schedulers.

Goal: *Purpose*   Identify
            Issue   (mutual) performance influences
           Object   of different time sharing properties
        Viewpoint   from the user's point of view.

The goal addresses the different performance influences of time sharing properties and their mutual dependencies. For example, fair run queues profit from priority-dependent timeslices. With this goal, we specifically target the user's perspective on software performance, i.e., externally observable performance metrics such as response time and throughput. The utilisation of resources, even though it is interesting for performance analysis, is only slightly affected by time sharing: The total amount of work a resource processes during a period is not affected by the time sharing policy.

In the following, we motivate the questions listed in Table 4.1. In Section 4.1.2, we describe the corresponding scenarios, metrics, hypotheses, and results.

Motivation of the Questions

Timeslices   Most GPOS schedulers use timeslices in combination with a variant of round-robin (RR) to share the available processing time among competing tasks. In software performance prediction, processor sharing (PS) is used to approximate such behaviour. PS abstracts from timeslices and cyclic resource assignment. From a theoretical point of view, it uses timeslices and context switch times that are infinitely close to zero [LZGS84]. As a result, processing time is equally distributed among competing tasks. However, GPOS schedulers may use strongly varying timeslice sizes to share processing time among tasks. If the requested processing times are smaller than a single timeslice, PS may not approximate task response times accurately. Furthermore, the effect of timeslices on response time distribution needs to be evaluated. Therefore, Question TS.1 (Table 4.1) addresses the influence of timeslices.

Performance influences of different time sharing properties from the user's point of view			
	TS.1	**TS.2**	**TS.3**
Questions	To what extent do timeslices influence task response times?	Under which conditions do fair/unfair run queues influence software performance?	How do priorities influence the processing time of tasks in fair run queues?
Experiment	Simulation	Measurement	Measurement
Scenarios	ContinuousLong ContinuousShort ExponentialShort	Closed Open	Close Medium Shifted Far
Metrics		Response Time and Throughput	
Hypotheses	Timeslices influence the variance but not the mean of response time distributions.	Fair run queues have a major influence for contiuous load. Otherwise they yield similar performance as unfair ones.	For fair run queues, priorities have a major impact on performance.

Table 4.1.: GQM plan – questions and expectations concerning the performance influence of time sharing policies.

Run Queues GPOS schedulers use different kinds of run queues to manage tasks that are waiting to be processed. In this section, we focus on the effect of fair and unfair run queues as implemented in the Linux 2.6 and Windows operating system series. Unfair run queues assign (almost) all processing time to the tasks with the highest priority. This policy can lead to starvation of lower priority tasks. By contrast, fair run queues are meant to prevent starvation and to assign a fair share of processing time to all tasks. In addition, Linux 2.6 scales timeslice sizes according to task priorities. This policy can directly affect task response time and throughput.

However, the scheduler may prefer I/O-bound and interactive tasks, to ensure a good overall system utilisation. This behaviour may countervail a run queue's fairness. Thus, tasks with lower priorities benefit only under certain conditions from the run queue's fairness. Question TS.2 (Table 4.1) addresses the influence of different run queue types.

Priorities Fair scheduling assigns larger timeslices to tasks with higher priorities in order to grant a larger share of processing time to them. However, the assignment of timeslices is not linear (cf. Table 2.2 on page 34). The actual share of processing time depends on the task's priority as well of the priorities of all concurrently running tasks. Due to the non-linearity, small changes of task priorities may lead to large differences in the observed performance. While the (pure) effect of priority-dependent timeslices may be derived from Table 2.2, its interactions with other scheduler properties require further investigation. Question TS.3 (Table 4.1) addresses the influence of priorities.

Experiment Design

The experiment design is focussed on the type of workload (open/closed), task priorities, and the performance metrics response time and throughput. The behaviour of a task is parametrised over the demanded processing time as well as its delay or inter-arrival time.

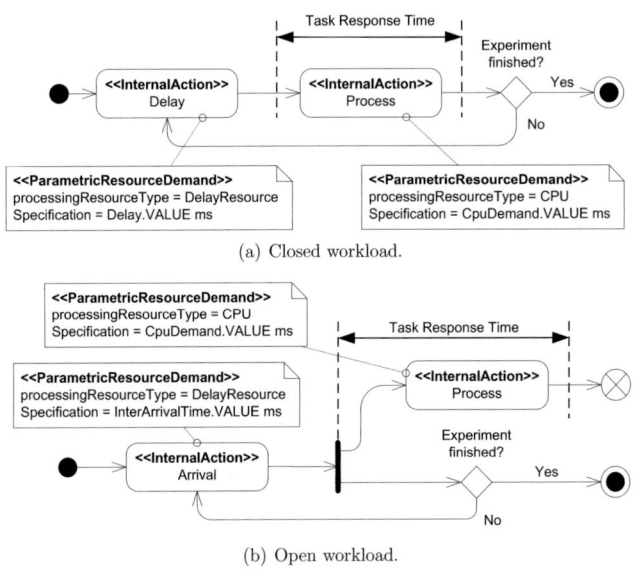

(a) Closed workload.

(b) Open workload.

Figure 4.1.: Task behaviour for closed and open workloads of the experiment.

Open and Closed Workload   Figures 4.1(a) and (b) depict the task behaviour for closed and open workloads in an RD-SEFF-like notation. RD-SEFFs are well-suited for this purpose, since they allow the parametrisation of resource demands (cf. Appendix A). The behaviour of closed workloads includes two internal actions executed in a loop. The first action (`Delay`) loads a delay server (`DelayResource`) that defers the task's execution for `Delay.VALUE` milliseconds. Internal action `Process` then requires `CpuDemand.VALUE` milliseconds of processing time on the processing resource `CPU`. The experiment is finished when either enough measurements have been taken, a certain time period has been exceeded, or a given confidence level has been reached (see [Jai91]) for details).

For open workloads, tasks behave analogously. The control flow is split after internal action `Arrival`. The first part executes internal action `Process` while the second part checks whether the experiment should be continued. Accordingly, it waits for the next arrival or finishes the experiment. The value of input parameter `InterArrivalTime` determines the inter-arrival time of the open workload.

For simulation, resource demands are directly linked to requests to the corresponding resources that defer the execution of the tasks. However, it is necessary to mimic the resource demands in order to measure the performance on real systems. Therefore, a set of algorithms typically used for CPU benchmarks, such as SPEC CPU2000 [Cor00, Hen00], generates the necessary load on the CPU. A detailed description of the resource demand generation can be found in [BDH08] and Appendix C.3. Furthermore, tasks are put to sleep to model the specified delays, e.g., by calling the Java function `Thread.sleep()`. Appendix C.2 describes the effect of this approach in more detail and discusses how accurate delays can be achieved.

Metrics The scenarios presented above require an exact definition of the performance metrics response time and throughput. For response time, the exact measurement points can strongly influence the results (see [Koz08b] for a discussion of different views on response time). Figure 4.1 depicts the start- and endpoints of response time measurements for open and for closed workloads. In the case of closed workloads, response time corresponds to the time for processing internal action `Process`. For open workloads, the response time includes the time passed from issuing a request until its completion. Thus, measurements start at the branch of the control flow and end at internal action `Process`. In addition to the pure (possibly contented) processing time, the measurement includes initial delays caused, for example, by other tasks occupying the CPU.

Throughput (X) is defined as the number of `Process` actions (N) completed during the entire experiment time (T), i.e., $X = N/T$ [LZGS84].

Nice-level	Priority	
	Windows	Linux
19	4	139
15	4	135
10	6	130
5	6	125
0	8	120
-5	10	115
-10	10	110
-15	13	105
-20	24	100

Table 4.2.: Mapping of nice-levels to operating system priorities.

Priorities To evaluate and quantify different time sharing properties, it is necessary to compare and to relate task priorities independent of the underlying operating system. In this section, we use nice-levels [BC05] for this purpose. Nice-levels are mapped directly to priorities and are available for most Unix-like systems. Furthermore, third party tools implement a mapping of nice-levels to priorities for all variants of the Windows operating system series [RH]. Table 4.2 shows the mapping of nice-levels to native operating system priorities. For Windows operating systems, it is necessary to map a set of nice-levels to the same priority. For the experiments presented here, we refer to nice-levels instead of operating system priorities and use both terms interchangeably.

4.1.2. Answering the Questions – Scenarios, Metrics, Hypotheses, and Results

In the following, we define scenarios, metrics, and hypotheses in order to answer the questions raised in the beginning of this section. The experiment results for the first question (TS.1) are determined by means of simulation. For the other two questions, measurements of a Linux 2.6.22 and Windows XP system provide the necessary results.

Question TS.1: To what extent do timeslices influence task response times?

Question TS.1 (cf. Table 4.1) is motivated by the abstraction of PS from RR, which is widely used in performance prediction. It targets the influence of time slices and round robin on the response time distribution's variance. It specifically evaluates the mutual influences of processing times, timeslice sizes, and the number of requests in the system.

Scenarios   The evaluation of Question TS.1 includes two major scenarios. The first scenario employs a closed workload with zero think time, with varying request sizes, and with different numbers of concurrent tasks. We focussed on influences of timeslices on response time. The demands of the tasks are either smaller than a single timeslice or significantly larger. Timeslices can be expected to have different effects on response time distribution for both cases. Furthermore, the closed workload keeps the processor's load constant and avoids disturbances by an increasing number of tasks in the system.

The second scenario resembles an open workload with short demands and an exponentially distributed inter-arrival time. We focussed on the influence of a fluctuating number of tasks. Since the influence of scheduling policies on response time is largest for open workloads and a high resource utilisation [SWHB06], the scenario is meant to point out differences and similarities of the scheduling policies with respect to response time.

Table 4.3 summarises the scenario configurations. The values given for the inter-arrival time and delay determine the valuation of the input parameters `InterArrivalTime` and `Delay` of the RD-SEFFs for open and closed workloads in Figure 4.1. Similarly, column

Name	Workload	Delay	Number of Tasks	CPU Demand
ContinuousLong	closed	0 ms	2, 16, and 32	450 ms
ContinuousShort	closed	0 ms	2, 16, and 32	20 ms

		Inter-Arrival Time		
ExponentialShort	open	ExponentialDist(1 / 21)		20 ms

Table 4.3.: Evaluation scenarios for Question TS.1.

CPU Demand stands for the valuation of input parameter CpuDemand. For the closed workload scenarios, the number of tasks is 2, 16, or 32. The inter-arrival time of scenario ExponentialShort is exponentially distributed with a rate of $\lambda = 1/21$, i.e., with a mean of 21 ms. Little's Law states that the utilisation s of a server with a mean service time $E[S]$ and an arrival rate λ is given by $u = \lambda * E[S]$, for queueing networks with an open workload. Therefore, the inter-arrival time and resource demand given in this scenario lead to a utilisation of $u = 1/21 * 20 = 0.952$ for the CPU. The combination of short requests, open workload, and high resource utilisation emphasises the (possible) differences of scheduling policies.

Response time is the only metric considered to answer Question TS.1. Special emphasis lays on its distribution. Thus, the standard deviation ($\text{sd}_{\text{RT}}[t]$) and the coefficient of variation ($\text{cov}_{\text{RT}}[t]$) are provided in addition to the mean value ($E_{\text{RT}}[t]$). The coefficient of variation aggregates the standard deviation and mean into a single value, i.e., the coefficient of variation is defined as the standard deviation of a data set divided by its mean.

Hypotheses For the scenarios ContinuousLong and ContinuousShort, Hypothesis TS.1.a expects the mean response time of each task to be the product of the number of concurrent tasks (N) and the request size. For scenario ContinousLong (ContinousShort), let t_l (t_s) be a task and N_l (N_s) the number of tasks, then

$$E_{\text{RT}}[t_l] \approx N_l * 450\,\text{ms} \quad \text{and} \quad E_{\text{RT}}[t_s] \approx N_s * 20\,\text{ms} \tag{TS.1.a}$$

In other words, PS, which assigns each task $1/N$th of the processor, is assumed to accurately predict the scenarios' mean response times. However, Hypothesis TS.1.b (see Table 4.1) expects the coefficient of variation for ContinuousShort to be much larger than for ContinuousLong. Let t_l (t_s) and N_l (N_s) be defined as above, then

$$\text{cov}_{\text{RT}}[t_s] \gg \text{cov}_{\text{RT}}[t_l] \quad \text{for all } N_s = N_l. \tag{TS.1.b}$$

Furthermore, Hypothesis TS.1.c expects the variation of the response time distribution to increase with the number of concurrently executing tasks for both scenarios. Let t_N be a task for a scenario with N concurrent tasks, then

$$\mathrm{sd}_{\mathrm{RT}}\, t_N < \mathrm{sd}_{\mathrm{RT}}\, t_{N+i} \text{ for all } i > 0. \tag{TS.1.c}$$

As a consequence, TS.1.d considers PS only a good approximation of RR-based time sharing policies if the coefficient of variation is below 0.2, i.e., the majority of observed response times deviates at most by 20% from the mean response time:

$$\mathrm{cov}_{\mathrm{RT}}[t_s] < 0.2 \quad \text{and} \quad \mathrm{cov}_{\mathrm{RT}}[t_l] < 0.2 \tag{TS.1.d}$$

For scenario `ExponentialShort`, Hypothesis TS.1.e expects FCFS, PS and RR scheduling to yield the same mean response time. The results should only differ in terms of variance. PS is expected to have the smallest standard deviation, followed by RR and then FCFS, i.e., let t_{fcfs}, t_{ps}, t_{rr} be a task of scenario `ExponentialShort` with FCFS, PS, and RR scheduling respectively, then:

$$\mathrm{E}_{\mathrm{RT}}[t_{\mathrm{ps}}] \approx \mathrm{E}_{\mathrm{RT}}[t_{\mathrm{rr}}] \approx \mathrm{E}_{\mathrm{RT}}[t_{\mathrm{fcfs}}]$$
$$\mathrm{sd}_{\mathrm{RT}}(t_{\mathrm{ps}}) < \mathrm{sd}_{\mathrm{RT}}(t_{\mathrm{rr}}) < \mathrm{sd}_{\mathrm{RT}}(t_{\mathrm{fcfs}}) \tag{TS.1.e}$$

In the following, we present the results of the experiments and evaluate whether the hypotheses listed above can be considered as valid.

Scenario	Number of Tasks	Mean [ms]	Standard Deviation [ms]	Coefficient of Variation
Continuous Short	2	40	8,2	0,21
	16	319	101,7	0,32
	32	649	203,6	0,33
Continuous Long	2	900	10,1	0,012
	16	7199	125,1	0,017
	32	14397	255,3	0,017

Table 4.4.: Characteristics of the measured response times for scenarios `ContinuousLong` and `ContinuousShort`.

Results Table 4.4 summarises the results for scenarios `ContinuousLong` and `ContinuousShort`. In all cases, the response time approximately equals the product of the number of tasks and the resource demand as expected by Hypothesis TS.1.a. The measured mean response time differs less than 1% from the expected result. In addition, the coefficient of variation is more than 10 times larger in scenario ContinuousShort compared to ContinuousLong. While the mean scales linearly with the request's size, the standard deviation increases only slightly for long requests compared to short ones. The similar standard deviation leads to large differences for the coefficient of variation and, thus, supports Hypothesis TS.1.b. Furthermore, the standard deviations listed in Table 4.4 suggest an almost linear increase with the number of concurrent tasks independent of the request size, which supports Hypothesis TS.1.c. In all cases, the coefficient of variation is below 0.2 for scenario ContinuousLong and above 0.2 for scenario ContinuousShort. Following Hypothesis TS.1.d, this suggests that PS sufficiently approximates the response time distribution of long requests, while smaller requests are stronger affected by timeslices. For the latter reason, Hypothesis TS.1.d has to be rejected.

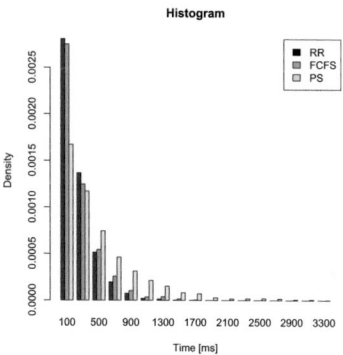

Figure 4.2.: Comparison between the response time distribution of scenario ExponentialShort for round-robin, first-come-first-served, and processor-sharing.

Figure 4.2 depicts the simulated response time distribution for scheduling policies RR (with a timeslice of 31.5 ms), FCFS, and PS. While RR and FCFS appear similar in the histogram, the response time distribution of PS has a heavier tail. A comparison between the mean response times of the three scheduling policies confirms this impression (cf. Table 4.5).

Scheduling Policy	Mean Response Time	Standard Deviation
RR	231.5 ms	208.4 ms
FCFS	254.7 ms	250.0 ms
PS	488.3 ms	491.4 ms

Table 4.5.: Simulation results for scenario ExponentialShort.

The mean response time predicted by PS is about two times larger than the mean response times predicted by RR and by FCFS. Newly arriving tasks delay the execution of all tasks currently in the queue under PS scheduling. Thus, tasks currently waiting in the queue complete their processing later and keep the load high for a longer time. When additional tasks arrive within this period, the effect is amplified. The newly arriving tasks further defer the tasks currently being processed. For FCFS (and RR in this case), newly arriving tasks do not affect the tasks currently waiting in the queue, which can proceed without disturbances. Thus, short periods of high load only affect the newly arriving tasks instead of all tasks waiting in the queue. The mean response times of FCFS and RR scheduling differ approximately 10% (23 ms). In comparison to PS scheduling, FCFS can be considered as a good approximation of RR.

The results presented above lead to a rejection of Hypothesis TS.1.e, which expected the means to be similar. Additionally, the ordering of the standard deviation differs from TS.1.e's expectation. In the results, RR has the least standard deviation directly followed by FCFS. The standard deviation of PS is (similarly to the mean) approximately twice as large. Furthermore, Hypothesis TS.1.e has to be rejected based on the results of scenario ExponentialShort. The results emphasise the effect of scheduling policies on (mean) response time also observed in [SWHB06].

To answer question TS.1, the relation between processing demands and timeslices of RR scheduling can have a strong influence on response time. PS can be an appropriate abstraction for RR based time sharing strategies if the resource demands are several times larger than the timeslices. For smaller resource demands, PS can lead to a large prediction error for the mean response time as well as the variation of the predicted response times. The extent of the error depends on the type of workload and the utilisation of the scheduled resource.

In the following experiments, we use resource demands that take significantly longer than a single timeslice, to minimise the effect on response times for the succeeding questions.

Question TS.2: Under which conditions do fair/unfair run queues influence software performance?

Fair run queues share the time between tasks according to their priority. However, operating systems, such as Linux, implement mechanisms to circumvent a run queue's fairness for I/O bound and interactive tasks. Question TS.2 evaluates how the type of workload (open-/closed) influences the behaviour of a run queue using measurements of the Windows XP and Linux 2.6.22 operating systems. In the following, we present the scenarios, hypotheses, and results of this question.

Scenarios Two scenarios, called Open and Closed, provide the necessary data to answer Question TS.2. Scenario Open uses a variant of the open workload in Figure 4.1(b) to mimic the effect of competing interactive tasks. It simultaneously starts two tasks with different priorities (low priority = -5 and high priority = 5) for each arrival. Both issue a resource demand of 450 ms (CpuDemand.VALUE = 450) to the processing resource called CPU. To exclude disturbing effects of an increasing number of tasks, the inter-arrival time is set to 1 second (InterArrivalTime.VALUE = 1000). This workload generates two tasks simultaneously and allows both to complete their resource demand before new tasks arrive. Since both tasks start simultaneously, their response time allows to draw conclusions about the share of processing time each task receives.

Scenario Closed uses closed workloads to generate a comparable load. It concurrently executes two tasks with different priorities. The higher priority task (t_h) requests no think time (Delay.VALUE = 0) while the lower priority task (t_l) waits for 450 ms after finishing a request (Delay.VALUE = 450). Both tasks request a processing time of 450 ms (CpuDemand.VALUE = 450) on the CPU. The priorities of tasks t_h and t_l are set to -5 and 5, respectively. The performance metrics, considered for tasks t_h and t_l, are mean response time ($\mathrm{E_{RT}}[t]$) and throughput ($\mathrm{TP}(t)$).

Hypotheses For scenario Open, Hypothesis TS.2.a (cf. Table 4.1) expects fair and unfair run queues to behave similar. In both cases, the higher priority task t_h suppresses the lower priority task t_l. Thus, the expected mean response time of task t_h is similar to the specified resource demand of 450 ms. For task t_l, the expected mean response time should increase by 450 ms to 900 ms. Since task t_h suppresses t_l, the latter has to wait for t_h to finish before it can start execution.

$$\mathrm{E_{RT}}[t_h] \approx 450\,\mathrm{ms} \quad \text{and} \quad \mathrm{E_{RT}}[t_l] \approx 900\,\mathrm{ms} \tag{TS.2.a}$$

For scenario Closed, Hypothesis TS.2.b expects the lower priority task to starve under unfair run queues. Due to starvation prevention mechanisms, low priority tasks receive a small share of processing time so that a few requests may be completed. Due to the overall preference of t_h over t_l, Hypothesis TS.2.b expects the mean response time of t_l to be larger than 30 seconds and its throughput less than 3 tasks per minute. Task t_l is explicitly not expected to starve completely, since Windows grants a small fraction of processing time to all tasks that could not run on the processor for more than 4 seconds.

$$\mathrm{E_{RT}}[t_h] \approx 450\,\mathrm{ms} \quad \text{and} \quad \mathrm{E_{RT}}[t_l] \geq 30\,\mathrm{sec}$$

$$\mathrm{TP}(t_h) > 120\,\mathrm{req/min} \quad \text{and} \quad \mathrm{TP}(t_l) < 3\,\mathrm{req/min} \qquad \text{(TS.2.b)}$$

For fair run queues, processing time is distributed between competing tasks according to their priority. Task t_h (priority -5) receives a timeslice of $500\,\mathrm{ms}$ while t_l (priority 5) receives $75\,\mathrm{ms}$. Thus, t_l should receive approximately 13% and t_h 87% of the total processing time. Hypothesis TS.2.c expects the following response time and throughput for t_h and t_l:

$$\mathrm{E_{RT}}[t_l] \approx 1/0.13 * 450\,\mathrm{ms} = 3450\,\mathrm{ms} \quad \text{and} \quad \mathrm{E_{RT}}[t_h] \approx 1/0.87 * 450\,\mathrm{ms} = 517\,\mathrm{ms} \quad \text{(TS.2.c)}$$

	Linux		Windows	
	Open	**Closed**	**Open**	**Closed**
Response Time [ms]				
High (-5)	435	503	440	451
Low (5)	867	3822	892	50670
Throughput [req / min]				
High (-5)	60	119	60	133
Low (5)	60	14	60	1

Table 4.6.: Mean response time and throughput for high and low priority tasks under open and closed workload.

Results   In the following, we present the results of the experiments for Windows and Linux. Table 4.6 summarises the measured mean response times and throughput for fair (Linux) and unfair (Windows) run queues. The resulting response times only exhibit a slight distribution, making the mean values sufficient for an interpretation of the results.

The results support all hypotheses of TS.2. For open workloads (scenario Open), the use of fair and unfair run queues does not affect the mean response time or throughput (Hypothesis TS.2.a). As a consequence of this observation, I/O-bound and interactive tasks can override the run queue's fairness property. Section 4.2 evaluates this effect in more detail. Furthermore, the measured response time of the high and low priority tasks are slightly below expectation, e.g., 435 ms compared to the defined 450 ms. This effect is a result of the employed resource demand generator that underestimates the computational effort necessary to generate a load of 450 ms (see Appendix C.3).

For closed workloads (scenario Closed), unfair run queues suppress lower priority tasks. The measured mean response time of task t_l is (with more than 50 seconds) even longer than expected in Hypothesis TS.2.b. Similarly, its throughput is close to 1 req/min. Furthermore, the higher priority task achieves a throughput of 133 req/min and a mean response time of 451 ms as expected in TS.2.b. In the case of fair run queues, lower priority task t_l

receives a slightly smaller share of processing time than expected (10.5% instead of 13%). Its mean response time is about 11% larger (3.8 sec compared to 3.4 sec) than expected in Hypothesis TS.2.c.

In this section, we have evaluated the conditions under which fair run queues can influence software performance. Based on the observation presented here, the next question addresses the mutual influences between task priorities and shares of processing time.

Question TS.3: How do priorities influence the processing time of tasks in fair run queues?

The results of Question TS.2 demonstrate that fair and unfair run queues can affect task response times and throughput. The scheduler of Linux 2.6.22 combines a fair run queue with priority-dependent timeslices, where a task's timeslice increases with its priority. The results of question TS.2 suggest that the share of processing time received by tasks can be computed from their timeslice sizes. Question TS.3 targets the validity of this assumption. It combines tasks that differ with respect to think time and priority to evaluate how these properties influence task response time and throughput.

Scenarios In the following scenario, we compare the performance of a higher priority task t_h and a lower priority task t_l for varying priorities under closed workloads, to evaluate the mutual influences of priorities and fair run queues. Both tasks t_h and t_l demand a processing time of 500 ms (CpuDemand.VALUE = 500). While task t_h has a zero think time (Delay.VALUE = 0), task t_l delays its execution for 500 ms once it finishes a request (Delay.VALUE = 500). Due to the long delay of 500 ms, the Linux scheduler classifies task t_l as interactive [TCM06]. The priorities of both tasks vary to determine the mutual influence of priorities, timeslices, and interactivity on software performance. Let p_h be the priority of task t_h and p_l the priority of task t_l. The four scenarios listed in Table 4.7 evaluate the influence of priorities on performance for fair run queues. Based on these scenarios, we define the following hypotheses.

Name	Distance	p_h	p_l
Close	5	0	5
Medium	10	0	10
Shifted	10	-5	5
Far	30	-15	15

Table 4.7.: Scenarios for Question TS.3.

Hypotheses Hypothesis TS.3.a expects the high and low priority tasks to receive processing time according to their timeslice sizes. For example, task t_l receives timeslices of 75 ms while task t_h receives 100 ms in scenario `PrioritySmall`. These timeslices lead to 43% and 57% shares of processing time for tasks t_l and t_h, respectively. To get the exact shares, both tasks must compute without interruption. Since task t_l additonally imposes a delay, the shares can only be considered as lower and upper bounds. Given these shares, the expected response time bounds can be estimated:

$$E_{RT}[t_h] \approx 500/0.57\,\text{ms} \approx 872\,\text{ms} \quad \text{and} \quad E_{RT}[t_l] \approx 500/0.43\,\text{ms} \approx 1163\,\text{ms}\,.$$

Similarly, the throughput of both tasks can be estimated by:

$$TP(t_h) \approx 120 * 0.57\,\text{req/min} \approx 68\,\text{req/min} \quad \text{and} \quad TP(t_l) \approx 120 * 0.43\,\text{req/min} \approx 52\,\text{req/min}$$

where 120 req/min is the maximum throughput for task processing times of 500 ms.

Scenario	Throughput [req / min]		Mean Response Time [ms]	
	$TP(t_l)$ $(<)$	$TP(t_h)$ $(>)$	$E_{RT}[t_l]$ $(>)$	$E_{RT}[t_h]$ $(<)$
`Close`	52	68	1163	872
`Medium`	40	80	1500	750
`Shifted`	17	103	3833	575
`Far`	4	116	14500	518

Table 4.8.: Expected response times and throughputs of Hypothesis TS.3.a.

Table 4.8 lists the expected outcome of all four scenarios. Due to the omission of t_l's delay in the computation, they can be considered as upper $(<)$ and lower $(>)$ bounds for both tasks. Hypothesis TS.3.a expects the actual response times and throughputs to improve for task t_h and to degrade for task t_l. In the following, we present the measurements of all four scenarios.

Results Figure 4.3 summarises the measurements for all four combinations of priorities. The results of scenarios `Medium`, `Shifted`, and `Far` support Hypothesis TS.3.a. However, Hypothesis TS.3.a does not hold for scenario `Close`. The mixture of waiting time and processing time for task t_l leads to the Linux scheduler overriding its run queue's fairness. After the waiting period, task t_l receives a higher dynamic priority than task t_h and completely suppresses t_h. This increase of t_l's priority leads to a mean response time of 500 ms for t_l and to a mean response time of about 1000 ms for t_h. In this scenario, t_l's behaviour changes the order of priorities for both tasks. Executing the same experiments without a delay for task

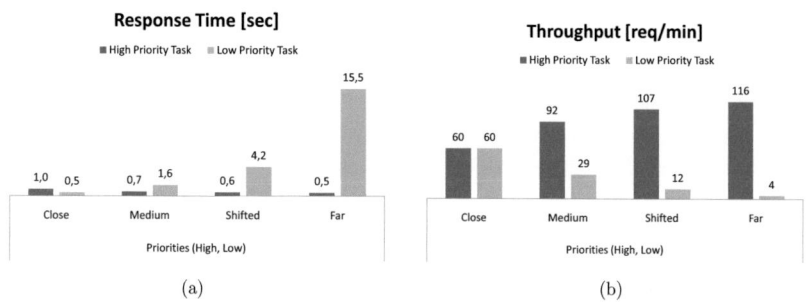

Figure 4.3.: Response time and throughput of task t_h and t_l with different priorities for the fair run queue with priority-dependent timeslices implemented under Linux.

t_l yields the expected behaviour. However, the results for scenario Close already point out the need for a detailed evaluation and modelling of interactivity policies (cf. Section 4.2).

A priority distance 10 suffices for the Linux scheduler to enforce a fair share of processing time. The measured response time and throughput follow the expected trend. Like expected in Hypothesis TS.3.a, the throughput and response time of t_h improve with a larger difference in priorities while t_l's performance degrades. Additionally, the shift of priorities from scenario Medium to scenario Shifted affects the response time and throughput of task t_h and t_l.

A comparison between the measurements (and estimates) of all four scenarios shows that at a certain point t_h benefits only little from the additional processing time, while t_l suffers heavily. For example, t_h's response time decreases by less than 10% from 559 ms to 514.4 ms from scenario Shifted to scenario Far. Task t_l is strongly penalised as its response time almost quadruples from 4 seconds to more than 15 seconds.

Conducting the same experiments for unfair run queues (Windows XP) yields the expected results. The actual priorities do not affect task response times and throughput. For all cases the results are similar to the results of scenario Closed. Due to the suppression of t_l by t_h, task t_l's mean response time is approximately 56 seconds. It only receives little processing time from the starvation prevention mechanism implemented by the Windows operating system scheduler. By contrast, the mean response time of task t_h approximates its uninterrupted processing time (502 ms). The throughput is with 119.6 req/min almost at the possible maximum throughput of 120 req/min. In the following, we continue the discussion of the results of questions TS.1 to TS.3.

Discussion

The questions and experiments that have been conducted to answer Questions TS.1 to TS.3 evaluated the mutual influences of timeslices, fair/unfair run queues, priorities and task behaviour. The results demonstrate that a task's behaviour can significantly affect the influence of a run queue's fairness. Especially the Linux 2.6.22 scheduler does not enforce fairness as strictly as expected. When a task spends a larger fraction of time waiting, fair run queues appear similar to their unfair counterpart with respect to task response time and throughput. However, the performance influence of both run queue types strongly differs if tasks spend most of their time processing. Fair run queues especially affect the performance of lower priority tasks, which risk starvation under unfair run queues.

The priority assigned to each task influences the throughput and response time of all tasks for fair run queues in combination with priority-dependent timeslices. A task's priority determines the share of processing time it receives, relative to its competitors. The results for question TS.3 suggest that priorities have to be chosen carefully. At a certain point, assigning a higher priority to a task yields only little benefit, while lower priority tasks are heavily penalised.

A continuous, closed workload where processing time and delay are well-balanced gives further insights in the interdependencies of task behaviour, run queues and priorities. If the priorities of the two competing tasks are close, the delayed task preempts the continuous one. This effect vanishes when the distance of the priorities increases. The Linux scheduler's interactivity handling classifies the continuously processing task as compute-bound and, hence, reduces its dynamic priority. By contrast, the task that is delayed is classified as I/O-bound and interactive. Therefore, it receives a higher dynamic priority. The increase leads to a change in the order of task preference if priorities differ only slightly.

The unfair run queues implemented in the Windows scheduler yielded the expected results. Unfair run queues suppress lower priority tasks for the sake of higher priority ones. To prevent starvation, Windows assigns a very small fraction of processing time to lower priority tasks. The main purpose of this behaviour is to prevent priority inversion.

4.1.3. The MOSS Prediction Model for Scheduler Time Sharing

In this section, we introduce MOSS' CPN model for performance-relevant time sharing properties which have been identified in the previous section. We enhance the model presented in Section 3.2.3. For this purpose, we focusse on the subnet of transition `Schedule` (cf. Figure 3.9). First, we give an overview of the scheduler's overall behaviour followed by a detailed description of the run queue, task processing, and task preemption. The description includes the modelling alternatives for each variation point (cf. Section 3.2.2).

Overview

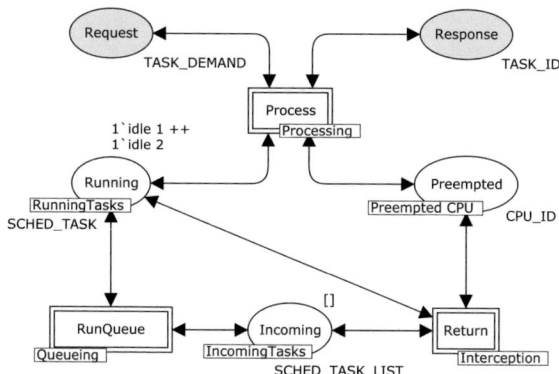

Figure 4.4.: Schematic overview of the scheduler's behaviour.

Figure 4.4 provides an overview of the scheduler's behaviour. It depicts the CPN underlying substitution transition Schedule in Figure 3.9. The depicted CPN schematically models the interactions of subnets Process, RunQueue, and Return. In the following, we describe the behaviour of the scheduler's CPN model in an abstract fashion. Details on the behaviour of each subnet follow in the next subsections.

The scheduler model accepts requests (TASK_DEMANDs) that require processing. Whenever the run queue assigns a task to a processor, its remaining demand is reduced by the time it spends processing. However, it may be preempted and returned to the run queue during its execution.

Transition Process communicates with the the task's behavioural model (i.e., the RD-SEFF) via places Request and Response. Whenever a task requires processing time on the scheduled resource it puts a TASK_DEMAND token on place Request. Transition Process tracks the remaining processing time and notifies the behavioural mdoel as soon as its request is finished by putting the task's identifier (TASK_ID) on place Response. To determine the processing time received by a task, transition Process continuously monitors place Running. This place contains the currently executing tasks for each processor. Figure 4.4 shows two idle tasks (idle 1 and idle 2) running on processors 1 and 2, respectively. The idle tasks on place Running represent available processors. Whenever a task releases its processor, a corresponding idle task takes its place.

Furthermore, transition Process manages the passage of time within the scheduler subnet. Following the modelling of time in CPN's, it defers the availability of tokens on the places

Response, and `Preempted`. When a task's timeslice expires, transition `Process` puts the identifier of its processor (`CPU_ID`) on place `Preempted` and, thus, notifies transition `Return` to remove the task from the processor. Transition `Return` removes the task's token from place `Running` and enqueues it in the list of incoming tasks of the run queue (place `Incoming`). The run queue (transition `RunQueue`) is responsible for assigning tasks to (idle) processors for execution. The task that has been chosen replaces the idle task's token on place `Running` and starts a new scheduling cycle.

Listing 4.1: Basic data types for time sharing.

```
colset PRIORITY = INT;
colset TIMESLICE = INT;
colset DEMAND = INT;
colset CPU_ID = INT timed;
colset TASK_ID = INT timed;

colset TASK_DEMAND = product TASK_ID * DEMAND timed;
colset SCHED_TASK = product CPU_ID * TASK_ID * PRIORITY * TIMESLICE timed;
colset SCHED_TASK_LIST = list SCHED_TASK;
colset PRIORITY_TIMESLICE = product PRIORITY * TIMESLICE;

colset RUNQUEUE = list SCHED_TASK;
colset CPU_RUNQUEUE = product CPU * RUNQUEUE;

fun idle cpu = (cpu, IDLE_TASK_ID, 0, 0);
```

Processing of Demands

The processing of resource demands requires the scheduler model to keep track of the remaining work for each task and its current state from the scheduler's perspective (e.g., the remaining timeslice). Tokens represent tasks within the model. MOSS uses the two distinct colour sets `SCHED_TASK` and `TASK_DEMAND` (cf. Listing 4.1) to represent the information necessary for the scheduler model and, thus, distinguishes the internals of the scheduler behaviour from the task's behaviour. A `TASK_DEMAND` and a `SCHED_TASK` token, which refer to the same task, can be joined by their unique identifier (`TASK_ID`) (identifier matching pattern and identifier manager pattern, cf. Section B.6). The `TASK_DEMAND` allows MOSS to keep track of a task's remaining demand, while `SCHED_TASKS` provides the necessary data for scheduling.

Figure 4.5 depicts the CPN describing substitution transition `Process`. Incoming demands arrive on place `Request` and are moved to the subnet's internal place `Demanding`, which manages all demands and their subsequent processing. The demand processing directly communicates with the run queue via the places `Running` and `Preempted`. Whenever a task demands processing time (`TASK_DEMAND` token on place `Demanding`) and receives a processor

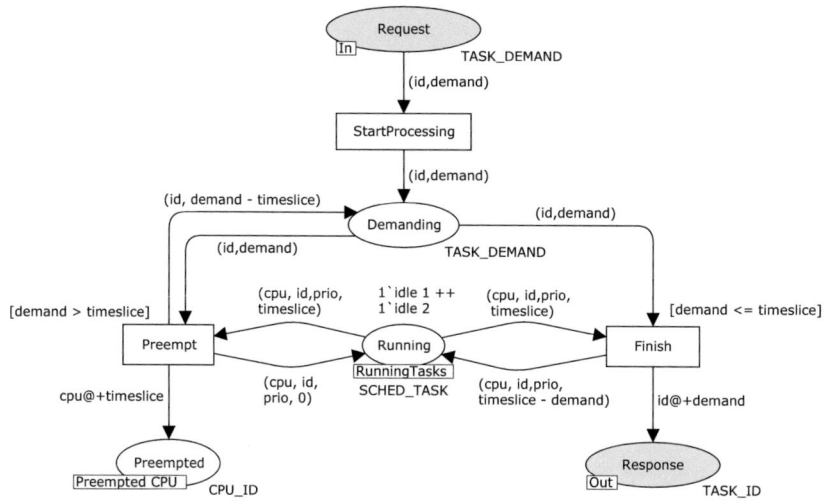

Figure 4.5.: Subnet of transition **Process** – the processing of resource demands.

(corresponding **SCHED_TASK** token on place **Running**), the task may either finish processing its demand within its remaining timeslice (transition **Finish** is enabled) or it is preempted (transition **Preempt** is enabled). In the first case, MOSS puts the task's identifier (**TASK_ID**) on place **Response** and notifies the task's behavioural model that its demand has been processed. The availability of the token for firing is deferred until the remaining demand's time passed. The task's timeslice is further reduced by the remaining demand. At this point, the task still occupies the processor even though its processing demand finished. This strategy allows the task's behavioural model to issue new demands without interruption, resembling the behaviour of real systems. When preemption is necessary, MOSS reduces the demand of the interrupted task by the remaining timeslice. Furthermore, it initiates the task's processor freeing by placing the processor's identifier on **Preempted**. The actual preemption is deferred by the task's remaining timeslice. Next MOSS needs to return the preempted task to the run queue and reset its timeslice as described in the following.

Returning Preempted Tasks

Once a task is preempted, transition **Return** (introduced in Figure 4.4, detailed view in Figure 4.6) is responsible for returning the task to the run queue and resetting its timeslice. Its subnet can vary with respect to the assignment of time slices, which can either be fixed or priority-dependent. In the case of fixed timeslices (Figure 4.6(a)), transition **Reset** simply

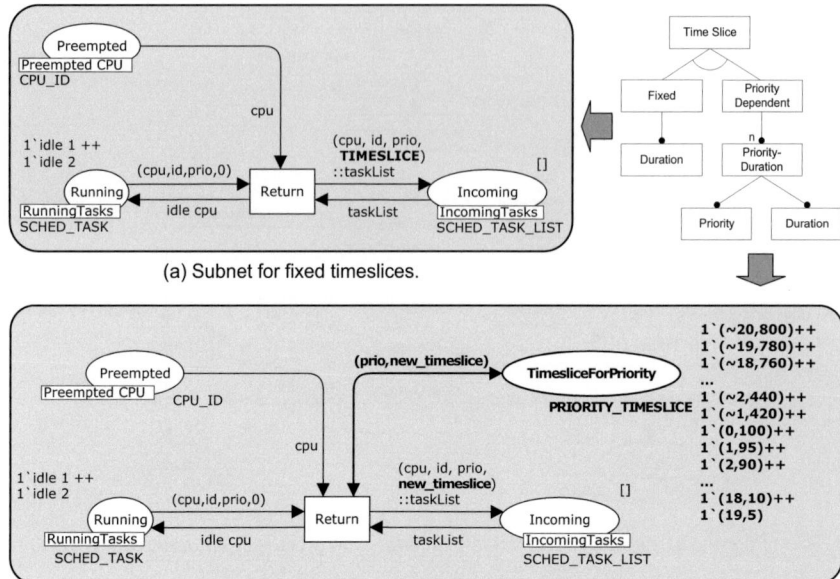

(a) Subnet for fixed timeslices.

(b) Subnet for priority dependent timeslices.

Figure 4.6.: Assignment of fixed and priority-dependent timeslices.

assigns a fixed value (TIMESLICE) to the task's timeslice. For priority-dependent timeslices (Figure 4.6(b)), the tokens on place TimesliceForPriority map each task priority to an individual timeslice. In this case, transition Return selects a task's new timeslice according to its priority (prio). When a processor's identifier token (CPU_ID) becomes available for firing on place Preempted, transition Return replaces the task currently running on the processor by the idle task. Furthermore, it resets the preempted task's timeslice (as discussed above) and inserts it into the list of tasks on place Incoming. These steps return the task to the run queue and prepares it for further processing.

Run queues

Run queues can either employ a fair (Figure 4.7(a)) or unfair (Figure 4.7(b)) policy to assign the available processors to competing tasks. Both policies differ mainly in their queueing of tasks which are ready for execution (places Ready, Active, and Expired), while their overall behaviour remains similar.

All tasks arrive at place `Incoming` of the run queue. They have to be enqueued before any other activity in the run queue can occur. This constraint guarantees that the run queue selects the correct task out of all tasks ready for execution. The inhibitor arc pattern (cf. Appendix B.6) ensures that all transitions (except `Enqueue`) are only enabled if the list of incoming tasks is empty.

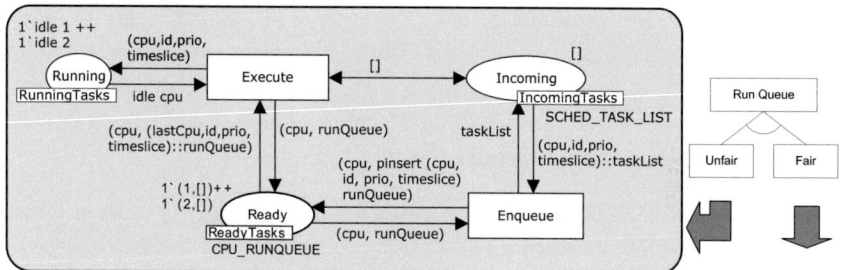

(a) Unfair run queue.

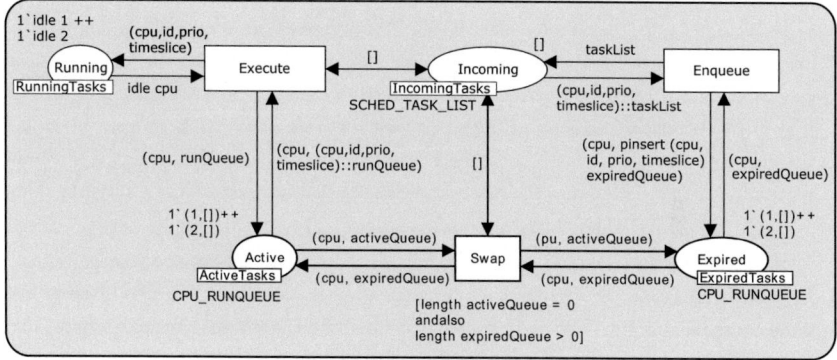

(b) Fair run queue.

Figure 4.7.: Model for fair and unfair run queues.

While unfair run queues manage waiting tasks in a single queue for each processor (place `Ready`), their fair counterpart distinguishes between active (place `Active`) and expired (place `Expired`) tasks. While active tasks still have a remaining timeslice, expired tasks already received their share of processing time. Thus, transition `Execute` only selects active tasks for processing. If the timeslice of a task is finished, the task is inserted into the expired run queue. Only if no active task remains, all expired tasks are reactivated (i.e., transiton `Swap` fires). Incoming tasks (usually the ones that just used up their timeslice) automatically join the expired queue. This behaviour resembles the fair time sharing of the Linux 2.6 scheduler.

Priorities

The range and meaning of priorities strongly varies for different GPOS schedulers. Therefore, MOSS models priorities by simple integer numbers. The priority of a task influences its position in the CPU_RUNQUEUE. In combination with function priorityInsert, it realises the priority queue pattern (cf. Appendix B.6). In priority queues, the head of the queue always contains the highest priority task. The order of priority values may be ascending or descending depending on the operating system. These differences are considered by the priority queues.

Preemption by Higher Priority Tasks

The CPN model presented so far does not reflect preemption of tasks by newly arriving ones with higher priorities. Whenever a higher priority task arrives at a processor's run queue, the scheduler preempts the currently executing task and adds it at the beginning of its previous run queue. It maintains the task's current timeslice and resource demand.

To include such a behaviour into MOSS, it is necessary to interrupt the delay of tokens on places Preempted and Response (see, for example, Figure 4.7). In CPNs, transitions can override a token's delay. A transition called Preempt (similar to transition Return in Figure 4.6) is enabled as soon as the run queue contains a task with a higher priority than the currently executing one. The transition returns the preempted task to the beginning of its run queue and determines the new values for the task's timeslice and processing demand.

So far, we assumed that tasks will not be preempted by higher priority tasks. MOSS adjusted timeslices and demands according to this assumption (subnet Process in Figure 4.5). In order to maintain the correct state of a task after preemption, transition Preempt recomputes its remaining timeslice and processing demand for the current simulation time. Finally, the transition returns the preempted task to the beginning of its previous run queue, so that it can directly continue execution as soon as the higher priority task releases the processor.

4.1.4. Validation of MOSS' Prediction Accuracy

In this section, we present a validation of MOSS' time sharing model introduced in the previous section. The validation compares the predicted response times and throughput of MOSS with measurements of the Windows Server 2003 and Linux 2.6 operating systems. In the validation, we target the prediction quality of fair run queues in combination with priority-dependent timeslices (Linux 2.6) as well as unfair run queues with different task behaviour and priorities (Windows operating system series). Therefore, we explicitly exclude scenarios affected by a scheduler's interactivity or starvation features.

Goal: *Purpose*   Assessment

               Issue   of MOSS' prediction accuracy

             Object   for time sharing features

      Viewpoint   from the software architect's point of view.

Similar to Section 4.1.1, the validation of MOSS' prediction accuracy employs the scenario-based GQM method introduced in Chapter 3.1. The differences between the predicted and measured response times and throughput indicate the prediction accuracy. Analogously to the experiments in Section 4.1.1, we focus on the performance metrics response time and throughput. In the following, we refine the goal by questions specific to time sharing.

The questions target the mutual influences of a run queue's fairness, the size of timeslices, and task priorities. Thus, the first question (TS.V1, where "V" stands for validation) asks whether MOSS accurately models the influence of fair and unfair run queues. The second question (TS.V2) evaluates MOSS' prediction accuracy of the mutual influences of priorities and timeslices for fair run queues. Table 4.9 summarises the scenario-based GQM plan of the validation introduced in the following.

MOSS' Prediction Accuracy for Time Sharing Features		
	TS.V1	**TS.V2**
Questions	Does MOSS accurately predict the effect of fair/unfair run queues?	Does MOSS accurately predict the mutual influence of priorities and timeslices?
Scenarios	Medium Open	Medium Shifted Far
Metrics	Prediction Error for Response Time and Throughput	
Hypotheses	MOSS predicts the performance of all tasks with an error less than 5%	

Table 4.9.: GQM plan for the validation of time sharing.

Question TS.V1: Does MOSS accurately predict the effect of fair/unfair run queues?

Question TS.V1 targets the influence of fair and unfair run queues in combination with priorities on response time and throughput. To assess MOSS' prediction accuracy, the predictions for scenarios `Medium` and `Open` (cf. Section 4.1.1) are compared to measurements.

We chose the relative prediction error of the mean values to answer the questions above. For any performance metric m, the relative prediction error is defined as follows. Let $E_p[m]$ be the predicted and $E_m[m]$ the measured mean, then $Error(m)$ is:

$$\text{Error}(m) = \frac{|E_p[m] - E_m[m]|}{E_m[m]} * 100$$

The prediction error is always given relative to the mean value of the measurements.

Hypotheses

$$\text{Error(TP)} < 5\% \quad \text{and} \quad \text{Error(RT)} < 5\% \qquad \text{(TS.V1.a)}$$

$$\text{Error(TP}(t_h)) \gg 5\% \quad \text{and} \quad \text{Error(RT}(t_l)) \gg 5\% \qquad \text{(TS.V1.b)}$$

For both scenarios (Medium and Open), Hypothesis TS.V1.a expects a prediction error of less than 5%. Since MOSS cannot predict the influence of starvaton prevention, Hypothesis TS.V2.b further expects a large prediction error in an exceptive case (scenario Medium, task t_l, unfair run queue).

(a) Unfair run queue (Windows Server 2003).

Scenario	Response Time [ms]			Throughput [req / min]		
	Prediction	Measurement	Error [%]	Prediction	Measurement	Error [%]
Open						
t_h	451	440	2,4	60,0	60,1	0,2
t_l	901	892	1,0	60,0	60,1	0,1
Medium						
t_h	500,5	501,5	0,2	107,8	106,6	1,2
t_l	360500	56300	540,3	0,2	1,0	83,3

(b) Fair run queue (Linux 2.6).

Scenario	Response Time [ms]			Throughput [req / min]		
	Prediction	Measurement	Error [%]	Prediction	Measurement	Error [%]
Medium						
t_h	0,65	0,65	0,3	92	92	0,3
t_l	1,54	1,60	3,8	29	30	2,8
Shifted						
t_h	0,56	0,56	0,1	107	107	0,1
t_l	4,07	4,25	4,2	12	13	4,9
Far						
t_h	0,52	0,51	0,4	117	116	0,4
t_l	14,69	15,44	4,9	4	4	3,6

Table 4.10.: Comparison between measurements and predictions for fair and unfair run queues with different priorities and timeslices.

Results The results summarised in Tables 4.10(a) and 4.10(b) do not reject Hypotheses TS.V1.a and TS.V1.b. The prediction error for almost all scenarios is less than 5%. Task t_l in scenario Medium forms the only exception as expected by Hypothesis TS.V1.b for unfair run queues. Scenario Open evaluates the performance prediction of lower priority tasks by MOSS for unfair run queues. The differences between measurements and predictions lie below 3% for throughput and response time of both tasks.

The remaining prediction error stems from caching and memory effects, from deviations of the defined and actual resource demands of the test application (cf. Appendix C.1), and from influences of the Java virtual machine (e.g., garbage collection) not captured by the prediction model. Section 5.3 further discusses the assumptions and limitations of MOSS.

Discussion The simulation lets higher priority task t_h fully suppress t_l. Thus, t_l starves completely as expected by Hypothesis TS.V1.b, while the measurements suggest that lower priority task t_l still receives a small share of processing time. In the simulation, t_l's processing time corresponds to the total duration of the experiment. The final cool down phase of the simulation allows all remaining tasks to finish execution. Thus, t_l's total execution time includes the experiment duration (360000 ms) plus its processing demand (500 ms). Usually, the results do not include observations during the cool down phase. In this case, it clearly demonstrates that t_l does not receive any processing time during the experiment run.

The results do not reject Hypotheses TS.V1.a and TS.V1.b. MOSS reflects the behaviour of fair and unfair run queues with the expected accuracy. The next question addresses the mutual influences of priorities and timeslices under fair run queues.

Question TS.V2: Does MOSS accurately predict the mutual influence of priorities and timeslices?

In the following, we focus on scenarios Medium, Shifted, and Far (cf. Section 4.1.2, Question TS.3) in order to assess MOSS' prediction accuracy for mutual dependencies of priorities and timeslices. We explicitly exclude scenario Close, which is strongly affected by the scheduler's interactivity handling (Section 4.2 examines the interactivity features of GPOS scheduler).

Hypothesis

$$\text{Error}(\text{TP}) < 5\% \quad \text{and} \quad \text{Error}(\text{RT}) < 5\% \qquad \text{(TS.V2.a)}$$

Similar to Hypothesis TS.V1.a, Hypothesis TS.V2.a expects MOSS to predict the response time and throughput of tasks t_h and t_l with an error of less than 5% in the selected scenarios. As a consequence of the hypothesis, MOSS should accurately predict the share of processing time received by each task.

Results Table 4.10(b) summarises the predictions, measurements, and errors for all three scenarios. MOSS fulfils the expectation of Hypothesis TS.V2.a in all cases. The prediction accuracy for task t_h exceeds the expectation with an error of less than 1%. The prediction error for lower priority task t_l ranges from $4-5\%$.

Figure 4.8 depicts the measured and predicted response time (Figure 4.8(a)) and throughput (Figure 4.8(b)) of lower priority task t_l. For higher priority task t_h, response time and throughput only change slightly and, thus, are not depicted here (cf. Table 4.10). In both

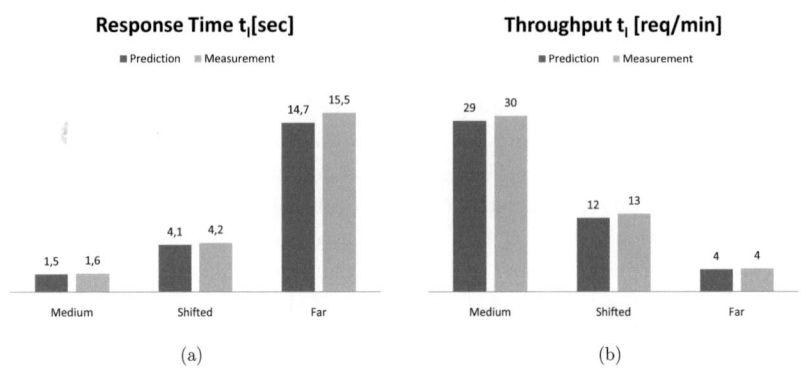

Figure 4.8.: Comparison between measurements and predictions for unfair run queues (Linux).

figures, the predictions trace the trend of scenarios Medium, Shifted, and Far. With an increasing difference in priorities, the response time of t_l increases and less requests get processed. The share of processing time received by each task can be computed from its throughput. For example, in scenario Medium, higher priority task t_h receives 75% (predicted and measured) of processing time while lower priority task t_l receives 25% (predicted and measured). MOSS estimates the share of processing time for all tasks with a deviation of less than 1%.

4.2. Interactivity

The experiments and predictions of GPOS schedulers (with respect to time sharing features) already point out the importance a scheduler's interactivity features for software performance. The mutual influences of task behaviour and a scheduler's interactivity policy require careful evaluation. In this section, we describe a series of experiments for the influence of interactivity policies as well as an extension and refinement of MOSS' CPN model. Analogously to Section 4.1, we employ the experiment-based derivation of performance models. First, we present an overview and motivation of the experiments (Section 4.2.1), then we describe their design (Section 4.2.2) and, finally, we summarise their results (Section 4.2.3). The proposed extension of MOSS (Section 4.2.4) is validated (Section 4.2.5) demonstrating the prediction accuracy of MOSS for different interactivity policies of GPOS schedulers.

4.2.1. Experiments – Overview and Motivation

The experiments conducted in the scope of this section evaluate two distinct interactivity policies realised in the Windows and Linux operating system series. The first policy (Windows) is based on the resources a task uses. Therefore, it is called *resource-dependent* policy. The second policy keeps track of a task's history (Linux). Its decisions are based on the previous behaviour of a task. Therefore, it is called *history-dependent* policy. Due to the inherently different characteristics of both policies, the following evaluation defines separate questions for both policies.

The Goal

Goal: *Purpose* Identify
Issue mutual performance influences
Object of interactivity features and task behaviour
Viewpoint from the user's point of view.

For both interactivity policies, the behaviour of a task determines its dynamic priority and, thus, its performance. The resources used determine the priority bonus of a task for the resource-dependent policy. Therefore, the evaluation focuses on resource usage as the most important factor of a task's behaviour. For the history-dependent policy, the previous waiting and processing times of a task determine its dynamic priority. Thus, the evaluation is focussed on the influence of waiting times and of processing times on software performance. The effect of both policies on externally observable performance metrics is of greatest interest. The goal targets the identification of influences that affect the performance perceivable by users of a system, e.g., response time. However, it is necessary to measure additional performance characteristics in order to design a performance model that reflects the influence of different interactivity policies on externally visible performance metrics correctly.

Motivation of the Questions

Resource-dependent Policy The resource-dependent interactivity policy increases the dynamic priority of tasks whenever they gain access to a resource. For example, when a task acquires a semaphore, it receives a priority bonus of one for its remaining timeslice. Whether the task benefits from the bonus (or not) depends on the other tasks running in parallel as well as the size of the bonus, which varies with the type of resource (cf. Section 2.3.4). Question IR.1 addresses the influence of different priority bonuses on software performance.

Whenever a task receives a priority bonus, the resource-dependent policy may reset its timeslice. The reset enables interactive and I/O-bound tasks to finish short requests of

processing without interruption. They can efficiently utilise external resources and maximise
the overall system utilisation. To prevent tasks from growing timeslices boundlessly (by
infinite series of resets), the resource-dependent policy considers a task's previous priority
bonus as well as its remaining timeslice. However, the exact behaviour of the policy is not
documented. Question IR.2 addresses the influence of timeslice resets for different resources
on software performance. Furthermore, Question IR.3 evaluates the effect of time penalties
for a set of resource acquisitions on software performance.

History-dependent Policy   The history-dependent policy determines the dynamic priority
of tasks based on their waiting time and processing times. It assigns bonuses to tasks with
long waiting times and penalties to tasks with long processing times. Question IH.1 addresses
the dependency of waiting and processing times and the dynamic priority of a task.

Additionally, the history-dependent policy explicitly distinguishes interactive and non-
interactive tasks. Tasks, which are classified as interactive due to their behaviour, are
preferred over non-interactive ones. Under Linux, for example, they circumvent the fair
policy of the run queue and, thus, are guaranteed to quickly receive processing time when
needed. Therefore, Question IH.2 addresses the conditions under which a task is classified
as interactive.

4.2.2. Experiment Design

In this section, we introduce the scenarios and metrics necessary to determine the influences
of a scheduler's interactivity policy on software performance. For this purpose, it is desirable
to measure the time for which a task receives a priority bonus. However, this metric cannot be
measured directly. It requires specific scenarios for indirect measurement. In the following,
we first describe the scenarios that allow us to determine the influence of priority bonuses on
software performance and then introduce a specific performance metric called high priority
time (HPT) for its measurement.

Scenarios

In order to measure the influence of resource-dependent interactivity policies, the closed
workload scenario introduced in Section 4.1.1 needs to be extended by the acquisition and
release of different resources. Figure 4.9 illustrates the behaviour for the acquisition of
a semaphore. An `AcquireAction` and `ReleaseAction` surround internal action `Process`
and model the acquisition and the release of `PassiveResource Semaphore`. The measured
response time includes possible contention delays of the resource acquisition.

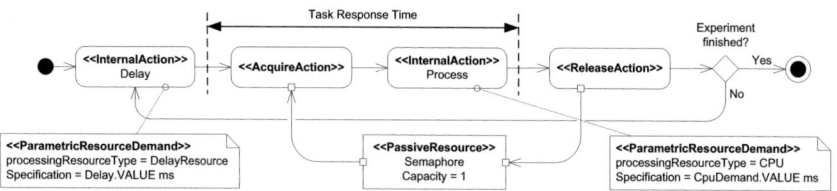

Figure 4.9.: Closed workload with acquisition and release of a passive resource (`Closed Interactive`).

The evaluation of different interactivity policies is focussed on three major scenarios which only differ in type of resources used. All scenarios subsume two competing tasks t_i and t_n. Task t_i resembles an interactive or I/O bound task, which uses different resources. Its behaviour is depicted in Figure 4.9. By contrast, task t_n is non-interactive. It behaves according to the closed workload specified in Figure 4.1(a).

Task	Priority	Workload
t_i	8	`Closed Interactive`
t_n	9	`Closed`

Table 4.11.: Priority and Workload of interactive task t_i and non-interactive task t_n.

Table 4.11 lists the workload and priority of both tasks. The priorities here are given in terms of the target operating system (Windows), since the mapping of nice-levels to operating system priorities is too coarse grained for this purpose. In the combination with Windows' unfair run queues, t_n suppresses task t_i due to its higher priority. However, if t_i receives a priority bonus, it may interrupt task t_n. We use this effect to determine the metrics of interest as described in the next section.

Name	Acquisition Action	Bonus	Workload of Task t_i
`No Boost`	–	0	`Closed`
`Semaphore`	Acquire semaphore	1	`Closed Interactive`
`Network`	Read data from network device	2	`Closed Interactive`

Table 4.12.: Scenarios for the evaluation of different interactivity policies.

Table 4.12 lists the three scenarios considered in the scope of this evaluation, which mainly differ with respect to the priority bonus and resource used. The scenarios allow a comparison between the performance of tasks t_i and t_n in similar settings with different priority bonuses. Scenario `No Boost` represents the neutral reference case for the resource-dependent inter-activity policy. The evaluation of the history-dependent interactivity policy only uses this scenario, since the type of resource does not affect performance, but only the processing and waiting times.

High Priority Time - A Performance Metric specific to Interactivity Policies

In the following, we introduces a performance metric specifically defined for the evaluation of resource-dependent interactivity policies, called **H**igh **P**riority **T**ime (HPT). This metric refers to the time a task's priority bonus keeps, i.e., the time its dynamic priority is larger than its static. Since this value cannot be measured directly, we introduce a heuristic method to estimate the time a task receives a higher priority in the following.

The scenarios above provide the necessary circumstances to indirectly measure the time that a task keeps a priority bonus. The non-interactive task t_n runs with a higher priority than interactive task t_i, more specifically $\text{prio}(t_n) = \text{prio}(t_i) + 1$. If t_i receives no priority bonus, it is delayed until task t_n is finished since Windows uses an unfair run queue (cf. Section 2.3.4). In other words, t_i can only preempt t_n if it receives a bonus. Thus, the delay of t_n quantifies the high priority processing time of t_i. However, this metric can be very vague, due to other disturbances of the measurement environment. The measurement of the time a task computes without interruption as well as the time it waits for the processor described in the following can yield much more accurate results.

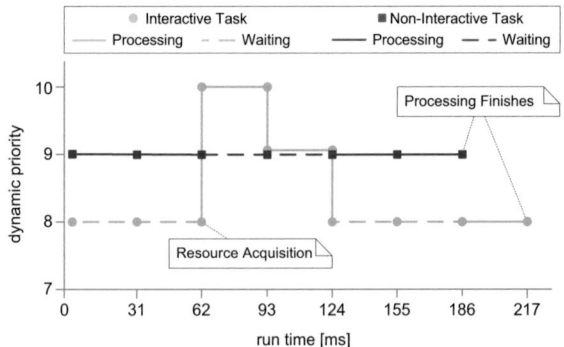

Figure 4.10.: The effect of priority bonuses on processing and waiting times.

Figure 4.10 illustrates the effect of priority bonuses for scenario `Network`. As soon as task t_i acquires its data from the network device, it receives a priority bonus of 2. This bonus increases its dynamic priority to 10 preempting task t_n. When t_i's next timeslice finishes (at 93 ms), the resource-dependent policy decreases its dynamic priority by 1. Now t_i and t_n compete for the processor on the same priority level. In the depicted case, t_i directly continues execution until its next timeslice is finished and until its dynamic priority decreases back to 8. Now, t_n takes over the processor again. The completion of t_i is deferred after t_n is finished. Thus, the high priority time of t_i corresponds to the time t_n is interrupted as well as the time t_i computes before t_n's execution is finished. The latter is the most reliable measure for HPT, since the interruption time of t_n suffers from similar disturbances like its response time. In the following, we introduce a heuristic method to measure the uninterrupted processing time as well as the waiting time of a task for scenarios No Boost, Semaphore, and Network.

A simple heuristic algorithm estimates the time a task is processing and waiting. It repeatedly measures the current system time using the most accurate clock (usually with the resolution of the processor's clock frequency). The heuristic estimates whether the task lost the processor between two subsequent measurements or not, based on the time passed between the measurements.

For this purpose, the heuristic measures the current time in a continuous loop. The time spend processing between to subsequent measurements is much smaller than 1 ms ($\ll$ 1 ms). Therefore, the heuristic assumes that the task has only been preempted if the time passed between two measurements is larger than 1 ms. In all other cases, it is assumed that the task could proceed without interruption. The heuristic aggregates continuous chunks of processing time, i.e., processing times not interrupted by waiting periods are summed up. Whenever a period of processing has been interrupted by a waiting period (i.e., two subsequent measurements differ more than 1 ms), a new measurement of waiting times and processing times is started.

Processing Time [ms]	31	31	31	**12**	**4**	31	31	31	31
Waiting Time [ms]		31	31	31	**5**	31	31	31	31

Table 4.13.: Sequence of processing times and waiting times measured.

The continuous measurement of subsequent processing and waiting times can yield a sequence as shown in Table 4.13. The table contains the measurements for a scenario with two tasks of equal priority under Windows Server 2003. The periods of processing and waiting times identified by the heuristic correspond to the timeslice size of 31 ms. The only disturbance (the sequence 12, 5, 4) is caused by an operating system interrupt. The sum of the times measured in the disturbed period yields a full timeslice of 31 ms. The interruption thus falls into the task's processing time and is not caused by competing tasks.

4.2.3. Answering the Questions – Scenarios, Metrics, Hypotheses, and Results

In the following, we refine the questions of the GQM-plan using the scenarios and metrics presented above. Furthermore, we present the results of the experiments that answer the questions.

Performance influences of task behaviour and the resource-dependent interactivity policy		
	IR.1	**IR.2**	**IR.3**
Question	Do priority bonuses influence software performance?	How long does a task profit from a priority bonus?	Does a series of resource acquisitions affect performance?
Scenario	No Boost Semaphore Network	Semaphore Network	Semaphore
Metric	Mean Response Time	High Priority Time of t_i	High Priority Time of t_i
Hypotheses	The response time of t_i decreases with a larger bonus while the response time of t_n increases.	Either t_i profits between 0 ms and 31 ms (Semaphore) or 31 ms to 62 ms (Network) from the bonus.	The more resouces aquisitions the shorter lasts the priority bonus.

Table 4.14.: GQM plan for the resource-dependent interactivity policy.

Question IR.1: Do priority bonuses influence software performance?

The resource-dependent policy grants priority bonuses to tasks according to the resources used. Question IR.1 targets the influence of these bonuses on software performance. In the following, we describe the scenarios, hypotheses, and result quantifying their effect.

Task		CpuDemand.VALUE	Delay.VALUE
t_i	interactive	20	20
t_n	non-interactive	500	20

Table 4.15.: Parameter characterisations for tasks t_i and t_n.

Scenarios   For all three scenarios (No Boost, Semaphore, and Network), Table 4.15 lists the resource demands and delays of Question IR.1. All scenarios use similar values in order to compare the influence of different bonuses on response times. The resource demand of interactive task t_i (20 ms) is smaller than a single timeslice (31 ms). This value should allow t_i to finish its demand within its bonus period. The significantly longer processing time (500 ms) of task t_n delays the remaining demand of t_i in case its boosted period does not suffice.

The delay of t_i is clearly visible, due to the large demand of t_n. The following hypotheses compare the response times of tasks t_i and t_n for all three scenarios.

Hypotheses In general, Hypotheses IR.1.a and IR.1.b expect task t_i to receive a larger share of processing time with an increasing priority bonus. This effect becomes visible in a decreasing response time for t_i and, thus, an increasing response time for t_n. Let t_i^{None}, t_i^{Sem}, t_i^{Net} be the interactive tasks of scenarios No Boost, Semaphore, and Network, respectively. Similarly, t_n^{None}, t_n^{Sem}, t_n^{Net} denote the corresponding non-interactive tasks of those scenarios, then Hypotheses IR.1.a expects:

$$\text{E}_{\text{RT}}[t_i^{\text{None}}] > \text{E}_{\text{RT}}[t_i^{\text{Sem}}] > \text{E}_{\text{RT}}[t_i^{\text{Net}}] \tag{IR.1.a}$$

Analogously, Hypothesis IR.1.b expects an increasing response time for t_n:

$$\text{E}_{\text{RT}}[t_n^{\text{None}}] < \text{E}_{\text{RT}}[t_n^{\text{Sem}}] < \text{E}_{\text{RT}}[t_n^{\text{Net}}] \tag{IR.1.b}$$

The next paragraph presents the results answering the question.

Results Figure 4.11 shows the mean response times (Figure 4.11(a)) of tasks t_i and t_n for all three scenarios as well as their distribution (Figures 4.11(b) – 4.11(e)). The results conform to the expectation of Hypotheses IR.1.a and IR.1.b. For scenario No Boost, task t_i is always delayed by the full processing demand of t_n (500 ms) resulting in a total response time of approximately 520 ms. The histogram and the cumulative distribution functions (Figures 4.11(b) and (c)) confirm this observation. Less than 3% of the requests deviate from the expectation.

In scenario Semaphore, task t_i receives a priority bonus of 1 for its remaining timeslice. Thus, t_i either finishes its demand within 20 ms (about 1/3 of all cases in Figure 4.11(b) and (c)) if its remaining timeslice is larger than 20 ms or it is delayed otherwise (2/3 of all cases). The bonus of t_i only affects the response time of t_n slightly. Compared to scenario No Boost, its mean response time increases by about 10 ms.

In scenario Network, the priority bonus of 2 always allows t_i to finish processing without interruptions caused by t_n. In addition to the shorter response time of t_i, its throughput increases from 2 req/sec (scenario No Boost) and 3 req/sec (scenario Semaphore) to about 23 req/sec. The increased load of t_i causes a significant delay for t_n leading to its mean response time of 727 ms.

The results suggest that priority bonuses can have a large influence on software performance, e.g., response time and throughput. The next question addresses the duration of priority bonuses.

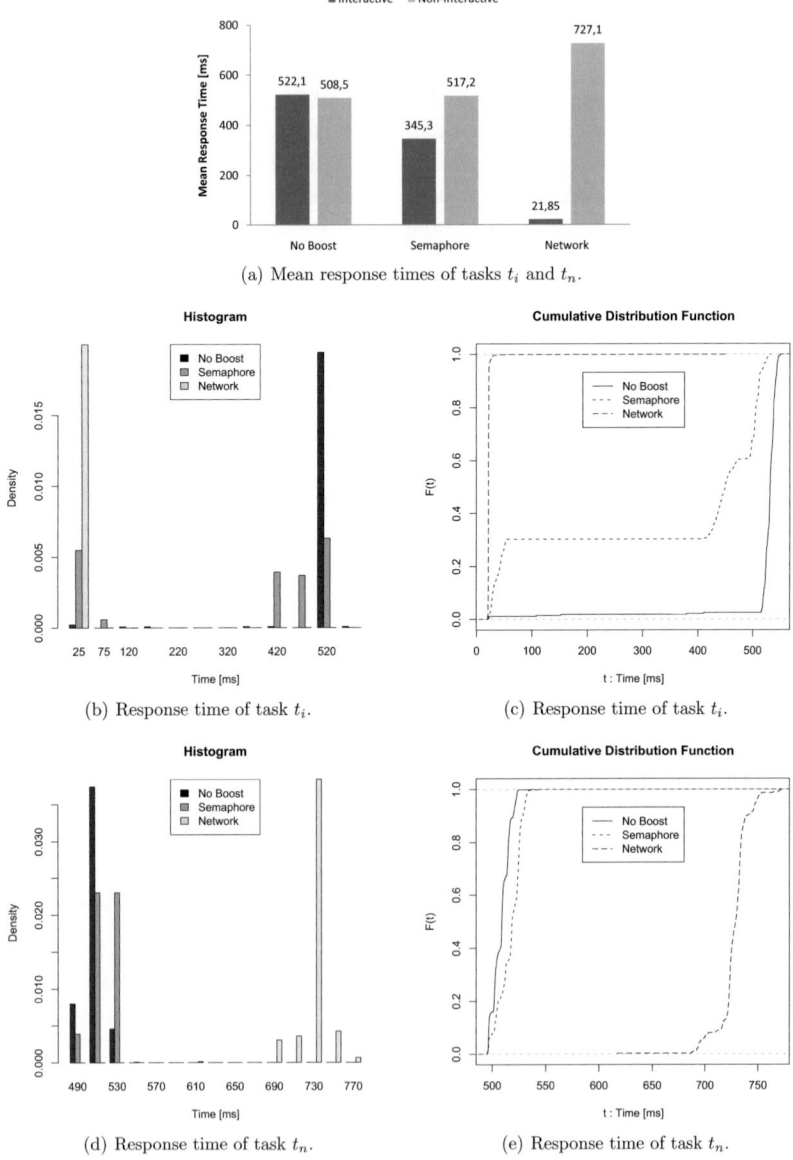

(a) Mean response times of tasks t_i and t_n.

(b) Response time of task t_i.

(c) Response time of task t_i.

(d) Response time of task t_n.

(e) Response time of task t_n.

Figure 4.11.: Mean response times and their distribution for tasks t_i and t_n.

Question IR.2: How long does a task profit from a priority bonus?

Whenever a task receives a priority bonus, the resource-dependent interactivity policy may reset its timeslice in order to finish its computation without interruption. Therefore, Question IR.2 targets the duration of priority bonuses quantifying the effect observed in the evaluation of Question IR.1.

	Task	CpuDemand.VALUE	Delay.VALUE
t_i	interactive	100	100
t_n	non-interactive	500	100

Table 4.16.: Parameter characterisations for tasks t_i and t_n.

Scenarios The evaluation of Question IR.2 focusses on scenarios Semaphore and Network. Scenario No Boost is omitted at this point, due to the absence of priority bonuses. Table 4.16 lists the valuations of the resource demand and delay for tasks t_i and t_n in both scenarios. The 100 ms of processing time of task t_i should capture the maximum possible high priority time of 62 ms. The high priority time of task t_i is the only performance metric relevant for answering Question IR.2. In the following, we present the hypotheses and results of this question.

Hypotheses The actual mechanisms for timeslice resets are vaguely documented. However, existing documentation suggests that a task's timeslice is always fully reset when acquiring a resource for the first time during its current timeslice [SR05]. By contrast, the results for Question IR.1 indicate that this statement may not hold. Therefore, we formulate two different expectations for the evaluation's outcome. The Hypothesis IR.2.a expects the documentation to be valid and, thus, expects a HPT of full timeslices only for t_i. Hypothesis IR.2.b is more general and just assumes a certain range for t_i's HPT. More precisely, IR.2.a expects a mean HPT of one timeslice for scenario Semaphore and a mean HPT of two timeslices for scenario Network:

$$\mathrm{E}_{\mathrm{HPT}}[t_i^{\mathtt{Sem}}] = 31\,\mathrm{ms} \qquad \text{and} \qquad \mathrm{E}_{\mathrm{HPT}}[t_i^{\mathtt{Net}}] = 62\,\mathrm{ms} \tag{IR.2.a}$$

Hypothesis IR.2.b weakens the previous expectation. It (only) expects the high priority time of task t_i to increase by a timeslice (31 ms) for an additional bonus of 1. This means that, for the scenario Semaphore, t_i receives a bonus of one timeslice at most. Analogously, the high priority time is expected to be larger than one (31 ms), but smaller than two timeslices (62 ms) for the scenario Network:

$$0\,\mathrm{ms} < \mathrm{HPT}(t_i^{\mathtt{Sem}}) \leq 31\,\mathrm{ms} \qquad \text{and} \qquad 31\,\mathrm{ms} \leq \mathrm{HPT}(t_i^{\mathtt{Net}}) \leq 62\,\mathrm{ms} \tag{IR.2.b}$$

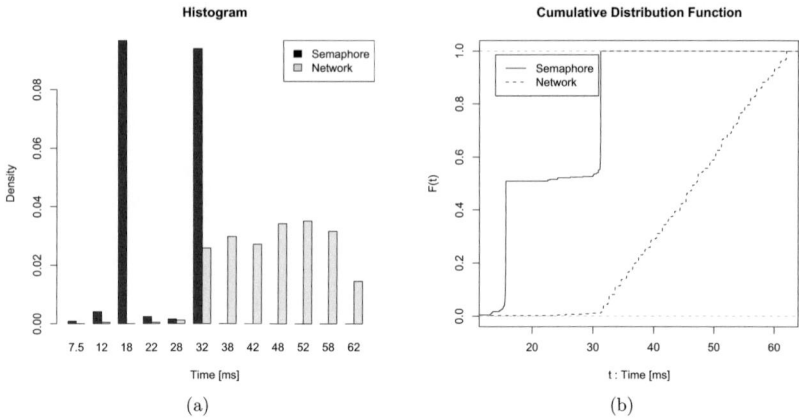

Figure 4.12.: Distribution of the high priority time of task t_i.

Results   Figure 4.12 depicts the distribution of task t_i's high priority processing time for scenarios Semaphore and Network. In scenario Semaphore, t_i's HPT is either half a timeslice (15.5 ms) with a probability of 0.5 or a full one (31 ms) with a probability of 0.5. For scenario Network, its HPT is approximately equally distributed between 31 ms and 62 ms. Due to this results, the resetting of timeslices is more complex than suggested by the documentation. Therefore, Hypothesis IR.2.a has to be rejected. However, the results support the more general expectation of Hypothesis IR.2.b.

The results for scenario Semaphore suggest that the timeslice is not fully reset in every case. In fact, the resetting of timeslices occurs on a more fine-grained level. Assuming that the remaining timeslices are equally distributed between 0 ms and 31 ms at the moment of resource acquisition, the resource-dependent policy rounds up the remaining timeslice to the next 15.5 ms.

For scenario Network, the equal distribution of the high priority time between 31 ms and 62 ms suggests that the timeslice is not reset. The high priority time of t_i (Figure 4.12) is a result of the remaining current timeslice and an additional full timeslice. Since t_i receives a priority bonus of 2, the remaining timeslice resembles the equally distributed part.

The next question addresses the effect of resource acquisitions on a task's high priority processing time.

Question IR.3: Does a series of resource acquisitions affect performance?

The resource-dependent interactivity policy should decrease the timeslice of a task which performs a series of resource acquisitions in a row [SR05]. In the following, we present the necessary scenarios, hypotheses and results.

Scenario   To answer Question IR.3, scenario `Semaphore` requires slight modification. After a delay of 100 ms (`Delay.VALUE = 100`), it acquires and releases the same semaphore multiple times in a loop to measure the influence of a series of resource acquisitions on the high priority time of task t_i. Its total processing time sums up to 100 ms. To measure the HPT for 1, 10, and 100 acquisitions, the resource demand within the loop (after acquisition) must be 100 ms, 10 ms, and 1 ms, respectively.

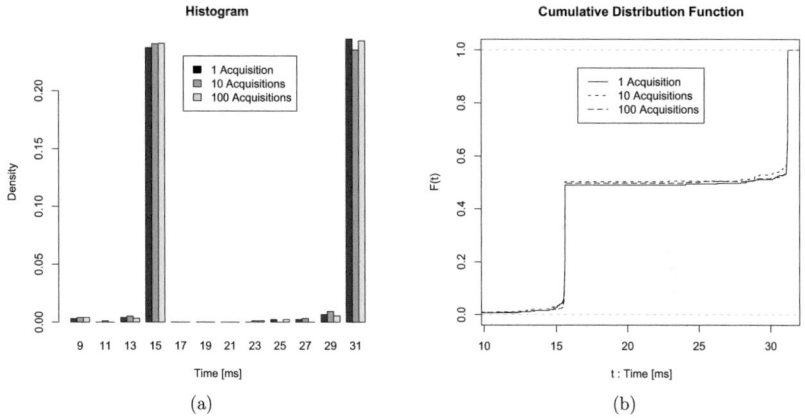

Figure 4.13.: High priority time of task t_i for an increasing number of semaphore acquisitions.

Hypotheses   Following the documentation [SR05], Hypothesis IR.3.a expects the high priority time of t_i to decrease with the number of semaphore acquisitions. Let t_i^1, t_i^{10}, and t_i^{100} denote the interactive task of scenario `Semaphore` with 1, 10, and 100 resource acquisitions respectively, then Hypothesis IR.3.a expects:

$$\mathrm{E}[HPT(t_i^1)] > \mathrm{E}[HPT(t_i^{10})] > \mathrm{E}[HPT(t_i^{100})] \qquad \text{(IR.3.a)}$$

In the following, we present the results for Question IR.3.

Results   Figure 4.13 shows the distribution of t_i's high priority time for an increasing number of semaphore acquisitions. In the considered scenario, the number of semaphore acquisitions does not affect the high priority time of t_i and, thus, contradicts Hypothesis IR.3.a. This observation refers to Java semaphores only and cannot be (directly) generalised for other semaphore implementations or resource types.

The next questions target the performance properties of the history-dependent interactivity policy implemented in the Linux 2.6. operating system.

Performance influences of task behaviour and the history-dependent interactivity policy		
	IH.1	**IH.2**
Question	How do longer waiting times influence a task's dynamic priority and thus its performance?	What is the shortest waiting time for a task to be classified as interactive?
Scenario	No Boost	No Boost
Metric	Dynamic priority Mean Response Time	Interactivity Threshold
Hypotheses	Dynamic priority increases and the mean response time decreases with longer waiting times	The interactivity threshold linearly increases with the the processing time.

Table 4.17.: GQM plan for the history-dependent interactivity policy.

Question IH.1: How do longer waiting times influence a task's dynamic priority and, thus, its performance?

History-dependent policies determine a task's dynamic priority based on its previous waiting and processing times. Question IH.1 addresses the mutual influences of both times on the response time and dynamic priority of a task.

	Task	CpuDemand.VALUE	Delay.VALUE	Priority
t_i	interactive	80	$0 - 20$	0
t_n	non-interactive	80	0	0

Table 4.18.: Parameter characterisations for tasks t_i and t_n.

Scenarios   To evaluate these mutual influences, we use scenario No Boost with a static priority of 0 (nice-level) for tasks t_i and t_n. Table 4.18 summarises the parameter valuations for the experiments. A resource demand of 80 ms prevents irregular disturbances by preemptions due to expired timeslices (100 ms) in measured response times. The waiting time of task t_i varies between 0 ms and 20 ms to evaluate its influence on t_i's dynamic priority. The performance metrics considered to answer Question IH.1 are t_i's average dynamic priority during the measurement period ($E[\text{prio}(t_i)]$) as well as its mean response time ($E[\text{RT}(t_i)]$). The latter indicates the performance gain of t_i for longer waiting times.

Hypothesis Hypothesis IH.1.a expects the priority to increase continuously with longer waiting times based on the realisation of the history-dependent interactivity policy in the Linux 2.6 scheduler (cf. Section 2.3.5). Let t_i^d denote the interactive task with a delay of d ms, then IH.1.a expects:

$$E[\text{prio}(t_i^d)] < E[\text{prio}(t_i^{d'})] \quad \forall \, d < d' \tag{IH.1.a}$$

Since task t_i and t_n run with the same static priority, the scheduler assigns an equal amount of processing time to both. Due to t_i's higher dynamic priority, Hypothesis IH.1.b expects its response time to decrease with an increasing delay:

$$E[\text{RT}(t_i^d)] > E[\text{RT}(t_i^{d'})] \quad \forall \, d < d' \tag{IH.1.b}$$

Hypotheses IH.1.a and IH.1.b do not state anything about the response time or dynamic priority of the non-interactive task t_n. However, t_i's increasing delay and dynamic priority should affect its performance. In the following, we describe the results to answer Question IH.1.

Results Figure 4.14 depicts the measured dynamic priorities (Figure 4.14(a)) and response times (Figure 4.14(b)). Both curves show an abrupt change between a delay of 8 ms and 9 ms. Delays of 8 ms or less lead to a penalty of approximately -5 on the dynamic priority of both tasks. When the delay further increases ($\geq 9\,\text{ms}$), task t_i's dynamic priority changes from a penalty of -5 to a bonus of +5. Similarly, its response time drops from 175 ms to 80 ms while t_n's response time rises from 145 ms to nearly 800 ms. The latter indicates that t_n receives the processor only during t_i's waiting periods. Such a behaviour is only possible if t_i circumvents the fairness properties of Linux' run queue. In fact, the scheduler classifies task t_i as interactive if their waiting time exceeds a certain threshold (cf. Section 2.3.5). In the following, the minimum time that a task must wait in order to be classified as interactive is called *interactivity threshold*.

Furthermore, t_i's dynamic priority (and consequently its response time) is penalised for delays smaller than 9 ms. In this case, the scheduler classifies t_i as a compute-bound tasks due to its large processing and small waiting times. For a delay of 0 ms, both tasks receive a similar share of processing time leading to a response time of approximately 160 ms for both. With an increasing delay, the response time of t_i (first) rises to 175 ms while the response time of t_n lowers to 145 ms. The dynamic priority of t_i remains close to -5. Only for delays

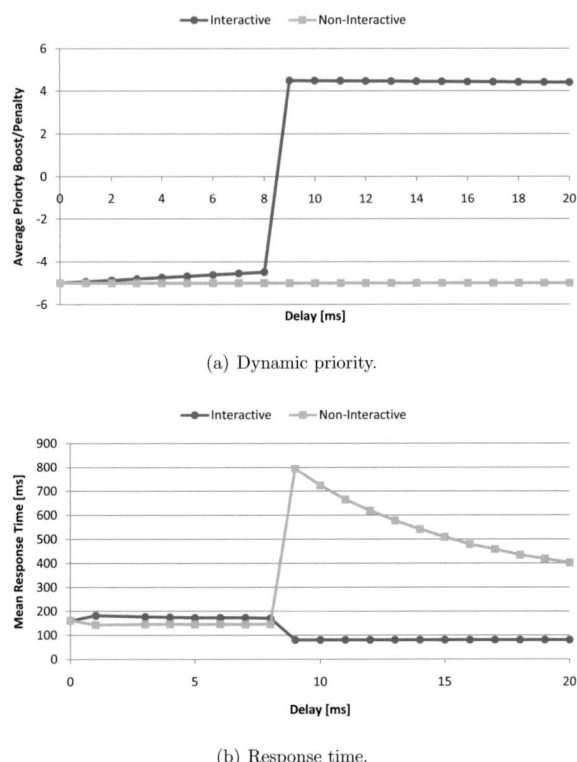

(a) Dynamic priority.

(b) Response time.

Figure 4.14.: Dynamic priority and response time of tasks t_i and t_n for an increasing delay of t_i.

of 9 ms and more does the situation change as discussed above. The increase in response times of t_i observed for small delays greater than zero is a consequence of the timeslices used by the scheduler. When t_i starts waiting it releases the processor and, thus, allows t_n to continue processing. However, when its delay is finished, the processor is still occupied by t_n. Since both tasks have the same priority in most cases, t_i must wait until t_n finished its timeslice. Thus, t_i's release of the processor leads to the long response times observed here.

To conclude, the dynamic priority of t_i does not increase continuously with longer delays as suggested by the documentation (Section 2.3.5). Thus, Hypotheses IH.1.a and IH.1.b have to be rejected. The next question addresses the abrupt changes in the dynamic priority and response time of t_i.

Question IH.2: What is the shortest waiting time for a task to be classified as interactive?

Since the experiment results of the question above require further investigation, Question IH.2 addresses the threshold of delays necessary to classify a task as interactive. Classifying a task as interactive refers to the abrupt change in priority and response time visible in Figure 4.14. In the following, we present the scenarios, hypotheses, and results for Question IH.2.

Task		CpuDemand.VALUE	Delay.VALUE
t_i	interactive	80, 160, 240, 320, 400, 480, 560	$0 - 100$
t_n	non-interactive	80, 160, 240, 320, 400, 480, 560	0

Table 4.19.: Parameter characterisations for tasks t_i and t_n.

Scenario Similar to Question IH.1, scenario No Boost provides the necessary results to answer Question IH.2. Therefore, its resource demands and delays are varied as listed in Table 4.19. The interactivity threshold of the interactive task t_i, denoted by $IT(t_i)$, is compared for the different scenarios of the evaluation. $IT(t_i)$ resembles the minimum delay for the abrupt change in priority and response time, e.g., $IT(t_i) = 9\,\text{ms}$ for the scenarios evaluated in the context of Question IH.1. In the following, we formulate two hypotheses on the expected outcome of the experiments.

Hypotheses In general, Hypotheses IH.2.a and IH.2.b expect the interactivity threshold of task t_i to increase for longer processing demands, i.e., the longer a task spends processing, the longer it has to wait to be classified as interactive. Hypothesis IH.2.b further expects the interactivity threshold to increase linearly (motivated by the results in [TCM06]).

Hypothesis IH.2.a expects the effect observed in Question IH.1 to occur for any task with any processing time. The interactivity threshold thus increases with t_i's resource demand. Let t_i^r denote the interactive task t_i with a resource demand of r ms, then

$$IT(t_i^r) < IT(t_i^{r'}) \quad \forall r < r' \tag{IH.2.a}$$

Hypothesis IH.2.a does not quantify the increase of the delay. Yet, Hypothesis IH.2.b does expect a linearly increasing interactivity threshold.

$$\exists c \in \mathbb{R} \; : \; \frac{IT(t_i^r)}{r} = c \quad \forall \, r \in \mathbb{R}_{>0} \tag{IH.2.b}$$

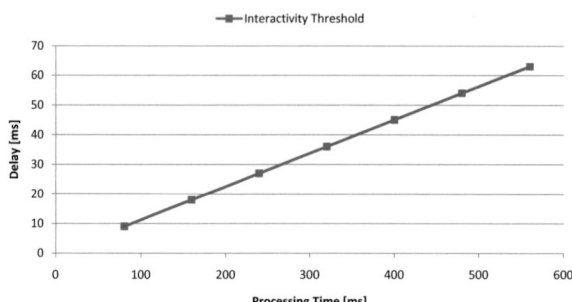

Figure 4.15.: Interactivity threshold for an increasing processing time.

Hypotheses IH.2.b assumes the ratio of the interactivity threshold and the resource demand of t_i to be constant. In the following, we present the results that answer Question IH.2.

Results   Figure 4.15 illustrates the interactivity threshold of task t_i in dependence of its processing time. For example, a task with an average processing time of 160 ms has to wait at least 18 ms on average to be classified as interactive. Similarly, a task with an average processing time of 400 ms hast to wait 45 ms. The interactivity threshold increases for larger resource demands (as expected by Hypotheses IH.2.a). Furthermore, the increase is constant leading to linear dependency of processing time and interactivity threshold (as expected by Hypotheses IH.2.b). In the considered scenarios, the slope of the function in Hypothesis IH.2.b is $c = 0.1125$.

In the following, we summarise and discuss the results for different interactivity policies.

Discussion

The experiments conducted within this section have evaluated the influence of resource-dependent and history-dependent interactivity policies on software performance. The first three questions have addressed the influence of different priority bonuses for the resource-dependent policy while the last two questions have targeted the influence of waiting and processing times for the history-dependent policy.

The results demonstrate that both policies react significantly different. The resource-dependent policy neglects a task's history focussing on its currently acquired resources. By contrast, the used resources play no role for the history-dependent policy, which only compares the waiting and processing time of a task. However, both policies strongly influence the response time of the interactive and non-interactive tasks.

For the resource-dependent policy, the priority bonus does not only affect the response time, but also the resetting of timeslices. This behaviour is of particular importance for the performance prediction of strong and weak semaphores [Hap07]. The necessary performance metric (high priority time) can only be measured indirectly in combination with non-interactive task t_n.

The results confirm the observation of Section 4.1.2 for the history-dependent policy that the interactivity policy affects the time sharing policy. The influence of processing and waiting times on a task's dynamic priority and performance have been different than its documentation and implementation suggest in the first place. Instead of a continuous increase in priority and, thus, performance for longer delays, the delay has almost no effect until it sharply rises the task's dynamic priority. Further evaluations of this behaviour have shown a linear dependency of the processing time and the interactivity threshold.

The questions, experiments and results presented above form the basis for the prediction model described in the next section.

4.2.4. Extending MOSS' Prediction Model for GPOS Schedulers by Interactivity Policies

In this section, we introduce MOSS' CPN model for resource- and history-dependent interactivity policies. The model extends the CPNs for time sharing described in Section 4.1.3. Furthermore, it introduces the acquisition and release of resources such as semaphores, connection pools, or network devices. In the following, we describe the CPNs for both policies. The CPN model presented here is geared to the implementations of Windows' resource-dependent and Linux' history-dependent interactivity policy.

Run Queue The changes necessary to model interactivity policies affect the scheduler's task preemption as well as its run queue. For the latter, the resource-dependent interactivity policy does not require any adjustments while the history-dependent policy needs to keep track of the tasks processing and waiting time. Figure 4.16 depicts a fair run queue for the history-dependent policy. The extensions to the original CPN model of fair run queues (Figure 4.7 on page 91) are printed in boldface.

Whenever transition `Execute` puts a task on place `Running` for execution, it also puts a new `TIMESTAMP` token (cf. Listing 4.2) on place `StartProcessingTimes`. The token contains the task's identifier (`TASK_ID`) and the current simulation time (`sim_time()`). It logs the time the processing started. Fusion place `StartProcessingTimes` allows other subnets (e.g., Figure 4.17 and 4.19) to use the information in order to determine the time a task spends processing.

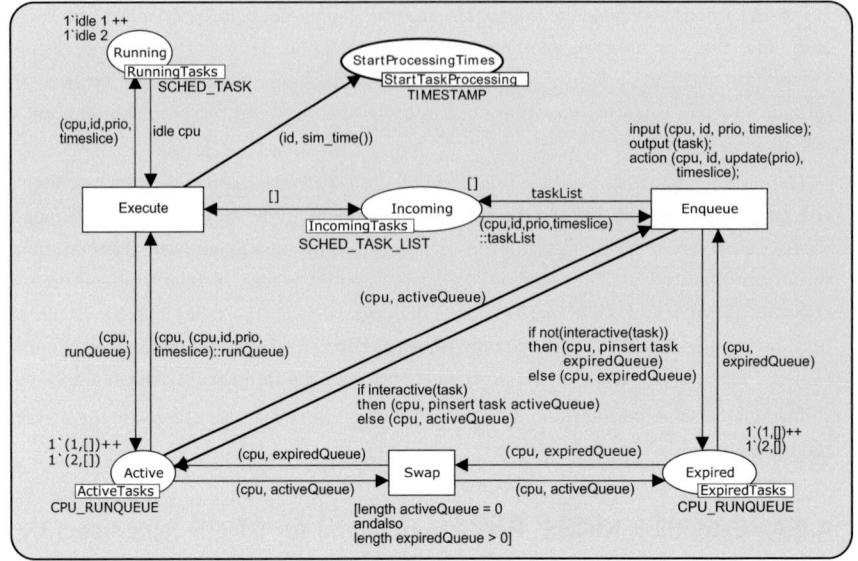

Figure 4.16.: CPN modelling a fair run queue with an history-dependent interactivity policy.

Furthermore, transition `Enqueue` updates a task's dynamic priority based on the time it spend waiting and/or processing. Its `input/output/action` declaration performs the necessary `update` operation. If a task is interactive (`interactive(task) = true`), transition `Enqueue` directly adds it to the active run queue. Otherwise (function `interactive(task) = false`), tasks are assigned to the expired run queue first.

Listing 4.2 shows the necessary colour sets, values and functions for the run queue's subnet. The functions listed here directly correspond to the Linux 2.6 scheduler's behaviour described in Section 2.3.5. A task's priority (`PRIORITY`) embodies three integers (instead of a single one, as is the case for the time sharing policies). The first resembles the task's static priority (`static_priority`), the seconds its dynamic priority (`dynamic_priority`), and the third its waiting time (`waiting_time`). The waiting time has to be modelled as an integer due to restrictions of CPNs (cf. Appendix B.4).

Function `priorityInsert` adds an incoming task into a run queue. It sorts the tasks according to their dynamic priority. The function is a realisation of the priority queue pattern (cf. Appendix B.6).

Function `update` determines the task's current `dynamic_priority` based on its `waiting_time` and `static_priority`. It linearly scales the `waiting_time` to the range of

Listing 4.2: Functions and colour sets for the history-dependent interactivity policy.

```
colset PRIORITY = product INT * INT * INT;
colset TIMESTAMP = product TASK_ID * INT;

(* The parameter values are defined in the feature configuration *)
(* of the history-dependent interactivity policy.                 *)
val MAX_PRIORITY = -20;
val MIN_PRIORITY = 19;
val MAXIMUM_BONUS = 10;
val MAXIMUM_DISTANCE = MIN_PRIORITY - MAX_PRIORITY + 1;
val MAX_WAITING_TIME = 1000

fun update(static_priority, dynamic_priority, waiting_time) =
let
    val bonus = MAXIMUM_BONUS * waiting_time div MAX_WAITING_TIME;
in
    (static_priority, min(MIN_PRIORITY, max(MAX_PRIORITY, static_priority
        - (bonus - MAXIMUM_BONUS div 2))), waiting_time)
end

fun delta(static_priority, dynamic_priority, waiting_time) =
    static_priority * MAXIMUM_BONUS div MAXIMUM_DISTANCE + 2

fun interactive(cpu, id, (static_priority, dynamic_priority,
                waiting_time), timeslice) =
let
    val (static_priority, dynamic_priority, waiting_time) =
        update((static_priority, dynamic_priority, waiting_time));
in
    (dynamic_priority <= static_priority -
        delta(static_priority, dynamic_priority, waiting_time))
end
```

priority bonuses (0 – **MAXIMUM_BONUS**). The upper limit (**MAX_WAITING_TIME**) ensures that the possible priority bonus (or penalty) stays within the predefined bounds. Furthermore, function **update** shifts the bonus's range from 0 – **MAXIMUM_BONUS** to -MAXIMUM_BONUS/2 – MAXIMUM_BONUS/2, leading to a penalty for tasks with low waiting times and with high processing times. The function finally ensures that the dynamic priority does not exceed the minimum (**MIN_PRIO**) and maximum priority (**MAX_PRIO**) for interactive tasks.

Furthermore, function **interactive** compares the current dynamic priority of a task to its interactivity threshold. If the dynamic priority is large enough, the task is considered as interactive and may be directly inserted into the active run queue, avoiding the run queues fairness. To consider the latest changes of the waiting time, the function first updates the dynamic priority of the considered task (calling function **update**). Furthermore, it needs to determine the interactivity threshold of the task, which depends on its static priority. The individual thresholds can either be explicitly modelled or – like in this case – be expressed as a function of the task's static priority. Therefore, function `delta` determines the threshold for a given static priority implementing the formula given in Section 2.3.5. Finally, function `interactive` compares the dynamic priority to the interactivity threshold (`static_priority` - `delta`). A task is considered as interactive if its dynamic priority is higher (i.e., the value is less or equal) than its interactivity threshold.

Task Preemption   The interactivity policies require changes of the scheduler's preemption mechanism which returns running tasks to their run queue. Figure 4.17 depicts the behaviour for the resource-dependent (Figure 4.17(a)) as well as the history-dependent (Figure 4.17(b)) interactivity policies.

Listing 4.3: Functions and colour sets for the resource-dependent interactivity policy.

```
colset PRIORITY = product INT * INT;

fun decrease((static_prio, dynamic_prio), timeslice) =
  if dynamic_prio > static_prio andalso timeslice = 0
    then (static_prio, dynamic_prio - 1)
    else (static_prio, dynamic_prio)

fun reset(timeslice, new_timeslice) =
  if timeslice > 0
    then timeslice
    else new_timeslice;
```

When returning a preempted task to the run queue, the resource-dependent policy needs to decrease the task's dynamic priority (function `decrease` in Listing 4.3) and reset its timeslice (function `reset` in Listing 4.3). Transition `Return` calls both functions when adding the task's token (`SCHED_TASK`) to the list on place `Incoming`. For the resource-dependent interactivity policy, a task's `PRIORITY` contains only its static priority and its dynamic priority omitting the waiting time. If a task's timeslice is expired and its dynamic priority is larger than its static, function `decrease` reduces a its dynamic priority by one. Otherwise, the function does not change the task's priorities. This behaviour ensures that whenever a task finishes its timeslice, its priority bonus (if it exists) is reduced. If a task's timeslice expired, function `reset` assigns a new timeslice to the task. The new timeslice may depend on external factors such as the the task's static priority and, thus, is given as a parameter to the function.

The history-dependent preemption (Figure 4.17(b)) continues the measurement of processing and waiting times started in the run queue. It uses the time stamps stored on place `StartProcessingTimes` (added by transition `Execute`) to determine the time a task spent processing. Transition `Return` selects the start time (`TIMESTAMP`) for the current task (which is uniquely identified by its `TASK_ID`) from place `StartProcessingTimes` and adds it to the

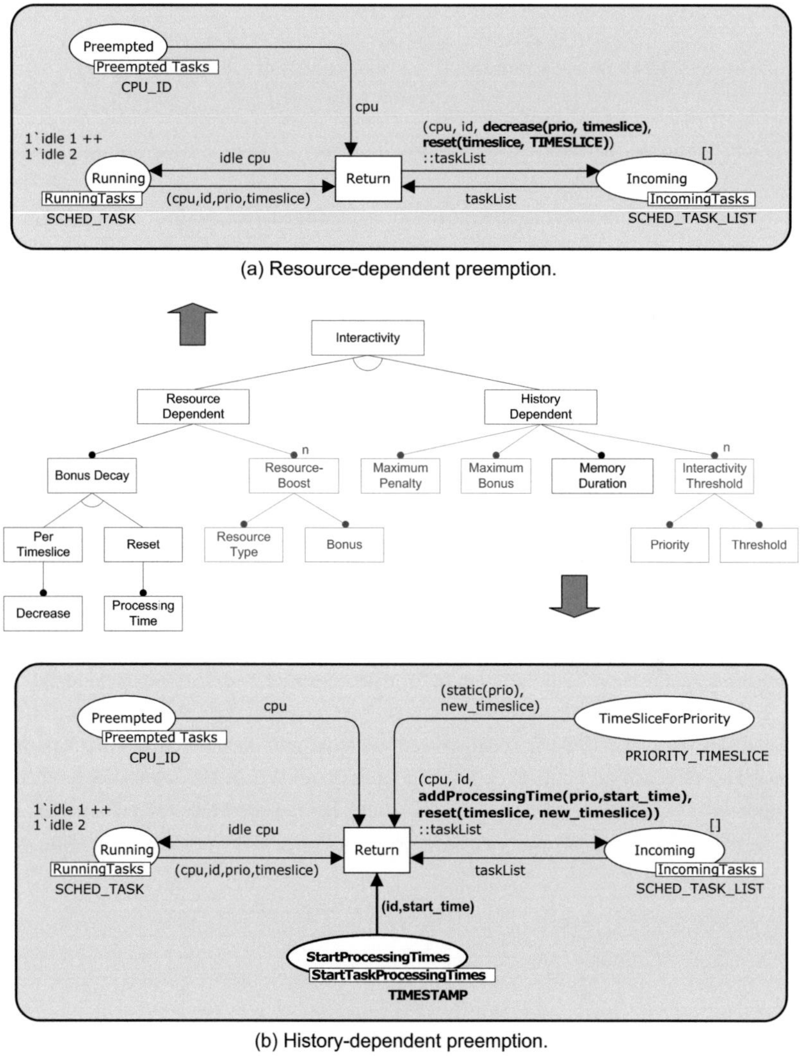

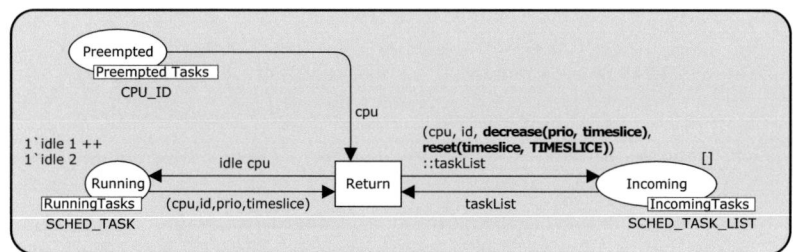

Figure 4.17.: CPN modelling task preemption.

Listing 4.4: Function `addProcessingTime`

```
fun addProcessingTime((static_prio, dynamic_prio, waiting_time), start_time) =
let
    val bonus = max(MAX_BONUS * waiting_time div MAX_WAITING_TIME, 1);
    val passed_time = (sim_time() - start_time) div bonus;
in
    (static_prio, dynamic_prio, max(0, waiting_time - passed_time))
end
```

task's current waiting time calling function `addProcessingTime` (cf. Listing 4.4). Parameter `prio` embodies the static and dynamic priority as well as the waiting time of the task (cf. Listing 4.2). The function determines the current bonus (not shifted) and divides the passed time (`sim_time()` - `start_time`) by the bonus. This division scales down the effect of longer processing times for tasks with a large priority bonus and contributes to the sharp change in priorities and response times observed during the experiments (cf. Section 4.2.3). As a consequence, a task needs only to spend a small fraction of its time waiting in order to receive a high priority bonus and in order to be classified as interactive. Finally, function `addProcessingTime` subtracts the scaled time value from the task's `waiting_time` and ensures that the result is not smaller than 0.

The history-dependent policy resets a task's timeslice in the same way as the resource-dependent policy. Only the new timeslice value (`new_timeslice`) depends on the tasks *static* priority.

Resource Acquisition   The acquisition of resources such as semaphores, connection pools, or network devices is central to both interactivity policies. Figure 4.18 depicts MOSS' behaviour for the acquisition of a semaphore. Tasks that require access to a semaphore put their identifier (`TASK_ID`) on input place `StartAcquisition`. When the acquisition is successfully completed, the acquisition's subnet puts the `TASK_ID` on output place `AcquisitionFinished`. In the mean time, the task may be put to sleep and wait for the resource to become available.

Listing 4.5: Function `available`.

```
fun available(semaphore, queue) =
(semaphore>0 andalso length queue = 0)
```

Furthermore, transitions `Acquire` and `Wait` require the demanding task to be currently running, i.e., its `SCHED_TASK` token has to lie on place `Running`. This condition is necessary since only tasks that are assigned to a processor can acquire passive resources. If the resource is currently available (`available(semaphore, queue)` = `true`), transition `Acquire` puts the task's identifier (`TASK_ID`) on place `AcquisitionFinished` and decreases the semaphore's

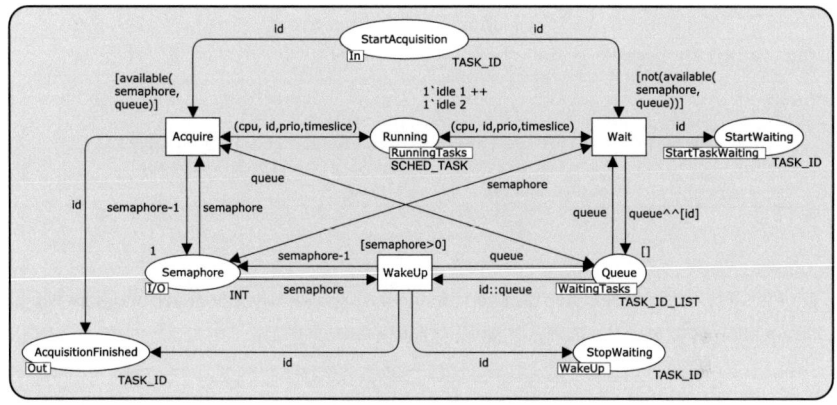

(a) History-dependent acquisition.

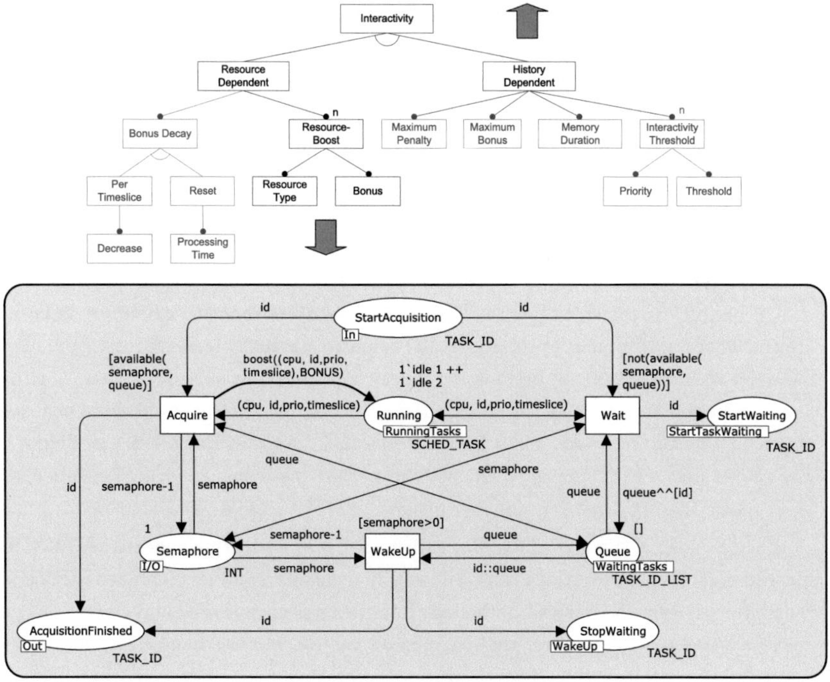

(b) Resource-dependent acquisition.

Figure 4.18.: CPN model for the acquisition of passive resources.

Listing 4.6: Function boost

```
fun conditional_reset (timeslice) = if timeslice > 15 then 31 else 15

fun boost((cpu, id, (static_priority, dynamic_priority), timeslice), bonus) =
  if (dynamic_priority >= static_priority + bonus)
    then (cpu, id, (static_priority, dynamic_priority), timeslice)
    else (cpu, id, (static_priority, static_priority + bonus),
                    conditional_reset(timeslice))
```

counter by one. Function `available` (Listing 4.5) checks whether the semaphore counter is larger than zero and the queue of waiting tasks is empty.

For the resource-dependent interactivity policy, transition `Acquire` assigns a bonus to the task that successfully acquired a resource. Function `boost` (Listing 4.6) checks the task's current dynamic priority. If the dynamic priority is already equal to or larger than the task's static priority plus the bonus, then the function does not change the task's dynamic priority or timeslice. Otherwise, it sets the task's dynamic priority to the static one plus the bonus and conditionally resets the task's timeslice. The term "conditional" refers to the type of resource and its behaviour. The experiments in Section 4.2.3 have demonstrated that the resource-dependent policy treats the timeslice differently for different types of resources. The function, printed in Listing 4.6, approximates the observed behaviour of semaphores. However, it is necessary to keep track of the remaining quanta (cf. Section 2.3.5) and compute the remaining timeslice accordingly, to achieve accurate predictions for the resource-dependent policy implemented in the Windows scheduler.

If a resource is currently not available (`available(semaphore, queue) = false`), the execution of a task that tries to acquire the resource needs to be delayed until the resource (semaphore in the example) becomes available. The treatment of waiting tasks is of major importance for the observed performance (see, for example, [Kou06]). To impose a specific order on the waiting tasks, place `Queue` stores their identifiers in a list. In Figure 4.18, the subnet uses a FIFO queue to manage the waiting tasks and, thus, implements a strong semaphore [Hap07]. However, different queueing policies can be considered here.

When a resource is not available, transition `Wait` inserts the task's identifier (`TASK_ID`) at the end of the list on place `Queue` and, additionally, puts its identifier on place `StartWaiting`. The latter triggers the removal of the task from its current processor and keeps track of the task's waiting time. Whenever the semaphore's value is increased and tasks are waiting in the queue, transition `WakeUp` takes the queue's first task and assigns it to the semaphore. The transition puts the tasks identifier on places `AcquisitionFinished` and `StopWaiting`. The first allows the task's behaviour to continue execution while the later notifies the scheduler that the task is no longer waiting.

Managing Waiting Tasks Figure 4.19 depicts the management of waiting tasks for
the resource- (Figure 4.19(a)) and history-dependent (Figure 4.19(b)) interactivity policy.
Whenever a task begins to wait for a resource, its identifier is put on place StartWaiting
and triggers the necessary operations of the scheduler. Transition PutToSleep removes a
task whose identifier lies on place StartWaiting from its processor (replacing its SCHED_TASK
token on place Running by an idle cpu token) and stores its scheduling data (SCHED_TASK)
on place Waiting. Once the requested resource(s) become available, the task's identifier is
placed on StopWaiting. Then transition WakeUp retrieves its SCHED_TASK token from place
Waiting and adds it to the list of tasks on place Incoming returning it to the schedulers run
queue. Transition WakeUp boosts the task's dynamic priority with a bonus specific to the
resource requested.

Listing 4.7: Function addWaitingTime.

```
fun addWaitingTime ((static_prio, dynamic_prio, waiting_time), start_time) =
let
    val passed_time = sim_time() − start_time;
in
    (static_prio, dynamic_prio, min(MAX_WAITING_TIME,
                                    waiting_time + passed_time))
end
```

The management of waiting tasks for history-dependent policies (cf. Figure 4.19(b))
needs to keep track of the waiting times and of the processing times. Therefore, transition
PutToSleep retrieves the time a task's processing started from place StartProcessingTimes
and incorporates the result with the task's current waiting time (as part of prio) by calling function addProcessingTime. Simultaneously, the transition puts an new TIMESTAMP
for the task on place StartWaitingTimes to measure the time it spends waiting for the
required resource. Tthe time stamp on place StartWaitingTimes is used to determine the
task's waiting time when the resource becomes available and transition WakeUp is enabled.
Function addWaitingTime (Listing 4.7) computes the passed time span and adds it to the
tasks waiting time while ensuring that the maximum waiting time (MAX_WAITING_TIME) is
not exceeded.

Releasing Resources Once a task finished its processing with respect to some required
resource, it may return the resource making it available for other tasks. Figure 4.20 depicts the subnet to release a semaphore. Whenever a task wants to release the semaphore
it puts its unique identifier on input place StartRelease. If the task is currently running
(i.e., its SCHED_TASK token lies on place Running), transition Release simply increases the
semaphores counter by one and places the task's identifier on FinishRelease allowing the

(a) Resource-dependent waiting.

(b) History-dependent waiting.

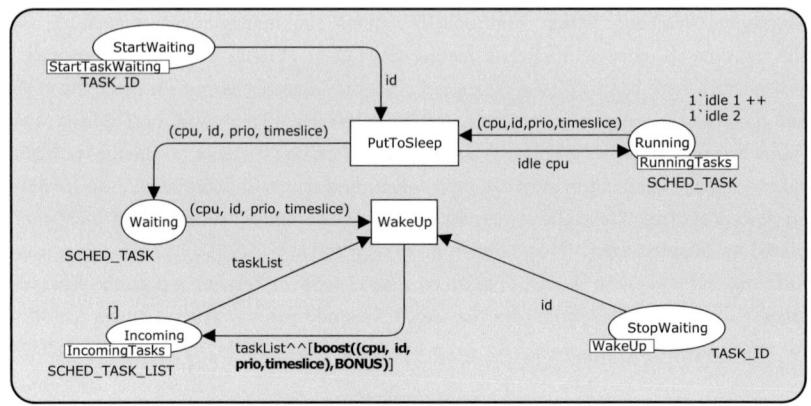

Figure 4.19.: CPN managing waiting tasks.

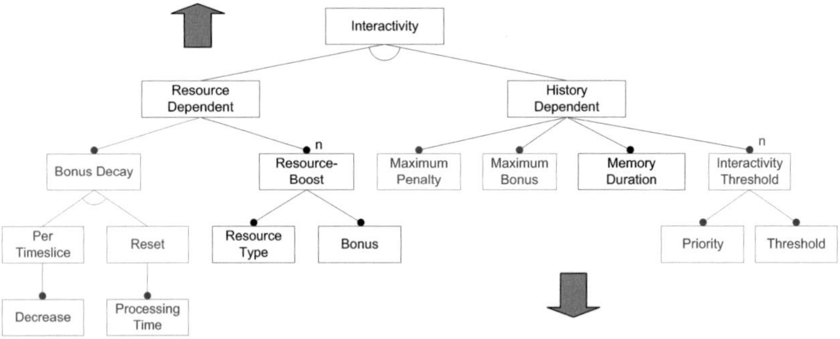

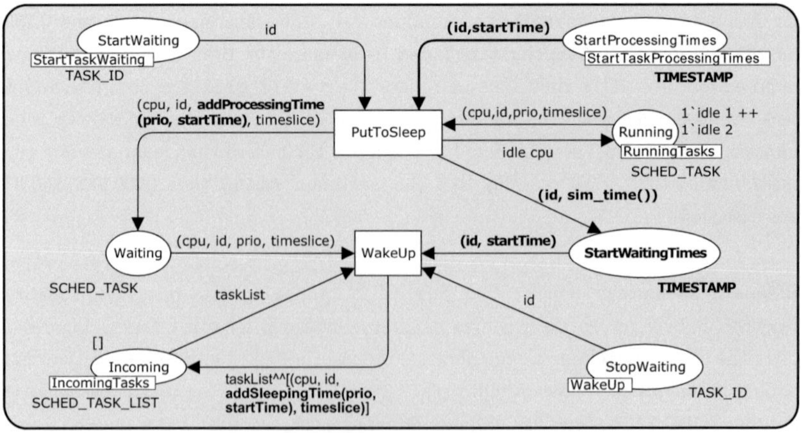

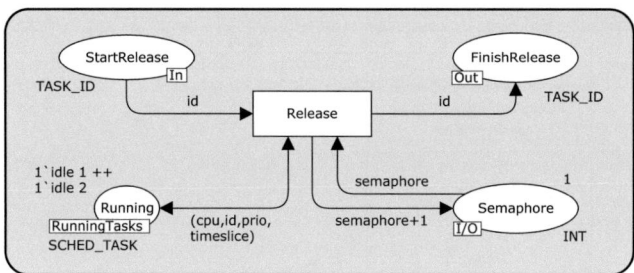

Figure 4.20.: CPN modelling the release or passive resources (e.g., semaphores).

task's behaviour to proceed. Increasing the semaphores counter automatically enables transition WakeUp of the acquisition's subnet (Figure 4.18) if other tasks are waiting for access to the resource. Transition WakeUp fires before the simulation time progresses.

4.2.5. Validation of MOSS' Prediction Accuracy

In this section, we present a validation of the prediction accuracy of MOSS's interactivity features based on the experiments presented in Section 4.1.1. The validation is focussed on the major features for resource-dependent and history-dependent interactivity policies. We compare the predictions of MOSS with measurements of Windows Server 2003 and Linux 2.6. In a complex case study (Section 5.2), we evaluate the mutual influences of different scheduler features.

Goal:	*Purpose*	Assessment
	Issue	of MOSS' prediction accuracy
	Object	for resource- and history-dependent interactivity policies
	Viewpoint	from the software architect's point of view.

In the following validation, the assessment of MOSS' prediction accuracy focusses on scenarios No Boost, Semaphore, and Network. The prediction error gives insights into the prediction accuracy of MOSS.

The questions listed in Table 4.20 address the prediction accuracy for different priority bonuses of the resource-dependent policy (Question IR.V1). Furthermore, the classification of interactive and non-interactive task (Question IH.V1) as well as the general prediction accuracy for tasks with different behaviour (Question III.V2) are of major relevance for the history-dependent policy.

Evaluation of the Prediction Accuracy for Interactive Tasks			
	IR.V1	**IH.V1**	**IH.V2**
Questions	How accurate does MOSS predict the influence of different priority bonuses on a task's performance?	Does MOSS correctly classify non-interactive and interactive tasks?	Does MOSS accurately predict the performance of interactive and non-interactive tasks?
Scenarios	No Boost Semaphore Network	No Boost	No Boost
Metrics	Error(RT) Error(HPT)	Error(IT)	Error(RT)
Hypotheses	Yes, the prediction error is less than 5%	Yes, the prediction error is less than 5%	Yes, the prediction error is less than 5%

Table 4.20.: GQM plan to evaluate the prediction accuracy of the developed model for interactive schedulers.

Question IR.V1: How accurate does MOSS predict the influence of different priority bonuses on a task's performance?

Question IR.V1 targets MOSS' prediction accuracy with respect to different resources used by tasks under a resource-dependent interactivity policy. Therefore, it represents the validation's counterpart of Questions IR.1 and IR.2. Consequently, it considers the prediction error (cf. Section 4.1.4) of the response time and high priority time for scenarios No Boost, Semaphore, and Network.

Hypotheses   As a result, Hypothesis IR.V1.a expects no deviation larger than 5% between the predictions and the measurements. Let t_i be the interactive and t_n be the non-interactive task in all three scenarios, then:

$$\text{Error}(\text{E}[\text{RT}(t_i)]) < 5\%, \quad \text{Error}(\text{E}[\text{RT}(t_n)]) < 5\%, \text{ and} \quad \text{Error}(\text{E}[\text{HPT}(t_i)]) < 5\%$$
$$\text{(IR.V1.a)}$$

for all three scenarios.

Results   Figure 4.21 depicts the predicted and measured response times (Figures 4.21(a) – (d)) and high priority times (Figures 4.21(e) and (f)) for the resource-dependent interactivity policy. The predicted and measured mean response times (Figures 4.21(a) and (b)) deviate only slightly. The corresponding distribution functions (Figures 4.21(c) and (d)) widely overlap. For scenario Semaphore, MOSS accurately predicts the fraction of tasks than can execute their processing demand without interruption as well as the fraction of tasks that are disrupted. However, the curve of the simulation shows less disturbances than the measurement. The peak found in the measurements, at about 450 ms, cannot be found

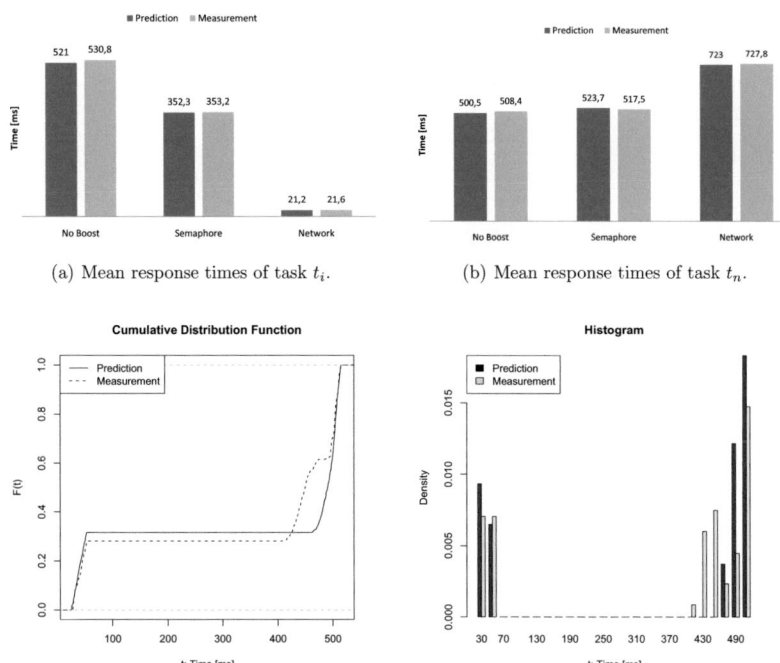

(a) Mean response times of task t_i.

(b) Mean response times of task t_n.

(c) Response time distribution of task t_i for scenario *Semaphore*.

(d) Response time distribution of task t_i for scenario *Semaphore*.

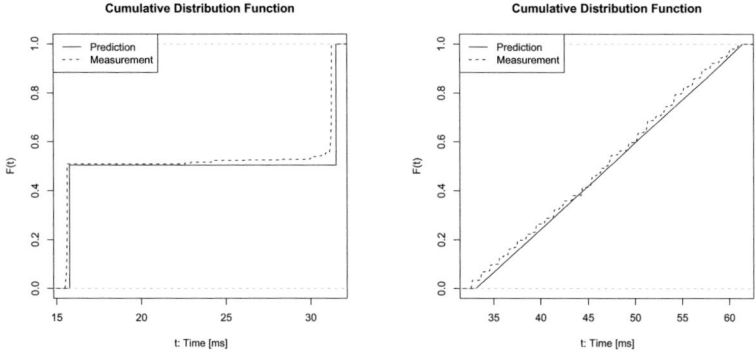

(e) High priority time distribution of task t_i for scenario *Semaphore*.

(f) High priority time distribution of task t_i for scenario *Network*.

Figure 4.21.: Predictions and measurements for interactive tasks under Windows.

in the predictions. Similarly, the distribution of the predicted and measured high priority processing times (Figures 4.21(e) and (f)) only deviate slightly. MOSS accurately predicts the timeslice reset as well as the effect of priority bonuses.

Error Response Time [%]		
	Interactive	Non-Interactive
No Boost	1,85	1,55
Semaphore	0,25	1,20
Network	1,85	0,66
Error High Priority Processing Time [%]		
Semaphore	2,16	-
Network	1,50	-

Table 4.21.: Prediction error for interactive tasks under Windows.

Table 4.21 summarises the prediction error for response times and high priority processing times. For the response times, the prediction deviates less than 2% from the measurements. A similar result is achieved for the high priority processing time in scenario `Network`. Only the prediction error for scenario `Semaphore` deviates slightly more than 2%. The results confirm Hypothesis IR.V1.a.

Question IH.V1: Does MOSS correctly classify non-interactive and interactive tasks?

This question addresses MOSS prediction accuracy with respect to the classification of tasks according to their behaviour. The question is motivated by the underlying question of whether MOSS models the history-dependent interactivity policy with sufficient detail or whether it requires further refinements. To answer this question, we consider measured and predicted interactivity thresholds of scenario `No Boost` with the valuations given in Table 4.19.

Hypothesis   Similarly to Hypothesis IR.V1.a, Hypothesis IH.V1.a expects a prediction error of less than 5% for the interactivity threshold:

$$\text{Error}(\text{E}[\text{IT}(t_i)]) < 5\% \qquad\qquad (\text{IH.V1.a})$$

Results   Table 4.22 summarises the predicted and measured interactivity thresholds for task t_i. Interestingly, predictions and measurements do not deviate at this point leading to a prediction error of 0%. This indicates that the interactivity threshold tolerates minor disturbances of the tasks execution and behaves exactly as reflected in MOSS. The absence of any prediction error is a consequence of the fact that the results only represent one decision after a long measurement or simulation run. The results support Hypothesis IH.V1.a. In this scenario, MOSS correctly classifies interactive and non-interactive tasks.

Demand [ms]	Delay [ms]		Error [%]
	Predicted	Measured	
80	9	9	0,0
160	18	18	0,0
240	27	27	0,0
320	36	36	0,0
400	45	45	0,0
480	54	54	0,0
560	63	63	0,0

Table 4.22.: Prediction and measurement t_i's interactivity threshold.

Question IH.V2: Does MOSS accurately predict the performance of interactive and non-interactive tasks?

While Question IH.V1 validates MOSS with respect to its prediction accuracy of the interactivity threshold, Question IH.V2 validates the more general prediction accuracy of interactive tasks (t_i) and of non-interactive tasks (t_n). We focus on the deviation of the predicted an measured response time in scenario No Boost with the a processing demand of 80 ms and a delay between 0 ms and 20 ms (cf. Table 4.18). In the following, we describe the question's hypotheses, the predictions, and the actual results.

Hypothesis   Similar to the hypotheses of the questions above, Hypothesis IH.V2.a expects a prediction error of less than 5% for task t_i and t_n:

$$\text{Error}(\text{E}[\text{RT}(t_i)]) < 5\% \quad \text{and} \quad \text{Error}(\text{E}[\text{RT}(t_n)]) < 5\% \tag{IH.V2.a}$$

Results   In the following, we present the predictions and measurements for interactive and non-interactive tasks with varying processing demands and delays. Figures 4.22(a) and (b) show the mean response times that have been predicted and measured for a task with 80 ms processing demand and varying delay between 0 ms and 20 ms. The response times largely overlap for task t_i (Figure 4.22(a)) and for task t_n (Figure 4.22(b)). The interactivity threshold of task t_i at 9 ms is clearly visible in both figures. The response time of t_i is reduced to 80 ms while the response time of t_n is increased to almost 800 ms. The overall prediction error is below 3%.

Figures 4.22(c) to (f) depict the response time distribution of tasks t_i and t_n with a processing demand of 80 ms and a delay of 8 ms. In this case, the history dependent policy does not (yet) classify task t_i as interactive, but rather it receives a higher dynamic priority than t_n. The response time predicted for t_i (Figures 4.22(c) and (d)) deviates only sightly from the measurements. MOSS accurately predicts the response time peaks at 80 ms, 172 ms, and 272 ms. The probability densities correspond to the measurements. However, the

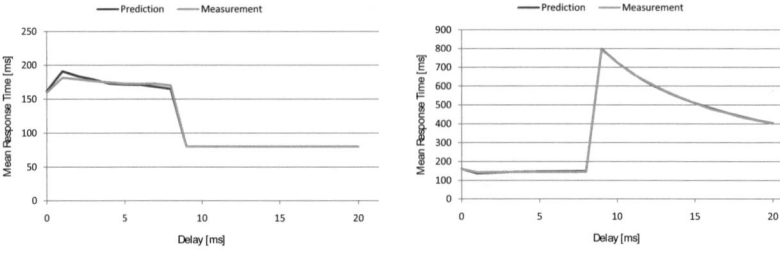

(a) Mean response times of task t_i with varying de- (b) Mean response times of task t_n with varying
lays.   delays.

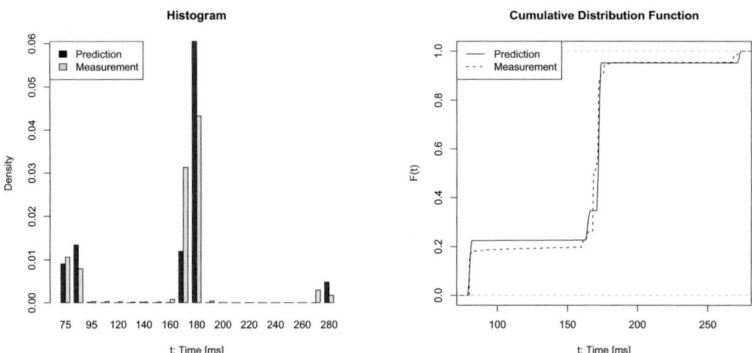

(c) Response time distribution of task t_i (80 ms (d) Response time distribution of task t_i (80 ms
demand, 8 ms delay).   demand, 8 ms delay).

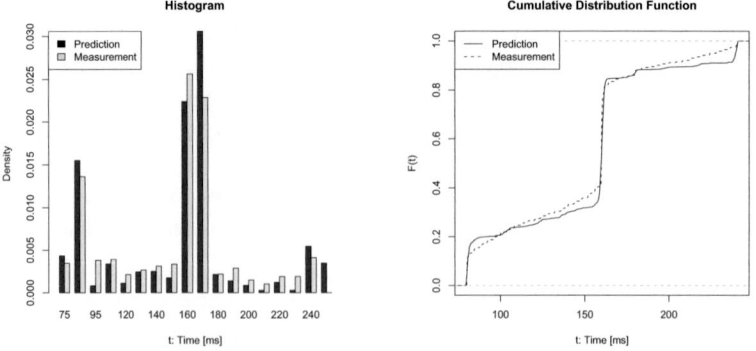

(e) Response time distribution of task t_n (80 ms (f) Response time distribution of task t_n (80 ms
demand, 8 ms delay).   demand, 8 ms delay).

Figure 4.22.: Predictions and measurements for interactive and non-interactive tasks for the
              history-dependent interactivity policy.

measurements show more disturbances than the predictions. The response time distribution predicted for task t_n (Figures 4.22(e) and (f)) widely overlaps with the measurements. The distribution captures the three major peaks at 80 ms, 160 ms, and 240 ms as well as the distribution between the peaks.

Altogether, MOSS predicts the mean response times of tasks t_i and t_n with an error of less than 5% in all cases. The predicted response time distribution accurately resembles measurements of the history-dependent interactivity and, hence, supports Hypothesis IH.V2.a.

4.3. Case Study

In this section, we present a case study to evaluate the applicability and prediction accuracy of MOSS for enterprise applications. Here, we focus on single processor systems. In Section 5.2, we continue the case study for multiprocessing environments. While each scheduling feature modelled in MOSS has already been extensively validated, this case study assesses the prediction accuracy of MOSS in a more complex setting. The setting contains various types of request as well as fluctuating workloads. However, the case study still requires some simplifications as discussed in the following.

The case study is focussed on the influence of different workloads and of different operating systems on performance. Therefore, we minimise the impact of other components and services that are typically used in the chosen application scenario. Simplification is necessary to avoid disturbances of other system components that cannot be modelled accurately with current performance prediction methods. This approach achieves a high internal validity of the results at the cost of external validity. However, case studies with a high external validity require performance models for databases, hard drives, and network connections of the same accuracy as MOSS. For this reason, we simplify the database used to store business data and manage the application state, which could easily become the limiting factor in the case study. Additionally, a load generator emulates the resource demands of the application (cf. Appendix C.1).

In the following, we describe the scenario of the case study (Section 4.3.1), its software architecture (Section 4.3.2), the performance questions (Section 4.3.3), the experimental setting (Section 4.3.4), and the results of the case study (Section 4.3.5).

4.3.1. Evaluated Use Cases

The case study is placed in the scenario of a supply chain management for supermarkets (as described in [SPE]). The whole scenario models a set of supply chain interactions between a supermarket company, its stores, its distribution centres, and its suppliers. In this case study, we focus on a sales statistics scenario (based on [WW04]) that includes business intelligence reporting to headquarters (HQ). Supermarkets send statistics to HQ that include, for example, the type and amount of goods purchased by customers visiting the store. HQ uses this data as a basis for data mining in order to study customer behaviour and to provide useful information to their marketing department. In this case study, we evaluate the performance of business intelligence reporting, online monitoring, and requests to static web pages described in the following.

Business Intelligence Reporting   HQ collects the necessary information about sales statistics from supermarkets and distribution centres. To support better business decision making, the business intelligence reporting integrates, analyses, and presents the supermarkets' business information. Statistical processing of data generates comprehensible overviews for managers and department heads (i.e., heads of the supermarket stores). Different managers and stores are interested in different information. Thus, business intelligence reporting supports various kinds of reports.

Online Monitoring   Online monitoring allows managers and department heads to track sales over the day. They can identify peak times or observe whether new marketing strategies had the expected impact. Department heads can directly react on changes and organise their personnel accordingly. The online monitoring updates whenever a supermarket sends new sales data to HQ. It generates static web pages which the supermarket market's personnel can access.

Requests to Static Pages   Requests to static web pages are an essential part of intranet applications. The intranet provides department heads, managers, accountants, and other employees with access to internal information such as marketing strategies, reports on new goods, or rankings of supermarket stores.

Workload

For the scope of this case study, the workload of the HQ's server consists of requests to static web pages, online monitoring, and business reporting. The number of supermarkets, the amount of products sold per supermarket, and the number of reporting and monitoring requests determine the workload of the HQ's server. In the case study, HQ manages 1500 supermarket stores all over the country. Depending on a store's size, 1 to 5 persons can access the HQ's server. Additionally, 50 employees at HQ use the business reporting system on a regular basis.

From observations of the current system, performance analysts expect a strongly fluctuating load of the system, with burst periods of 5 to 10 minutes. They approximate this
behaviour by the curve shown in Figure 4.23. Even though the curve does not reflect the
exact behaviour of the system, it allows the effect of peak loads on software performance to
be determined. The arrival rate ranges from 60 to 180 requests per minute depending on
the time of day, i.e., at noon the load is generally low but several peaks can be observed
during the early afternoon. In most cases, users request static web pages via intra-net (70%
of all requests). Business reports are requested in 10% of all cases. The remaining 20%
of the requests stem from supermarkets, which send new sales reports to HQ. Thus, online
monitoring is updated 12 (= 60 * 0.2) to 36 (= 180 * 0.2) times a minute.

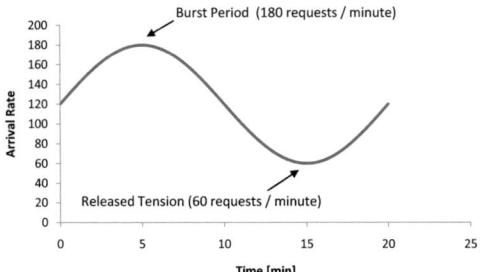

Figure 4.23.: Function modelling the fluctuating workload of HQ's business reporting.

To analyse the influence of load peaks on the applications performance, performance analysts must use fluctuating arrival rate of 60 to 180 requests per minute. The modelled
workload continuously fluctuates following a sinus curve with a period length of 20 minutes (cf. Figure 4.23). Its low periods reflect the system's usual workload of 60 requests
per minute, its high periods reflect the burst conditions where the workload triples. This
workload allows performance analysts to estimate the influence of burst periods on system's
response times, resource utilisation and throughput. Furthermore, the load of HQ's application is expected to double during the next two years. To ensure a good performance of the
application in the long term, performance analysts need to evaluate the system's scalability
for an increasing load.

The architecture of the HQ's server application described in the following section efficiently
handles the high load of computation intensive requests.

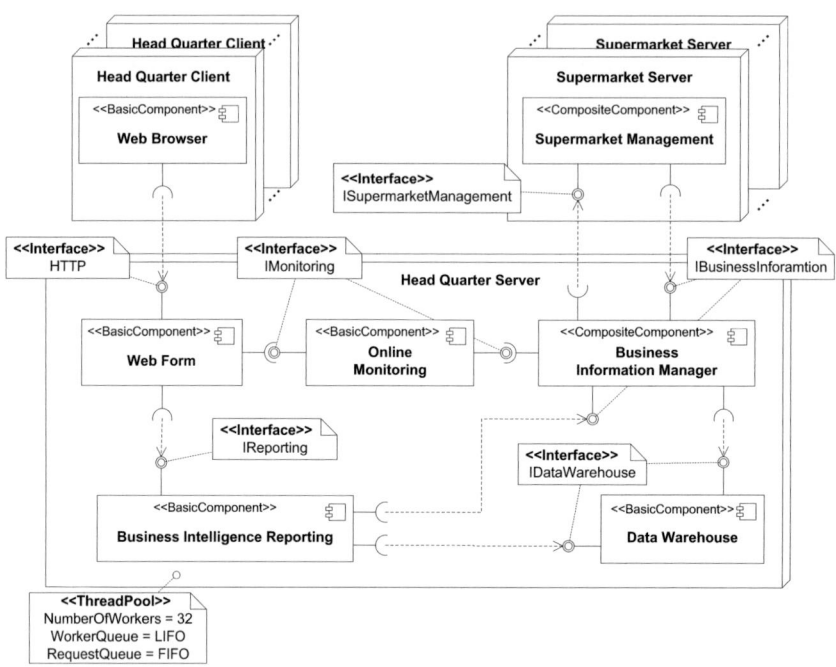

Figure 4.24.: Static and deployment view of the HQ's server application.

4.3.2. Architecture of HQ's Application

Static Architecture View   The hardware environment of the HQ's server system presented in Figure 4.24 contains the HQ's server as well as several supermarket servers and HQ clients. The software system consists of several components distributed among the hardware nodes. For the case study, the architecture has been modelled using the PCM (cf. Appendix A).

Supermarket servers are responsible for managing the warehouse inventory, order goods from distribution centres, and communication with HQ. Figure 4.24 abstracts their software system into a single composite component called Supermarket Management. Figure 4.24 only shows the interfaces relevant for the HQ's server application. The provided interface ISupermarketManagement allows the Business Information Manager to request information on the supermarket's state, update prices, distribute product announcements, or request sales statistics. Furthermore, supermarkets actively inform HQ on their current state via the IBusinessInformation interface. The Business Information Manager stores infor-

mation about supermarkets in the Data Warehouse and updates the Online Monitoring
of the supermarket stores. When requested, the Online Monitoring provides an overview
of the current state of the supermarket stores. For more detailed information, the Business
Intelligence Reporting generates individually configured business reports.

The application server running the HQ's application uses a thread pool to limit the number
of concurrent requests in the system. It uses a dynamic pool with a maximum number of
32 worker threads per processor or processor-core. The performance model approximates
the pool's dynamic behaviour with a thread pool of fixed size. To reduce context switch
overheads, the application server manages worker threads in a Last-In-First-Out (LIFO)
queue. This strategy increases the chance of finding necessary data in the processor's caches.
Additionally, workers can continue processing requests without context switches if requests
queue up. To treat requests similarly, the application server queues incoming requests in a
First-In-First-Out order.

Dynamic Architecture View RD-SEFFs (cf. Appendix A) specify the dynamic architecture of the HQ's application (Figure 4.25) relevant for performance evaluation. The RD-
SEFFs include the dispatching of requests by the Web Form (Figure 4.25(a)), the generation
of reports by the Business Intelligence Reporting (Figure 4.25(b)), and the Online
Monitoring (Figure 4.25(c)). The Web Form dispatches incoming HTTP requests to the
Business Intelligence Reporting or serves requests to static web pages. The RD-SEFF
in Figure 4.25(a) models the choice as a guarded branch action. The guards evaluate the
value of input parameter RequestType, which represents a performance abstraction of the
HTTP protocol. It only contains the types Reporting, Monitoring, and StaticPage, for
the considered scenario. The guarded branch action contains an alternative for each possible value. Its branching probabilities depend on the probability distribution of the values
of parameter RequestType. In the PCM, an EnumPMF specifies the probability distribution
over an enumeration of values. For example, a valuation

   EnumPMF[('Reporting';0.1) ('Monitoring';0.2) ('StaticPage';0.7)]

of the input parameter RequestType leads to branching probabilities of 0.1, 0.2, and 0.7
for reporting, monitoring, and static pages, respectively. To handle reporting and monitoring, the Web Form calls the generateReport and updateMontioring methods on the
IReporting and IMonitoring interface respectively. For requests to static pages, an internal action models the corresponding resource demand with a normal distribution. Figure 4.25(a) specifies the distribution's mean value as 50 CPU units with a variance of 1. In
the PCM, CPU or workload units allow the abstraction from the underlying hardware plat-

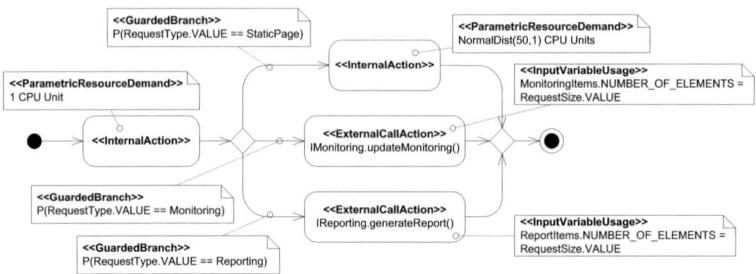

(a) Service `processHttpRequest` of component `Web Form`.

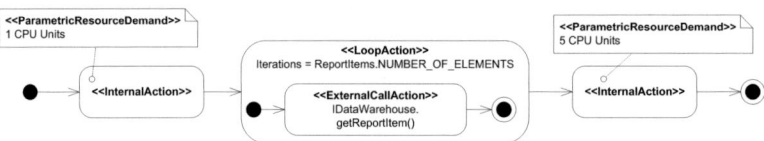

(b) Service `generateReporte` of component `Business Intelligence Reporting`.

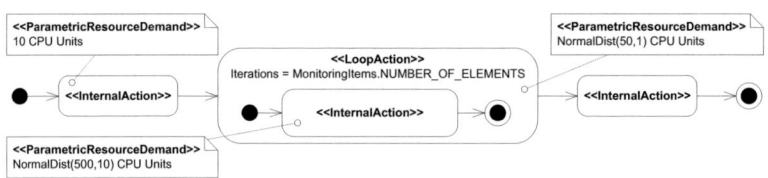

(c) Service `updateMonitoring` of component `Online Monitoring`

Figure 4.25.: Behaviour (RD-SEFFs) of the HQ's server components.

form [RBH+07, KB07]. For the sake of simplicity, we assume that 10 CPU units correspond to 1 ms of processing time for all considered processor types.

In method `generateReport` of component `Business Intelligence Reporting`), a loop action iterates over a set of `ReportItems` and includes them into the report. The caller (i.e., component `WebForm` in the case study) passes a collection of `ReportItems` to the method. The collection contains, for example, references to the supermarkets which are included into the report. The size (i.e., `NUMBER_OF_ELEMENTS`) of collection `ReportItems` determines the number of loop iterations (see Figure 4.25(b)). Method `generateReport` retrieves the report items from the `Data Warehouse`. This specification is an abstraction of different types of report items and contains only a single method call for all possible types. Finally, `generateReport` combines the report items into a single web page and returns it to the caller.

To update the current statistics, the `Business Information Manager` calls the `Online Monitoring` whenever new status information arrives from a supermarket. It calls the method `updateMonitoring` on the `IMonitoring` interface to generate new static pages which summarise the status of the supermarkets. The behaviour of `Online Monitoring` is similar to report generation. However, the processing is completely internal. In the next section, we discuss the performance questions relevant for the HQ's server application.

4.3.3. Performance Questions

The HQ's server system has to handle an intensive workload while retaining high responsiveness. Thus, it can easily become a bottleneck for management and accounting of the supermarket company. Performance analysts decide to conduct an initial performance study before deploying the application. They want to answer the following questions given the high and strongly fluctuating workload of the HQ's server system:

1. Can the new software system handle the workload with the given hardware?

2. How does the system react under overload conditions?

3. Which operating system (Linux 2.6 or Windows Server 2003) provides the best performance under heavy load?

The questions are motivated by the possible overload conditions that can occur due to the strongly fluctuating load. Scheduling is one possibility to improve performance without buying additional hardware [SWHB06]. Thus, performance analysts want to make sure that the system's performance meets the requirements for intensive load. Furthermore, they are mainly interested in the response times for different requests (business intelligence reporting, online monitoring, and static pages). The acceptable response time bounds strongly depend on the type of request. For example, requests to static pages must be served immediately (i.e., with a response time of a few milliseconds) while requests to the business reporting can be delayed by several seconds.

In the following section, we present the experimental settings of the case study. This includes a description of the measurement environment as well as the prediction model and chosen solution method.

4.3.4. Experimental Settings

Measurements For the case study, we implemented the HQ's application in Java and instrumented it for measurements. The specified resource demands (cf. Figure 4.25) have been generated by a resource demand generator (cf. Appendix C.3). The generator loads the CPU using typical algorithms found in benchmark applications for processors, such as SPEC

CPU2000 [Hen00, Cor00]. A workload generator has simulated the user behaviour, i.e., the calls to the HQ's application. The implementation thus ensures that the case study focusses on effect of scheduling and excludes disturbances of the environment. The confidence level of the measurements is 90% for requests `generateReport` and `updateMonitoring` in Section 4.3.5. For the relatively short requests to static pages, the confidence level is 80%, since small disturbances (of a few milliseconds) already have a large impact. All measurements were taken on a single machine with the accuracy of the machines clock frequency (i.e., 1.87 GHz in for the measurements on a single core processor).

Predictions For performance prediction, a discrete event simulation technique [LMV02, LB05] specialised for MOSS has been implemented and integrated with the Palladio Component Model. The simulation employs the method of overlapping batch means [Jai91] to achieve reliable results. The confidence levels for the predictions are 95% for `generateReport` and `updateMonitoring`, and 90% for requests to static pages (same argumentation as above). A simulation run lasted from 45 to 60 seconds and simulated a run time of approximately 8 hours. The customisations of MOSS used to predict the influences of the Linux and Windows scheduler are listed in Table 3.2 on page 63.

To allow a better interpretation of the measurements and predictions, the parameters of the application (resource demands and number of report items) have been adjusted so that the total resource demands of all request have the following means:

Static Page Requests: 5 ms
Online Monitoring: 250 ms
Generate Report: 3000 ms

Outlier Removal Due to the periods of transient overload in the scenario, measurements (and predictions) contain strong outliers that heavily contribute to the predicted and measured mean response times. In order to achieve stable results (for predictions and measurements), we consider only predictions and measurements for which the topmost 5% to 10% of outliers have been removed. Additionally, the confidence intervals for the predictions and measurements are based on the results after outlier removal. Even though the outlier removal leaves some room for discussion, it is unavoidable to achieve stable measurements and predictions for scenarios with transient overload as considered here.

In the next section, we present the results (predictions and measurements) to answer the questions and to assess the accuracy of the prediction model proposed in this chapter.

4.3.5. Results

The results summarised in the following demonstrate the differences and similarities of the Windows and Linux operating systems with respect to software performance as well as the prediction accuracy of MOSS. The prediction quality varies strongly for the commonly used scheduling policies FCFS and PS. In this case study, their prediction errors range from more than 70% to up to 40000%. By contrast, MOSS predicts the influence of Windows and Linux schedulers on software performance with an error of less than 5% to 10% in most cases. The prediction error does not exceed 30%. MOSS represents a significant increase of the prediction accuracy compared to commonly used scheduling policies in performance prediction. In the following, we present the experimental setting for the case study and discuss the prediction accuracy of MOSS with respect to PS and FCFS.

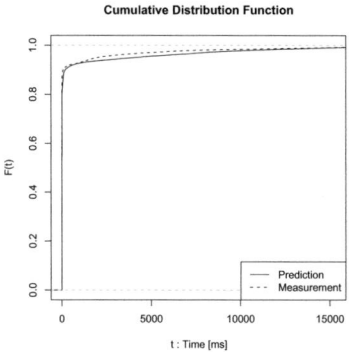

Figure 4.26.: Predictions and measurements for static page requests under Linux 2.6.22.

Prediction Accuracy Figure 4.26 shows the cumulative distribution functions predicted and measured for the response time of static page requests under Linux 2.6.22. The figure illustrates the role of outliers in the results of this case study. Approximately 90% of all requests are processed within 5 ms for predictions and measurements. However, processing of the upper 10% of all requests is delayed for several seconds (up to 15 seconds in the cumulative distribution function shown). The heavy tail of their response time distribution significantly influences its mean value. Due to this heavy tail, the mean value of the response time distribution is rather unstable. Tight confidence bounds are only reached very slowly. The upper 5% of outliers have been removed from the distribution to reduce the influence of the response time distribution's tail. The prediction error is less than 5% for Windows and Linux (see Table 4.23).

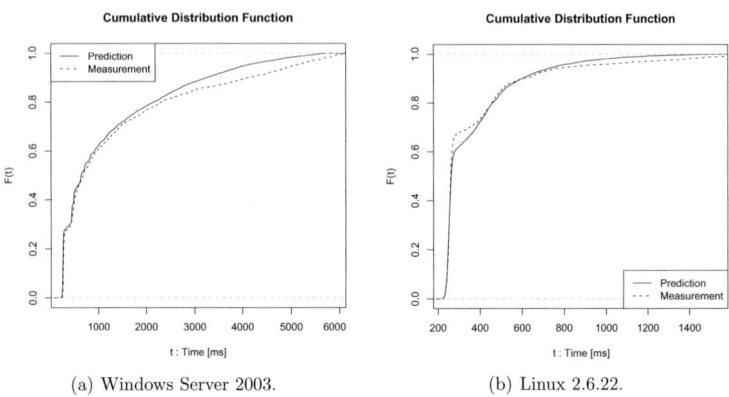

(a) Windows Server 2003.   (b) Linux 2.6.22.

Figure 4.27.: Predictions and measurements for monitoring requests.

Figure 4.27 shows cumulated distribution functions of the response times for online monitoring. The predictions and measurements widely overlap for the Linux and Windows operating system. Furthermore, the predicted and measured mean values and medians deviate no more than 15% (Table 4.23).

The response times for monitoring requests differ significantly for both operating systems. Linux limits the distribution to 250 ms to 1600 ms, while the response time under Windows ranges from 250 ms to 6000 ms. The differences in response times are visible in the mean value and median. The response time of monitoring requests under Linux is less than one third of the response time under Windows (see Table 4.23).

Table 4.23 summarises the predicted and measured mean response times for all request types and scenarios. The prediction error is approximately 5% – 10% in the most cases and does not exceed 30%. As discussed above, MOSS accurately predicts the mean and median of the response time for static page and monitoring requests. Due to the the heavy tail of the response time distribution for static page requests under Linux, its mean value (50 ms) is much larger than its counterpart under Windows (5 ms). However, the median is similar for both operating systems.

Furthermore, the measured response times of the business reporting are comparable for both operating systems. However, the predicted and measured response times deviate by 32% for the business reporting under Linux. One cause of the deviation lies in the artificial load driver used in the experiment setting. Under Linux, the load driver cannot maintain its pace for the arriving requests during peak loads. It freezes several times for a period of 1 to 10 seconds loosening the system's tension. The simulator does not suffer from such

Median						
		MOSS		**Processor Sharing**		**FCFS**	
	Measurement	**Prediction**	**Error [%]**	**Prediction**	**Error [%]**	**Prediction**	**Error [%]**
Windows							
Static Pages	5,4	5,0	7,2	14,3	163,3	30,9	469,2
Monitoring	814,1	704	13,5	736	9,6	289,6	64,4
Reporting	12100	9546	21,1	8538	29,4	3027	75,0
Linux							
Static Pages	5,1	5,5	7,4	14,3	180,8	30,9	507,1
Monitoring	261,4	266,2	1,8	736	181,6	289,6	10,8
Reporting	11480	13720	19,5	8538	25,6	3027	73,6
Mean Value							
		MOSS		**Processor Sharing**		**FCFS**	
	Measurement	**Prediction**	**Error [%]**	**Prediction**	**Error [%]**	**Prediction**	**Error [%]**
Windows							
Static Pages	5,2	4,9	5,0	24,3	372,6	2180,0	42230,1
Monitoring	1398,0	1226,0	12,3	1233,0	11,8	2398,0	71,5
Reporting	19520,0	17480,0	10,5	14630,0	25,1	5075,0	74,0
Linux							
Static Pages	48,5	47,9	1,3	24,3	49,8	2180,0	4396,7
Monitoring	438,9	438,9	0,0	1233,0	180,9	2398,0	446,4
Reporting	18520,0	24460,0	32,1	14630,0	21,0	5075,0	72,6

Table 4.23.: Prediction accuracy for single-core system running under Linux and Windows.

difficulties, since it can easily maintain the defined pace. Especially long requests suffer from the additional load due to their decaying priority bonus. This behaviour contributes to the additional delay of the reporting requests observed in the simulation. Furthermore, the deviation of the resource demand generator (cf. Appendix C.1) increases for larger processing demands. The generator uses previously calibrated algorithms to emulate the necessary computation demand on a processor. While it yields accurate results for short requests, its error increases for longer resource demands. Both effects together explain the deviation predictions and measurements observed for the business reporting requests.

A comparison between the medians for both operating systems (Table 4.23) yields the impression that Linux performs much better than Windows. However, it is important to notice that Linux suffers from a large number of outliers for static page and monitoring requests that significantly lower its performance with respect to the overall response time distribution.

Comparison with Models using Processor Sharing and First-Come-First-Serve MOSS can accurately predict response times of requests to static web pages, online monitoring, and business reporting. Figure 4.28 gives an impression how MOSS improves prediction accuracy with respect to scheduling policies commonly used in software performance prediction, namely PS and FCFS. In the following, we compare the measurements for Windows and Linux with their prediction results.

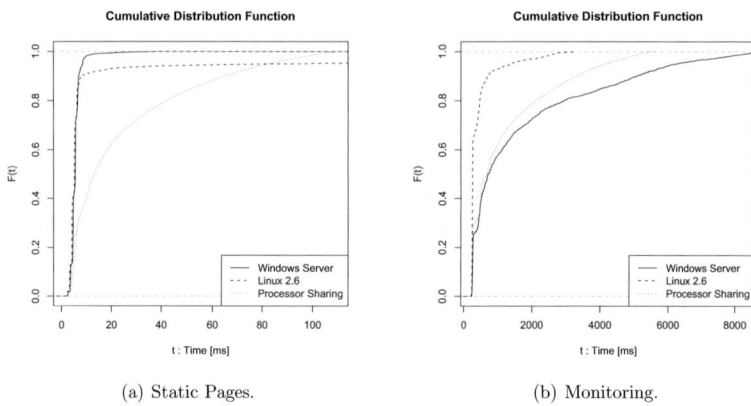

(a) Static Pages.   (b) Monitoring.

Figure 4.28.: Differences between Windows, Linux, and processor sharing.

Figure 4.28 depicts the cumulative response time distributions of requests to static pages (Figure 4.28(a)) and online monitoring (Figure4.28(b)). Both figures show measurements for Linux and Windows on a single-core system and the corresponding predictions for PS.

PS predicts a strong delay for most of the requests for requests to static web pages (cf. Table 4.23). The additional delay induced by PS leads to a prediction error factor of up to 5 for mean values and 3 for medians. While the response time distribution and median for Linux appears similar to the one for Windows, its mean value is nearly 10 times larger due to the heavy tail of the distribution. This example illustrates the importance of response time distributions. While a mean response time of 50 ms is acceptable for requests to static web pages, timeouts for 10% of the requests are not. In the following, we briefly explain the causes of this effect, which MOSS accurately predicts (see Table 4.23).

The long delays for 10% of the requests result from Linux' dynamic priority assignment in combination with the application server's thread pool. The application server uses an unfair (also called weak) semaphore [GPB+06] to manage its worker threads. It basically prefers worker threads which have been running recently over those waiting in the queue. Linux lowers a thread's priority according to the time it spent processing. Thus, continuously processing threads receive a lower priority than threads waiting in the queue. If such a thread processes a request to a static page, other threads can easily preempt it due to its lower priority. Additionally, a higher load increases the chance that a lower priority thread serves static page requests. This behaviour leads to the heavy tail of the response time distribution.

For requests to the online monitoring (Figure 4.28(b)), Linux outperforms Windows by a factor of 2 to 3. Linux' slowly decaying priorities ensure that requests to the online monitoring are only interrupted by requests which received a similar amount of processing time (assuming they started at similar priorities). Therefore, it preempts all reporting requests that received more than (approximately) 250 ms of processing time.

Windows grants a similar priority boosts to all tasks. The boost is independent of their previous processing time and lasts two timeslices (approximately 60 ms) at most (cf. Section 2.3.4). While short requests (smaller than 60 ms) benefit from this policy, longer requests, which cannot be completed within this period, may be delayed. Thus, requests to online monitoring (that last approx. 250 ms) compete with each other and the business intelligence reporting. For these reasons, the results shown in Figure 4.28(b) suggest that processor sharing can approximate the response time of the online monitoring under Windows.

The differences in the response times of both operating systems already suggest that scheduling policies such as FCFS or PS can predict response times only with limited accuracy. Especially FCFS shows large deviations between the predicted and the measured response times (see Table 4.23). In the case of static pages, it predicts a mean response time of more than two seconds, while the measured mean response time is about 5 ms (Windows) and 50 ms (Linux). The results demonstrate how FCFS prefers long requests. The mean response time of the business intelligence reporting is only 1/4 of the measured mean response times for both operating systems.

In the beginning of this section, performance analysts asked whether the system can fulfil the performance requirements with the existing systems. In the following, we discuss the results of the case study with respect to the questions.

Answers to the Performance Questions   Performance analysts predicted the response times of the HQ's application. They come to the following conclusions based on the results discussed in this section.

The current hardware environment can handle the application's workload only insufficiently. Especially during peak load, the response time increases by several orders of magnitude. Under Linux, such heavy load can lead to timeouts for requests to static pages for more than 10% of all requests. Windows poses a significant delay on the online monitoring (up to 6 seconds) which is not acceptable. Thus, further performance analysis is necessary to evaluate the performance of the applciation in multiprocessing environments. The results of this evaluation are presented in Section 5.2. In the next section, we discuss the limitations and assumptions of MOSS for single processor systems.

4.4. Discussion of Assumptions and Limitations

Focus on Linux and Windows Operating System Series   MOSS is focussed on the Linux
and Windows operating system series. It can predict the performance influence of Windows
XP and Windows Server 2003 as well as the Linux Kernel versions 2.5 to 2.6.22. With the
introduction of Windows Server 2008 and Windows Vista, Microsoft changed the implementation of their operating system schedulers [Rus07]. The changes require further evaluations
and adjustments of MOSS in order to accurately reflect the new scheduler's performance
influences. However, the prediction validation in Section 5.1.5 demonstrates that Vista's
multiprocessor load balancing is not affected with respect to its influence on software performance.

Additionally, the implementation of the Linux has been changed with Kernel version
2.6.23. Linux now uses a so-called **C**ompletely **F**air **S**cheduler [Tra] which is based on the
fair queueing [Nag87] scheduling policy. The scheduler approximates the shortest remaining
processing time (SRPT) policy. However, it uses similar heuristics as the O(1) scheduler
modelled by MOSS to identify interactive processes (called *sleeper fairness*). Extending
MOSS to the new CFS scheduler requires new evaluations. Following the documentation, it
may be sufficient to replace the run queue model by a model for fair scheduling to enable
good performance predictions for the CFS scheduler.

Simulation-based Solution Method   We used timed Coloured Petri Nets to model the
performance-relevant features of GPOS schedulers in MOSS. While CPNs provide a high
flexibility and expressiveness, they can only be solved by simulation for performance prediction [Wel02]. Simulation provides an efficient solution for complex systems. However, it carries the risk of inaccurate or of unrepresentative results. Kounev et al. [Kou06, KB06, KB03]
have used simulation-based as well as analytical methods to predict the performance of distributed component-based software systems. They come to the conclusion that simulation
is the only feasible option for solving large performance models. Due to their computational
complexity, analytical solution techniques require strong simplifications of the system under
study, which may lead to invalid results.

Independent and Identically Distributed Random Variables   From a mathematical perspective, MOSS assumes that resource demands of different tasks are independent and identically distributed (iid) random variables. Thus, subsequent resource demands of a task do
not depend on each other. Additionally, the resource demands of two concurrently running
tasks are assumed to be independent. These assumptions do not have to hold in reality. For
example, subsequent resource demands of a task may depend on the same input parameters,

e.g., a task first sorts an array and then prints it. In this case, both associated resource demands depend on the size of the array. This assumption is addressed in [Koz08a, Bec08].

The independence of concurrently executing tasks holds for specific cases only. Whenever two tasks run on separate processors (or cores), they may produce contention on low-level resources of the processor and execution environment. These contentions include caching effects and the memory bus (see Section 5.3 for discussion). Furthermore, tasks may access shared memory on a fine grained level. While MOSS supports coarse-grained synchronisation mechanisms based on semaphores, it cannot predict the performance influence of atomic actions, such as test-and-set operations. Therefore, the performance influences of low-level resource contention requires further investigation.

Limited Synchronisation Methods   The performance influences of process synchronisation and communication are tightly coupled to features of operating system schedulers. MOSS accurately predicts the effect of strong and weak semaphores on software performance. However, operating systems and middleware platforms provide a wide range of different synchronisation mechanisms (e.g., reader writer looks and different resource pools). While many synchronisation mechanisms are based on semaphores and, thus, can be modelled and predicted with MOSS, others tend to use entirely different operations. It is necessary to evaluate the performance influences of the most relevant synchronisation methods and to extend MOSS towards them for a general prediction method in multiprocessing environments.

No Real-Time Capabilities   MOSS explicitly does not support real-time schedulers. Furthermore, its predictions are only stochastic approximations of the performance metrics of the system under test. Thus, MOSS does not guarantee a correctly predicted upper and lower performance bound as required in real-time environments. Literature [BMdW⁺04, BKR95, EE00, FNNS06, HZS01, LM99, MPC04, YW98] reports on numerous approaches that allow performance predictions of real-time system with different scheduling policies.

Constant Processing Power   MOSS assumes that the processing power of the available cores and processors does not change over time. Most modern processors implement some power-saving functionality that allows the operating system to throttle the processing power when the system is lightly loaded. Furthermore, emerging virtualisation technologies share the available processing power among a set of concurrently running operating systems. In both cases, MOSS cannot predict the effect of fluctuating processing power on software performance. Instead, it assumes a constant processing power of all processors and cores of the system. Since scheduling becomes most important in situations where the processor's load is high, power-saving should not effect the relevant cases for performance evaluation. However, in lightly loaded situations MOSS is likely to overestimate the performance of the system under study.

4.5. Summary

In this chapter, we have evaluated the performance-relevant factors of time sharing and interactivity policies implemented in GPOS schedulers. The evaluation has pointed out major differences in the behaviour of the Windows and Linux schedulers.

- *Linux* employs a fair policy to distribute the processing time among all tasks. However, tasks can circumvent this property if they spend a small fraction of their processing time ($\approx$12%) waiting. In this case, they are classified as *interactive* and gain a significantly larger share of processing time as they are entiteled to. The task's dynamic priority increases (or decreases) aprubtly when the waiting time crosses a narrow border around 12%.

- *Windows* strictly prefers higher priority tasks over lower priority ones and, thus, employs an unfair policy. It only grants brief periods of processing time to low priority tasks in order to prevent starvation. Furthermore, the resource-dependent interactivity policy of Windows boosts a task's dynamic priority and resets its timeslice. Especially the reset of timeslices follows different strategies for different resources, e.g., to either 15 ms or 31 ms for semaphores and no reset for accesses to network devices.

Furthermore, we have presented a customisable performance model for single processor systems that is based on the evaluation results. In the case study, we have demonstrated that both operating systems can yield significantly different response times. MOSS accurately predicted the performance of both operating systems. In the following chapter, we further refine MOSS with respect to the influences of symmetric multiprocessor systems on software performance.

5. Multiprocessor Scheduling

In this chapter, we continue the experimental evaluation and the modelling of performance-relevant features of GPOS schedulers from Chapter 4. We extend the model for time sharing and interactivity towards symmetric multiprocessing environments like multi-core processors (Section 5.1). Furthermore, we continue the case study of Section 4.3 and extend it towards symmetric multiprocessing environments (Section 5.2). A discussion of the model's benefits and drawbacks concludes this chapter (Section 5.3).

5.1. Multiprocessor Load Balancing

In this section, we extend MOSS towards symmetric multiprocessing environments. Section 5.1.1 accounts for the experiments that are necessary to determine the performance influences of multiprocessor load balancing policies. The experiments are based on the specification of the Windows and Linux operating systems (cf. Section 2.3). We systematically evaluate the different features of both operating system with respect to load balancing. The experiment design is described in Section 5.1.2. In Section 5.1.3, we refine the goal by means of question, scenarios, and hypotheses. Furthermore, we present the experiment results which provide the necessary answers. The results prepare the extension of MOSS to multiprocessing environments in Section 5.1.4. In a final validation in Section 5.1.5, we demonstrate the prediction accuracy of MOSS for symmetric multiprocessor systems.

5.1.1. Experiments – Overview and Motivation

In this section, we evaluate two distinct load balancing policies implemented in the Windows Server 2003 / Vista and the Linux 2.6.0 - 2.6.22 operating systems. Windows Server 2003 and Vista use a receiver-initiated load balancing policy that is only triggered when a processor becomes idle (cf. Section 2.3.4). Therefore, it tolerates major imbalances in the system and is referred to as *lazy-balancing*. By contrast, Linux 2.6.22 actively balances the system's load trying to keep the load imbalances below a certain level. Its load balancing policy is called *active-balancing*.

The Goal

Goal: *Purpose*   Identify
         Issue   the relevant performance properties
         Object   of multiprocessor load balancing policies
         Viewpoint from the user's point of view.

The goal is focussed on the evaluation of different multiprocessor load balancing policies realised in today's GPOS schedulers. We are especially interested in the effect of load balancing on the performance perceived by users. The lazy- and active-balancing policies are inherently different concepts and lead to different response times and throughputs given the same workload.

Motivation of the Questions

Identify the relevant performance properties of multiprocessor load balancing policies		
	LB.Lazy.1	**LB.Lazy.2**	**LB.Lazy.3**
Questions	How does continuous load influence load balancing?	Do waiting times influence load distribution and software performance?	What happens when system load decreases?
Scenario	Heavy Load	Moderate Load	Decaying Load
Metric	RT, Load(CPU$_i$)	RT, Load(CPU$_i$), COV(E[RT(t)])	RT, Load(CPU$_i$)
Hypothesis	The scheduler does not change the initial load distribution and imbalances (even a strong ones) remain.	The System stayes balanced.	The scheduler moves one task from the busiest processor to the idle one.

Table 5.1.: GQM plan for the evaluation of lazy-balancing.

Lazy-Balancing   Lazy-balancing is a receiver-initiated policy, which is only triggered when a processor becomes idle. The system's load characteristics are thus of major importance for the performance influence of this policy. The heavier the system's load, the less balancing attempts occur and the more imbalances remain. Questions LB.Lazy.1 and LB.Lazy.2 (Table 5.1) address the performance influence of different load conditions for lazy-balancing. Furthermore, load balancing only reacts if the system's load changes, e.g., tasks arrive or leave the processor. Therefore, Question LB.W.3 addresses the influence of a decreasing system load on performance.

Active-Balancing   Active-balancing is a symmetrically initiated, active load balancing policy. The scheduler triggers balancing attempts as soon as differences in the system's load distribution exceed a predefined threshold (cf. Section 2.3.5). Thus, active-balancing leads to an equally distributed load. Question LB.Act.1 (Table 5.4) evaluates its achieved balance under different load conditions. Furthermore, the active-balancing policy adapts its balancing activities according to the system's state. For example, the interval length of load balancing attempts increases with an increasing system load. Question LB.Act.2 addresses the time necessary to balance heavily loaded systems. Finally, the Linux scheduler prefers interactive tasks over non-interactive ones (cf. Section 4.2). Question LB.Act.3 targets the influence of interactive load on software performance in combination with load balancing.

5.1.2. Experiment Design

In this section, we extend the experiment design of Section 4.1 and 4.2 for symmetric multiprocessing environments. We describe the generation of unevenly distributed load as well as the estimation of a processor's load based on task response times. The first is necessary to evaluate the effect of different load balancing policies under controlled conditions. The latter allows to determine a processor's load independent of the underlying operating system.

Generating Unevenly Distributed Load   To evaluate the influences of different load balancing policies, it is necessary to intentionally produce situations in which the load is unevenly distributed among the available processors. The imbalanced situation is used for the scenarios throughout the experiments. It assigns all tasks to a single processor while all other processors stay idle. The scheduler's load balancing policy then distributes the load among the available processors.

Name	Workload of Task t_i	CpuDemand.VALUE	Delay.VALUE
Heavy Load	Closed	250	0
Moderate Load	Closed	250	10
Decaying Load	Closed	250	0

Table 5.2.: Scenarios for the evaluation of different multiprocessor load balancing policies.

Main Scenarios   The evaluation is focussed on three scenarios called Heavy Load, Moderate Load, and Decaying Load (Table 5.2). In all three scenarios, the tasks are executed in a closed workload with a processing demand of 250 ms. For scenario Heavy Load, the delays are set to 0 ms in order to evaluate the influence of load balancing policies for compute-bound tasks (cf. Section 2.3). The delay of 10 ms of scenario Moderate Load allows the load balancing policy to redistribute the load among the available processors. Finally, scenario Decaying Load limits the number of repetitions for each task. Instead of endless processing, tasks finish execution after a predefined number of iterations, which is equal for all tasks.

Since the system is imbalanced, the tasks that can solely execute on a processor without interruption finish first. When their processor becomes available, the scheduler allocates a task from the busiest CPU to the now idle processor.

Estimating a Processor's Load   It is necessary to measure or estimate the load of the processors to answer some of the questions in Table 5.1 and 5.4. In this context, the term "load" refers to the number of tasks running on a specific processor. Since the measurements or estimations should not influence the underlying operating system, we propose an heuristic approximation in the following.

Furthermore, the estimation allows to determine the processor's load for operating systems, which do not support the measurement of a single processor's queue length (such as Windows Server 2003). The load of a processor is estimated based on the response times of the currently running tasks. The approximation computes the number of simultaneously running tasks by dividing the task response times by the uncontented processing time, which is 250 ms for the scenarios defined above. For example, the estimation computes a load of two tasks for a response time of 500 ms. This approximation is possible, since all tasks are executed with the same priority and, thus, share the processor equally. However, the execution of multiple tasks can overlap and a task's delay can further shift the overlap. Therefore, the approximation clusters response times around multiples of the processing time. For example, if the resource demand of a task is 250 ms, then two concurrent tasks without waiting time yield a response time of 500 ms. We use tolerance bounds of ± 125 ms and, thus, consider all response times from 375 ms to 625 ms as concurrent execution of two tasks. This approximation is only a rough estimate of the actual load distribution, but it already shows the large imbalance of the system's load.

5.1.3. Answering the Questions – Scenarios, Metrics, Hypotheses, and Results

In this section, we present the necessary experiments to evaluate and answer the questions of the GQM plan in Table 5.1 for GPOS schedulers in symmetric multiprocessing environments.

Question LB.Lazy.1: How does continuous load influence load balancing?

Lazy-balancing is only initiated when a processor becomes idle. Question LB.Lazy.1 addresses its load balancing capabilities under continuous heavy load, which should avoid all load balancing attempts and should maintain initial imbalances.

Scenario Scenario `Heavy Load` provides the initial load imbalances to evaluate the influence of lazy-balancing in combination with continuous load. The response time distribution (Hist(RT)) of each task as well as the number of tasks running on a processor (Load) provide the necessary information to answer Question LB.Lazy.1.

Hypotheses Since lazy balancing can only be initiated by a receiver (i.e., idle processor), Hypothesis LB.Lazy.1.a expects an initial balancing attempt where each idle processor receives one task from the busiest processor. The load distribution then does not change any further and imbalances remain. Formally, let m be the number of processors, n number of tasks, and CPU_i with $i \in \{1 \ldots m\}$ the processors where CPU_1 is the initially loaded processor, then Hypothesis LB.Lazy.1.a expects:

$$\text{Load}(CPU_j) = \begin{cases} n - m + 1 & \text{, for } j = 1 \\ 1 & \text{, for all } j > 1 \end{cases} \qquad \text{(LB.Lazy.1.a)}$$

Furthermore, the mean response time of a task t_j with $j \in \{1 \ldots n\}$ is expected to be:

$$\text{E}[\text{RT}(t_j)] = \begin{cases} (n - m + 1) * 250\,\text{ms} & \text{, if } t_j \text{ is running on } CPU_1 \\ 250\,\text{ms} & \text{, if } t_j \text{ is running on } CPU_i \text{ with } i \in \{2 \ldots m\} \end{cases}$$

$$\text{(LB.Lazy.1.b)}$$

The first case represents the shared execution time of all $(n - m + 1)$ tasks running on CPU_1. The second case resembles the uninterrupted execution time on an uncontended CPU_i. The following presents the measurements of scenario `Heavy Load` with seven tasks on a dual-core system.

Results Figures 5.1(a) and (b) show the response times measured for tasks t_1, t_2, and t_3 of scenario `Heavy Load` with two processors ($m = 2$) and seven tasks ($n = 7$). For reasons of clarity, the figures are limited to the response times of the first three tasks. The cumulative distribution function (Figure 5.1(a)) as well as the histogram (Figure 5.1(b)) show two peaks of the response times: One at 250 ms and one at 1500 ms. The results correspond to Hypothesis LB.Lazy.1.b, which expects a task response time of either 250 ms or 1500 ms ($= (7 - 2 + 1) * 250$ ms) for $n = 7$ tasks and $m = 2$ processors. Estimating the load distribution from these values complies to the expectation of Hypothesis LB.Lazy.1.a.

For each task, Hypothesis LB.Lazy.b expects either a response time of 250 ms or 1500 ms. However, the measurements show mixed response times of 250 ms and 1500 ms for single tasks. These values suggest that the task is executed on different processors during the experiment.

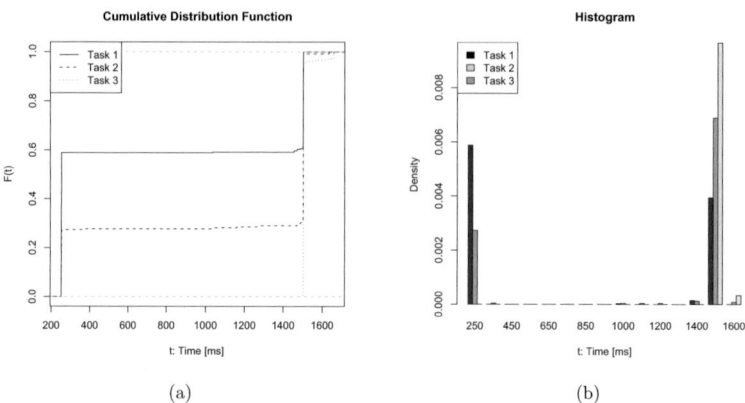

Figure 5.1.: Response time distribution for scenario Heavy Load.

Figure 5.2 supports this observation. It shows the response time measurements of one task during the experiment. The task runs on CPU_1 for the first 120 iterations. It shares the processor with five other tasks, which yields a response time of 1500 ms. It then executes on CPU_2 for more than 200 iterations and does not have to share the processor with other tasks. However, the overall load distribution is not affected, since all resource demands are either processed within 250 ms or 1500 ms. During the whole execution of scenario Heavy Load, CPU_1 has been processing six tasks while CPU_2 has been executing one task. The results confirm Hypothesis LB.Lazy.1.a.

While Hypothesis LB.Lazy.1.b correctly reflects the general behaviour of lazy-balancing, it does not capture the observed effect of "random task switches" shown in Figure 5.2. The effect leads to a rejection of the hypothesis. However, the measurements confirm the fact that lazy-balancing does not distribute the system's load equally if all processors are busy.

Discussion   The "random task switches" result from the realisation of user-level threads (either in the Java virtual machine or the operating system). Scenario Heavy Load uses Java threads to implement the concurrently running tasks, which need to be mapped to light-weight processes (or kernel-level threads) to execute. Windows uses a one-to-one mapping of user-level threads and light-weight processes [SGG05], but their association can change during runtime. These changes are not visible to the scheduler's load balancer, which deals only with light-weight processes, but affect the response times measured for single tasks. Section 5.1.5 discusses this effect in more detail.

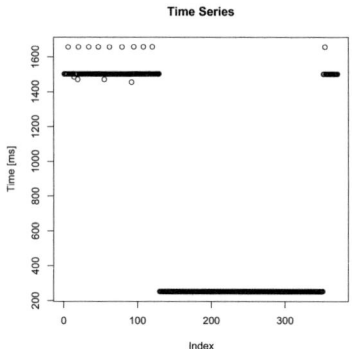

Figure 5.2.: Evolution of the measured response times during the experiments (`Heavy Load`).

Question LB.Lazy.2: Do waiting times influence load distribution and software performance?

Question LB.Lazy.1 is intentionally focussed on compute-bound tasks that limit the capabilities of the lazy-balancing policy. This question targets its influence on load distribution and performance for less loaded systems. Lazy-balancing requires a processor to become idle in order to initiate load balancing. If tasks successively demand short periods of processing and waiting time, then the load of the processor changes continuously and, thus, should trigger load balancing. In the following, we describe the scenarios, hypotheses, and results for Question LB.Lazy.2.

Scenarios   In scenario `Moderate Load`, tasks execute a resource demand of 250 ms followed by a waiting period of 10 ms. This short interruption should allow the scheduler to initiate load balancing.

Hypotheses   Hypothesis LB.Lazy.2.a expects the system to reach a balanced state and, hence, distribute its load evenly among the available processors. As a consequence, the response times of all tasks are expected to be similar, i.e., only differ within a certain range. Let m be the number of processor, n the number of tasks, and d the delay of task t_i, then Hypothesis LB.Lazy.2.a expects the following mean response time for all tasks:

$$\mathrm{E}[\mathrm{RT}(t_j)] = n/m * 250\,\mathrm{ms} - d \text{ for all } t_i \text{ with } i \in \{1 \dots n\}. \qquad \text{(LB.Lazy.2.a)}$$

This formula yields a response time of 865 ms for $n = 7$ tasks, $m = 2$ processors, and a delay of 10 ms. To compare the response times of all tasks, the coefficient of variation (COV) of the tasks *mean* response times is expected to be below 5%:

$$|\,\mathrm{COV}(\mathrm{E}[t_i])| < 5\% \text{ for all } t_i \text{ with } i \in \{1\dots n\} \qquad \text{(LB.Lazy.2.b)}$$

This equation expresses that all tasks receive the same amount of processing time on average. Furthermore, Hypothesis LB.Lazy.2.c expects the load of the processors to differ within predefined bounds:

$$|\,\mathrm{Load}(\mathrm{CPU}_j) - \mathrm{Load}(\mathrm{CPU}_k)| < n/(2*m) \text{ for } \mathrm{CPU}_j \text{ and } \mathrm{CPU}_k \text{ with } j \neq k \quad \text{(LB.Lazy.2.c)}$$

For example, for a system with two processors ($m = 2$) and seven tasks ($m = 7$), the load of the processors is expected to differ no more than 1.75 tasks in average. The bounds are given by the deviation from the ideal distribution, e.g., $n/m = 3.5$ for the previous example. Hypotheses LB.Lazy.2.c expects the load distribution to deviate less then 50% from the ideal distribution.

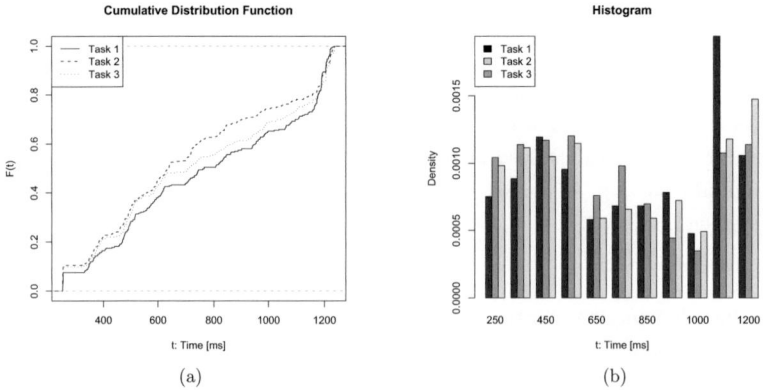

Figure 5.3.: Response time distribution for scenario `Moderate Load`.

Results   Figures 5.3(a) and (b) show the response time distributions for scenario `Moderate Load` with seven concurrently running tasks ($n = 7$) on a system with two processors ($m = 2$). For clarity, the figures only show the first three tasks. The task response times are distributed between 250 ms and 1200 ms. This distribution is a considerable difference to the results of scenario `Heavy Load`, where the response times bundled at two values.

Task	1	2	3	4	5	6	7
Mean Response Time [ms]	786,0	724,4	760,1	768,6	785,1	750,5	712,0

Table 5.3.: Mean response times of tasks t_1 to t_7 for scenario Moderate Load.

Table 5.3 lists the mean response time of all tasks of scenario Moderate Load. The co-efficient of variation of the mean response times listed there is 3.7% and, thus, below the threshold of 5% specified in Hypothesis LB.Lazy.2.c. However, the average response time of all tasks is with 755.5 ms about 110 ms below the expected value of 865 ms rejecting Hypothesis LB.Lazy.2.a. The task waiting time is responsible for this difference in measurement and expectation. Even though the specification of the scenario demands a delay of 10 ms, the actual delay during the execution is approximately 135 ms. Due to the high load of seven simultaneously running tasks, the operating system is not able to adhere to the specified waiting times. Computing the expected mean response time with a value value of 135 ms yields an expected response time of 740 ms, which is much closer to the actually measured value.

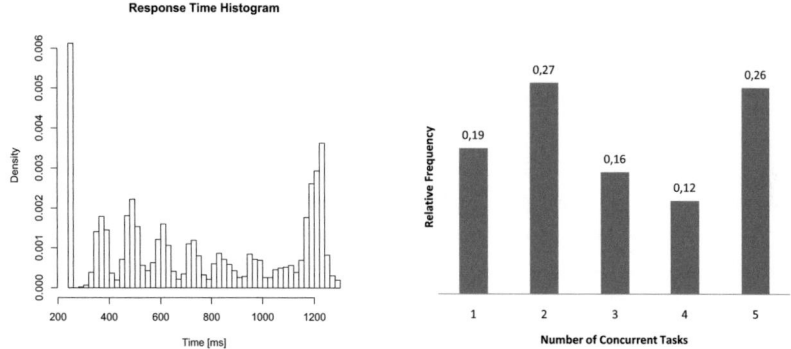

(a) Combined response time histogram of tasks t_1 to t_7.

(b) Relative frequency of concurrently executing tasks.

Figure 5.4.: Response time and load distribution for scenario Moderate Load.

Figure 5.4(a) depicts the histogram of joined response times for tasks t_1 to t_7. Despite the stronger distribution of the response times compared to scenario Heavy Load, the histogram contains multiple peaks in the response time distribution. Especially for 250 ms, 500 ms, and 1250 ms, the histogram shows high densities.

Figure 5.4(b) approximates the load distribution for scenario Moderate Load based on the response times of tasks t_1 to t_7 (cf. Section 5.1.2). It depicts the resulting relative frequencies for the number of simultaneously running tasks. As expected from the response time distribution, the undisturbed execution of a task has a relative frequency of 20%. However, the concurrent execution of six tasks (the expected counterpart when seven tasks are running in parallel) does not occur. The effect is caused by long waiting times of each task, which reduces the overall load of the system. In Figure 5.4(b), two (27%) and five (26%) tasks are most likely to be executed concurrently. However, the optimal load distribution of three and four tasks has the least relative frequency of 16% and 12%. Lazy-balancing distributes the load more evenly in scenario `Moderate Load` than in scenario `Heavy Load`, but still allows strong imbalances to occur. Thus, Hypothesis LB.Lazy.2.c must be rejected.

Question LB.Lazy.3: What happens when system load decreases?

Question LB.Lazy.3 targets the behaviour of lazy-balancing under decreasing load. If tasks finish successively, the policy needs to move tasks from the busiest to the new idle processor.

Scenarios   Scenario `Decaying Load` resembles such a behaviour (cf. Section 5.1.2). The concrete scenario subsumes six tasks running in parallel on a two processor system. Each task issues 400 resource demands of 250 ms and a waiting time of 0 ms in a loop and then terminates. The initial load distribution of the scenario consists of five tasks running on the first processor and one on the second processor.

Hypotheses   Hypothesis LB.Lazy.3.a expects the number of tasks running on the busiest processor to decrease continuously until each processor executes a single task.

Let m be the number of processors, CPU_i with $i \in \{1 \ldots m\}$ be a single processor, where CPU_1 denotes the busiest processor and n be the current number of running tasks with $n > m + 1$. Furthermore, let $\text{Load}_t(CPU_i)$ denote the loads of processor CPU_i at time t, then:

$$\forall \ \text{Load}_t(CPU_1) = n - m + 1 \text{ and } \text{Load}_t(CPU_i) = 1 \text{ with } i > 1, \exists \ \Delta \ \in \mathbb{R}_{>0} :$$
$$\text{Load}_{t+\Delta}(CPU_1) = (n - m) \text{ and } \text{Load}_{t+\Delta}(CPU_i) = 1 \quad\quad \text{(LB.Lazy.3.a)}$$

In other words, whenever a task finishes, the number of tasks on the busiest processor is reduced. If the task is running on a lightly loaded processor ($\text{Load}(CPU) = 1$), then the processor becomes idle and receives a task from the busiest processor. Otherwise, the task has already been running on the busiest processor ($\text{Load}(CPU) = n - m + 1$). In both cases, the busiest processor looses one of its tasks. Analogously to Question LB.Lazy.2, the number of concurrently running tasks is determined on the basis of the task response times (cf. Section 5.1.2).

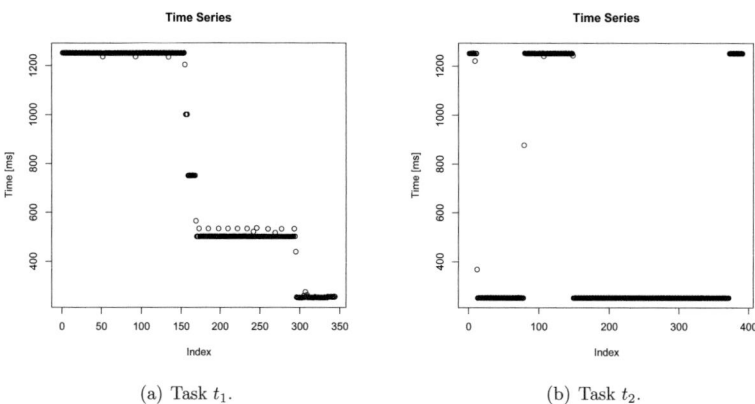

(a) Task t_1.   (b) Task t_2.

Figure 5.5.: Response time measurements for the scenario `Decaying Load`.

Results Figure 5.5 depicts the evolution of response times for two tasks as a series of measurements. Figure 5.5(a) shows a series of response times for a task running on the busiest processor. For the first 160 iterations, the task has a response time of 1250 ms and, thus, shares its processor with four other tasks. Then, during a period of 10 iterations, the task's response time decreases from 1250 ms to 500 ms in intervals of 250 ms. Each decrease corresponds to the completion of another task. The sudden termination of three tasks in a brief period suggests that not only a single task runs on the second processor as expected by Hypothesis LB.Lazy.2.a, but the second processor executed (at least) three tasks. From the measurements, three tasks can be identified that exhibit "random task switches" already observed in scenario `Heavy Load` (Question LB.Lazy.1). Their total execution time matches the time of the first 160 iteration in Figure 5.5(a).

Figure 5.5(b) depicts the response time of a task executing for a long period on the second, uncontended processor. However, the task switches multiple times between short (250 ms) and long (1250 ms) response times. In total, it executes 290 requests in 250 ms and 101 requests in 1250 ms. Even though the number of uncontended iterations exceeds the number of contended ones, the task spends only 36% of its processing time on the uncontended processor compared to 64% on the contended one. Likewise, two other tasks of scenario `Decaying Load` show a behaviour similar to the task depicted in Figure 5.5(b). Furthermore, their total execution time sums up to approximately 200 seconds which corresponds to the execution time of the first 160 iteration of the task shown in Figure 5.5(a). These measurements suggest, that three tasks randomly share the uncontended processor. After

200 seconds, the three tasks finish in a relatively short period, which leads to the decreasing response time shown in Figure 5.5(a).

Despite the "random task switches" between the contended and uncontended processor, the tasks in the scenario behave as expected. Only one task at a time is running on the uncontended processor, whereas all other tasks share the other processor. Furthermore, the lazy-balancing polices moves only one task at a time if a processor becomes idle.

Identify the relevant performance properties of multiprocessor load balancing policies			
	LB.Act.1	**LB.Act.2**	**LB.Act.3**
Questions	How well does the scheduler balance the system?	How long does the scheduler need to balance the system's load?	Does interactive load influence load balancing?
Scenario	Heavy Load	Heavy Load	Moderate Load
Metric	RT, Load(CPU$_i$)	RT, E[transient], Pr(Imbalance)	RT, Load(CPU$_i$), COV(E[RT(t)])
Hypothesis	The System stayes balanced	The system balances during the first seconds.	Interactive Load allows better balancing than continuous load.

Table 5.4.: GQM plan for load balancing under Linux 2.6.22.

Question LB.Act.1: How well does the scheduler balance the system?

Question LB.Act.1 addresses the capabilities of the active-balancing policy for compute-bound tasks. It expects the policy to evenly distribute the load among the available processors.

Scenario   Scenario Heavy Load answers Question LB.Act.1. The resulting load distribution as well as the task response times give hints on the capabilities of the active-balancing policy.

Hypotheses   Hypothesis LB.Act.1.a and LB.Act.1.b expect the active-balancing policy to evenly distribute the load among the available processors. Thus, the load of all processors should at most differ by one task. For a system with n tasks and m processors, the expected load of a processor CPU$_i$ with $i \in \{0 \ldots m\}$ is:

$$\text{Load(CPU}_i) = \begin{cases} \lfloor n/m \rfloor & \text{, for } m - (n \bmod m) \text{ processors} \\ \lceil n/m \rceil & \text{, for } (n \bmod m) \text{ processors} \end{cases} \quad \text{(LB.Act.1.a)}$$

Furthermore, Hypothesis LB.Act.1.b expects the response time of a task t_j with $j \in \{1 \ldots n\}$ to be a multiple of the load of the processor CPU$_i$ executing t_j. The actual task response time depends on the number of interruptions of task t_j. In the experiment, all tasks have the same priority and timeslice (prio(t_k) = 0 and $TS(t_k) = 100$ ms $\forall\ k \in \{1 \ldots n\}$, cf. Table 2.2 page 34).

For task t_j, which demands a processing time of $d_j = 250$ ms, the scheduler interrupts its processing time either two or three times for a timeslice of 100 ms. Due to the fair run queues of the Linux scheduler, all other tasks have to finish their timeslice, before t_j resumes its execution. This behaviour yields the following expected response times for all tasks:

$$\text{RT}(t_j) = \begin{cases} \lfloor d_j / \text{TS}(t_j) \rfloor * \text{Load(CPU}_i) * \text{TS}(t_j) + (d_j \bmod \text{TS}(t_j)) \\ (\lceil d_j / \text{TS}(t_j) \rceil * \text{Load(CPU}_i) - 1) * \text{TS}(t_j) + (d_j \bmod \text{TS}(t_j)) \end{cases} \qquad \text{(LB.Act.1.b)}$$

The actual response time depends on the number of interruptions of the task's execution expressed by $\lfloor d_j / \text{TS}(t_j) \rfloor$ and $\lceil d_j / \text{TS}(t_j) \rceil$. The first case represents the response time for the minimum number of interruptions, while the second case yields the maximum number of interruptions.

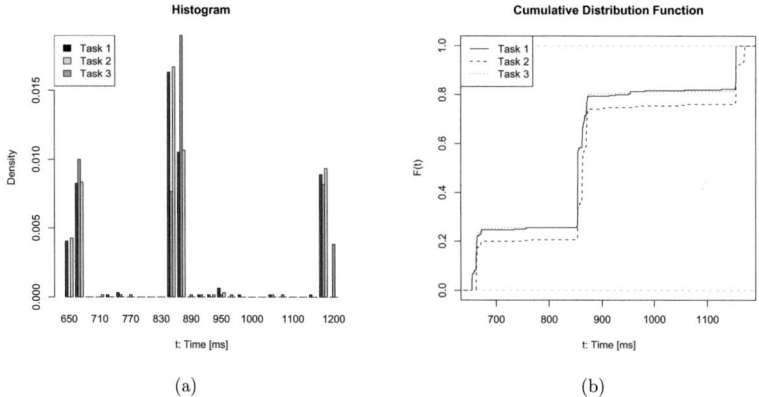

Figure 5.6.: Response time distribution for scenario Heavy Load.

Results Figures 5.6(a) and (b) present the results for scenario Heavy Load and active-balancing. The scenario was executed on a two processor system with seven concurrent tasks. For clarity, the figures depict the response time of the first three tasks. The response times of the remaining four tasks are similar to the depicted ones. Hypothesis LB.Act.1.b expects a response time of either 650 ms or 850 ms for the processor loaded with three tasks and either 850 ms or 1150 ms for the processor loaded with four tasks. The following formula

computes the task response time for three concurrent tasks to illustrate the interpretation
of Hypothesis LB.Act.1.b:

$$\mathrm{RT}(t_1) = \begin{cases} \lfloor 250\,\mathrm{ms}\,/100\,\mathrm{ms} \rfloor * 3 * 100\,\mathrm{ms} +50\,\mathrm{ms} & = 650\,\mathrm{ms} \ \ (\text{lowest RT}) \\ (\lceil 250\,\mathrm{ms}\,/100\,\mathrm{ms} \rceil * 3 - 1) * 100\,\mathrm{ms} +50\,\mathrm{ms} & = 850\,\mathrm{ms} \ \ (\text{highest RT}) \end{cases}$$

The results presented in Figures 5.6(a) and (b) confirm the expectation of Hypothesis
LB.Act.1.b. In the experiment, the load balancer assigns three tasks to the first and four to
the second processor. Furthermore, the task response times lie around 650 ms, 850 ms, and
1150 ms as anticipated. Thus, Hypotheses LB.Act.1.a and LB.Act.1.b cannot be rejected.

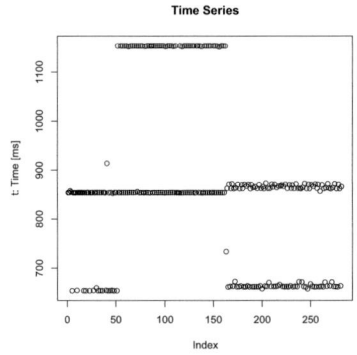

Figure 5.7.: Measurements of the task response time for load balancing under Linux.

However, the series of measured response times (Figure 5.7) suggests that the load distribution changes during the measurements. For the first 50 iterations, the task runs on a
processor with two other tasks yielding a response time of 650 ms and 850 ms. Then the
number of concurrently executing tasks increases to four for the next 110 iterations leading
to a response time of 850 ms and 1150 ms. For the last 120 iterations, the load drops back
to three tasks, but the response time shows more disturbances.

To answer Question LB.Act.1, active-balancing equally distributes the running tasks
among the available processors. The next question addresses the time a system needs to
reach a balanced state.

Question LB.Act.2: How long does the scheduler need to balance the system's load?

The results of Question LB.Act.1 suggest that active-balancing equally distributes the load over the available processors. However, the system's load in scenario Heavy Load is relatively high. Balancing events occur only during task creation and active load balancing intervals. Thus, Question LB.Act.2 addresses the time necessary for active-balancing in heavily loaded environments. Its hypotheses expect balancing to occur during the first seconds of scenario execution. During this initial transient phase, imbalances occur irregularly until the scenario reaches a steady state.

Scenarios   Like for Question LB.Act.1, we consider scenario Heavy Load with m processors and n tasks in the following. The duration of the initial transient phase provides sufficient information to answer Question LB.Act.2.

Hypotheses   Hypothesis LB.Act.2 expects the initial transient phase to last longer with an increasing number of tasks. A system reaches its steady state when the systems load disperses as specified in Hypothesis LB.Act.1.a and the response time of all tasks falls into the categories defined in Hypothesis LB.Act.1.b for the remaining execution time. The first time the requirements above are fulfilled, then, for the remainder of the experiment, the requirements above mark the end of the transient phase and the beginning of the steady state behaviour.

Hypothesis LB.Act.2.a expects the transient time of scenario heavy load to increase with the number of tasks in the system. Let $E[\text{trans}_n]$ be the expected transient time for n concurrent tasks, then

$$E[\text{trans}_n] \leq E[\text{trans}_k] \text{ with } n < k \text{ and } n, k \in \mathbb{N} \qquad \text{(LB.Act.2.a)}$$

Furthermore, Hypothesis LB.Act.2.b states that imbalances occur irregularly during the transient phase and the number of imbalances increases with the number of tasks in the system. To distinguish balanced from imbalanced requests, the expected response times of Hypothesis LB.Act.1.b define the upper and lower bound for the range of balanced requests. For a task t_j with a processing demand d_j, the lower bound is the minimum response time on the least loaded processor. Similarly, its upper bound is the maximum response time on the most loaded processor:

$$\text{lower}(t_j) = \lfloor d_j / \text{TS}(t_j) \rfloor * \lfloor n/m \rfloor * \text{TS}(t_j) + (d_j \bmod \text{TS}(t_j))$$
$$\text{upper}(t_j) = (\lceil d_j / \text{TS}(t_j) \rceil * \lceil n/m \rceil - 1) * \text{TS}(t_j) + (d_j \bmod \text{TS}(t_j))$$

For example, a system with $m = 2$ processors, $n = 7$ tasks, and a demand of 250 ms has a lower bound of $2 * 3 * 100\,\text{ms} + 50\,\text{ms} = 650\,\text{ms}$ and an upper bound of $(3 * 4 - 1) * 100\,\text{ms} + 50\,\text{ms} = 1150\,\text{ms}$. All response times within this range are considered as balanced, while all others are considered as imbalanced. Due to disturbances of single response time measurements, the tolerance bounds may be extended by half a timeslice, e.g., to 600 ms and 1200 ms.

Formally, let $\text{Pr}_n(\text{Imbalance})$ be the probability that the response time of a task t_j with $j \in \{1 \ldots n\}$ is not within the balanced range for a system with n tasks and m processors, i.e., $\text{Pr}_n(\text{Imbalance}) = \text{Pr}((\text{RT}(t_j) > \text{upper}(t_j)) \lor (\text{RT}(t_j) < \text{lower}(t_j)))$, then

$$\text{Pr}_n(\text{Imbalance}) \leq \text{Pr}_k(\text{Imbalance}) \text{ with } n < k \text{ and } n, k \in \mathbb{N} \qquad \text{(LB.Act.2.b)}$$

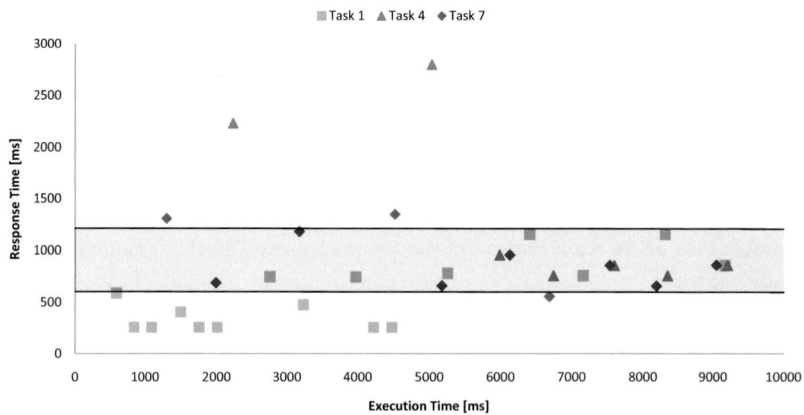

Figure 5.8.: Response time series for three tasks on a dual-core processor.

Results Figure 5.8 shows the initial transient phase during the experiment's execution. It depicts the response times of three out of seven tasks. Its x-axis represents the execution time of the experiment and its y-axis a task's measured response times. Hypotheses LB.Act.2.a and LB.Act.2.b consider the measured response times that fall into the range from 650 ms to 1150 ms as balanced. The light grey area in Figure 5.8 emphasises the balanced region. During the first 5 seconds of the experiment, several of the measured response times lie below or above this region. After this initial phase, the response time measurements scatter less and start forming a regular pattern within the balanced range.

Tasks	Transient Time [sec]	Imbalanced Requests [%]
1	0	0
2	0	0
3	1,6	5
4	2,5	7,5
5	3,3	22,5
6	5,1	32,5
7	6,7	40

Table 5.5.: Changes of load balancing with an increasing number of tasks.

Table 5.5 lists the average transient times for $n = 1$ to 7 tasks as well as the relative amount of imbalanced requests during that period. Like Hypotheses LB.Act.2.a and LB.Act.2.b expect, the initial transient phase as well as the probability of imbalanced requests increases with the number of tasks in the system. Thus, both hypotheses cannot be rejected.

Question LB.Act.3: Does interactive load influence load balancing?

Questions LB.Act.1 and LB.Act.2 are focussed on the performance influences of active-balancing for compute-bound tasks. Question LB.Act.3 targets its balancing capabilities for interactive tasks, since interactivity strongly influences the Linux scheduler's behaviour (cf. Section 4.2).

Scenarios   In the following hypotheses and experiments, we employ scenario `Moderate Load` to answer Question LB.Act.3. Its results give an impression on the mutual influences of interactivity and multiprocessor load balancing. We use a waiting time of 50 ms (`Delay.VALUE = 50`) instead of 10 ms in order to force the Linux scheduler to classify all tasks as interactive.

Hypotheses   In general, Hypothesis LB.Act.3.a expects a stronger variation of response times and processor loads compared to scenario `Heavy Load`. Thus, the peaks in response time distributions are expected to disappear. The load of a processor is expected to vary between three and four concurrent tasks in most cases. Even though the task response times are less regular, the coefficient of variation (COV) for the response times of all tasks is expected to be less than 5%. In other words, the system is expected to be balanced:

$$| \operatorname{COV}(\operatorname{E}[t_i])| < 5\% \text{ for all } t_i \text{ with } i \in \{1 \ldots n\} \qquad \text{(LB.Act.3.a)}$$

Furthermore, the load is expected to be equally balanced. The following hypotheses formulate the expectations on mean response times and the load distribution for scenario Moderate Load.

For a system with n tasks and m processors, each processor CPU_i with $i \in \{1 \ldots m\}$ has the following load in 90% of all cases:

$$\text{Load}(CPU_i) = \begin{cases} \lfloor n/m \rfloor & \text{, for } m - (n \bmod m) \text{ processors} \\ \lceil n/m \rceil & \text{, for } (n \bmod m) \text{ processors} \end{cases} \qquad \text{(LB.Act.3.b)}$$

For seven tasks ($n = 7$) and two processors ($m = 2$), this yields an expected load of 3 to 4 tasks per processor during 90% of the measurement period. For a processing time of $d_i = 250\,\text{ms}$, and a delay (waiting time) of $w_i = 50\,\text{ms}$ for all tasks t_i with $i \in \{1 \ldots n\}$, the expected mean response time is given by:

$$E[\text{RT}(t_i)] = d_i * n/m - w_i. \qquad \text{(LB.Act.3.c)}$$

For the system above, the equation yields an expected mean response time of 825 ms for all tasks. To reject Hypothesis LB.Act.3.c, the measured mean response time of all tasks must deviate more than 5% from the expected value. Since active-balancing should lead to an equal distribution, Hypothesis LB.Act.3.d expects 90% of all tasks to execute their resource demand within the lower (650 ms for the system above) and the upper (1150 ms for the system above) response time bounds:

$$\Pr(\text{RT}(t_i) < \text{upper}(t_i) \wedge \text{RT}(t_i) > \text{lower}(t_i)) > 0.9 \qquad \text{(LB.Act.3.d)}$$

Results   Figures 5.9(a) and (b) show the response time distributions of the first three tasks for scenario Moderate Load with seven concurrently running tasks ($n = 7$) on a system with two processors ($m = 2$). In this scenario, the response times are distributed between 350 ms and slightly more than 1100 ms.

Task	1	2	3	4	5	6	7	COV
Windows	786,0	724,4	760,1	768,6	785,1	750,5	712,0	3,8
Linux	812,6	826,8	805,2	834,8	814,0	792,9	841,8	2,1

Table 5.6.: Mean response times of tasks t_1 to t_7 for scenario Moderate Load for Windows and Linux.

Table 5.3 lists the mean response time of all tasks of scenario Moderate Load for Windows (lazy-balancing) as well as for Linux (active-balancing). For active-balancing, the

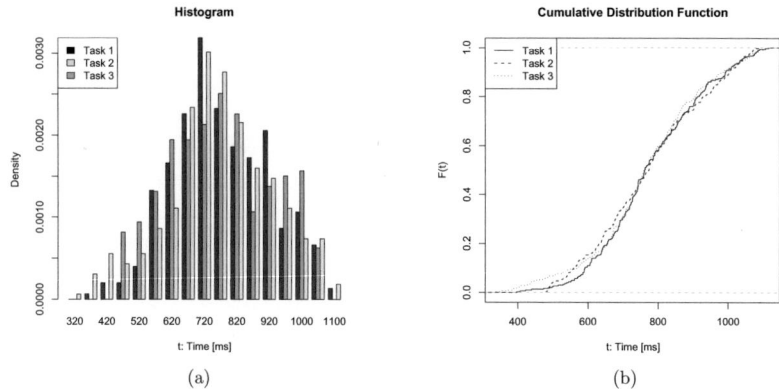

Figure 5.9.: Response time distribution for scenario `Moderate Load`.

coefficient of variation of the mean response times is 2.1% meeting the exception of hypothesis LB.Act.3.a of 5%. The average response time of all tasks is 816.9 ms and deviates less than 1% from the expected response time of 825 ms. The difference is below the specified threshold of 5%. Thus, Hypothesis LB.Act.3.c cannot be rejected.

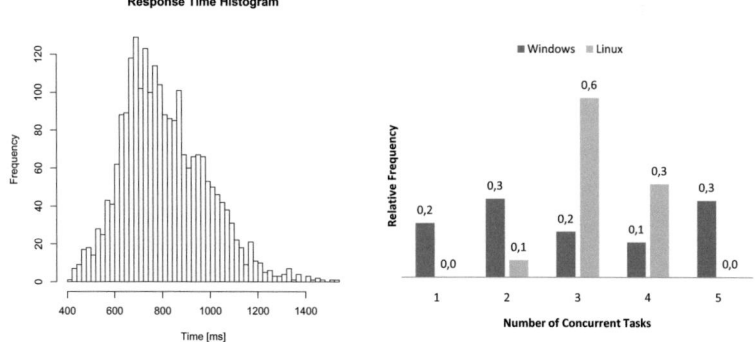

(a) Combined response time histogram of tasks t_1 to t_7.

(b) Relative frequency of concurrently executing tasks.

Figure 5.10.: Load distribution for scenario `Moderate Load`.

Figure 5.10(a) shows a histogram of accumulated response times for tasks t_1 to t_7 under Linux 2.6.22. Hypothesis LB.Act.3.d expects 90% of all values to fall in the range of 650 ms to 1150 ms. For the experiment, 1462 response time measurements of a total of 1614

measurements lie in this range. Thus, 90.6% of all response times lie in the expected range
and Hypothesis LB.Act.3.d. cannot be rejected.

Estimating the load distribution of the processors based on the task response times (cf.
Section 5.1.2) yields the number of simultaneously running tasks depicted in Figure 5.10(b).
The active-balancing policy of Linux concurrently executes three and four tasks in most
cases (90%). Only in 10% of all cases do two tasks share one processor. The figure depicts
the results for the lazy-balancing policy of Windows. The comparison between both policies
shows, that the Linux scheduler keeps a good balance of all tasks most of the time. By
contrast, Windows minimises its balancing effort and, thus, tolerates larger imbalances in
the system, but minimises its overhead for moving tasks.

5.1.4. Extending MOSS to Symmetric Multiprocessor Systems

In this section, we extend the CPN model of MOSS introduced in Sections 4.1.3 and 4.2.4 by
different load balancing policies for symmetric multiprocessing environments. The prediction
model reflects the variation points presented in Section 3.2.2.

Static Load Balancing

Static load balancing policies assign newly created tasks to a processor. Figure 5.11 depicts
the static load balancing policies available in the context of MOSS: *cyclic splitting*, *random*,
and *same as parent*. The static load balancing policy is part of the subnet `InitialiseTask`
(cf. Figure 3.9 page 67) and, hence, is responsible for assigning an initial processor to
the newly created task. Place `New` holds newly created tasks, which already received a
unique identifier (`id`), static and dynamic priority (`prio`), and timeslice (`timeslice`). The
subnets for the static load balancing policy assign an initial processor to the new tasks and
hand them over to the scheduler. Therefore, transitions `CyclicSplitting`, `Random`, and
`SameAsParent` take the new task's `SCHED_TASK` token with its `UNDEFINED` processor from
place `New`, determine the initial processor of the task, and enqueue it in the list of incoming
tasks of the scheduler on place `Incoming`.

Transition `CyclicSplitting` (Figure 5.11) uses the CPU token on place `NextCPU` to determine the new task's processor. Place `NextCPU` contains a single token of colour `CPU`, which
specifies the identifier of the next available processor. When transition `CyclicSplitting`
fires, it removes one of a newly created task from place `New`, takes the next processor's identifier from place `NextCPU` and the list of the scheduler's incoming tasks from place `Incoming`.
It appends a new token to the scheduler's list of incoming tasks (`taskList`). The token
contains the identifier, priority, and timeslice that have already been defined. Its initial processor is set to the value of `cpu`. Furthermore, transition `CyclicSplitting` determines the

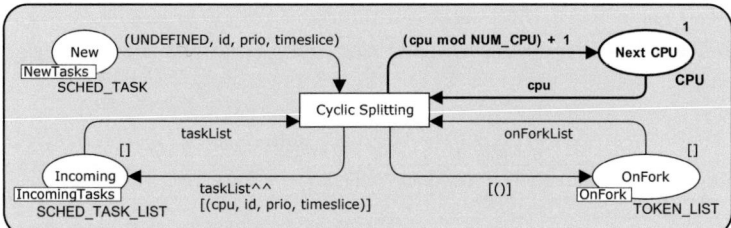

(b) Subnet for the "Cyclic Splitting" policy.

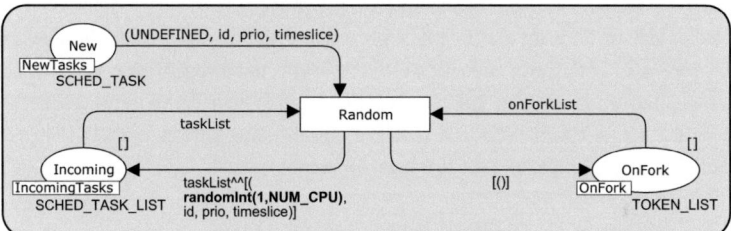

(c) Subnet for the "Random" policy.

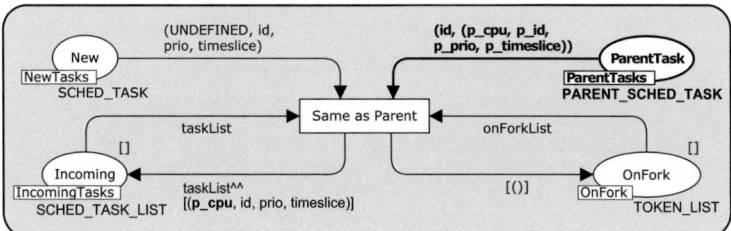

(d) Subnet for "Same as Parent" policy.

Figure 5.11.: Static load balancing.

processor for the next arriving task ((cpu MOD NUM_CPU) + 1). The computation ensures that the set of processor identifiers ranges from 1 to NUM_CPU. A processor identifier of 0 stands for an undefined processor (UNDEFINED).

The subnets for the *random* and *same as parent* policies follow the same structure. Transition Random calls function randomInt to generate a uniformly distributed random number between 1 and NUM_CPU, which represents the selected processor of the new task. Transition SameAsParent looks up the SCHED_TASK token of the task which created the new task, i.e., its parent.

Listing 5.1: Colour set PARENT_SCHED_TASK.
_____
colset PARENT_SCHED_TASK = **product** TASK_ID * SCHED_TASK;
_____

Place ParentTask contains the SCHED_TASK tokens of the parent tasks associated to the identifier (TASK_ID) of the created task (cf. Listing 5.1). This tokens allows transition SameAsParent to look up the parent's processor (p_cpu) and assign the new task to the same processor. All three transitions of the static balancing policy subnets retrieve the token onForkList from place OnFork. Independent of the list's current content, they return a list with a single token. The new token on fusion place OnFork notifies the dynamic load balancing policy that a new task has been created.

Dynamic Load Balancing

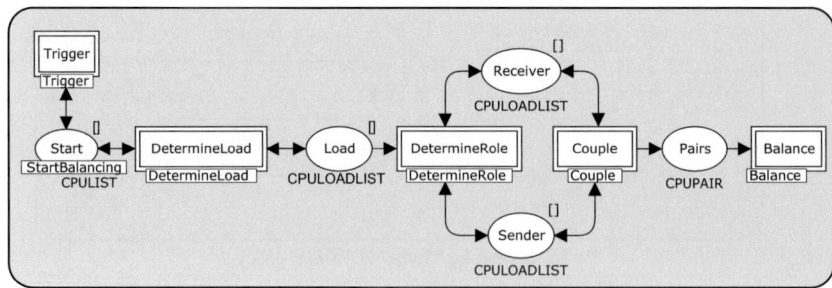

Figure 5.12.: Overview of dynamic load balancing.

MOSS reflects the influence of various features for dynamic multiprocessor load balancing policies. It includes different load indices as well as transfer, location, information, and selection policies. MOSS requires a high flexibility as it allows various configurations of different features. In Figure 5.12, the CPN for dynamic load balancing policies is split into multiple subnets, which are represented by substitution transitions, to support such a flexibility. In the following, we give an overview of the overall dynamic load balancing behaviour.

When load balancing has been activated (i.e., transition `Trigger` fired), transition `DetermineLoad` determines the current *load index* for all processor identifiers on place `StartBalancing` and stores the result on place `Load`. Next transition `DetermineRole` partitions the processors into senders and receivers based on their current load. Whether a processor needs to participate in load balancing as well as its role depend on the specified *transfer policy*. When all processors have been partitioned and a sender and a receiver are available, transition `Couple` creates pairs of potential senders and receivers. The transition's behaviour depends on the *information policy* of the load balancer. Transition `Balance` models the movement of tasks from one processor to another. It chooses the tasks for transfer according to the defined *selection policy*. In the following, we present the realisation of each substitution transition in detail.

Activating Dynamic Load Balancing

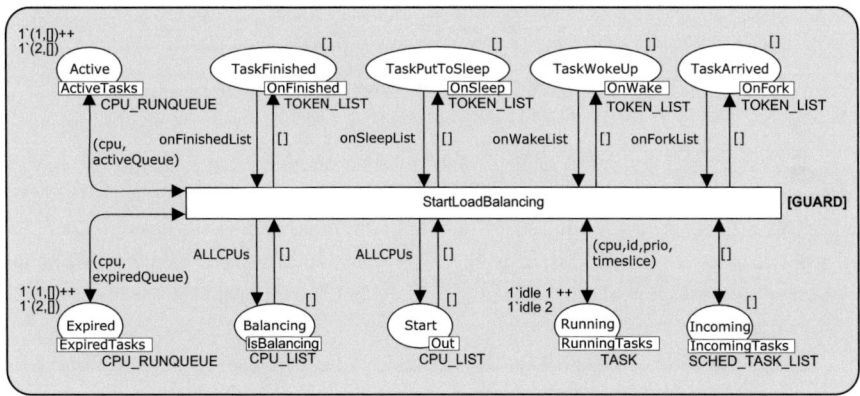

Figure 5.13.: Subnet `Trigger` for the state change driven activation of load balancing.

Figure 5.13 depicts the general behaviour of subnet `Trigger`. The `GUARD` of transition `StartLoadBalancing` depends on the selected *information policy*. The places `TaskFinished`, `TaskPutToSleep`, `TaskWokeUp`, and `TaskArrived` belong to the fusion sets `OnFinished`, `OnSleep`, `OnWake`, and `OnFork`, respectively, and represent state changes of the scheduler important for load balancing. Whenever one of these events occurs, the scheduler puts a token on the respective event's place.

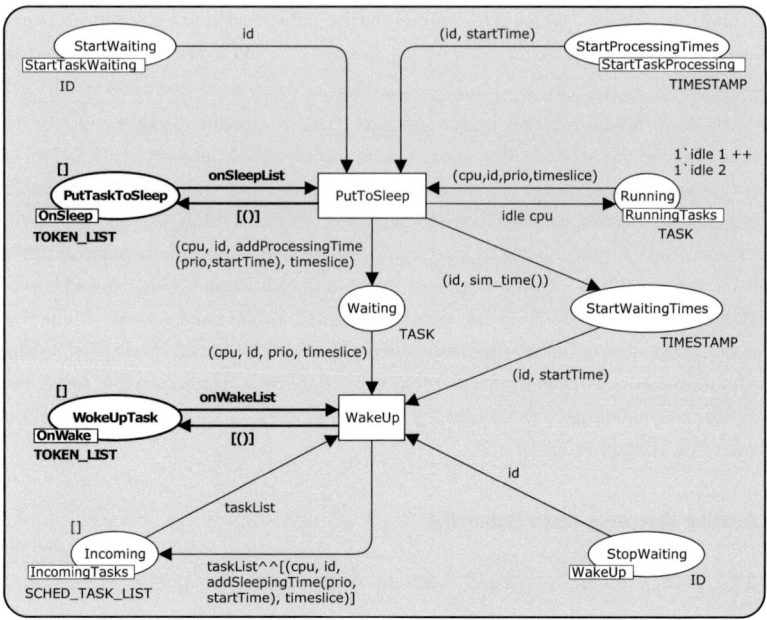

Figure 5.14.: Load balancing activation.

For example, Figure 5.14 depicts the extended subnet for the management of waiting tasks from Section 4.2.4. Additionally to their original behaviour, transitions `PutToSleep` and `WakeUp` insert tokens into the lists on places `PutTaskToSleep` and `WokeUpTask` of fusion sets `OnSleep` and `OnWake` respectively. Thus, when a task is put into the waiting queue during the acquisition of a semaphore, the subnet notifies the load balancer that an `OnSleep` event occurred.

Each event place contains a single list of tokens. Transition `StartLoadBalancing` retrieves all lists and concatenates the ones of interest. If the concatenated list contains at least one element, then an event of interest occurred. When transition `StartLoadBalancing` fires, it removes all tokens from the event places and inserts all processor identifiers into the list on place `Start`. The latter belongs to the fusion set `StartBalacing`, which finally triggers the load balancing. The inhibitor arc to place `Incoming` ensures that all incoming task are placed in the run queue before load balancing is initiated. The inhibitor arc prevents wrong load balancing decisions for the events `OnWake` and `OnFork`.

The different feature configurations of the *state-change-driven information policy* influence the guard of transition `StartLoadBalancing`. Listing 5.2 shows the conditions for the state-change driven information policies implemented in Windows Server 2003 and Linux 2.6.22. The condition modelling the behaviour of the Windows Server 2003 operating system reacts when a processor becomes (or currently is) idle (*OnIdle*). Whenever an event occurs (i.e., the concatenated event list is greater than zero) transition StartLoadBalancing checks whether a processor is idle (i.e., it executes the idle task with id = IDLE_ID) and whether its run queue is empty (i.e., length(runQueue) = 0). The transition ensures this condition by its bidirectional arcs to the places Ready (or Active and Expired) and Running. The arcs select the currently executing task and the run queue of a processor. Only if the run queue is empty and a processor is idle, then transition StartLoadBalancing fires.

Listing 5.2: Different variants of the guard of transition Trigger Load Balancing.

```
val NUM_CPU = 2;
val UNDEFINED = 0;
colset CPU = int with 0..NUM_CPU;
val ALLCPUs = CPU. all () -- 1'UNDEFINED;

(* OnIdle   (Windows Server 2003) *)
[length onFinishedList^^onSleepList^^onWakeList^^onForkList > 0
 andalso id = IDLE_ID andalso length runQueue = 0]

(* OnWake, OnFork, and OnIdle   (Linux 2.6.22) *)
[(length onFinishedList^^onSleepList > 0 andalso id = IDLE_ID
   andalso length (activeQueue^^expiredQueue) = 0)
   orelse length onWakeList^^onForkList > 0]
```

Similarly, transition StartLoadBalancing for Linux 2.6.22 waits for tokens on places TaskFinished, TaskPutToSleep, TaskWokeUp, and TaskArrived. While the latter two directly conform to the events *OnWake* and *OnFork*, respectively (like their fusion set is called), event *OnIdle* is triggered if the number of executable tasks in the system reduces and, hence, a processor becomes idle. Condition length onWakeList^^onForkList > 0 enables the transition if either a token lies on place TaskWokeUp of fusion set onWake or on place TaskArrived of fusion set onFork. To initiate load balancing whenever a processor becomes idle, condition length(onFinishedList^^onSleepList) > 0 checks whether event onFinished or onSleep occurred. Furthermore, condition id = IDLE_ID requires the idle tasks to currently execute on one of the processors whose active and expired run queues are empty (length (activeQueue ^^ expiredQueue) = 0). These conditions enable transition StartLoadBalancing, whenever a task finishes or starts waiting and a processor becomes idle.

Transition StartLoadBalancing encapsulates the complex load balancing activation to guarantee atomicity. Furthermore, its inhibitor arc to place Incoming of the scheduler only allows to start balancing if all scheduling operations have been finished. Using a single transition that is only activated if the scheduling is terminated ensures that no invalid balancing operations are executed, e.g., the processors are balanced even though not all tasks have been placed in run queues. Furthermore, the transition reduces the simulation overhead necessary, since it combines a set of events into a single scheduling attempt.

Determining the Load

If load balancing has been initiated, then the load of each processor has to be determined next. Figure 5.15 depicts two subnets for substitution transition DetermineLoad.

The first subnet (Figure 5.15(a)) determines the current *CPU queue length*. It collects the necessary information from places Ready and Running and stores the resulting load in the list on place Start. The second subnet (Figure 5.15(b)) computes the *ageing CPU queue length* using the subnet in Figure 5.15(a). It incorporates the current load with the previously determined one.

For the computation of the current CPU queue length, transition DetermineCurrentLoad is enabled as soon as an element is added to the CPU_LIST on place Start. Furthermore, a bidirectional arc with an empty list ensures that the TASK_LIST on place Incoming is empty (inhibitor arc patter, cf. Appendix B.6). When firing, transition DetermineCurrentLoad removes the first element from the CPU_LIST on place Start and gets the corresponding run queue (from place Ready) as well as the currently running task (from place Running). Furthermore, it adds a new token of colour CPULOAD (cf. Listing 5.3) to the list on place Load. The CPULOAD embodies a CPU representing the processor's identifier and an integer representing its load. Function insertAscending (cf. Listing 5.3) realises the priority queue pattern (cf. Appendix B.6) and ensures that processors on place Load are ordered according to their current load. Finally, transition Determine Current Load uses function determineLoad to compute the processor's load from the run queue and the executing task's identifier (cf. Listing 5.3).

The age based load index (Figure 5.15(b)) requires multiple steps to determine the ageing load from the current and last load of a processor. Furthermore, it is necessary to determine the load for all processors on place Start before transition DetermineRole is enabled. Place DetermineLoad of fusion set IsDeterminingLoad contains a list of processor identifiers whose load has not yet been computed. The realisation of transition DetermineRole employs an inhibitor arc on this place to ensure that the load of all processors is available.

When a list of processor identifiers is put on place Start, transition StartDetermineLoad is enabled. It removes the list of processors from place Start and puts a copy on place IsDetermingLoad and on place GetCurrentLoad. While the latter ensures, that the load balancer determines the load of all processors, before it assigns roles (i.e., sender or receiver)

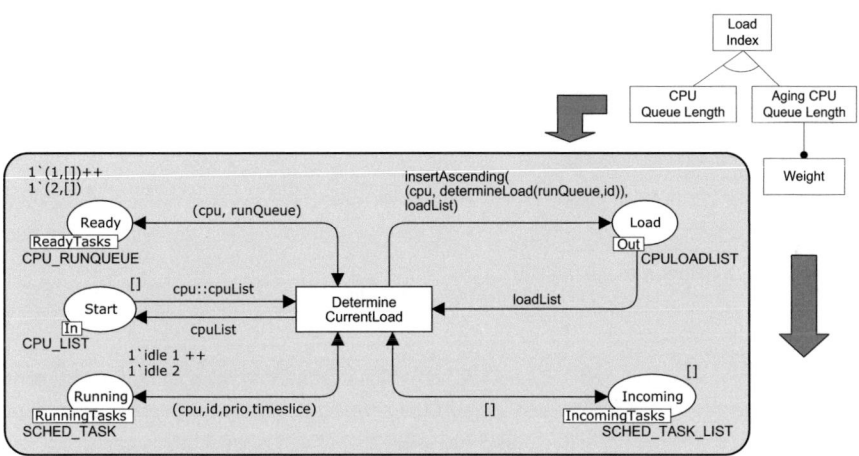

(a) Subnet determining the current processor load (CPU Queue Length).

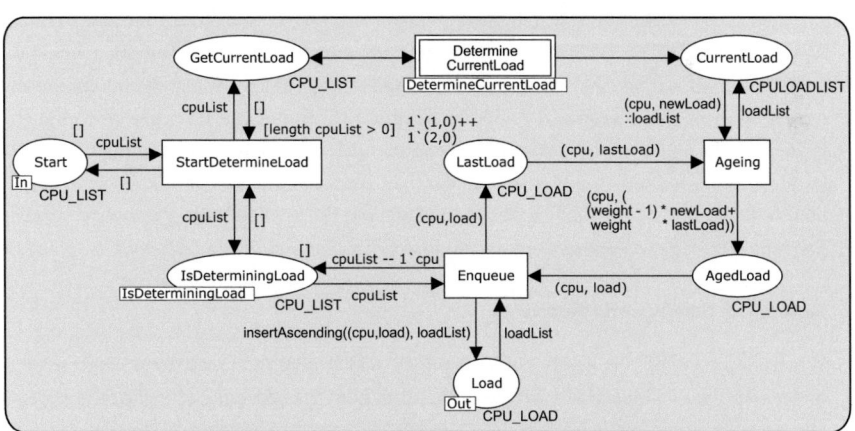

(b) Subnet determining the aging processor load (Ageing CPU Queue Length).

Figure 5.15.: Subnets for different load indices.

Listing 5.3: Functions `determineLoad` and `insertAscending`.

```
colset CPULOAD = product CPU * INT;
colset CPULOADLIST = list CPULOAD;

fun determineLoad (runQueue, id) =
if id = IDLE_ID
   then length runQueue
   else length runQueue + 1;

fun lowerLoad ((cpu1, load1), (cpu2, load2)) =
      (load1 < load2);

fun insertAscending (elm,[]) = [elm]
   | insertAscending (elm,(q::queue)) =
        if lowerLoad (elm,q)
           then elm::q::queue
           else q::(insertAscending(elm, queue));
```

to each processor, the first initiates the actual load computation. When a list of processors is put on place `GetCurrentLoad` substitution transition `DetermineCurrentLoad` sums up the length of the (active and expired) run queue including the currently running process. Its subnet is similar to the one for the feature *CPU queue length* in Figure 5.15(a).

When a new `CPULOAD` token is inserted into the list on place `CurrentLoad`, transition `Ageing` is enabled. It takes the processor's newly computed load (token `(cpu, newLoad)`) and its last known load (token `(cpu, lastload)`) from place `LastLoad` and computes the aged load from both values. Parameter `weight` determines the influence of the past and current load's value. Finally, transition `Enqueue` adds the resulting load in the `CPULOADLIST` on place `Load`, removes the processor's identifier from the list on place `IsDeterminingLoad`, and stores the resulting load on place `LastLoad` for the next balancing attempt. Transition `Enqueue` uses function `insertAscending` to add the computed load to the list on place `Load`.

Determine Senders and Receivers

When the load of all processors has been determined, senders and receivers for balancing need to be identified. The *transfer policy* determines how the scheduler classifies the processors based on their current load index. Figure 5.16 shows the subnets of the *threshold-based* (Figure 5.16(a)) and *relative* (Figure 5.16(b)) transfer policies.

For the *threshold-based* policy (Figure 5.16(a)), either transition `IsReceiver`, `IsBalanced`, or `IsSender` fires depending on the processor's load. If the lower bound is smaller than the upper bound, the guards of all three transitions are disjoint and only one transition is enabled at a time. In case both bounds are equal, only transitions `IsReceiver` and `IsSender` can be enabled.

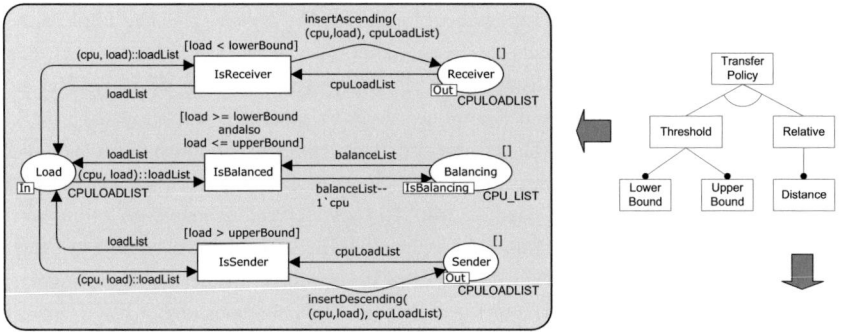

(a) Subnet for the threshold-based transfer policy.

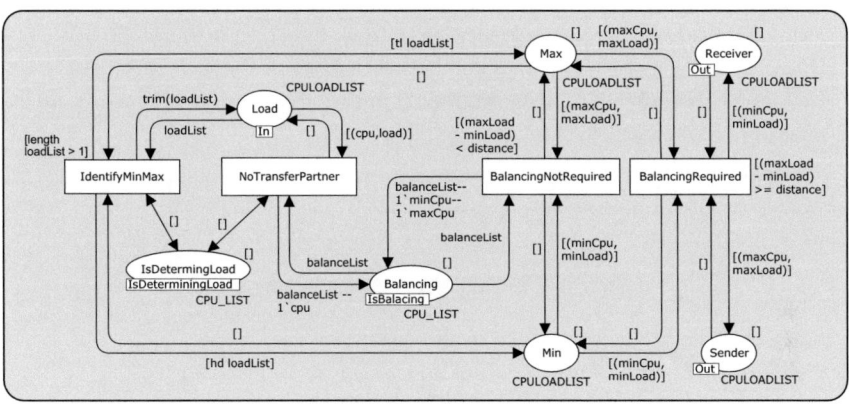

(b) Subnet for the relative transfer policy.

Figure 5.16.: Subnets to determine senders and receivers for load balancing.

If the load of a processor lies below the `lowerBound`, transition `IsReceiver` considers the processor as a receiver and inserts it into the list on place `Receiver`. For the insertion, transition `IsReceiver` calls function `insertAscending`. Analogously, transition `IsSender` fires if a processor's load lies above the `upperBound`. Function `insertDescending` adds the tuple (`cpu`, `load`) to the list on place `Sender` in descending order (cf. Listing 5.4). By sorting the receivers in an ascending order and the senders in a descending order, MOSS allows the direct identification of the highest and least loaded processors for balancing. Finally, transition `IsBalanced` fires if no balancing for the selected processor is necessary. The transition simply removes the processor from the list of currently balanced processors and, thus, aborts balancing for this processor.

Figure 5.16(b) shows the role assignment for the *relative transfer policy* as implemented in Linux 2.6.22. Once the load of all processors is determined, either transition IdentifyMinMax or NoTransferPartner is enabled. While the first requires at least two processors in the CPULOADLIST on place Load and determines the list's minimum and maximum, the latter is responsible for removing a single processor from the list, for which no proper partner can be found. Transition IndentifyMinMax takes the list of processor loads (loadList) from place Load and puts its head on place Min and its tail on place Max. Finally, function trim(loadList) (cf. Listing 5.4) returns the list without its head and tail to place Load. Since the list of processor load tokens in loadList is sorted in an ascending order, its first and last elements are the minimum and maximum of the list, respectively. Once the minimum and maximum are available, either transition BalancingRequired or BalancingNotRequired is enabled. In the first case, the load difference of the minimum and maximum loaded processor is equal to or larger than the predefined distance and load balancing is required. When transition BalancingRequired fires, it moves the minimum loaded processor token ((minCpu, minLoad)) to place Receiver and the maximum loaded processor token ((maxCpu, maxLoad)) to place Sender.

Listing 5.4: Functions insertDescending and trim.

```
fun higherLoad ((cpu1, load1), (cpu2, load2)) =
        (load1 > load2);

fun insertDescending (elm,[]) = [elm]
  | insertDescending (elm,(q::queue)) =
        if higherLoad(elm,q)
        then elm::q::queue
        else q::(insertDescending(elm,queue));

fun trim(head::l) = List.take(l, length l - 1)
  | trim([]) = [];
```

If instead transition BalancingNotRequired is enabled, the difference of the minimum and maximum load is smaller than the predefined distance. Thus, transition BalancingNotRequired terminates the balancing attempt for both processors. It removes their tokens from places Min and Max as well as their processor identifiers minCpu and maxCpu from the list on place Balancing.

Finding Partners for Transfer

To eventually create a balanced situation for all processors of a system, the load balancing policy needs to identify transfer partners, i.e., senders and receivers, so that tasks can be moved from one to the other. The subnet of substitution transition `Couple` realises the identification of fitting transfer partners in the context of MOSS.

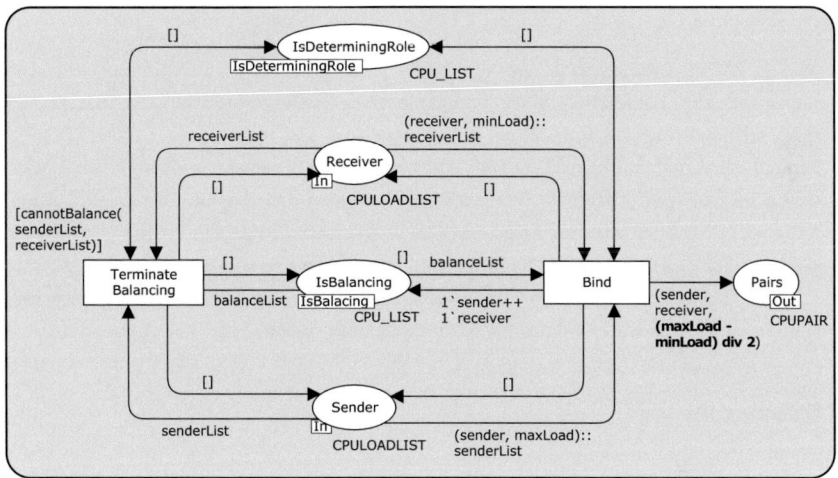

Figure 5.17.: Subnet for substitution transition `Couple`.

Figure 5.17 depicts its subnet with the input places `Sender` and `Receiver` and the output place `Pairs`. It contains two fusion places `IsBalancing` and `IsDeterminingRole`, which ensure that the role of all processors involved in load balancing has been determined. If this is the case, either transition `TerminateBalancing` or `Bind` is enabled. The first ensures that the balancing attempt is terminated if no redistribution of load is possible. Its guard calls function `cannotBalance` which checks whether the `receiverList` or whether the `senderList` is empty while its counterpart still contains at least one element. In this case, the system is either overutilised (contains only senders) or underutilised (contains only receivers) and balancing is not possible. Thus, transition `TerminateBalancing` terminates the balancing attempt, removes all senders and receivers, and empties the list of currently balanced tasks on place `IsBalancing`.

If, otherwise, the lists on places `Sender` and `Receiver` contain at least one element each, transition `Bind` is enabled. It takes the first sender and receiver token from the lists on places `Sender` and `Receiver` and puts a new `CPUPAIR` token on place `Pairs`. The token contains the sending and receiving processor's identifiers as well as the number of tasks to move. By

Listing 5.5: Function `cannotBalance`.

```
colset CPUPAIR = product CPU * CPU * INT;

fun cannotBalance (senderList, receiverList) =
(length receiverList = 0 andalso length senderList > 0)
 or else
(length senderList = 0 andalso length receiverList > 0)
```

default, MOSS assumes that threshold based policies just move a single task while relative policies equalize the load of the sender and receiver. Furthermore, transition Bind terminates the load balancing attempts for all other processors and removes their tokens from places Sender, Receiver, and IsBalancing. The termination is necessary, since the load balancing of the two selected processors changes the overall load distribution. If further balancing is required, a whole new balancing attempt must be started to determine the new senders and receiver. For example, one of the processors involved in the current load balancing attempt may still be the busiest processor after balancing is finished. Continuing load balancing with the remaining processors would not resolve such situations.

Balancing the Load

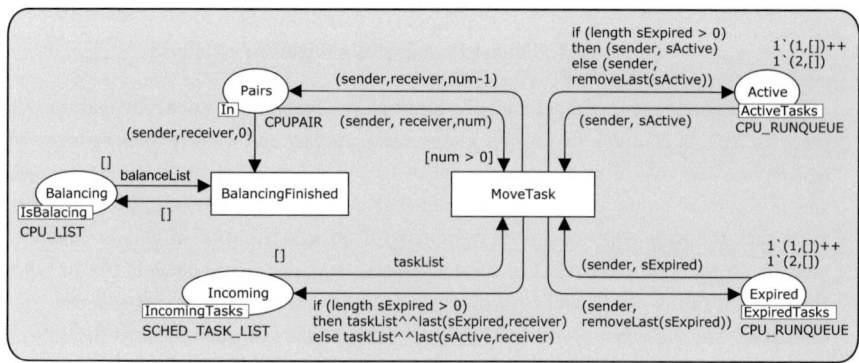

Figure 5.18.: Subnet for substitution transition Balance.

After substitution transition Couple identified two transfer partners, transition Balance (Figure 5.18) can select and move tasks from the sender to the receiver. For each pair on place Pairs, it moves the specified number of tasks from the sending to the receiving processor. The task transfer is executed in multiple steps. During each step, transition

`MoveTask` moves one task from the sender to the receiver until no further tasks have to be moved. Then transition `BalancingFinished` terminates the load balancing operation.

Transition `MoveTask` takes a `CPUPAIR` token from place `Pairs`, whose number of tasks to move is greater than zero (`num > 0`). Furthermore, it selects the sender's (active and expired) run queue from places `Active` and `Expired`. Transition `MoveTask` first tries to move the last task of the expired queue. If such a task exists (i.e., `length sExpired > 0`), transition `MoveTask` removes it from the sender's expired run queue and adds it to the list of tasks on place incoming (`taskList^^last(sExpired, receiver)`), where function `last` returns the last element of a run queue and sets its processor identifier to the specified one (cf. Listing 5.6). The functions `last` and `removeLast` realise the *selection policy* of the load balancer. Its preferred priority is low, its preferred waiting time is short, and processor as well as cache affinities are not considered.

Listing 5.6: Functions `update` and `interactive`.

```
fun last ([] , newCpu) = []
  | last ([(cpu,id,prio,timeslice)], newCpu) = [(newCpu, id, prio, timeslice)]
  | last (q::queue, newCpu)= last(queue, newCpu);

fun removeLast [] = []
  | removeLast [elm] = []
  | removeLast (q::queue) = q::removeLast(queue);
```

The scheduler's subnet automatically places the tasks in the list on place `Incoming` in the correct run queue of the receiving processor. If the expired run queue of the sender is empty, transition `MoveTask` switches to its active run queue performing the same operations as for the expired one. Finally, it return the `CPUPAIR` token to place `Pairs` reducing its number of tasks by one. If the number is still greater than zero, transition `MoveTask` is enabled again and can move the next task.

As soon as the number of tasks to move reaches zero, transition `BalancingFinished` is activated. It empties the list of currently balanced processors on place `Balancing`. This terminates the balancing operation.

For MOSS, we considered the configurations of information policies, load indices, transfer policies, and selection policies. However, we neglected the different location policies. Location policies have only a limited influence on software performance, since the load balancing itself does not consume simulated time. In the next section, we validate the prediction accuracy of MOSS for symmetric multiprocessing environments.

5.1.5. Validation of MOSS' Prediction Accuracy

In this section, we present a validation of MOSS' prediction accuracy for symmetric multiprocessing environments following the same structure as in Sections 4.1.4 and 4.2.5. The validation is based on the experiments in Section 5.1.3 and targets the prediction accuracy of the multiprocessor load balancers of Windows Server 2003 and Linux 2.6.22 under different load conditions. In the validation, we compare predictions and measurements for single-, dual-, and quad-core systems and, thus, extend the scenarios of Section 5.1.2.

Goal:	*Purpose*	Assessment
	Issue	of MOSS' prediction accuracy
	Object	for symmetric multiprocessing environments
	Viewpoint	from the software architect's point of view.

Evaluation of the Prediction Accuracy for Multiprocessor Load Balancing		
Questions	Can the model predict the influence of heavy load?	Can the model predict the influence of moderate load?
Scenarios	Heavy Load 250 ms Demand 0 ms Delay 7 Tasks	Moderate Load 250 ms Demand Windows: 10 ms Delay Linux: 50 ms Delay 7 Tasks
Metrics	Err(RT), Err(Load(CPU))	Err(RT), Err(Load(CPU))
Hypotheses	Yes, the prediction error is less than 5% Err(RT) < 5% Err(Load(CPU)) < 5%	Yes, the prediction error is less than 5% Err(RT) < 5% Err(Load(CPU)) < 5%

Table 5.7.: GQM plan for the multiprocessor load balancing prediction model.

Table 5.7 shows the scenario-based GQM plan of the validation. The first question addresses the influences of initial imbalances under heavy load conditions. While the imbalances are expected to remain under Windows, the Linux scheduler is expected to balance the system (cf. Section 5.1.3). The second question addresses MOSS' prediction accuracy for moderately loaded systems, where both operating systems achieve a more balanced state. In the following, we answer both questions for the considered operating systems and discuss the effect of changes in the prediction model on performance results. For brevity, we only list the scenarios and hypotheses in Table 5.7 omit a detailed description.

Prediction Accuracy for Lazy Load Balancing

MOSS accurately predicts the effect of Window's lazy-balancing policy on software performance. Figure 5.19 depicts the response time distributions for scenarios Heavy Load and

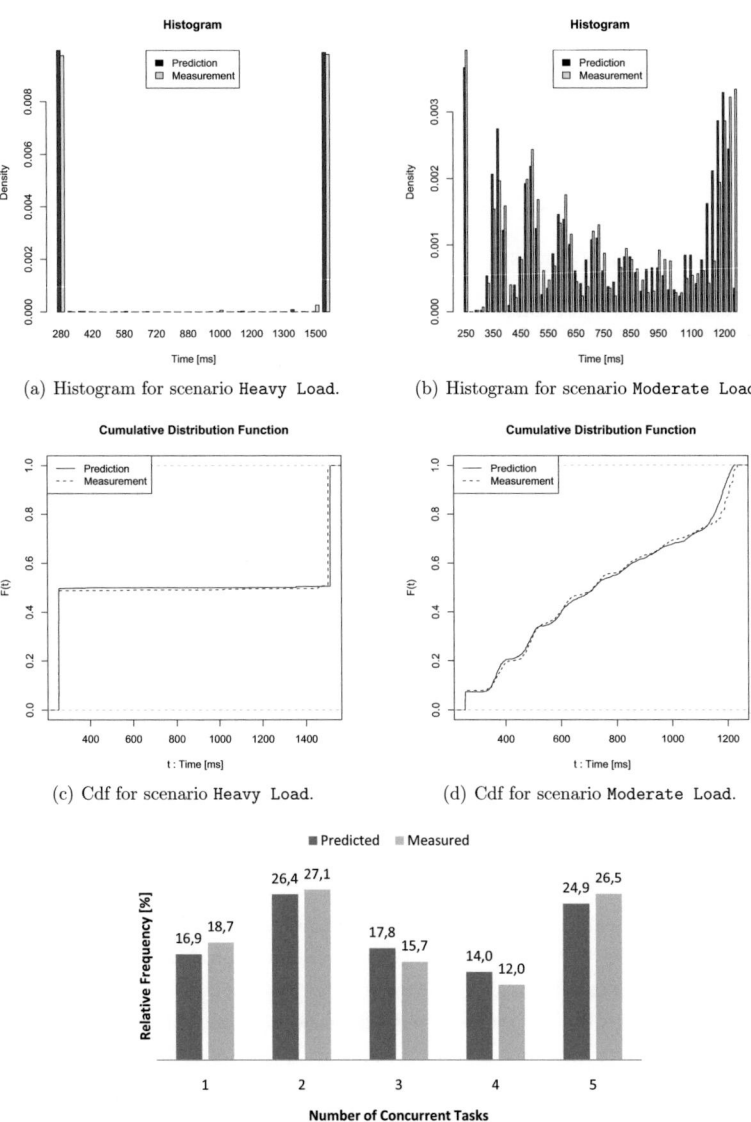

(a) Histogram for scenario Heavy Load.

(b) Histogram for scenario Moderate Load.

(c) Cdf for scenario Heavy Load.

(d) Cdf for scenario Moderate Load.

(e) Comparison between predicted and measured load distribution.

Figure 5.19.: Predictions and measurements for load balancing under Windows.

Moderate Load. MOSS predicts the task response times for both scenarios with an error of less than 1% (Table 5.8(b)). Figures 5.19(a) and 5.19(c) show the accumulated response time distributions of all seven tasks for scenario Heavy Load. As expected, one task is executed without preemptions on one processor while the remaining six tasks share the second processor. This behaviour yields the depicted response time distribution, where 50% of all requests finish within 250 ms and 50% in 1500 ms. Analogously, Figures 5.19(b) and Figure 5.19(d) show the accumulated results for scenario Moderate Load.

(a) Estimated load distribution for scenario Moderate Load.

Tasks	Relative Frequency [%]		Error [%]
	Predicted	Measured	
1	16,9	18,7	1,86
2	26,4	27,1	0,74
3	17,8	15,7	2,14
4	14,0	12,0	2,05
5	24,9	26,5	1,59

(b) Measured and predicted response times for scenarios Heavy Load and Moderate Load.

Task Response Time [ms]			
Scenario	Prediction	Measurment	Error [%]
Moderate Load			
Min.	251,9	251,8	0,0
1st Qu.	471,5	476,1	1,0
Mean	753	754,5	0,2
3rd Qu.	1124	1123	0,1
Max	1224	1237	1,1
Heavy Load			
Min.	251,8	251,8	0,0
1st Qu.	251,9	251,8	0,0
Mean	881	886	0,6
3rd Qu.	1512	1502	0,7
Max	1513	1503	0,7

Table 5.8.: Prediction accuracy for Windows Server 2003.

Tables 5.8(a) and 5.8(b) summarise the prediction error for both scenarios. The predicted load distribution among the available processor (Figures 5.19(e)) matches the measurements with an error of approximately 2% for scenario Moderate Load and less than 1% for scenario Heavy Load.

Prediction Accuracy for Active Load Balancing

Similar to the lazy load balancing policy, MOSS accurately predicts the task response times and load distribution for scenarios Heavy Load (Figures 5.20(a) and 5.20(c)) and Moderate Load (Figures 5.20(b) and 5.20(d)). However, the predictions for scenario Moderate Load show a larger variance than the corresponding measurements. This difference becomes evident in the predicted and measured load distribution (Figure 5.20(e)).

For scenario Heavy Load, MOSS predicts the response time with an error of less than 1% (Table 5.9). It predicts the mean response time for scenario Moderate Load with the same accuracy. However, the quantiles show larger differences due to the larger variance of the predicted response times compared to the measured response times. The first quantile of both distributions differs by 12% and the third by 17%. Furthermore, the minimum and

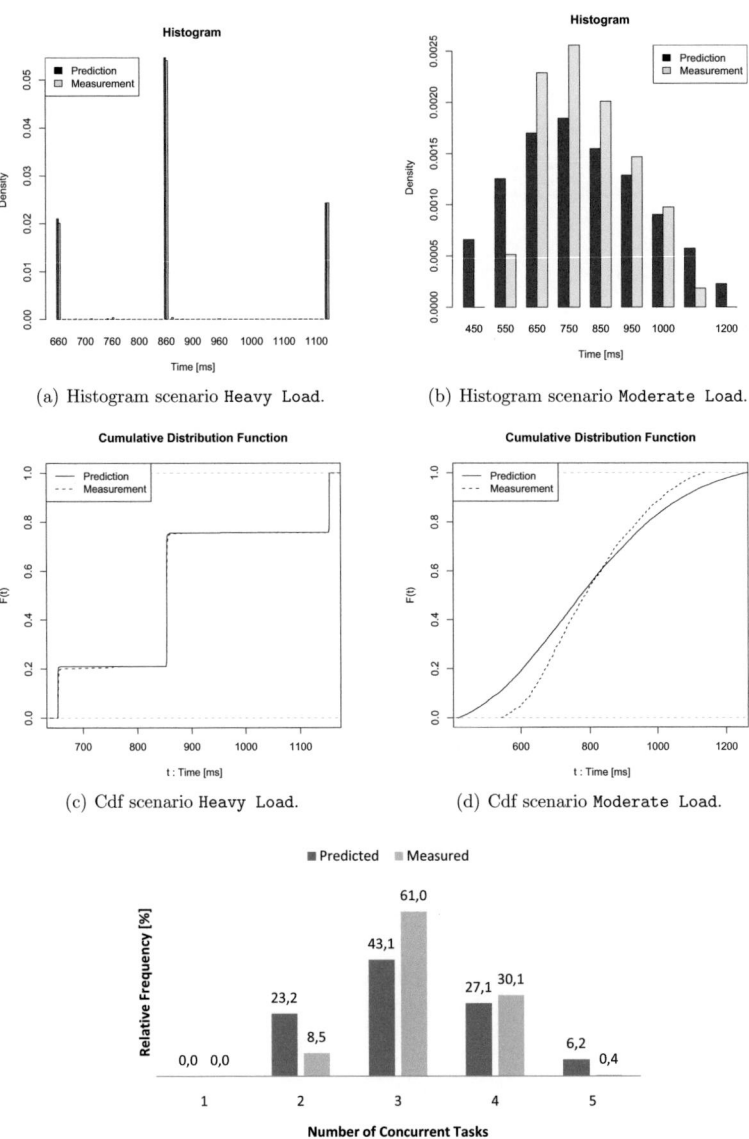

(a) Histogram scenario Heavy Load.

(b) Histogram scenario Moderate Load.

(c) Cdf scenario Heavy Load.

(d) Cdf scenario Moderate Load.

(e) Comparison between predicted and measured load distribution.

Figure 5.20.: Predictions and measurements for load balancing under Linux.

(a) Estimated load distribution for scenario Moderate Load.

	Relative Frequency [%]		Error [%]
Tasks	Predicted	Measured	
1	0,0	0,0	0,00
2	23,2	8,5	14,63
3	43,1	61,0	17,85
4	27,1	30,1	2,94
5	6,2	0,4	5,73

(b) Measured and predicted response times for scenarios Heavy Load and Moderate Load.

Task Response Time [ms]			
Scenario	Prediction	Measurment	Error [%]
Moderate Load			
Min.	419,0	541,6	22,6
1st Qu.	635,0	693,0	8,4
Mean	790,6	804,4	1,7
3rd Qu.	934,0	909,3	2,7
Max	1261,0	1136,0	11,0
Heavy Load			
Min.	653,6	653,8	0,0
1st Qu.	853,4	853,5	0,0
Mean	884,8	885,9	0,1
3rd Qu.	855,9	859,9	0,5
Max	1154,0	1154,0	0,0

Table 5.9.: Prediction accuracy for Linux 2.6.22.

maximum response times deviate by 17% and 16% respectively. While the measurements show a load of 3 and 4 tasks in most cases, the prediction expects a load distribution ranging from 2 to 5 tasks. Hence, MOSS does not achieve the same degree of balancing as the Linux scheduler.

Thread vs. Process Load Balancing

In this section, we examine the effect of "random task switches" observed in Section 5.1.3. The effect is caused by the dynamic remapping of light weight processes (LWPs [SGG05]) or kernel-level threads and user-level threads. The mapping affects the performance metrics observed for the tasks in scenarios Heavy Load and Moderate Load. For scenario Heavy Load, the response time predicted for a single task strongly deviates from the measurements, while the accumulated response time of all tasks is predicted accurately. The histogram in Figure 5.21(a) compares the predictions and measurements. While MOSS predicts an almost constant response time of 1500 ms, the measurements alternate between 250 ms and 1500 ms. Thus, the task switched processors during its execution. However, it did not affect the overall response time of all tasks as the results depicted in Figures 5.19(a) and (c) show.

A changing association between user-level threads and light weight processes (or kernel-level threads) explains this effect. In general, Windows uses a separate LWP for each user-level thread. However, the relation can change in multiprocessing environments. Whenever a user-level thread has to wait for a resource, its associated LWP looks for a new user-level thread of the same heavy weight process to execute. Such situations lead to the "random task switches" observed in scenario Heavy Load. In this case, two user-level threads switch

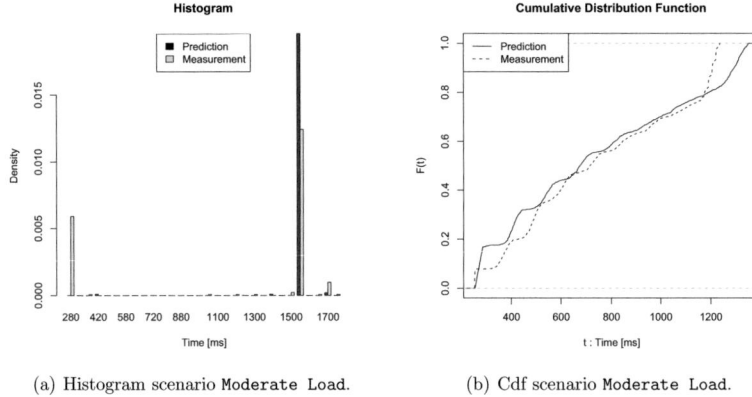

(a) Histogram scenario `Moderate Load`.   (b) Cdf scenario `Moderate Load`.

Figure 5.21.: Differences in predictions and measurements for load balancing under Windows.

processors without affecting the overall balancing situation, i.e., one processor still executes a single task while the other processor executes the remaining six.

The "random task switches" also occur in scenario `Moderate Load`. Lazy-balancing alone is not sufficient to explain the measurements shown in Figure 5.19(b) and 5.19(d). Consider, for example, the predicted response times for scenario `Moderate Load` with lazy-balancing (Figure 5.21(b)). Compared to the measurements, the predictions show a higher variance, i.e., short requests are interrupted less often while long requests are additionally delayed.

To better understand the effect, consider the results of a simplified version of scenario `Moderate Load` in Figures 5.22(a) and (b). The figures compare predictions for process load balancing with measurements for thread load balancing. In the first case, an idle processor moves an available light weight process from the busiest processor to its run queue. In the second case, a light weight process (whose user-level thread starts waiting) looks for a new user-level thread to execute in exchange for its waiting one. The predictions depicted in Figure 5.22 demonstrate the different performance influences of both strategies, which affect the delay of each task (Figure 5.22(a)) as well as its response time (Figure 5.22(b)).

The delay distribution (Figure 5.22(a)) provides information on how often and at what times the load balancing policy moves tasks between the available processors. For process load balancing, tasks wait for one timeslice, in most cases ($\approx 80\%$). A task only waits for a full timeslice if the scheduler does not move it to another processor, assuming that the scheduling interupts of both processors occur independently. If the task would be moved, the remaining timeslice of the currently running task is most likely to be less than a full

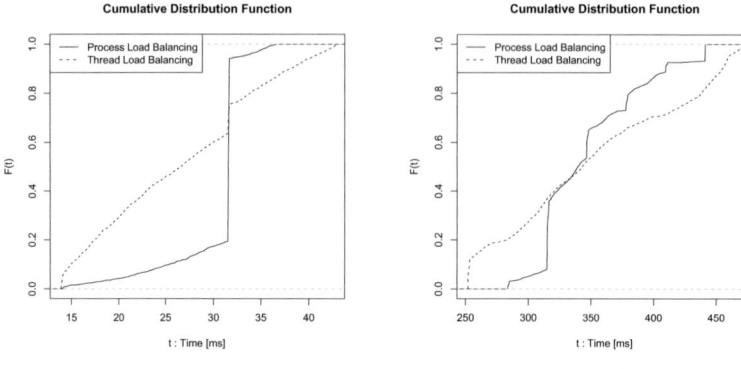

(a) Predicted and measured delay.　　　　(b) Predicted and measured response time.

Figure 5.22.: Prediction results for load balancing with 3 tasks (and no LWP-thread switches).

timeslice. Only if the task remains on the same processor, then it either has to wait for a full timeslice or wait until the currently running task on the same processor finishes execution.

For thread load balancing, a task has to wait less than a full timeslice in 60% of all cases. This is only possible if the scheduler moves the thread to another processor (where the currently running task's timeslice already progressed). However, the lazy-balancing policy is not sufficient to explain this effect. The measurements and predictions in Figure 5.22(a) suggest that the processing of a task must start before the timeslice of the currently running task is finished and before the second processor becomes idle. Both can only happen if the task is already in the other processor's run queue. Such a reallocation of tasks is not possible with the lazy-balancing policy of Windows. Only a change in the association of light weight processes and user-level threads explains the observed effect. If two LWPs switch their executing threads, then this keeps both processors busy and adds the currently waiting user-level thread to the busiest processor's run queue. The change in the association explains the "random task switches" in scenario Heavy Load.

Lifting MOSS to Different Environments.

MOSS has been validated and modelled according to the measurement results on a dual-core
system with Windows Server 2003 and Linux 2.6.22. In the following, we present predictions
and measurements of scenarios `Heavy Load` and `Moderate Load` for a quad-core system with
Windows Vista to emphasise its transferability to other platforms. The experiments address
the following two questions: (i) Does the number of symmetric multiprocessors influence load
balancing? (ii) Do newer operating system versions implement a more efficient (or different)
load balancing strategies?

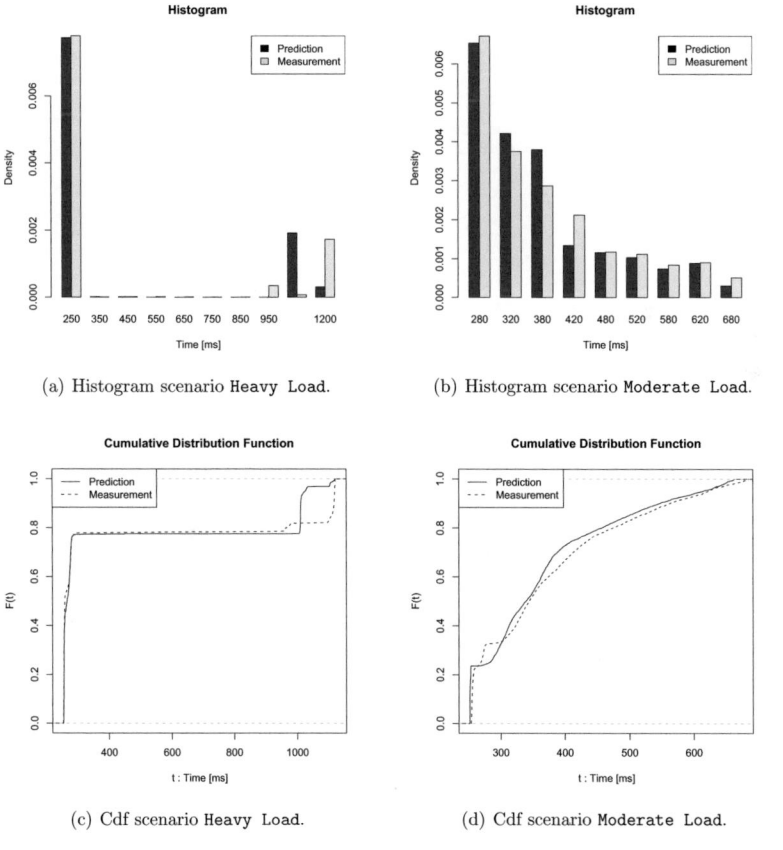

(a) Histogram scenario `Heavy Load`.

(b) Histogram scenario `Moderate Load`.

(c) Cdf scenario `Heavy Load`.

(d) Cdf scenario `Moderate Load`.

Figure 5.23.: Predictions and measurements for a quad-core system with Windows Vista.

Figure 5.23 shows the resulting measurements and predictions. As predicted by MOSS, the imbalances generated in scenario `Heavy Load` remain and, thus, yield the extreme response times of 250 ms and 1000 ms. The predicted long response times (i.e., four tasks sharing one processor) deviate approximately 12% from the measurements (Figures 5.23(a) and 5.23(d)). The relative large deviation of about 100 ms results from an additional preemption of the tasks, which does not occur in the predictions. The task is preempted by its three competing tasks and, thus, prolongs the response time by three timeslices (94.5 ms) plus its remaining processing time. The additional interruption is a result of the approximated generation of resource demands (cf. Appendix C.1) and of disturbing influences in multiprocessing environments explained in the following.

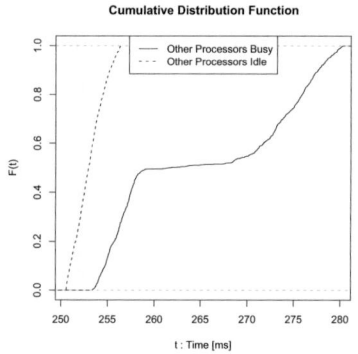

Figure 5.24.: Influence of the load on other processors on task response time.

In multiprocessing environments, the response time of a task solely running on its own processor is influenced by the activity of the other processors. If all processors in the system are busy processing a single task, the response time of each task increases compared to its response time in a system where all other CPUs are idle. Figure 5.24 illustrates this effect. The initially specified response time of 250 ms increases up to 280 ms. The task executes a computation intensive algorithm that only rarely accesses main memory. Therefore, possible contention effects of the main memory and memory buses cannot cause this effect (cf. Section 5.3). The additional processing time yields the delay observed in Figures 5.23(a) and (c).

Table 5.10 summarises the prediction quality of MOSS for quad-core processors with Windows Vista. The predictions and measurements for the quantiles and mean deviate by less than 5%. The results demonstrate that the model is capable of predicting the performance of tasks on platforms with more processors as well as newer versions of the

Task Response Time [ms]			
Scenario	Prediction	Measurment	Error [%]
Moderate Load			
Min.	251,8	254,1	0,9
1st Qu.	282,1	268,8	4,9
Mean	365,9	374,1	2,2
3rd Qu.	414,7	436,1	4,9
Max	663,7	685,6	3,2
Heavy Load			
Min.	253,4	253	0,2
1st Qu.	255,3	254,9	0,2
Mean	434,2	442	1,8
3rd Qu.	279,9	280,5	0,2
Max	1122	1122	0,0

Table 5.10.: Prediction error Windows Vista quad-core.

Windows operating system. However, it may be necessary for other platforms to reexecute the defined scenarios in order to validate the validity of the scheduler performance model on the new platform.

5.2. Case Study

In this section, we continue the case study of Section 4.3, which is placed in the scenario of a supply chain management for supermarkets. For the business intelligence reporting use case evaluated in Section 4.3, the predictions and measurement showed that a single-core system cannot handle the load of the HQ application. With the given hardware, the HQ server can easily become a bottleneck for management and accounting of the supermarket company. In the following, we continue the performance evaluation, discusse the relevant performance questions (Section 5.2.1), and present the results (Section 5.2.2). Please see Section 4.3 for an introduction to the overall scenario of the case study.

5.2.1. Performance Questions

Driven by the performance problems discovered in the previous case study (Section 4.3), performance analysts decide to continue the evaluation. In order to resolve the bottleneck, they evaluate the benefit of a multiprocessor system for the HQ application. They want to answer the following questions:

1. How would a new multiprocessor system improve performance?
2. Which operating system (Linux 2.6.22 or Windows Server 2003) provides the best performance under heavy load?

A multiprocessor system could be used to improve performance if the processor was the bottleneck. However, overload conditions can occur even with additional hardware due to the strongly fluctuating load. Thus, performance analysts want to further ensure, that the system's performance meets the requirements for intensive load.

5.2.2. Results

In this section, we discuss the predicted and measured response times for a dual-core processor running with the Windows Server 2003 and Linux 2.6.22 operating systems. The results demonstrate the differences and similarities in performance of single- and multi-core systems as well as the prediction accuracy MOSS.

	180 req / min			360 req / min		
	Prediction	Measurement	Error [%]	Prediction	Measurement	Error [%]
Windows (Dual)						
Static Pages	5,0	5,1	2,5	5,0	5,1	1,8
Monitoring	256,6	256,5	0,0	463,3	458,4	1,1
Reporting	3191,0	3028,0	5,4	4584,0	4653,0	1,5
Linux (Dual)						
Static Pages	5,2	5,3	1,8	5,3	5,2	2,0
Monitoring	252,6	255,6	1,2	259,3	258,5	0,3
Reporting	3018,0	3009,0	0,3	5739,0	4445,0	29,1
Windows (Single)						
Static Pages	5,0	5,4	7,2			
Monitoring	704,0	814,1	13,5			
Reporting	9546,0	12100,0	21,1			
Linux (Single)						
Static Pages	5,5	5,1	7,4			
Monitoring	266,2	261,4	1,8			
Reporting	13720,0	11480,0	19,5			

Table 5.11.: Predicted and measured median of the response time distribution under Linux 2.6.22 and Windows Server 2003.

Prediction Accuracy   To illustrate MOSS's prediction accuracy, the predictions and measurements of the following four scenarios are compared:

1. Dual-core   Windows   180 requests / minute
2. Dual-core   Linux   180 requests / minute
3. Dual-core   Windows   360 requests / minute
4. Dual-core   Linux   360 requests / minute

Figure 5.25 shows the cumulated distribution functions of the response times of the online monitoring in all four scenarios. Furthermore, Table 5.11 summarises the predicted and measured median of response times for all request types and scenarios. The prediction error

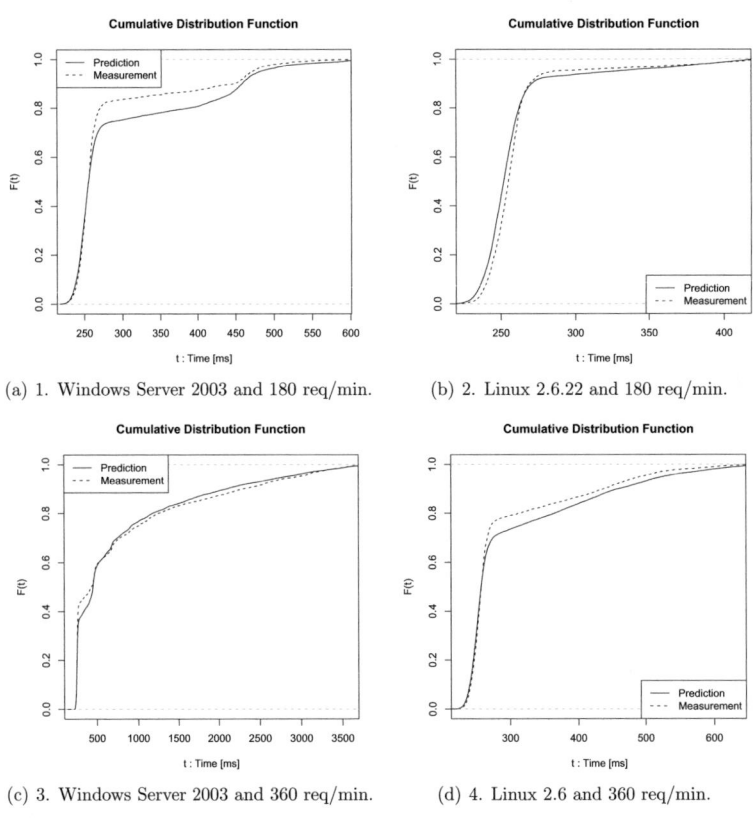

(a) 1. Windows Server 2003 and 180 req/min.

(b) 2. Linux 2.6.22 and 180 req/min.

(c) 3. Windows Server 2003 and 360 req/min.

(d) 4. Linux 2.6 and 360 req/min.

Figure 5.25.: Monitoring requests, results for a single-core system.

ranges from 5% to 10% in most cases and does not exceed 30%. The prediction error for business reporting under Linux is caused by the same influences as discussed in the previous case study (cf. Section 4.3.5).

The results for the dual-core scenario suggest a significant improvement in response time for all request classes when compared to a single-core system. Even though the load doubles (360 requests per minute), the system shows a much better response time than the single-core system with the original load (180 requests per minute).

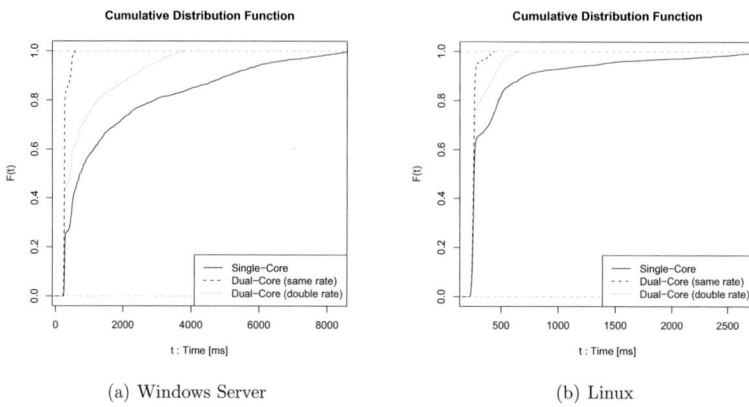

(a) Windows Server   (b) Linux

Figure 5.26.: Comparison between single-core and dual-core performance.

Single- versus Dual-core Processors Using a system with an additional processor core in the HQ server represents a significant performance gain for the whole application (cf. Table 5.11). If the load conditions stay similar, then Windows maintains a mean response time of 5 ms for static pages, while Linux reduces it from 50 ms to 5 ms (factor of 9.5). However, the median response time stays similar for both operating systems (5 ms). This performance gain indicates that the response time distribution for the dual-core processor does not have a heavy tail as the one for the single-core system. The additional processor core reduces contention and allows Windows and Linux to serve incoming requests to static pages immediately. The number of threads in the pool increases with the additional processor core. The threads reduce the contention of the thread pool and further decrease the delay of incoming requests.

For online monitoring under Windows, the median of the response time decreases from 814 ms to 256 ms. By contrast, the additional processor does not affect the response time's median under Linux, but rather reduces its mean value. Similar to the static page requests, the heavy tail of the distribution vanishes which yields the reduction of mean response times. Finally, the response time of the business reporting benefits by a factor of 3 to 4 for both operating systems.

The reduced contention leads to a significant performance gain for all request types. The response time not only halves (as one might expect) but improves by a factor ranging from 2 to 5. This large gain is a consequence of the reduced contention. The additional processor reduces waiting times and, thus, significantly increases the performance perceived by users.

If the server's load doubles from 180 to 360 requests per minute, the response times listed in Table 5.11 still suggest an overall performance-gain of a factor up to 2. For the mean values the factor is even larger, ranging from 1 to 6. All request types benefit from the second core even though the system utilisation is similar to the single-core scenario. This effect may not be expected in the first place, but it is a direct result of the operating system scheduler's behaviour. Figure 5.26 compares the response times of the online monitoring for a single- and dual-core system. It depicts the cumulative distribution functions of the response time under Windows Server 2003 (Figures 5.26(a)) and Linux 2.6.22 (Figures 5.26(b)). For the scenarios `single-core` and `dual-core` (`same rate`), requests arrive at a rate of 180 requests per minute, for `dual-core` (`double rate`) with 360 requests per minute.

The speedup of the dual-core processor is a consequence of the multiprocessor load balancing implemented in the Windows and Linux operating systems. It significantly reduces the waiting time for all tasks executing currently. For a single-core processor, the execution of one task delays all others waiting in the queue. In a dual-core system, the operating system scheduler moves tasks as soon as one of the processors becomes idle (Windows) or is less loaded (Linux). Load balancing between the processor cores reduces the delay for each request. In this case, delays are determined by the tasks currently running on both cores. If a request is finished, the scheduler moves tasks from the busier to the more idle core to balance the load. This balancing affects the delay of all requests. Since the load of the (previously) busier core is reduced, the remaining tasks can process with shorter waiting times. The tasks moved to the second core find a less contended processor and receive a larger share of processing time. As a result, a major decrease of the response times can be observed, especially under Windows.

In the beginning of this section, performance analysts asked whether a dual-core system can provide sufficient performance for the HQ application. In the next paragraph, we answer the questions that the performance analysts posed before this case study.

Answers to the Performance Questions Performance analysts predicted the response times for multiprocessing environments of the HQ application. Based on the results, they suggest to deploy the application on a new dual-core processor system running Windows Server 2003. This execution environment profits from the major performance gain of the second core even under heavy load conditions and ensures fast responses to static web pages. However, from the performance analyst's perspective, the risk of timeouts for static page requests under Linux is significantly larger than possible delays in the online monitoring under Windows. Hence, the performance analysts prefer the Windows Server 2003 system over Linux 2.6.

5.3. Discussion of Assumptions and Limitations

In the case study presented in the section above, we demonstrated the good prediction accuracy of MOSS. MOSS increases the accuracy of the predicted response times of the business reporting use case by several orders of magnitude compared to scheduling policies classically used in performance prediction. However, MOSS still requires several assumptions and simplifications to make multiprocessing environments predictable. In this section, we discuss the assumptions and limitations underlying MOSS.

No Memory Access In symmetric multiprocessing environments, different processors and cores may share common caches and memory buses. These contented low-level resources can become a limiting factor for the scalability of software applications. Therefore, the task's memory usage, the processor cache sizes, and the memory bus together determine the influence of memory access on software performance. Thus, the effect varies for different processor architectures. The first dual-core processors showed strong influences of concurrent memory access on software performance [HKR06]. The concurrent execution of memory intensive tasks could actually prolong task response times instead of reducing it. Even though today's multi-core processor architectures still show a similar effect, its influence on software performance has been strongly reduced [BDH08]. Current research in processor design is directed towards the optimisation of memory buses for concurrent memory access [AS01, IZG+07].

MOSS explicitly neglects contentions of the memory bus, varying memory access times, and caching effects. While these factors can have a large influence on software performance, the actual influence depends on the underlying processor architecture. Thus, we assume that memory access times are uniform (uniform memory access, UMA) and do not depend on the memory location. Consequently, we do not consider the influence of non-uniform memory access (NUMA) in MOSS. Furthermore, predicting the contention at the memory bus requires a behavioural model for tasks (such as RD-SEFFs, cf. Appendix A) that reflects the type and degree of memory access and keeps track of the data's location in memory. Modelling memory access requires much additional effort for the software architects, which cannot be justify by the small benefit for software performance prediction. With the rapid development of multi-core processors, contentions of the memory bus are likely to vanish or become marginal in the near future.

Focus on Symmetric Multiprocessing Environments MOSS has been designed for performance predictions in symmetric multiprocessing environments. Therefore, it assumes that all processors and cores in the evaluated system are similar with respect to their performance properties. MOSS cannot accurately predict performance in asymmetric multiprocessing environments such as IBM's cell processor [IBM]. In such processor architectures, a single main processor executes (parts of) the operating system and delegates work to other, specialised processors.

Furthermore, MOSS cannot predict the influence of simultaneous multi-threading (SMT, also called hyper-threading) on software performance. SMT systems allow multiple threads to run concurrently on a single processor utilising internal resources of the processor. Due to these shared internal resources, the influence of SMT processors on software performance is hard to estimate. In [BP04], Bulpin and Pratt evaluate the performance of different SPEC CPU2000 benchmarks on a Pentium 4 with hyper-threading. They systematically execute different combinations of benchmarks concurrently. The results show that the actual performance gain or loss caused by SMT technology strongly depends on the properties of the combined benchmarks. The observed effect ranges from a performance gain of more than 30% to a slowdown of more than 20%. Determining the relevant properties of a software application beforehand is nearly impossible for software architects. Thus, MOSS does not reflect the performance influences of SMT systems.

Simplified Model of Linux' Multiprocessor Load Balancing Policy Linux uses a hierarchical model that reflects the structure of the underlying hardware to make load balancing decisions. It uses different decision policies on each level of the hierarchy. The policies reflect the varying costs for moving tasks between the processors. The costs include the task's transfer itself as well as its dependencies to the local memory or any other resource. While MOSS reflects the decision policies of all layers, it does not model the hierarchical processor structure. Instead, it focusses on a single level of the hierarchy and treats all processors equally. This restriction is closely related to the focus on symmetric multiprocessing environments.

Furthermore, the results of the case study as well as the validation of MOSS prediction accuracy in Section 5.1.5 suggest that MOSS does not reflect all performance-relevant properties of Linux' multiprocessor load balancing policy. In general, the measurements show a more balanced load distribution than the predictions of MOSS. The effect can be caused by Linux load balancing policy as well as other scheduler features such as the interactivity policy or starvation prevention.

5.4. Summary

In this chapter, we have presented an extension of MOSS to symmetric multiprocessing environments. Similarly to Chapter 4, we have systematically evaluated the influences of multiprocessor load balancing on software performance. Furthermore, we have introduces a CPN model to address the performance-relevant factors identified in the evaluation.

A comparison between the results for the active-balancing policy and the results for the lazy-balancing policy implemented in the Linux and Windows schedulers shows that active-balancing leads to more evenly distributed load than lazy-balancing. As a consequence, response times show less variance under Linux than under Windows. However, the throughput and mean response times are similar for both systems in the scenarios that have been considered.

A closer examination of the results shows that not only load balancing itself influences the response time of the tasks, but the association of kernel- and user-level threads also plays a major role. For both systems, the association can change during execution. As soon as a user-level thread starts waiting, its kernel-level thread looks for a new task to execute for the remaining timeslice. Interestingly, this behaviour – an effect of the thread library used by Java – further reduces the variance of response times.

6. Message-based Communication

Details about the underlying Message-oriented Middleware (MOM) are essential for accurate performance predictions for software systems using message-based communication. The MOM's configuration and usage strongly influence its throughput, resource utilisation and timing behaviour. However, the inclusion of MOM in software architecture models requires additional effort as well as detailed knowledge of the infrastructure used. As a consequence, software architects might omit its influence. However, this can lead to erroneous or even misleading predictions. Detailed performance models for MOM (such as [LG05]) are difficult to apply for software architects, especially if they are not integrated into proper architecture description languages. Prediction models need to reflect these effects and allow software architects to evaluate the performance influence of MOM that has beed configured for their needs. In the context of the Palladio Component Model (PCM, cf. Appendix A), performance completions (cf. Section 2.1.4 or [WPS02, WW04, Bec08]) provide the general concept to include low-level details of execution environments into performance models.

In this chapter, we present a meta-model extension to the PCM for Message-oriented Middleware [HFBR08] using the concept of performance completions. Our performance completion for message-based communication integrates abstract descriptions for MOM based on messaging patterns [HW03] in software architecture models. The messaging completion allows software architects to specify message-based communication in a pattern-based language tailored to their vocabulary. The use of pattern-based configurations in combination with model transformations reduces the model complexity (from the software architect's perspective) and increases prediction accuracy. For performance evaluation, a model-to-model transformation integrates the low-level details of a MOM into software architecture models.

In a case study based on the SPECjms2007 Benchmark [SPE], we evaluate the prediction accuracy of the messaging completion. The benchmark models a typical supply chain management scenario of a supermarket. The case study evaluates three design alternatives with varying pattern selections for message based communication as well as varying message sizes. In the case study, predictions and measurements deviate less than 20%.

This chapter is structured as follows. Section 6.1 introduces the GQM plan for the performance evaluation of messaging patterns. In Section 6.2, we elaborate their influence on software performance and describe parametrisation of messaging completion. In Section 6.3, messaging completion is introduced to the PCM. In Section 6.4, we evaluate the prediction accuracy of the messaging completion in a case study. The assumptions and limitations of the messaging completion are discussed in Section 6.5. In Section 6.6, we summarise the main results of this chapter.

6.1. Performance Evaluation of Messaging Patterns

In this section, our goal is the identification of performance-relevant patterns for message-based communication. Analogously to Chapters 4 and 5, a detailed performance evaluation provides the information necessary to design a performance model for MOM. However, this section differs in several aspects from our previous evaluations:

- Message-oriented middleware has multiple dependencies between parameters (e.g., message sizes, number of message consumers, or number of messages in a transaction) and performance. The evaluation needs to study the influence of these parameters systematically.

- The evaluation targets the definition of a general performance model for MOM that does not depend on its underlying implementation and is sustainable for future implementations. Thus, the model is based on measurements and messaging patterns only.

- Different patterns can lead to different performance models (i.e., different behaviour of the MOM) or just affect the model's resource demands.

Due to the combination of models and measurements, it is necessary to determine resource demands for each execution environments independently. In Section 3.1.4, we already presented the general idea of parametric performance completions. We apply this concept for the design of the messaging completion. Before the performance prediction can take place, an automated test driver evaluates the resource demands of the specific MOM platform used. The results are added to the performance model skeletons defined in Section 6.3.

For the sake of brevity, this section is limited to the most relevant results of the evaluation. A full description of the evaluation that includes the implementation of the benchmark application and all results can be found in Holger Friedrich's master's thesis [Fri07].

The Goal

Goal:	*Purpose*	Identify
	Issue	the performance influence of MOM
	Object	for different messaging patterns
	Viewpoint	from the user's point of view.

Similar to the evaluation of GPOS schedulers, this evaluation should identify the performance-relevant features. However, in the case of MOM, the level of abstraction is considerably higher. Instead of looking at the implementation details of each MOM, we focus on the more general messaging patterns that are realised in most MOM platforms (e.g., most patterns can be found in the Java Message Service standard [HBS+08]). This abstraction is possible since the actual implementation of a pattern influences the MOM's resource demands but not its general behaviour. For GPOS schedulers, the resource demands of the scheduler are dispensable for software performance. Only its behaviour determines the response time and throughput of a software application. Thus, for MOM, it is sufficient to model the general behaviour as specified by the messaging patterns and determine the necessary resource demands by measurements.

Questions

MOM enables loosely-coupled components to communicate via the exchange of messages. The messaging patterns summarised in [HW03] structure the various implementation and configuration possibilities for message-based communication. They present standard solutions for different types of senders, receivers, and message channels. From these messaging patterns, the evaluation has to be focussed on those patterns useful in the context of Java Message Service [HBS+08, MHC02]. Furthermore, the performance model should contain only options that have an actual influence on performance or provide special features for message-based communication.

Therefore, the questions address the influence of each messaging pattern (described below), the combination of different patterns, and the influence of variable parameters, such as message sizes or the number of message consumers. For the sake of brevity, we only present the most relevant questions. All other questions are analogous. The performance metric for MOM used in the evaluation is the delivery time of a message, i.e., the time passed from sending a message until its processing starts (the `onMessage` method is executed).

1. How does *guaranteed delivery* influence the delivery time of a message?

2. How does an increasing *message size* influence the delivery time of a message?

3. How does an increasing *message size* influence the delivery time of a message with *guaranteed delivery*?

The first question addresses the influence of a single feature (guaranteed delivery) on the delivery time of a message. The pattern *guaranteed delivery* persistently stores messages before they are delivered to ensure their arrival even in the case of failures. Its performance influence is determined by comparing the delivery time of the same message with enabled/disabled guaranteed delivery. Depending on the results, the pattern's performance influence is classified.

The second question addresses the influence of message sizes. The delivery time is expected to grow with an increasing message size. This effect requires several measurements for different message sizes. It is important to notice that the delivery time is unlikely to grow linearly with an increasing message size due to the general overhead of the transmitted message and due to packet sizes of the network.

The third question targets the mutual dependency of two different influencing factors. For an efficient evaluation of all parameter combinations, a k-factorial analysis [Jai91] allows to determine the mutual influences of various parameters with a minimum set of experiments.

6.2. The Performance Influence of Messaging Patterns

Messaging Pattern	Influence Factor			
	~0	< 0.1	<= 1.0	> 1.0
Point-to-Point	x			
Publish-Subscribe	(x)			
Guranteed-Delivery			x	
Idempotent-Receiver	x			
Selective Consumer		x		
Transactional Client				x
Durable Subscriber			x	
Competing Consumer				x
Message Size				x
Remote Receiver/MOM				x

Table 6.1.: Messaging patterns and features categorised according to their performance influence.

In this section, we describe the evaluation results for all message patterns for the JMS implementation Sun Java System Message Queue 3.6 conducted within a master's thesis [Fri07]. Table 6.1 lists the resulting classification for the evaluated messaging patterns. We distinguish features without performance influence (mean delivery time not changed), features with a small influence (below 10%), features with a moderate influence (between 10% and 100% change of mean delivery time), and features with a large influence (more than 100% change of mean delivery time). For the last category, all of its features depend on input parameters, e.g., message size, number of messages in a transaction, or number of compet-

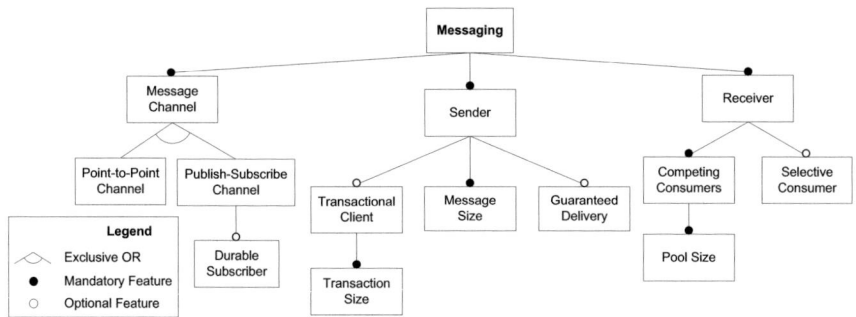

Figure 6.1.: Feature diagram of the relevant messaging patterns.

ing consumers. A benchmark application measured the *delivery time* for each messaging pattern. The results of the benchmark form the basis for the pattern selection presented in Figure 6.1. In the feature diagram, we distinguish patterns for message channels, receivers, and senders. In the following, we explain the patterns and their performance influences in more detail.

Message channels   *Message channels* are logical connections between communicating components. They can be considered as queues. While *point-to-point* channels only allow a single receiver for messages, multiple receivers can subscribe to *publish-subscribe* channels. Optionally, a receiver can *durably subscribe* to the latter. In this case, the MOM keeps all published messages until they can be delivered if a receiver disconnects from a messaging channel.

The influence of multiple receivers on performance is not considered in this thesis (see Section 6.5 for a discussion). For a single receiver, the choice between publish-subscribe and point-to-point channels has no considerable effect on the delivery time. However, this distinction is necessary for modelling multiple receivers and, thus, is included in the model. Furthermore, durable subscription leads to longer delivery times even if the receiver always stays connected.

Senders   *Senders* add messages to a message channel. The sender of a message determines its size, transaction boundaries, and type of delivery. The *message size* depends on the data that needs to be transferred from the sender to the receiver. A message is a simple data structure containing a header and a body. However, message size refers only to the body of a message neglecting the influence of possible overheads in the message, such as its header. To *guarantee the delivery* of a message, the MOM stores messages persistently during their transfer. The implementation of the MOM determines how the message is stored, for example, using a database or file system. Stored messages can survive system crashes and, if possible, are delivered after a restart. A *transactional client* sends one or multiple messages as a single transaction. The transaction boundaries are specified by the sender.

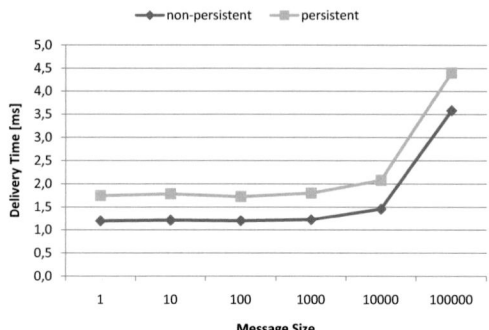

(a) Persistent vs. non-persistent message transfer.

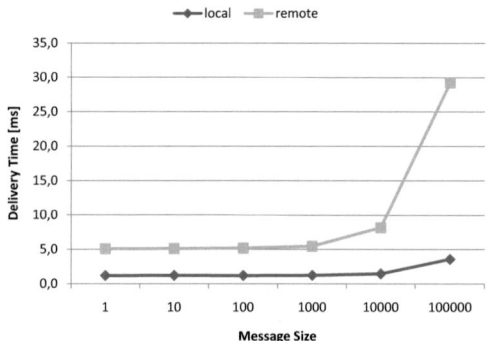

(b) Local vs. remote message transfer.

Figure 6.2.: The influence of message size on the delivery time.

The size of a message significantly influences its delivery time. Figure 6.2 illustrates this effect. With an increasing message size the delivery time of a message increases as well. While the slope of the curves is rather small for short messages, its impact grows for messages larger than 10000 bytes. The influence of the message size strongly depends on the evaluated platform. For the evaluated system in Figure 6.2, the message size influences the delivery time, but its effect is limited. However, its influence becomes clearly visible for the system depicted in Figure 6.5.

For guaranteed delivery (Figure 6.2(a)), the access to additional resources, e.g., the hard disk, leads to longer delivery times. Compared to the delivery time without guaranteed delivery, Figure 6.2(a) yields a factor of approximately 25% for its increase. If the MOM or the message receiver is deployed on a remote machine, the necessary transfer over the network further delays the delivery of a message (Figure 6.2(b)). The network's influence is much larger and cannot be captured by a single factor. For transactional clients, the

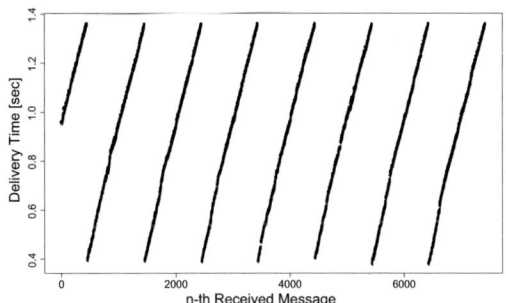

Figure 6.3.: Delivery time of messages in a transaction set with 1000 messages.

delivery time of a message strongly depends on the number of messages in a transaction and the message's position in the transaction set. The delivery time increases linearly with the message's position in the transaction set (see Figure 6.3) The MOM stores all messages until it receives the last message of a transaction set and then executes the message sequentially. Since the generation of a message is much faster than its processing, successive tasks exceed the accounted waiting time of the first message (0.4 seconds). The sequential processing of messages leads to the observed linearly increasing delivery times.

Receivers   *Receivers* remove messages from a message channel. They can employ multiple, *competing consumers* to process incoming messages concurrently. The consumers wait for incoming messages. When a message arrives, it is processed by the next waiting consumer. If no consumer is available, messages queue up until a consumer finishes processing its current message. Furthermore, message receivers can filter messages delivered via its subscribed channels. These *selective consumers* only accept messages, which match their filter criteria.

Competing consumers can have a large impact on performance. If too few consumers are available, congestion is likely and will lead to long delivery times. For example, if messages are received and processed sequentially by a single consumer, the consumer can easily become a bottleneck leading to congestion on receiver side. In Figure 6.4(a), a single consumer processes all incoming messages. However, it cannot keep pace with the arriving

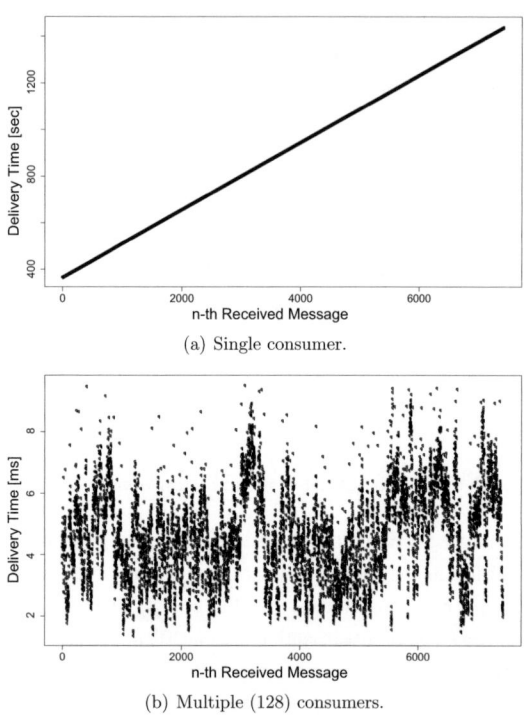

(a) Single consumer.

(b) Multiple (128) consumers.

Figure 6.4.: The effect of competing consumers on delivery time.

messages. Message delivery times increase constantly up to 1400 seconds. When multiple consumers are used to processing the same load (Figure 6.4(b)), the system can maintain the pace of message arrivals and yields acceptable message delivery times of less than 10 ms. Thus, multiple competing consumers can avoid congestion on the receiver end.

The influence of selective consumers depends on the complexity of the filters used. For their simple filters considered in this evaluation, the influence on delivery times was marginal.

In the next section, we describe how parameter dependent resource demands can be derived from measurements and be included in the performance completion.

Parameter Dependent Resource Demands

The size of a message's content strongly influences its delivery time. With an increasing message size, the usage of resources increases. Figure 6.5 shows how the message size affects the average delivery time. Here, the sender, receiver, and MOM are deployed on the same machine. A single regression analysis [Fre05] over the measured times yields the linear function in Figure 6.5(a). While the approximation is good for large messages, it largely deviates for small ones. To achieve better prediction results, multiple regression functions are necessary: One for messages smaller than 1000 bytes and one for messages larger than 1000 bytes. The more fine grained approximations yields the curve shown in Figure 6.5(b) and reduces the estimation error to 5% – 30%.

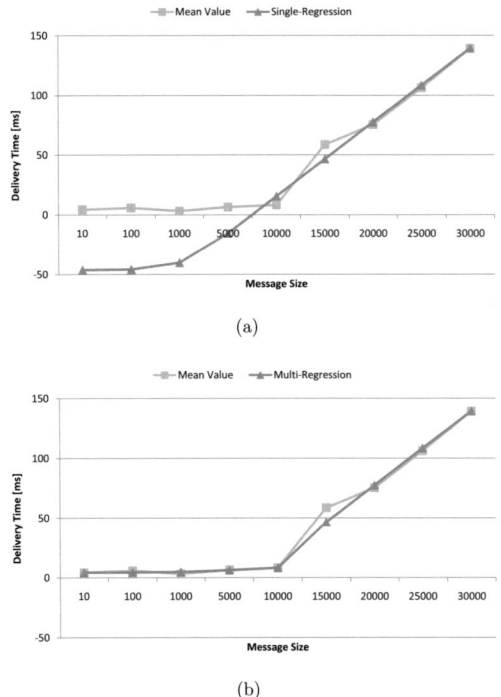

(a)

(b)

Figure 6.5.: Regression analysis for different message sizes.

In the PCM, stochastic expressions [BKR07, RBH+07] reflect the influence of different parameters on software performance and, thus, can model resource demands depending on messages sizes. Stochastic expressions support basic arithmetic operations on probability

distributions and parameters (cf. Appendix A). For example, the average delivery time of
messages larger than 1000 bytes can be computed by a linear function with a slope of 0.02
and a y-intercept of -32.8 yielding the following stochastic expression:

```
0.02 * message.BYTESIZE - 32.8
```

In the prediction model, a branch condition selects the correct regression for a specific
message size. The stochastic expressions resulting from the regression analysis are integrated
in the messaging completion described in the following.

6.3. PCM Completion Models

The messaging completion takes into account the patterns described in Section 6.1 together
with message sizes and the allocation of the MOM. An annotation model allows software architects to easily choose among different design alternatives regarding the messaging service.
Completion components realise the performance-relevant messaging patterns.

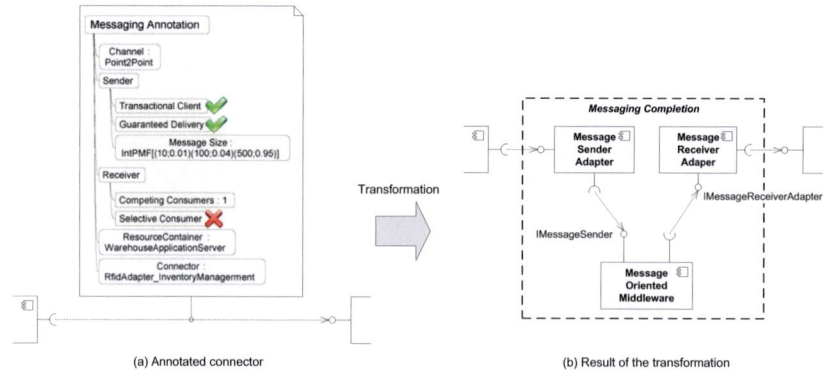

(a) Annotated connector   (b) Result of the transformation

Figure 6.6.: Replacement of an annotated connector by completion components.

Messaging Annotation Model Message-based communication affects the connectors between components in the software architecture. An *annotation model* allows to select and
customising connectors for message-based communication. Figure 6.6(a) shows an example
for a messaging annotation. The annotation references a connector between two communicating components. The possible configurations are defined by the feature diagram in
Figure 6.1. In the example, we configured the communication between the components as

a point-to-point channel. The transfer of messages is transactional and messages are stored persistently during the transaction (guaranteed delivery). The message size is specified by a probability mass function over the domain of integers. With a probability of 0.01 the message size is 10 bytes, with a probability of 0.04, 100 bytes, and with a probability of 0.95, 500 bytes. The receiver uses a single consumer to process messages and does not filter the incoming messages.

In addition to the options shown in the feature diagram, the annotation contains a reference to a connector and a resource container where the MOM is deployed. In the example, the annotation references the connector with identifier `RfidAdapter_InventoryManagement` and the resource container with identifier `WarehouseApplicationServer`. As shown in figure 6.6, a transformation replaces annotated connectors by completion components, which are described in the following.

6.3.1. Messaging Completion Components

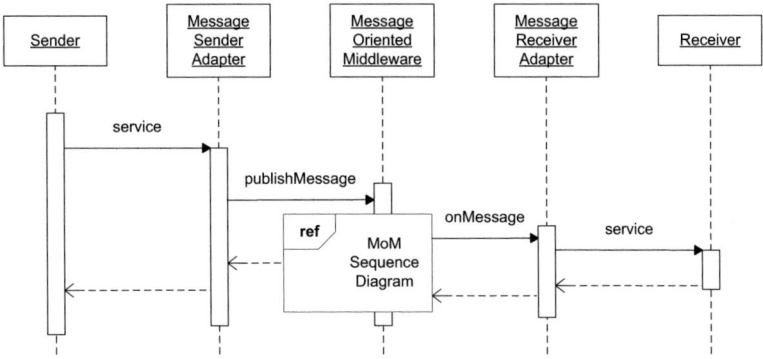

Figure 6.7.: Interactions of the messaging completion components.

Figure 6.6(b) and 6.7 show the components generated by the transformation as well as their interactions. The transformation selects a platform-specific `MOM component` corresponding to the configuration of the messaging annotation. Furthermore, it generates the adapters necessary to hide the message-based communication from the sender and receiver.

A `MessageSenderAdapter` provides the same interface as required by the sender. When the sender calls a service on this interface, the adapter generates a message of the size specified in the annotation model and starts the message transfer by calling `publishMessage`. As soon as the message has been added to its channel, the control flow returns and allows the sender to continue its execution.

The MOM component loads the CPU and hard disk of its resource container with
the resource demands caused by the message. Then, it forwards the call to the
MessageReceiverAdapter, which hides the messaging service from the called component.
Its onMessage method calls the corresponding service on the receiver component.

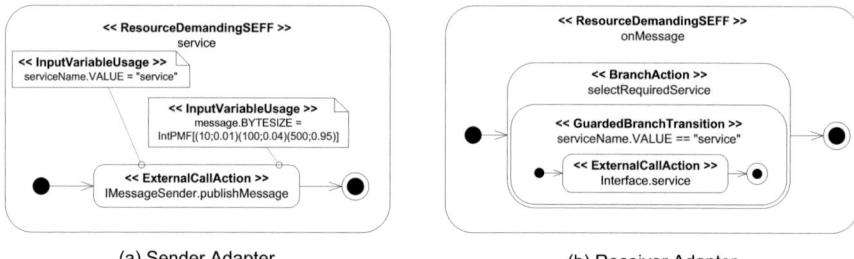

(a) Sender Adapter   (b) Receiver Adapter

Figure 6.8.: Behavioural specification for the completion's basic components.

In the PCM model of the messaging completion, RD-SEFFs specify the communication
and resource demands of the components. Furthermore, they model the data flow between
the components. Figure 6.8 shows the RD-SEFFs of the sender and receiver adapters.
Since an interface can contain multiple services, the sender adapter (Fig. 6.8(a)) needs to
pass a unique identifier of the called service. Furthermore, it sets the size of the message according to the size specified in the annotation model. The ExternalCallAction
of service publishMessage passes this information to the MOM Component with two
InputVariableUsages. The first sets the value of parameter calledService to the service's name, which is assumed to be unique.

The receiver adapter uses this parameter in its onMessage method (Figure 6.8(b))
to identify the service addressed by the message. The BranchAction contains a
GuardedBranchTransition for each available service. If the serviceName's value complies
with the identifier specified in the condition, then the transition calls the selected service.
The second InputVariableUsage of the sender adapter sets the size of the message. The
MOM component uses this value to determine the resource demand for delivering the message. The size of a message can be a probabilistic distribution over different message sizes
as shown in Figure 6.6(a).

MOM Completion Components

The component `MessageOrientedMiddleware` decouples the receiving process from the sending process and generates resource demands according to its configuration. Figure 6.9 shows its internal structure and the interaction of its subcomponents.

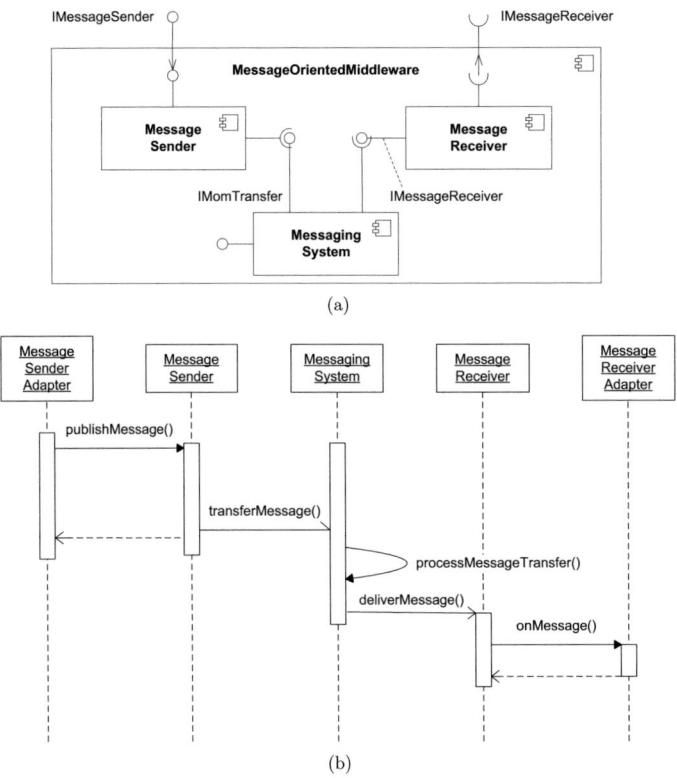

Figure 6.9.: Subcomponents of the `MessageOrientedMiddleware` component and their interactions.

Component `MessageSender` asynchronously invokes service `transferMessage` on the `MessagingSystem`. This decouples the delivery of a message from the sender process. After internally processing the message transfer, the `MessagingSystem` asynchronously calls the service `deliverMessage` of the `MessageReceiver`. Figure 6.10(a) shows its RD-SEFF. The transfer of a message starts with an `InternalAction`, which represents the internal processing of the `MessagingSystem`. The resource demand of this action is a stochastic expression, whose resource demand increases with the message size (cf. Section 6.2). The whole resource demand is assigned to a single resource (instead of hard disk drive, memory, and processor), which does not reflect the actual load distribution in distributed scenarios (discussion in Section 6.5). When the internal processing finishes, a `ForkAction` starts a new thread which calls service `deliverMessage`. As the property `synchronize` is set to `false` the execution of `transferMessage` continues immediately and does not wait for the `ForkActions` behaviour to finish. This models the asynchronous call of `deliverMessage` in the PCM.

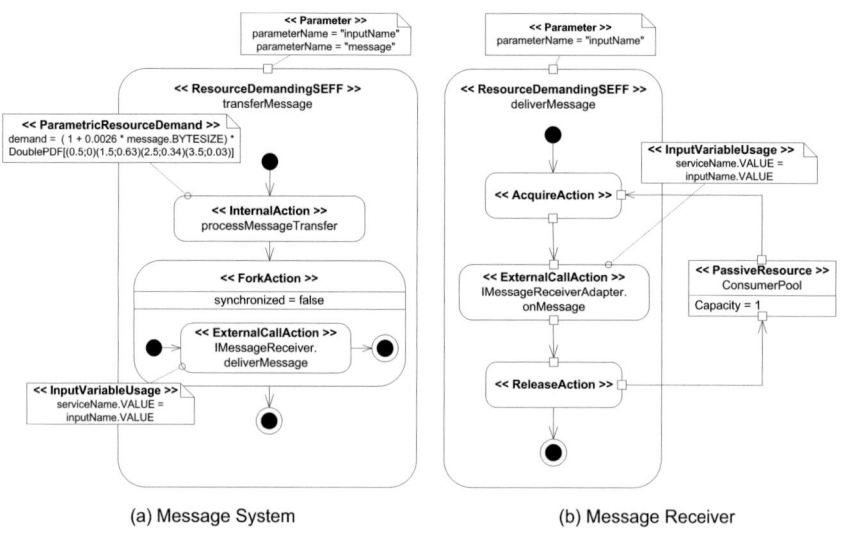

(a) Message System   (b) Message Receiver

Figure 6.10.: Behavioural specification for the MOM-model's basic components.

Next, `deliverMessage` calls the `onMessage` service of the `MessageReceiverAdapter`. Its RD-SEFF (Fig. 6.10(b)) models the influence of competing consumers. The passive resource `ConsumerPool` contains the maximum number of competing consumers specified in the annotation model. Before calling `onMessage`, the method acquires one of the consumers from the pool. `AcquireAction` blocks until a consumer becomes available. When the processing of `onMessage` finishes, the `ReleaseAction` returns the consumer to the pool. This limits the number of concurrently processed messages.

6.3.2. Transformation

An in-place model-to-model transformation [(OM07a] integrates the messaging completion components into the architecture model. Following the scheme of a Y-transformation, it takes as input a PCM instance (software architecture model) and an instance of the messaging annotation model. The latter references a connector in the software architecture model which needs to be replaced. The transformation is implemented in plain Java code. Both models are specified in Ecore, the meta-modelling language of the Eclipse Modelling Framework[1] (EMF).

The transformation (1) generates adapter components for the sender and receiver, (2) selects a MOM component for the annotated configuration, (3) connects the new components to the sender and receiver, and finally (4) allocates the new components to its resource containers. See [Fri07] for a more detailed description of the transformation.

6.4. Case Study

In this section, present a case study that evaluates the prediction quality of the messaging completion described in Section 6.3. A comparison between predictions based on architectural specifications and measurements of an implementation gives an impression of the prediction accuracy on messaging completion. The case study is based on the SPECjms2007 Benchmark [SPE, SKCB07, SKBB07] and is focussed on the influence of the MOM on performance. Since the messaging completion should support early design decisions, the case study evaluates three design alternatives for one of the benchmark's interactions. The case study should answer the question: Are the predictions of our messaging completion good enough to support design decisions and to identify the MOM configuration with the best actual performance?

The SPECjms2007 Benchmark [SPE, SKCB07, SKBB07] provides suitable scenarios for the case study. It is a standard industry benchmark for performance analyses of JMS developed by SPEC's OSG-Java subcommitee (including IBM, TU Darmstadt, Sun, Sybase, BEA, Apache, Oracle, and JBoss). SPECjms2007 reflects the way messaging services are used in real-live systems including the communication style, the types of messages, and the transaction mix. Furthermore, it is focussed on the influence of the MOM's implementation and configuration. The benchmark minimises the impact of other components and services that are typically used in the chosen application scenario. For example, the database used to store business data and manage the application state could be easily become the limiting factor of the benchmark and, thus, is not represented in the benchmark. This design allows

---

[1]http://www.eclipse.org/modeling/emf/

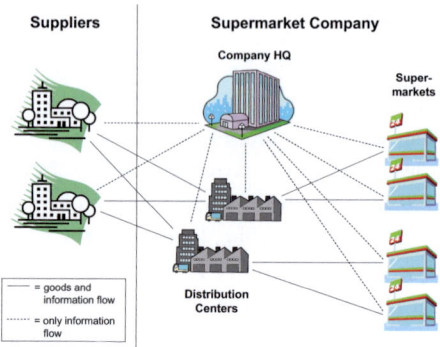

Figure 6.11.: Overview of the interactions of the supermarket supply chain [SKBB07].

us to focus our evaluation on the influences of the MOM without possible disturbances of other infrastructure components.

The SPECjms2007 Benchmark resembles a typical scenario of the supply chain management domain. It models a set of supply chain interactions between a supermarket company, its stores, its distribution centres, and its suppliers (Figure 6.11). In the following, we describe the involved parties, their responsibilities, and a business reporting use case for the company headquarters.

The *company headquarters* are responsible for managing the accounting of the company. This includes managing information about goods and products offered in the supermarkets like their selling prices. HQ monitors the flow of goods and money in the supply chain. *Distribution centres* supply goods to supermarket stores in a given area. They take orders from supermarkets and deliver goods on demand. In addition, they order goods from external suppliers and provide statistical data to HQ for data mining. *Supermarkets* sell goods to consumers and manage the inventory of their warehouses. The different supermarket stores vary in size and range of products. Some supermarkets do not have enough room for all products and, thus, have to order goods on demand. Other supermarkets are specialised for some product groups (e.g., food). A supermarket receives its goods always from a single distribution centre. Finally, external *suppliers* deliver goods to distribution centres. Each supplier offers different groups of products and has its own product catalogue. Suppliers deliver goods on demand.

The case study is focussed on the inventory management of a supermarket. *Inventory management* is necessary when goods leave the warehouse of a supermarket, to refill a shelf. RFID readers register goods leaving the warehouse and notify the local warehouse application, which updates its inventory.

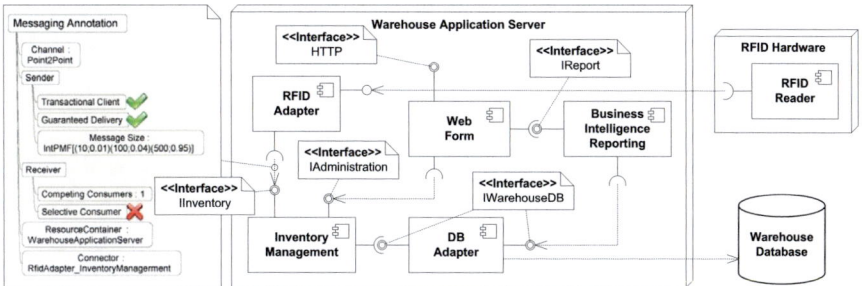

Figure 6.12.: Architecture of the warehouse application.

Architecture of the Warehouse Application   Figure 6.12 shows the static architecture of the warehouse application. A hardware `RFID Reader` is directly connected to the `Warehouse Application Server`. An `RFID Adapter` component manages the connection to the RFID reader. It converts and forwards the read data to the `Inventory Management`. A `Messaging Annotation` configures the connector between the `Inventory Management` and the `RFID Adapter` as persistent and transactional messaging channel. The message service allows `RFID Adapter` to quickly accept new requests from the `RFID Reader` as it will not block its execution. Persistency ensures that no inventory update is lost in case of failures. When notified, the `Inventory Management` updates the inventory data using the `DB Adapter` component.

Usually, many goods leave the warehouse at once, e.g., an employee brings a lorry with goods into the supermarket to refill the shelves. In this case, the RFID reader sends many messages in a short time period. Experts estimate the number of messages up to 100 in a second. The software architect now wants to know whether such a high load can be handled by the Message-oriented-Middleware. In addition, it needs to be ensured that the warehouse application itself is not affected.

Design Alternatives   The software architect considers three design alternatives of the warehouse application (Table 6.2). The original architecture (alternative 1, Persistent) sends the complete data, i.e., `message.BYTESIZE = Full` from the `RFID Reader` to the `Inventory Management`. Alternative 2 (Non-Persistent) uses a reconfigured message service, since persistency and transactionality might produce too many overheads. However, turning both off carries the risk of loosing messages in case of failures, but might solve possible performance problems. Alternative 3 (Small) reduces the message sizes. Instead of transmitting all data kept on an RFID chip to the inventory management, the message could be limited to a single product identifier. This strategy reduces the message size, but also requires changes

	Alternative	Arrival Rate	Message Size	Configuration
1.	Persistent	100	Full	Persistent, Transacted
2.	Non-Persistent	100	Full	
3.	Small	100	Identifier	Persistent, Transacted

$$\texttt{Full} := \texttt{IntPMF[(10;0.01)(100;0.04)(500;0.95)]}$$
$$\texttt{Identifier} := \texttt{IntPMF[(10;0.95)(100;0.04)(500;0.01)]}$$

Table 6.2.: Design alternatives.

of the **Inventory Management** component. Thus, this alternative should only be considered if really necessary.

To make a decision, the software architect defines performance requirements for the warehouse application. The RFID reader should not affect the rest of the application too much, so it should not utilise the system more than 50%, which enables the other components to keep working properly. Furthermore, the system must be able to handle 100 RFID reads per second, which is the expected maximum number of goods taken out of the warehouse at once. Finally, the delivery time of a message must not exceed 1 second in 90% of all cases.

Results A simulation of the model for each alternative predicted the delivery times and CPU utilisations. Each simulation run lasted 5 minutes and simulated the delivery of over one million messages. A warm-up period of the first 2500 measurements was not included in the prediction results.

The measurements were conducted with the SPECjms2007 Benchmark version 1.0. The benchmark was deployed on a single machine, to focus on the effects of message sizes and the message service's configuration. Sun's Java System Message Queue 3.6 provided the necessary infrastructure for the measurements. During the measurement period, the benchmark executed only the inventory movement interaction. The upper 5% of measured values were removed, to exclude disturbances from the results. All other interactions were disabled and, thus, not considered in the case study. A warm-up period of 10 minutes preceded the measurement period of 30 minutes.

Figure 6.13 summarises the predictions and measurements for the three design alternatives. It shows the average and percentile 90% of the delivery time as well as the CPU utilisation. Measured values are printed in dark grey, predicted values in light grey. The prediction error for the average delivery time (Fig. 6.13(a)) as well as the percentile 90% (Fig. 6.13(b)) is below 15% in all cases. The messaging completion predicts the CPU utilisation (Fig. 6.13(c)) with an error below 2% for design alternatives 1 (Persistent) and 2 (Non-Persistent). For alternative 3 (Small), the prediction error is nearly 20%. In the scenarios considered, the usage of persistent message transfer has a major influence on the delivery time of a message. While the measured and predicted average delivery times for alternative 2 (Non-Persistent)

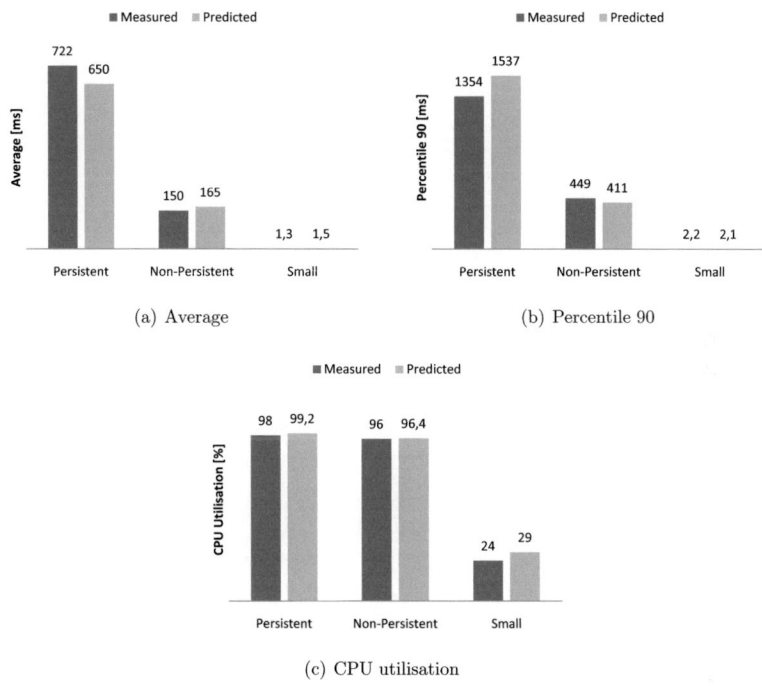

(a) Average   (b) Percentile 90

(c) CPU utilisation

Figure 6.13.: Predictions and measurements of the three design alternatives.

are 150 ms and 165 ms, respectively, they are 722 ms and 650 ms for alternative 1 (Persistent). The percentile 90% of the latter exceeds the upper bound of 1 second. The delivery time for measurements is 1354 ms and for the prediction 1537 ms.

To allow a visual comparison, Figure 6.14 shows the cumulative distribution function (cdf) of the predicted and measured delivery times for design alternative 2 (Non-Persistent). The measured time is printed in dark grey and the predicted time in light grey. Both functions match to a large extent. The model predicted that 90% of all messages are delivered in less than 411 ms. This estimate is confirmed by the measurements, where 90% of all messages are delivered in less than 449 ms. In this case, the prediction error is 8.5%. However, the predicted and measured CPU utilisation (Figure 6.13(c)) of about 96% for alternative 2 exceed the required maximum utilisation of 50%.

Alternative 3 (Small) shows the best performance. Its measured and predicted delivery times are much smaller than for the other alternatives. For example, 90% of all messages are

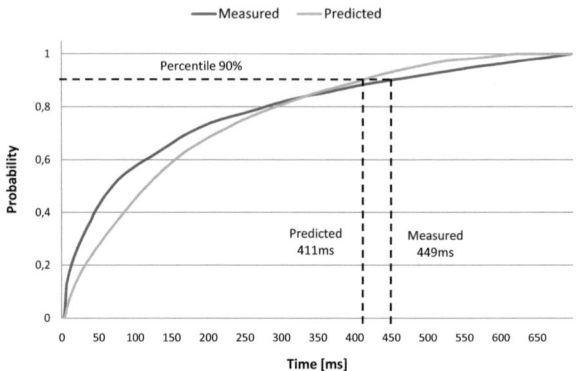

Figure 6.14.: Delivery time of alternative 2 (cdf).

delivered in less than 2.2 ms (measured) and 2.1 ms (predicted). The measured and predicted CPU utilisation is in the range of 24% and 29% and, thus, below the required upper bound of 50%. Alternative 3 is the best choice for the software architect with respect to performance. Coming back to the question posed in the beginning of this section, messaging completion can correctly rank different design alternatives concerning message services. It can predict the delivery time of messages with an error of less than 15% and the resource utilisation with an error less than 20%. In the following section, we discuss the results of the case study as well as the design of the messaging completion.

6.5. Discussion of Assumptions and Limitations

Case Study   The case study in section 6.4 demonstrated the prediction accuracy of the messaging completion. The different configurations of alternative 1 and 2 significantly influence performance. Furthermore, the delivery time of a message strongly depends on its size. Especially in highly loaded systems, different message sizes can change the delivery time by several orders of magnitude. Therefore, the MOM's configuration as well as message sizes are important factors for performance of systems using message-based communication.

The case study showed that predictions and measurements can deviate up to 20%. This deviation is mainly caused by the abstraction of the model compared to a real system. In the model, demands to multiple resources, e.g., processor, hard disk, and network, are summarised into a single resource demand. Furthermore, the model does not represent the actual arrival rates of messages in the benchmark. The benchmark tries to achieve the specified rate of messages. However, if the system is overloaded, the benchmark reduces the pace, since the workload driver does not get enough processing time. The approximation of the resource demands by linear regression introduces another abstraction to the model. Therefore, the uncontended resource demands derived from a linear function already deviate from the demands in a real system.

Measurement-based Model The resource demands of the completion's internal actions are based on measurements. To predict the performance of a MOM system on different hardware platforms, it is necessary to re-execute the benchmark application for each platform in order to determine its resource demands. If the target platform is available, then it is no longer a problem. However, the necessary hardware might not be available if the performance of an application should be evaluated during early development stages.

Relying on measurements of time consumption leads to further challenges. The MOM might access different resources during the measured period. For example, a persistent message channel will access the hard drive. Measuring the whole period makes it challenging to assign the correct load to single resources, but requires to assign all load to a single resource. This simplification can lead to false predictions if another resource than the loaded one becomes a bottleneck. Here, detailed measurements for each resource are needed.

Not only the assignment of load to different resources is challenging, but also the allocation of load to involved components is difficult. Since the MOM is considered as a black box, its internal time consumptions cannot be measured. Thus, the proper load of the sender, receiver, and MOM components cannot be determined. Instead, all load is assigned to the MOM. It might be possible to measure the time consumption of each component for open source MOM implementations. However, such an approach would impose a lot of effort and would be limited to open source systems.

Limitations of the Messaging Completion While constructing the performance completion for message oriented middleware, several assumptions and simplifications were necessary.

The type of a message (Object, Map, or Text) might influence its delivery time. The MOM completion does not reflect this effect and is focussed on text messages with varying sizes. The delivery time of object messages and map messages may depend on the object that is send. To include such effects on performance, the messaging completion can be combined with a marshalling completion developed by Becker [Bec08]. Most of the additional resource consumption will be produced by the marshalling and demarshalling of messages. Using an already evaluated marshalling completion would easily allow to predict the performance of other message types.

In the description of the SPECjms2007 Benchmark, Kounev and Sachs [SKBB07] distinguish horizontal and vertical scaling. For horizontal scaling, the number of receivers for a message is varied, while for vertical scaling the number of messages in the system is varied. As demonstrated in the case study presented in Section 6.4, messaging completions can successfully predict the influence of additional messages in the system. The influence of additional message receivers can however only be predicted with limited accuracy.

Furthermore, the model does not consider service parameters. So, software architects need to specify the size of a message in the annotation model. Ideally, the specification should be derived automatically from the parameters of a service. A similar problem is the forwarding of parameter characterisations from the sender to the receiver. Forwarding of parameters is not supported by current messaging completion.

6.6. Summary

In this chapter, we have presented a performance completion for Message-oriented Middleware. The completion is customisable for different messaging patterns, like publish-subscribe or competing consumers. Messaging annotations allow software architects to specify message-based communication in software architecture models in a language specific to their domain. An in-place model-to-model transformation generates components, which represent the MOM as well as adapters for the communication components. The behaviour of generated components reflects the configuration of the MOM. Parameter dependencies model the influence of varying message sizes on performance. The MOM is treated as a black box. This approach makes the model independent of the MOM's actual implementation, but requires to initially measure the performance of the MOM. The measurements determine the resource demands of messaging completion. Regression analysis approximates the influence of message sizes on resource demands. A case study based on the SPECjms2007 Benchmark has demonstrated the prediction quality of messaging completion. For the three design alternatives: Persistent, Non-Persistent, and Small, the delivery time of a message was predicted with an error less than 15%. The predictions of the CPU utilisation showed an error of at most 20%.

The messaging completion supports software architects to predict the influence of message services on the performance of their applications. The messaging annotations for the PCM hide the underlying complexity and allow an easy integration of different message services.

7. Related Work

In this chapter, we summarise the state-of-the-art of software performance evaluation with respect to scheduling. In Section 7.1, we discuss recent analytical solutions for queueing models with various scheduling policies and their implications for software performance. From a more practical perspective, we present measurements and prediction results for specific features of general purpose operating systems in Section 7.2. Furthermore, we provide an overview of the existing work on scheduling in real-time systems and high performance computing. In Section 7.3, we outline approaches that integrate infrastructure performance models into architectural specifications.

7.1. Performance Evaluation of Scheduling Policies in Queueing Theory

A significant part of ongoing work in the area of queueing theory is devoted to assessment and evaluation of performance influences of different scheduling policies. The overall aim of this work is the identification of optimal scheduling policies with respect to mean response time, fairness, and resource utilisation. In the following, we describe the current research for single-server (Section 7.1.1) and multi-server queues (Section 7.1.2).

7.1.1. Performance Properties of Scheduling Policies in Single-Server Queues

Advanced policies for single-server systems prefer shorter jobs over longer ones or extend processor sharing with priorities and job classes. Such policies can provide an initial approximation of specific features of GPOS schedulers, like their preference of I/O-bound and interactive tasks or task priorities. In the following, we discuss the performance influences of policies which are biased towards small jobs. Furthermore, we describe recent results regarding their fairness properties compared to other scheduling policies. Finally, we summarise existing work on performance evaluation with extended processor sharing.

Bias Towards Small Jobs   Wierman et al. [WHBO05] introduced a class of scheduling policies called SMART policies, which are biased towards jobs with small sizes. Such scheduling policies promise better interactivity and responsiveness for desktop and server systems. Thus, these polices can approximate the behaviour of GPOS schedulers which prefer interactive and I/O-bound tasks over compute-bound ones. SMART policies subsume the well known Shortest Remaining Processing Time (SRPT) [Sch68] and Preemptive Shortest Job First (PSJF) policies. If the job sizes are not known, Least-Attained-Service (LAS, also known as feedback scheduling) is typically used to approximate SRPT [YWSHB06]. LAS prioritises jobs with a short life span (little attained service) so that short jobs (which always have little attained service) tend to have the server for themselves. If several jobs received the same service, they share the processor via PS.

Yang et al. [YWSHB06] have shown that the mean delay of any SMART policy is near optimal under all service distributions. Furthermore, they have proved that all SMART policies have the same response time distribution as SRPT, which is well-known to be optimal for mean delays [Sch68]. Additionally, they have come to the conclusion that the delay distribution of SMART policies improves upon the delay distribution of LAS. However, LAS still provides an improvement over FCFS for most job sizes [YWSHB06] and over PS for specific job size distributions [WBHB03].

The applicability LAS and SMART policies has been evaluated in empirical studies. Harchol-Balter and Schroeder [HBSBA03, SHB02] compared the performance of a webserver under a fair scheduling policy and a variant of SRPT. They found that the performance can be dramatically improved for short jobs using SRPT. In their experiments, long jobs experienced only negligibly higher response times. Inspired by the use of SRPT for webservers, Rawat and Kshemkalyani [RK03] introduced the so called SWIFT scheduling policy for web servers. Additionally to the job size, SWIFT considers the network and server characteristics. Taking these effects into account, the SWIFT scheduling policy can improve response times of long jobs by additional 2.5% to 10%.

Fairness   Scheduling policies which are biased towards small jobs optimise mean response times. However, SMART policies tend not to be used in practice due to their expected unfairness. This trade-off also occurs for age based policies such as LAS. Wierman and Harchol-Balter [WHB03] address the question of fairness for different scheduling policies and classify them accordingly. They define three classes of fairness: Always fair, sometimes fair, and always unfair (cf. Table 7.1). Based on a formal definition of the fairness classes, they show that SRPT (being an instance of the SMART policies) is only unfair under certain service time distributions and under certain load distributions. Interestingly, LAS (being an approximation of SMART policies) is classified as always unfair, since it disproportionately penalises long jobs independently of service times and load distributions.

Name	Description	Policies
Always Fair	Policies that are fair under all load and all service distributions	Processor Sharing, Preemptive Last Come First Serve
Sometimes Fair	Policies that are unfair for some load and some service distributions, but are fair under other loads and other service distributions	Shortest Remaining Processing Time, Shortest Job First
Always Unfair	Policies that are unfair under all load and all service distributions	First Come First Served, Least Attained Service, Preemptive Shortest Job First

Table 7.1.: Fairness classification of scheduling policies [WHB03].

Beyond Processor Sharing   Processor sharing is commonly used in software performance evaluation to approximate the behaviour GPOS schedulers. However, PS does not consider the performance influence of priorities and different classes of tasks (or jobs). To predict such influences, extended processor sharing policies have been introduced (surveyed by [AAB+07]). These policies can discriminate different job classes and assign different service-levels to jobs depending on their class. Common extensions to processor sharing are **D**iscriminatory **P**rocessor **S**haring (DPS), **G**eneralised **P**rocessor **S**haring (GPS), and **M**ultilevel **P**rocessor **S**haring (MLPS) explained below.

DPS assigns a positive weight factor to each job class. The service capacity is shared among all jobs present in proportion to the respective class-dependent weights. Therefore, DPS can be used to abstractly model the behaviour of Linux' run queue. Linux uses priority-dependent timeslice sizes that can be approximated by DPS weights.

Unlike DPS, GPS uses class-dependent weights to share the service capacity among all non-empty classes (i.e., classes that currently have jobs waiting). It does not consider the actual number of jobs present for a class. Thus, all jobs of one class share the capacity assigned to their class. This policy guarantees a minimum capacity to each class and isolates competing classes. GPS is mostly used in telecommunications to reflect the behaviour of routers with shared bandwidth.

Finally, MLPS exploits the variability in service demands to improve the overall system performance. It gives precedence to shorter requests over longer ones. It assigns arriving jobs to classes based on their service time. Within a class, jobs are served by ordinary PS policy. Therefore, MLPS is an approximation of simple multi-level feedback queue schedulers.

Discussion   The analytical solutions for queueing networks with generally distributed service times are becoming increasingly powerful. However, they are still limited to simple scheduling policies that do not reflect the complexity of GPOS schedulers.

Policies that are biased towards small jobs (SMART policies) provide the best mean response times when job sizes are known a priori. These policies are not as unfair as expected. However, job sizes cannot be known a priori in GPOS. Furthermore, tasks use processors as well as other resources alternately so that the same task enters and leaves a processor's queue several times during its lifetime. Some GPOS schedulers (such as the O(1) and CFS implemented in Linux 2.6) consider the task's past waiting and processing times in order to make good scheduling decisions. Therefore, models that only consider the duration of a job are not sufficient for performance prediction.

The implementations of GPOS schedulers, such as the Windows and Linux operating system series, are based on MLFQ to prefer I/O-bound and interactive tasks. The dynamic priority of a task decreases with the time a task spends computing. However, the priority decay depends on the scheduling policy and significantly determines the share of processing time received by a task (cf. Section 4.2). Static priorities additionally favour specific tasks independent of their behaviour or size.

The performance influences of GPOS schedulers mentioned above affect the applicability of extended processor sharing policies. DPS, GPS, and MLPS partially model the run queue of GPOS schedulers, but neglect influences of its interactivity and multiprocessor load balancing policies. The focus on specific features only allows good performance estimates for specific scenarios only. Furthermore, the prediction accuracy of PS (or one of its variants) for GPOS schedulers strongly depends on the workload characteristics. For example, PS yields large prediction errors for small requests (e.g., that are smaller than a single timeslice), while FCFS provides a good approximation for such cases (cf. Section 4.1)

In the next section, we summarise and discuss current research on the performance evaluation of different scheduling and routing policies in multi-server queueing models.

7.1.2. Performance Properties of Scheduling and Routing Policies for Multi-Server Queues

While scheduling policies for single-server systems are well understood and analytically tractable, multi-server queueing models pose several new challenges [Squ07]. For example, the SRPT policy, which is proven to be the optimal scheduling policy with respect to mean response time for single-server queues, is not optimal for multi-server systems [LR97]. An optimal strategy for multi-server systems is yet unknown. Furthermore, analytical solutions have a limited availability, i.e., for specific combinations of scheduling and routing policies.

For multi-server systems with immediate dispatching, the routing policy is crucial for achieving good utilisation and low response times. However, its mutual influences with local scheduling of service centres is not yet fully understood. Accurate models for load distribution in multi-server systems are essential for performance evaluation of symmetric multiprocessing and distributed systems. In such environments, the dynamic re-distribution of load plays a major role for software performance. Thus, researchers address the question of how analytical models of load balancing policies, such as cycle stealing or coupled processor models [Oso05], can improve the overall system performance.

In the following, we describe work devoted to the analysis of multi-server systems with different routing and scheduling policies. First, we present approaches that evaluate the performance influence of priorities in multi-server systems. Second, we discuss analytical approaches for the performance evaluation of load balancing and/or load distribution.

Priorities Harchol-Balter et al. [HBOSWW05] analysed multi-server systems with prioritisation and compared the resulting response times with their single-server counterparts. Priority queueing is difficult to analyse in a multi-server setting, since jobs of different priorities may be in service (at different servers) at the same time, which leads to complex Markov chains. They came to the conclusion that the effects of prioritisation in multi-server systems cannot be predicted by considering a comparable single-server system. Furthermore, the authors state that a set of servers provides a strong benefit in dealing with highly variable job sizes, yet they hinder performance under light load. Finally, SMART prioritisation has much stronger effect in a single-server system than in a multi-server system of equal capacity.

Choosing a Queue – The Routing Policy In multi-server systems, the distribution of jobs among the available servers is one of the most important design questions. The central queue model and the immediate dispatching model are two different concepts addressing this question.

In the immediate dispatching model, random and round-robin are the simplest assignment strategies. While the random policy assigns an incoming job to each server with probability $1/k$, where k is the number of servers, round-robin distributes jobs to servers in a cyclic order. However, they neither maximise utilisation nor minimise mean response times. Under the Join-the-Shortest-Queue (JSQ) policy, incoming jobs are immediately dispatched to the host with the fewest number of jobs in the queue. This policy has been shown to be optimal for exponentially distributed service times and unknown job sizes [Win77, TSC92, MS91, EVW80].

In the central queue model, the $M/G/k/FCFS$ policy has been proven to minimise mean response time and maximise utilisation for exponentially distributed service times and unknown job sizes [Wol89]. The $M/G/k/FCFS$ policy holds all jobs in a central queue. When a host becomes free, it receives a job from the central queue in the order of their arrivals.

While policies like Join-Shortest-Queue and $M/G/k/FCFS$ perform well when job sizes are exponentially distributed, they perform poorly when the job size distribution has higher variability [KST99, Whi86]. It has been shown analytically and empirically that the so-called dedicated routing policy outperforms both policies with respect to mean response time [SHB04, HBCM99]. The dedicated policy designates some servers as "short servers" and others as "long servers". It always routes short jobs to the "short server" and long jobs to the "long server". The dedicated policy is defined for both the immediate dispatching model and the central queue model, which behave similarly under the dedicated policy. The dedicated policy performs well when job sizes have high variability, because it isolates short jobs from the long jobs as waiting behind the long jobs is costly [OHBSW05].

The unnecessary idling of some servers is the major disadvantage of the dedicated policy. For example, if many short but no long jobs arrive the "long servers" remain idle while the "short servers" become saturated with the load. Cycle stealing provides first concepts to overcome this shortage.

Balancing the Load – Cycle Stealing   In his Phd-Thesis [Oso05], Osogami addressed the problem of imbalanced situations for the dedicated policy. He introduced the concept of cycle stealing to combine the variance reducing benefit of the dedicated policy with the high utilisation property of $M/G/k/FCFS$ and Join-the-Shortest-Queue. Basically, cycle stealing enables one server to help another one when its own queue is empty. For example, if the "long server's" queue is empty while the "short server" is under heavy load, the latter may steal the "long servers's" idle cycles to serve short jobs.

However, cycle stealing grants short jobs access to the long server only when the long server is free. It must not let long jobs starve causing them undue delay. Since jobs are not preemptive, there is a penalty to a long job which arrives to find a short job using the long server. Osogami shows that cycle stealing can provide an boundless benefit over the simple dedicated policy.

To be a good estimator for real systems, cycle stealing needs to reflect the costs of moving jobs between servers [OHBSW05]. The additional costs may be caused by reloading memory, the resumption of processing of donor jobs, remote execution costs, loading memory to the donor machine. Thus, cycle stealing may pay off only if the beneficiary's queue is sufficiently long. Osogami analysed the optimal thresholds on the beneficiary and donor queue [OHBSWZ04].

Discussion In this section, we have presented current research on queueing theory which addresses the performance evaluation of scheduling and routing policies. The analytical solutions for multi-server systems are still limited to specific combinations of routing and scheduling policies. For example, just recently solutions for multi-server queues with JSQ routing and PS scheduling have been proposed. The dedicated policy promises the best performance for multi-server systems which have to process load with a high variance of service times. However, the analytical solutions for different combinations of routing and scheduling policies as well as the load balancing models are still an initial step towards the analytical solution of multi-server queueing systems.

Regarding the assumptions made by queueing network models, it is still unclear under which conditions a multi-server queue yields accurate performance predictions for symmetric multiprocessors. The scheduling and routing policies used in queueing theory are strong abstractions of the scheduling policies of real systems [RUKVB04]. To make good performance predictions, it is necessary to understand the conditions for the applicability of a specific queueing model.

7.2. Performance Evaluation of Operating System Schedulers

In this section, we summarise work involved in the performance evaluation of operating system schedulers. These approaches include the performance evaluation of multiprocessor load balancing policies for GPOS schedulers (Section 7.2.1), their interactivity features (Section 7.2.2), real-time operating systems (Section 7.2.3), and high-performance computing (Section 7.2.4).

7.2.1. Multiprocessor Load Balancing of General Purpose Operating Systems

Chanin, Correa et al. [CCF+06, CZS06] analysed the influence of different load balancing polices for NUMA systems on software performance focussing on the effect of different memory access times. They proposed an optimised multilevel load balancing algorithm and demonstrated with simulations, measurements and formal analyses of stochastic automata networks [PA91] the possible performance gain of the new algorithm. However, the results of the simulation and formal analysis are contradicting. While the simulation and measurements yielded a performance gain of 2.2% to 10% depending on the underlying hardware architecture [CZS06], the analytical results predicted an improvement of no more than 1% [CCF+06].

The contradicting results are a consequence of an oversimplified analytical model. Chanin et al. [CCF+06] modelled the behaviour of processes by alternating periods of I/O and computation. The period durations were approximated by exponential distributions. Furthermore, the model contains only one explicit task. All other tasks in the system have a fixed influence on the waiting time of the explicit task, i.e., the task's waiting time in the different processor queues does not change over time. The modelled load-balancer can only move a single task between the available processors. This restriction strongly limits the capabilities of the modelled load balancer compared to real systems. The simulation results and measurements in [CZS06] suggest that the analytical model does not reflect the performance-relevant properties of the system under study accurately.

The work presented above demonstrates the need for performance model validation, which compares predictions to measurements. The authors neglected performance-relevant details of the load balancer, which were essential for their approach. Omitting the model validation led to misleading conclusions about the performance of the system under study.

Ahmad et al. [AGM+94] evaluated the influence of various load balancing policies and of their parameters on software performance using neural networks. They trained a neural network using simulation results of different load balancing policies for distributed multi-computer systems. The simulation model is based on a simple queueing network with FCFS scheduling and exponentially distributed service times. The neural network predicts the response time of the system under study with different parameters for various load balancing strategies. The prediction error is below 5% in most cases. While the usage of neural networks to predict the influence of scheduling and load-balancing policies seems promising, the examined system still contains strong restrictions, such as exponential distributions, FCFS scheduling, and the restriction of the considered metrics to mean response times.

Kluge et al. [KN07] developed a framework for monitoring the Linux scheduler called VAMPIR that observes the number of task movements in multiprocessor environments. In a larger case study, they observed the scheduler's load balancing behaviour for an MPI application in three different scenarios. In the first scenario (big blocks of work), the system was balanced quickly and it remained balanced for the whole experiment. The second scenario (small blocks, busy waiting) required repetitive balancing attempts of the scheduler, but still achieved a balanced state. Finally, the third scenario (small blocks, yield CPU) led to continuous task movement during the whole experiment and the system did not reach a balanced state. However, even though the third scenario was not stable with respect to load balancing, it yielded the fastest overall response times. The results of Kluge et al. pointed out strong mutual dependencies between multiprocessor load balancing and the interactivity policy of the Linux scheduler. The usage of different synchronisation methods as well as the partitioning of the overall work into differently sized blocks affected the overall response times.

7.2.2. Interactivity and Processor Reservation in GPOS Schedulers

In their experiments, Torrey et al. [TCM06] focus on the performance of interactive and I/O-bound tasks under Linux 2.6.3. One of the main aims of the Kernel developers was the improvement of interactivity in the Linux 2.6 scheduler. However, the MLFQ implementation of Torrey et al. outperforms the Linux scheduler with respect to interactivity. The observed performance gain comes at the cost of losing priority levels and starvation prevention. Furthermore, the performance of batch processes and server systems was not evaluated. In their experiments, Torrey et al. observed a fixed ratio of processing and sleeping times for tasks to be classified as interactive. If a task sleeps for at least one quarter of its processing time, the Linux scheduler considers it as interactive. While Torrey et al. evaluated many performance properties of the Linux scheduler, the underlying concepts that cause the observed results remain unclear. Their study particularly emphasises the difference between the Linux scheduler and formal scheduler models as described in Section 7.1.

Kawasaki et al. [KGC⁺06] proposed an extension of the Linux operating system scheduler, which reserves a percentage of the processor's capacity to specific tasks. The reservation ensures responsiveness and predictability of these tasks. The authors used a simple Markov model to capture the behaviour of the Linux scheduler. The model demonstrates the improvements of their approach compared to the current scheduler implementation. The evaluation of their performance model is limited to a comparison with a simulation which contains similar simplifications and assumptions like the proposed Markov model. According to their results, the reservation of processor capacity for specific tasks can improve the performance of these tasks. However, this reservation leads to a performance degradation of other tasks.

7.2.3. Real Time Operating Systems

There are numerous approaches for the performance evaluation of real-time systems available in literature, e.g., [BMdW⁺04, BKR95, EE00, FNNS06, HZS01, LM99, MPC04, YW98, MPC04, SG06, JLT85]. While the performance evaluation of real-time systems and component-based enterprise applications may exhibit some common problems, their level of abstraction, their assumptions about the underlying hard- and software infrastructure as well as the performance metrics they consider vary significantly. For example, simulators of real-time operating systems (such as [MPC04, SG06]), which allow system designers to evaluate the influence of different scheduling policies on the performance of their system, include many low level details, such as the saving and loading of tasks context, context-switch times, and scheduling latency, which are negligible for GPOS schedulers. The performance metrics considered are mostly related to the meeting of hard and soft deadlines. The scheduling policies available for modelling are often limited to the most basic policies such as RR, FCFS, or SRPT. Their simplicity on the one hand and the large number of low-level details on the other make them inapplicable for performance evaluation in enterprise applications.

7.2.4. High Performance Computing

In the past several decades, various scheduling policies for multiprocessing systems have been evaluated in order to identify the critical factors for performance in high performance computing applications (e.g., [MEB88, Maj92, GTU91, LV90, AD96, RSSS98]). Table 7.2 summarises the most important scheduling policies of this area. The findings differ depending on the focus of the authors. While Majumdar et al. [MEB88, Maj92] rate policies with a priori job knowledge (especially Smallest Number of Processes First) best, Gupta et al. [GTU91], who emphasise the influence of caching effects, favour co-scheduling. Leutenegger and Vernon [LV90] observe the best performance for dynamic partitioning and round

Name	Description	Time Sharing	Space Sharing	Known Job Size
Batch Scheduling / FCFS	All processes of an arriving job are placed consecutively in a shared queue. If a processor becomes empty it fetches the first process from the queue.	-	-	-
Dynamic Partitioning Policy	Assign an equal fraction of processors to each available job. Jobs are at most assigned as many processors as there are parallel processes.	-	yes	-
Gang Scheduling / Coscheduling	All runnable processes of an application are scheduled to run on the processors at the same time. When a time slice ends all running processes are preempted simultaneously, and all processes from another application are scheduled for the next time slice.	yes	-	-
Smallest Number of Processes First (SNPF)	Process the job with the least number of processes first.	-	-	yes
Preemptive Smallest Number of Processes First (PSNPF)	Similar to SNPF, but preempts the currently running job, if a new job with less processes arrives.	yes	-	yes
Preemptive Shortest Cumulative Demand First (PSCDF)	Process the job with the least cumulative demand (sum of the demands of all processes)	yes	-	yes
Process Round-Robin (Rrprocess)	Round robin strategy that assigns an equal share of processing power to each process.	yes	-	-
Job Round-Robin (RRjob)	Round robin strategy that assigns an equal share of processing power to each job.	yes	-	-

Table 7.2.: Overview of scheduling policies for high performance computing [LV90].

robin job policy (where a job subsumes several processes). Au and Dandamudi [AD96] evaluated effects of a program's structure on the performance of scheduling policies for UMA systems. They observe the best performance for preemptive shortest cumulative demand first scheduling. Rosti et al. [RSSS98] include I/O accesses into their evaluation of scheduling policies. They demonstrate that the contention of disk resources can become a dominating factor which significantly influences scheduler performance.

7.3. Infrastructure Performance Models

In this section, we describe model-driven performance prediction approaches that add platform-specific performance specifications to software architectures. Furthermore, we discuss performance prediction models for middleware infrastructures. The considered approaches provide the necessary concepts to integrate MOSS as well as other infrastructure performance models into high-level architectural models for performance prediction.

Including Infrastructure Models into Abstract Software Architectures Inspired by the ideas of component-based software engineering, Woodside and Wu [WW04] proposed the reuse of performance (component) specifications. These previously calibrated sub-models or "performance components" can be used flexibly in the system model. This approach allows the straightforward integration of middleware details into prediction models. The envisioned concept is in line with their earlier proposition of performance completions [Woo02], which supply additional information not needed for functional specification but rather required for performance prediction.

Following the same idea, Grassi et al. [GMS06] used refinements from model-driven technologies to integrate aspects of performance (and reliability) into their prediction model KLAPER. In the considered example [GMS06], they integrate the overhead of remote procedure calls into a performance specification of a distributed application. Woodside and Wu as well as Grassi et al. focus on the concepts of completions and refinements.

Verdickt et al. [VDGD05] developed a framework to automatically include the impact of CORBA middleware on the performance of distributed systems. Transformations map high-level middleware-independent UML models to other UML models with middleware-specific information. Their work is focused on the influence of Remote Procedure Calls (RPCs) as implemented in CORBA, Java RMI, and SOAP. Their integration of delays imposed by RPCs is based on the mean values of simple measurements. The proposed transformation approach extends the architectural specification by performance models of the infrastructure. While this method enables the usage of various solutions for annotated UML specifications, infrastructure specification are constrained by the capabilities of UML. Thus, complex data dependencies or scheduling algorithms are hard or even impossible to express.

Cortelessa et al. [CPR07] developed a framework that combines architectural performance specifications with simulation prototypes of resources. In their case study, they evaluate the influences of schedulers and webserver components on a web application. Resource prototypes are reusable basic blocks for platform models. Their framework includes prototype models of some of the most used resource types like CPU, mass memory, and network. To include resources into software architecture, resource prototypes can be either directly instantiated or specialised adding additional performance or behavioural information. These resource prototypes embed specific probes to collect performance data. Resource prototypes can be assembled to processing nodes or to whole platform models. For this purpose, special dispatching components standardise the management of resource service requests.

Behaviour of resources is specified in terms of UML state-charts. Resources communicate via ports, which can be regarded as the interface of a resource. For example, to specify a simple scheduler, an external port accepting resource requests has to be modelled. When a request arrives, a set of elementary jobs (required to satisfy the request) is enqueued (e.g., a disk reading can be partitioned as a set of block reading jobs). When the scheduler selects a job for execution, its behavioural specification (i.e., the statechart) moves to another state (e.g., "busy") for a specific time. Such transitions simulate the time spent by the physical resource to execute the job. When all the jobs that are related to a request have been processed, the caller is notified that its request has been satisfied.

Cortelessa et al. [CPR07] only give prototypical description of schedulers in their framework. The state-charts are just an abstract representation of what happens inside the simulation. For example, the authors do not model the queueing of jobs necessary for the scheduler. Furthermore, they do not validate their prototypical resource models. However, validation is essential for reliable prediction models.

Measurement-based Development of Infrastructural Models Gorton and Liu [LFG05, GL03] as well as Denaro et al. [DPE04] studied the influence of middleware on software performance. Both considered middleware as the determining factor for performance in distributed systems and, thus, focused on its modelling and evaluation.

Gorton and Liu [LFG05, GL03] proposed a measurement-based approach in combination with mathematical models to predict the performance of J2EE applications. Measurements provide the necessary data to compute the input values of a queueing network model. The computation reflects the behaviour of the application under concern. The queueing network is solved to derive performance metrics, such as response time and throughput for the application.

Denaro et al. [DPE04] completely focused on measurements and did not rely on predictions. They assumed that the infrastructure of a software system is available during early development stages. They use test cases based on architecture designs to provide performance estimates of a software system. Both approaches strongly simplify the behaviour of an application neglecting its influences on software performance. For measurements, they require the complete infrastructure which may not be available during the design phase.

7.4. Summary

In this chapter, we have discussed approaches closely related to this thesis. We have addressed approaches from (i) mathematical analysis of scheduling policies, (ii) performance evaluation of operating system schedulers, and (iii) performance models for middleware platforms.

1. *Formal analyses of scheduling policies* have achieved interesting results about the influence of scheduling policies on software performance. They point out possible performance gains by the improvement scheduling policies. Unfortunately, the models are still simple compared to the behaviour of real operating systems schedulers. However, the results guided the experiments in Chapter 4 and 5.

2. Experiments on the performance influences of *GPOS schedulers* have provided interesting insights into the performance influences of Linux' interactivity and load balancing policies. However, all performance prediction models for GPOS schedulers discussed here lack a thorough validation. The lack of validation leads to oversimplified performance models and, thus, erroneous predictions.

3. *Performance models for middleware platforms* provide background of the performance completion for message-oriented middleware (MOM). However, at their current state, significant expertise is necessary for their application. The steep learning curve hinders their usage in practice.

In this thesis, we have addressed the shortcomings of existing approaches and have proposed a performance model for GPOS schedulers that accurately predicts their influence on software performance (Chapters 3, 4, and 5). In addition, we have developed a performance completion for MOM that allows software architects to include influences of MOM in their architectural model (Chapter 6).

8. Conclusions

8.1. Summary

In this thesis, we have presented performance modelling frameworks for general purpose operating system schedulers and message-based communication in symmetric multiprocessing environments. Their design followed a novel iterative method that experimentally derivates performance models from specification and documentation. The models have been extensively validated and contain only those factors that influence software performance. Software architects can customise the models according to the requirements of the system under study. The proposed techniques help software architects to predict response time, throughput, and resource utilisation with an error of less than 5% to 10% in most cases and, thus, decrease the prediction error by several orders of magnitude compared to today's prediction methods. In the following, we summarise the main contributions of our work.

Experiment-based Model Derivation For accurate performance predictions, model design needs to be goal-oriented and tightly coupled with measurements. For this purpose, we have proposed and employed a systematic approach to the experimental derivation of performance models from initial specification and documentation. The method focuses the modelling effort and identifies the performance-relevant factors before model design. An explicit validation of assumptions identifies counter-intuitive performance-factors of the system under study and directs further investigation if necessary. Based on the results, a performance model can be designed. Finally, a comparison between predictions and measurements further ensures that the model captures all important influences and has been defined on an appropriate level of abstraction.

Furthermore, performance models can be parametrised over the execution environment. Parametrisation enables software architects to customise models for their specific target platform. To determine the resource demands of that platform, automated test drivers execute a series of predefined measurements. The results determine the parameter values of the model. Additionally, parametrisation allows the definition of generic performance models for a class of middleware platforms. Model-driven techniques integrate the models into architectural specifications and, thus, hide their complexity from software architects.

Performance Model for GPOS Schedulers   We extensively employed the experiment-based derivation method during the construction of MOSS, a performance model for general purpose operating system schedulers. MOSS reflects the mutual influences of different time sharing, interactivity, and multiprocessor load-balancing policies on the performance of software applications. MOSS specifically addresses the influence of GPOS schedulers in symmetric multiprocessing environments, such as today's multi-core processors. In a series of goal-oriented experiments, we have evaluated the performance influences of the Windows and Linux operating system series. Based on the results, we have determined the performance-relevant properties of GPOS schedulers described in the scope of this thesis.

On an abstract level, feature diagrams model the performance-relevant properties of GPOS schedulers. Feature characteristics reflect, for example, the different types of run queues, dynamic priorities, and dynamic load balancing policies employed in both systems. Software architects can customise the GPOS scheduler models based on the identified features.

For performance prediction, CPNs formally describe the behaviour of GPOS schedulers and of their feature characteristics. These CPNs are hierarchically structured so that each subnet represents a different feature. This separation of concerns allows the straightforward integration of different feature characteristics in a single CPN. In a final validation of MOSS, we have compared predictions to measurements and ensured that the model captures all important performance-influences.

To hide the complexity of MOSS from software architects and from performance analysts, MOSS has been integrated with the PCM, which is an architectural modelling language that supports performance predictions during early development stages. For the integration, we have implemented a discrete event simulation technique specialised for MOSS. Software architects can either choose from existing scheduler configurations, e.g., Windows Server 2003 or Linux 2.6, or provide their own configuration. Depending on the configuration, the simulation chooses different time sharing, interactivity and multiprocessor load balancing policies. This approach hides the complexity of the scheduler model from software architects while significantly increasing prediction accuracy.

However, MOSS also requires several assumptions on the task behaviour and underlying execution environment. For example, memory access is not considered. Caching effects, possible bottlenecks at memory buses, or varying memory access times for different memory spaces can have a significant effect on software performance.

Messaging Completion   Message-passing is widely used for communication in distributed enterprise applications. To model and predict the performance of such applications, we have proposed a parametrised performance model for Message-oriented Middleware. Software architects can customise a so-called messaging completion that models the behaviour of the underlying MOM using a language specific to their domain. The model as well as its specification language are based on design patterns for message-based communication. To a large extent, these patterns are realised in standards for message-oriented middleware, such as Java Message Service [HBS+08].

For model design, we have identified those patterns that significantly influence the delivery time of a message in a series of experiments. The proposed performance model only reflects the behaviour specified in the messaging patterns and abstracts from the actual implementation. Measurements determine the necessary resource demands of a specific MOM platform in the target environment. For this purpose, an automated test driver measures the necessary data for the new platform. To reflect the influence of different usage profiles (e.g., message and transaction sizes), regression analyses extract the parametric dependencies of input parameters and resource demands from the measurements. The resulting functions determine the resource demands in dependency of the current input parameters.

Messaging can be customised for different execution environments and implementations of MOM. The combination of pattern-based models with measurements allows accurate performance predictions for different vendor implementations using the same performance model. Software architects can customise the prediction model according to a feature diagram modelling the performance-relevant messaging-patterns (e.g., publish subscribe or guaranteed delivery).

The abstract modelling of complex middleware also requires several assumptions. For example, demands to individual resources cannot be determined exactly by this approach. Thus, it is assumed that the message delivery time is sufficient to model the performance of MOM. Even though the assumption holds in the considered case study, more complex scenarios may require a detailed resource demand breakdown to individual resources.

Validation   In the scope of this thesis, we have validated the performance models by means of a series of case studies all placed in the scenario of a supermarket supply chain management. The case studies have provided detailed performance evaluations of HQ's business reporting and a supermarket's warehouse applications. Both involve different types of requests as well as message-based communication. The overall scenario of the case studies has been introduced in the context of the SPECjms2007 benchmark [SPE, SKCB07]. We have extended the benchmark to reflect additional classes of requests and support more elaborate scenarios.

The benefit of MOSS for performance prediction of business applications has been demonstrated by a business reporting use case for HQ's application. Supermarket managers as well as employees of HQ can request different kinds of business reports. The reports are generated on the fly from the collected data. The case study evaluates the performance of the system for different types of requests and for different execution environments including a dual-core system under Linux and Windows. MOSS predicts the response time for all types of requests with an error of less than 5 – 10% in most cases. Compared to commonly used prediction models, MOSS increases the prediction accuracy up to several orders of magnitude.

The performance completion for Message-oriented Middleware has been evaluated in the context of the supermarkets warehouse management. An RFID-reader notifies the system whenever goods leave the warehouse. The application keeps track of the stored goods and notifies the supermarket management whenever new goods have to be ordered. In the case study, we have evaluated the performance influence under peak load conditions that may occur when many goods leave the warehouse at once, e.g., a lorry of goods is brought into the shop. The performance model has predicted the message delivery time with an error of less than 15%. The resource utilisation has been predicted with an error of 20%. The case study has demonstrated that some of the assumptions underlying the messaging completion affect prediction accuracy and should be weakened in the future. However, a prediction error of less than 30% is considered a good performance prediction [MAD04] in general.

8.2. Benefits

The results of this thesis support software architects and performance analysts to i) focus their modelling effort on the performance-relevant factors of the system under study, ii) transparently evaluate the performance influences of different GPOS schedulers, and iii) include message-based communication into their software performance models.

The proposed experimental derivation of performance models supports performance analysts designing goal-oriented performance models. Its support for parametrisation allows abstracting from the underlying hard- and software layers. Software architects can use the parametrised models to predict performance properties of their software application in different environments with little additional modelling effort.

The performance model for GPOS schedulers (MOSS) allows accurate predictions of influences of the Windows and Linux operating system series on software performance. Such predictions are especially useful in symmetric multiprocessing environments which become more common with today's multi-core technology. The model increases the prediction accuracy by several orders of magnitude reducing the risk of erroneous performance predictions. It supports software architects judging different design alternatives correctly. Based on the predicted results, software architects can identify the operating system best suited for their needs. Especially in heavy load situations, operating systems differ significantly in their influence on software performance. Depending on the scenario and the performance requirements, either equal distributions of processing time or large differences may be preferable. While the first guarantees similar response times for all tasks, the latter can be used to minimise the overall mean response time [WHBO05].

MOSS can further support operating system developers to predict the effect of changes in scheduling algorithms on software performance a priori. Assessing the influence of changes without measurement and/or simulation is a difficult or even impossible task. Today's GPOS schedulers target a wide range of systems with largely varying requirements. They must perform well on desktop systems with few processors only and with high requirements to interactivity as well as on sever systems with a large number of processors and tasks. Evaluating the influence of changes to a scheduler in a set of representative scenarios reduces risk lowering the performance for one user group while increasing the performance for another. Furthermore, it focuses the development effort on the relevant scheduler features.

The messaging completion proposed in Chapter 6 enables software architects and performance analysts to model and to predict the influence of asynchronous communication via message passing on performance of their application. They can configure the messaging completion using a language specific to their domain that reflects the performance-relevant messaging patterns, e.g., durable subscription or competing consumers.

8.3. Lessons Learned

In the following, we summarise some of the lessons learned during the course of this thesis with respect to software performance engineering.

For the design of accurate performance models, an initial validation of the model's assumptions is essential. Performance influences are often counterintuitive. Especially, mutual influences of different system parts are difficult to track. For concurrent software systems, just the understanding of the functional behaviour can be challenging [Lee06]. Therefore, formal analyses techniques, such as model checking, are essential to ensure correctness. It is mandatory for performance prediction to understand the mutual influences of – on the first glance – independent system behaviour, to design models that accurately reflect the behaviour of the overall system. Goal-oriented experiments can guide the identification of such mutual dependencies. They help performance analysts and software architects to get the complexity of today's enterprise applications under control. The experiment-based derivation of performance models proposed in Chapter 3 systematically challenges expert intuition by comparing their expectations to measurements. This method supports performance analysts to focus their attention on the most critical parts of the system under study.

However, not only counter-intuitive influences are a threat to validity for software performance engineering but also the experimental settings selected for evaluation. For example, the workload type (i.e., open or closed) is of major importance for the performance influence of scheduling policies. While scheduling has a limited impact for closed workloads, it affects response times up to several orders of magnitude for open workloads. Identifying the right experimental setting for performance evaluation is challenging. The settings have to provide proper results answering specific questions, but must not be too specific so that their results can still be generalised.

While measurements are essential to build valid performance models for software systems, they can also lower model complexity. In Chapter 6, simplified models were used to capture the influence of Message-oriented Middleware. While this work has been focused on the basic concepts underlying the simplification (parametrised performance models), the general approach has much more potential for software performance engineering. With the increasing complexity of software systems, strong abstractions are necessary for performance modelling. Parametrised models in combination with measurements could help to get control over today's complexity of software systems.

While abstraction is necessary and helpful for some infrastructure models, such as message-oriented middleware, it can hurt prediction accuracy for others. The design of MOSS has demonstrated that some details can have a large impact on the overall software performance. Schedulers affect all software artefacts running on the system under study, since they access and manage most resources of a system. The identification of the relevant factors requires detailed measurements to get a proper understanding of the mutual influences of scheduler features and task behaviour.

The validation of MOSS by multiple experiments and case studies captures a wide range of possible influencing factors. However, a broader application of MOSS in different environments and contexts is necessary to identify those factors not yet included.

8.4. Future Work

In the following, we propose several improvements of MOSS, parametrised performance completions, as well as performance modelling and model solution techniques.

MOSS - Performance Model for General Purpose Operating System Schedulers

Further Case Studies for Validation   At the time of writing, a larger case study that continues the supply chain management scenario for supermarket stores [SPE, SKBB07] is being conducted. The validation integrates the performance modelling techniques prosed in this thesis. It includes message passing, multi-core processors, different operating systems, and various types of requests. The case study will give an impression on how the techniques can be combined and what the expected prediction accuracy can be.

Support a boarder range of GPOS schedulers In this thesis, the design of MOSS has been focussed on the Linux and Windows operating system series. For the future, we plan to support a much wider range of operating systems common in the server and desktop market. MOSS is planned to include the new Completely Fair Scheduler (CFS) of Linux as well as the operating system schedulers of FreeBSD, Open Solaris, and AIX.

Integration with other simulation-based performance models Currently, MOSS is integrated into the Palladio Component Model (PCM). However, its functionality is independent of the PCM. Other performance simulation environments, such as Queueing Petri Nets (QPNs), are planned to include MOSS to improve their prediction accuracy for GPOS schedulers. Furthermore, an integration with more powerful simulation environments is possible. For example, MOSS may be implemented as a module for OMNeT++ [omn], which is a powerful and widely used simulation environment for distributed systems. On the one hand, this allows MOSS to benefit from OMNeT++'s network simulation capabilities and, on the other hand, OMNeT++ provides an easy access to MOSS for a broad user community.

Many-core processors If today's trend of multi-core processors will continue, the number of processors on a single chip is likely to increase according to Moore's Law. Thus, the future generations of processors will not only contain two, four, or eight cores, but several hundreds or thousands of specialised processor cores. This expectation poses new challenges for operating system development, programming language design, and software performance prediction. Appropriate abstractions of such processors need to be identified for accurate software performance prediction. MOSS is a first step in this direction. However, its prediction capabilities have to be refined with the evolution of operating systems and processor technology.

NUMA architectures MOSS' current support for symmetric multiprocessors (SMP) environments needs to be extended to non uniform memory access (NUMA) architectures as a major step in this direction. Compared to SMP, NUMA architectures are connected to multiple memory banks with different access times, which strongly influence software performance. The extension of MOSS and the PCM towards such influencing factors requires the PCM to specify the used memory and its location, i.e., the position of a task's data in distributed memory, as well as different memory access times.

Virtualisation of resources Furthermore, the increasing virtualisation of processing resources poses new challenges to software performance prediction. Companies try to optimise the usage of their existing hard- and software resources. Virtualisation provides the necessary technologies to offer mutually independent software environments to different customers sharing the underlying hardware resources. In such environments, the environment hosting the virtual operating systems also influences task performance. In the long term, we plan to extend MOSS by an additional virtualisation layer that allows predicting software performance in such dynamic environments.

Parametrised Performance Completions

Automated generation of platform-specific completions from measurements Parametric performance completions use measurements of predefined performance metrics on the target environment to predict the performance of the system under study. Within this thesis, a parametric messaging completion has modelled the influence of different messaging patterns on the delivery time of a message. For a broader application of parametric performance models, it is necessary to automate the entire process of measuring the required performance metrics, executing regression analyses, and creating platform-specific completions from measurements. This approach makes the process transparent for software architects and provides the necessary prediction accuracy for the target platform.

Additional infrastructure completions Furthermore, additional parametric performance models for other infrastructure layers are planned, e.g., for databases and application servers. However, databases require more sophisticated models for input parameters, since the processing time of requests mainly depends on the query and the database state.

Performance characteristic curves The messaging completion assumes that resource contention can be approximated by assigning the whole delivery time to single shared resource. However, the discussion in Chapter 6 has shown that the approximation is not always sufficient. It may be necessary to measure delivery times with respect to the number of concurrent messages in the system and their size to increase prediction accuracy. The resulting function captures – similar to characteristic curves in physics – the influences of different parameters on the observed performance. While this approach increases the prediction accuracy for the message delivery time, it does not capture contention effects with other services using the same resources. Queueing theory provides the necessary mathematics to compute the resource demands of a single request from the observed resource utilisation and the message's delivery time. However, measuring times in distributed environments is challenging. The delivery time of a single message is often smaller than the clock drift between the involved hardware nodes.

Regression splines Finally, the messaging completion uses linear regression to extract the functional dependencies of the message delivery time and the message's size. While this was appropriate for the scenarios considered, better regression analyses for parameter dependencies of infrastructure performance models are desirable. Courtois and Woodside [CW00, WVCB01] propose regression splines to model the functional dependencies between input parameters and observable performance metrics. Applying this technique to parametrised performance completions allows extracting much more complex functional dependencies from measurements.

Performance Modelling and Model Solution Techniques

Design patterns for concurrent software systems With the rise of multi-core processors in the common server and desktop market, concurrency becomes ubiquitous in software development. To ease performance modelling and implementation of concurrent software architectures, design patterns can support the definition of software behaviour on an abstract level. Performance completions in combination with model-driven techniques (as proposed by Becker [Bec08]) enable the automatic transformation of abstract pattern-based models to complete behavioural specifications. The pattern-based approach encapsulates the implementation knowledge and allows software architects to reason about systems on an abstract level. The transformation into full behavioural specifications further enables the performance evaluation of the system under study as well as automated code generation.

Variance reduction With the ubiquity of concurrency in multiprocessing environments, the need for efficient analysis and simulation methods rises. As a first step, the use of statistical methods for variance reduction can lower the simulation effort needed and aid the simulation of more complex models.

Combining simulation and analytical methods A next step to increase the solution capabilities for performance models is the combination of simulation and analytical methods. It is often not necessary to predict all parts of the software architecture with similar (high) accuracy. Therefore, it may be useful to select different solution techniques for different parts of a model. Especially, the currently emerging fluid models that approximate solutions of continuous time Markov chains (e.g., [Hil05, CDGH06, BP07]) are promising for highly concurrent software systems. Furthermore, efficient solutions for different types of GI/GI/n queues have been proposed recently (e.g., [Oso05]). Combining such methods with discrete event simulation can help to cope with the ever increasing complexity of performance models.

Acknowledgements

This page is most likely one of the first pages you are reading (and it's actually the last one I wrote). You want to know what you meant in a PhD-candidate's life. A tough task for me. However, this page gives me the possibility to reflect a long time of experimenting, discussing, modelling, and writing. Many of you accompanied this work. We discussed ideas, gave feedback to each others work, listened to talks and wrote papers together. I want you to know how much I enjoyed that time!

First of all, I would like to thank Lucka for being an incredible girlfriend. Lucka, I love you for your endless patience, your reassurance, and for showing me what is really important in life. And, yes, I'm back now.

Furthermore, I would like to thank my parents for their absolute support which goes way beyond my PhD-studies. I'm grateful for your motivation and your help. It is good to know that there is someone you can rely on no matter how good or bad things go.

This thesis was accompanied by two great professors: Prof. Dr. Ralf Reussner and Prof. Dr. Eike Best. Ralf, without your guidance and support, I would never have come this far. You gave me a good feeling for what research is about. Your constructive feedback and advice helped me to accomplish my goals, the large ones as well as the smaller ones. Furthermore, I would like to thank Eike Best for supervising this thesis and for his detailed and constructive comments.

Moreover, this work would not have been possible with the continuous support of my PhD-fellows Heiko Koziolek and Steffen Becker who accompanied my PhD-studies for the best part. I really loved (and still love) the intensive and constructive discussions, the long days of paper writing, and – not to forget – the beers we had (and the cocktails, by the way).

During the course of this thesis, I worked with many great people from various projects at the University of Oldenburg and at the University of Karlsruhe (TH). From the University of Oldenburg, I would like to thank Martin Fänzle and Willhelm Hasselbring as well as my colleagues and TrustSoft fellows (note the alphabetic order): Marko Boskovic, Abhishek Dhama, Viktoria Firus, Simon Giesecke, André van Hoorn, Henrik Lipskoch, Roland Meyer, Karl-Heinz Pennemann, Astrid Rakow, Matthias Rohr, Christian Storm, Mani Swaminathan, Timo Warns, Daniel Winteler for their fruitful comments and constructive discussions. Not to forget our secretaries Ira Wempe and Manuela Wüstefeld: You have your heart in the right place!

In Karlsruhe, the people of the Chair of Software Design and Quality strongly contributed to this work. I would like to thank (again, in alphabetic order) Franz Brosch, Samuel Kounev (Thanks for the very good atmosphere you brought to our office!), Klaus Krogmann, Michael Kuperberg, Anne Martens, Christof Momm, Thomas Goldschmidt, Henning Groenda, Christoph Rathfelder, Johannes Stammel for your constructive discussions, the great Dagstuhl sessions we had, and the long nights in the wine-cellar. Furthermore, I would like to thank the good souls of our institute, Elena Kienhöfer and Elke Sauer, who took the responsibility of finalising my education and helped me out in any situation.

During the course of this work, I supervised the diploma theses of Henning Groenda and Holger Friedrich whose contributions are also part of this work. Henning, you started the evaluation of operating system schedulers and by this laid some of the fundamentals of this work. Holger, you investigated message-based communication. Many thanks to both of you! I really enjoyed (and still enjoy) working with you. I would also like to thank all students that worked with me during the last years: Tobias Dencker, Ihssane El-Oudghiri, Rainer Scheuerer, and Wenyun Zhou. Your work and your input helped me to keep things going.

Last but not least, I would like to thank my Czech and Slovak colleagues Barbora Zimmerova, Jan Kofron, and Lucia Kapova for the great time we had together in Karlsruhe. I'm already missing our (almost) Check/Czech evenings. It was great to have you here!

To all of you, who are not listed here but have the strong feeling that they actually should be: Please let me know. I guess I won't be able to change these acknowledgements, but I'm definitely able to buy you a beer.

A. The Palladio Component Model

The Palladio Component Model (PCM) [RBH$^+$07, KBHR07, BKR08] is an architecture description language supporting design time performance evaluations of component-based software systems. The PCM provides transformations to stochastic regular expressions [FBH05, KBH07], discrete-time Markov chains [Hap05b], Layered Queueing Networks [RS95, Fra99], and an event-based simulation framework [BKR07]. The modelling and evaluation of the PCM is supported by a tool called PCM Bench [Pal06]. In this section, we introduce the necessary concepts for the messaging completion introduced in Chapter 6.

A.1. CBSE Development Process

In component-based software engineering (CBSE), the development of a software system is typically distributed over multiple independent roles. Each role takes different responsibilities and contributes to the overall software system. In the context of the PCM, we distinguish four developer roles who produce artefacts of a software system [KH06]:

- *Component developers* specify and implement components. The specification contains an abstract, parametric description of a component and its behaviour.

- *Software architects* assemble components in order to build applications. For the evaluation of extra-functional properties, such as performance or reliability, they retrieve component specifications from a repository. Based on these specifications, simulation-based and analytical methods predict the expected behaviour of a system.

- *System deployers* model the resource environment and the allocation of components to different resources.

- Business *domain experts*, who are familiar with the customers or the users of a system, provide usage scenarios as well as typical parameter values.

The PCM provides a domain specific modelling language for each developer role. It supports a mixture of top down and bottom up development for component-based software systems [KBHR08]. For performance evaluation, all model parts are combined and transformed into a single performance model that can be solved using different analytical or simulation-based solution techniques.

A.2. Component Specification (Component Developers)

Component developers specify and implement components, whose artefacts (e.g., specifications and binaries) are stored in repositories. Additionally, they may assemble so-called composite components from existing (sub-)components. To enable performance predictions, component developers create abstract descriptions of service behaviour.

Interfaces In the PCM, components communicate via interfaces which they can provide or require. An interface serves as a contract between a client requiring a service and a server providing the service. Components implement services specified in their provided interfaces and may use services specified in their required interfaces during execution. The role of an interface (i.e., provided or required) is thereby determined by its relation to a component. Note that an interface can take multiple roles.

Components Software components are the core entities of the PCM. Basic components contain an abstract behavioural specification called Resource-Demanding Service-Effect-Specification (RD-SEFF) for each provided service. RD-SEFFs describe how component services use resources and call required services using an annotated control flow graph. Basic components cannot be further subdivided. Composite components are assembled from other components introducing hierarchy into the model. To connect components, a connector binds a required interface of one component to the provided interface of another component.

Resource Demanding Service Effect Specification RD-SEFFs are stochastic abstractions of the control flow of a service. For each provided service of a component, an RD-SEFF describes how the service uses hardware/software resources and how the service calls the component's required services.

Resource demands in RD-SEFFs abstractly specify the consumption of resources by the service's internal behaviour, e.g., in terms of CPU units needed, or in terms of bytes read or written to a hard disk. Resource demands as well as calls to required services are included in an abstract control flow specification, which captures call probabilities, sequences, branches, loops and forks. In the following, we describes the elements of RD-SEFFs in more detail.

Internal actions model resource demands and abstract from computations performed inside a component. For performance prediction, component developers need to specify demands of internal actions to resources, like CPUs or hard disks. Demands can depend on parameters passed to a service or return values of external service calls.

External call actions represent invocations by a component of services provided by other components. For each external service call, component developers can specify performance-relevant information about the service's parameters. For example, the size of a collection passed to a service can significantly influence its execution time, while the actual values may have only little effect. Modelling only the size of the collection keeps the specification understandable and the model analysable. Apart from input parameters, the PCM also deals with return values of external service calls.

External service calls are always synchronous in the PCM, i.e., the execution is blocked until a call returns. This is necessary for considering the effect of return values on performance. However, asynchronous calls can be modelled by a combination of external service calls and fork actions that allow parallel execution.

Control flow elements allow component developers to specify branches, loops, and forks of the control flow. *Branch actions* represent "exclusive or" splits of the control flow, where only one of the alternatives can be taken. In the PCM, the choice can either be probabilistic or determined by a guard. In the first case, each alternative has an associated probability giving the likelihood of its execution. In the latter case, boolean expressions on the service's input parameters guard each alternative. With a stochastic specification of the input parameters provided by the caller, the guards are evaluated to probabilities.

Loop actions model the repetitive execution of a part of the control flow. A probability mass function specifies the number of loop iterations. For example, a loop might execute 5 times with a probability of 0.7 or 10 times with a probability of 0.3. The number of loop iterations can depend on the service's input parameters. Furthermore, iterations over a collection are also modelled explicitly where the number of repetitions depends on the size of a collection.

Fork actions split the control flow into multiple concurrently executing threads. The control flow of each thread is modelled by a so-called forked behaviour. The main control flow only waits for forked behaviours that are marked as synchronised. Its execution continues as soon as all synchronised forked behaviours finished their execution (barrier pattern [Dou02]).

Acquire and *release actions* model the acquisition and release of limited passive resources, e.g., semaphores or connection pools (see pooling pattern [Dou02]). Passive resources can have a significant influence on the execution time of a service due to waiting times and, hence, are included in the PCM.

Parametric Dependencies In the PCM, parameter dependencies [KHB06, KBH07] abstractly specify input and output parameters of component services with a focus on performance-relevant aspects. For example, the PCM allows to define the VALUE, BYTESIZE, NUMBER_OF_ELEMENTS, or TYPE of a parameter. The characterisations can be stochastic, e.g., the byte size of a data container can be specified by a probability mass function:

$$\texttt{data.BYTESIZE = IntPMF[(1000;0.8) (2000;0.2)]}$$

where `IntPMF` is a probability mass function over the domain of integers. The example specifies that `data` has a size of 1000 bytes with probability 0.8 and a size of 2000 with probability 0.2.

Stochastic expressions model data flow based on parameter characterisations. For example, the stochastic expression

$$\texttt{result.BYTESIZE = data.BYTESIZE * 0.6}$$

specifies that a compression algorithm reduces the size of `data` to 60%. The expression thus yields: `IntPMF[(600;0.8) (1200;0.2)]`. Stochastic expressions support arithmetic operations $(*,-,+,/,...)$ as well as logical operations for boolean expressions $(==,>,<,\texttt{AND},\texttt{OR},...)$ on random variables.

A.3. Architecture Model (Software Architect)

Software architects usually build systems from existing components. Similarly, component developers create composite components. Within these composed structures, the connection of required and provided interfaces specifies the flow of control between different components. Furthermore, delegation connectors forward incoming and outgoing requests from the surrounding structure to the internal components and vice versa.

Architects and developers can use multiple instances of the same component in the same composite structure. Components are embedded in unique contexts [BHK06], which separate the component specification from its environment. All information that depends on a component's environment (i.e., parameter valuations, service times for specific resources) are held by its context.

A.4. Resource Model (System Deployer)

System deployers model the resource environment of a component-based software architecture and allocate individual components to resources. According to the PCM, they instantiate abstract resource types from a global resource repository to describe their concrete resources. The PCM distinguishes between processing (or active) resource types (e.g., CPU, HD, Memory, etc.) and passive resource types (e.g., semaphores etc.). Component developers specify RD-SEFFs which reference resource types without knowing concrete resource instances.

Resource environments contain a number of resource containers (called nodes in UML) connected by linking resources. Resource containers include processing resource specifications (e.g., a CPU with a processing rate 1000 work units per second) or passive resource specifications (e.g., a data base connection pool with a capacity of 10). System deployers group resources in resource containers. For example, a resource container that models a server contains multiple CPUs, memory, and caches. To model distribution, the PCM provides link resources that model network connections between multiple resource containers.

A component that is embedded in a specific software architecture (its so-called assembly context) can be allocated to the concrete resources. The abstract resources referred to by the RD-SEFFs can be substituted by the concrete resources from the resource environment to compute actual resource demands.

A.5. Usage Model (Domain Expert)

Domain experts specify a system's usage in terms of workload (i.e., the number of concurrent users), user behaviour (i.e., the control flow of user system calls), and parameters (i.e., stochastic characterisations of input data).

Usage models contain multiple scenarios, each of which models a single use case of the system. For each scenario, a workload describes its usage intensity and a behavioural model describes its flow of user actions (analogously to RD-SEFFs). Similar to queueing networks, the workload may be open or closed (cf. Section 2.1.2).

Modelling alone is not sufficient to design performance models that accurately predict the performance characteristics of interest. Therefore, performance modelling needs to be combined with systematic experiments that support the model design [Jai91, Kou06].

B. Timed Coloured Petri Nets

In this appendix, we described the concepts and features of timed Coloured Petri Nets (CPNs) [Jen92] for the purpose of software performance evaluation. Further information on the formal background of CPNs as well as their analytical capabilities can be found in the literature [Jen92, Jen94, JKW07].

CPNs are a formally well-founded modelling language for the evaluation of functional and extra-functional properties of concurrent systems. They support the modelling of concurrent behaviour as well as the specification of data flow and data manipulation. Thus, CPNs provide high flexibility with respect to performance modelling. For example, they support generally distributed service and transition times as well as customised performance monitors which collect the performance metrics of interest. To ease the design of complex models, CPNs additionally allow the definition of hierarchically structured nets. Modelling and evaluation of CPNs described in this section have been implemented in a tool suite called *CPN Tools* [JKW07]. The tool determines the performance characteristics of a CPN model by means of simulation. The expressive power and modelling support for complex systems make CPNs well suited for the design of performance models of operating system schedulers presented in Chapter 3 to Chapter 5.

In the next section, we informally introduces the basic modelling concepts of CPNs. Section B.2 describes their dynamic behaviour. In Section B.3, we introduce hierarchical modelling with CPNs. Sections B.4 and B.5 describe the modelling of time and the collection of data in CPNs. Both are fundamental concepts for software performance evaluation. In Section B.6, we summarise CPN-patterns, i.e., typical solutions of problems in CPN modelling employed in the context of this thesis.

B.1. Overview of the Structure of CPNs

Similarly to ordinary Petri nets [Pet62], places (denoted by circles or ellipses), transitions (denoted by rectangles), and directed arcs connecting places and transitions constitute the structure of a coloured Petri net. An arc always connects a place to a transition or a transition to a place. Thus, arcs are not allowed between two nodes of the same kind, i.e., between two transitions or two places. Furthermore, names are associated to places and transitions. For CPNs, the names have no formal meaning but improve the readability of the net.

In addition, textual inscriptions are associated to places, transitions, and arcs. The inscriptions have to be specified in a variant of Milner's functional programming language Standard ML [MTHM97] called CPN ML. In the graphical notation, inscriptions are written next to their transition, place, or arc.

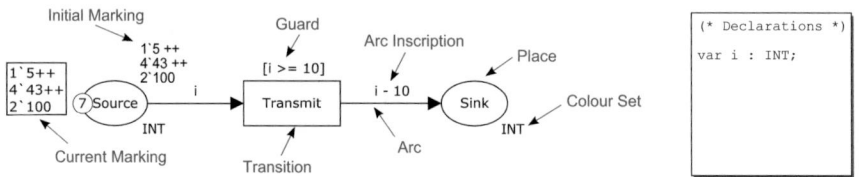

Figure B.1.: Example of the basic concepts of CPNs.

Figure B.1 exemplarily shows a CPN. It consists of two places (Source and Sink) and a single transition (Transmit). By convention, the inscription below a place denotes the set of token colours (data values) allowed on that place. The set is specified by means of a type (similar as in programming languages) called the *colour set* of a place (colset in CPN ML). In Figure B.1, places Source and Sink can hold tokens of the colour set INT, i.e., all integer values.

Each place can contain zero or more tokens of its colour set. Each token has an attached data value called *token colour* or simply *colour*. For example, place Source in Figure B.1 can contain tokens with integer values. These tokens represent the current state of a place also called its *marking*. The initial marking is, by convention, written above the place. The state of the system, i.e., the marking of the whole CPN model, is the combined marking of the individual places.

The marking of a place subsumes its current number of tokens as well as their colours. In Figure B.1, the current number of tokens on place Source is denoted by the number (7) in the circle next to it. The individual token colours are listed in the box. The listing specifies a *multi-set*, which contains multiple instances of the same token colour. The operators ' and ++ combine multiple token colours into a single set. The left argument of the infix operator ' is a positive integer which denotes the number of appearances of the element specified as the right argument. The ++ operator returns the union of two multi-sets (sum). Furthermore, multi-sets can be multiplied, compared, and subtracted, which allows a straightforward manipulation of tokens with CPNs. The initial (and current) marking of place Source (Figure B.1) contains seven tokens: One token with value 5, two tokens with value 100, and 4 tokens with value 43.

Transitions represent the events that can take place in the modelled system. When a transition fires, it removes tokens from its input places (those places that have an arc leading to the transition) and adds new tokens to its output places (those places that have an arc coming from the transition). Arc expressions (textual inscriptions next to the arcs) determine the colours of tokens removed from input places and added to output places. Guards (written next to the transition) restrict the enabling of transitions.

In Figure B.1, transition Transmit removes a token from place Source, which is bound to variable i in the scope of the transition. Variable i is declared as "var i : INT;" and has thus to be bound to a value of type INT. A concrete binding of variable i for transition Transmit is denoted by:

$$(\texttt{Transmit}, \langle \texttt{i = 100} \rangle)$$

Here, variable i receives the value 100 for the scope of transition Transmit. The transition's guard (i >= 10) restricts the binding of variable i to tokens colours whose value is equal to or greater than 10 in the example. Only if tokens are available which fulfil this condition, transition Transmit is enabled. When transition Transmit fires, it removes a token from place Source and puts a new token on place Sink. The new token's value is defined by the arc inscription i-10, i.e., the value of the new token is 90 for the above binding (i = 100).

CPNs also allow to model double-headed arcs as a shorthand notation for two arcs in opposite directions between a place and a transition with the same arc expression. Formally, the place is both an input place and an output place for the transition. In practical terms, such arcs only check the existence of specific token(s) in the respective place.

B.2. Dynamic Behaviour

Enabling and Firing of Transitions Transitions represent events of a studied system in its CPN model. The expressions on the input arcs of a transition together with the tokens on the input places determine whether the transition is enabled, i.e., is able to fire in a given marking. Therefore, a binding of the variables that appear in the adjacent arc expressions of the transition must be found. The arc expressions of each input arc must evaluate to a multi-set of token colours that is present on the corresponding input place.

When a transition fires with a given binding, it removes the multi-set of token colours to which the corresponding input arc expression evaluates from each input place. Analogously, it adds the multi-set of token colours to which the expression on the corresponding output arc evaluates to each output place. In the following, we describe how CPNs resolve non-determinism and conflicts of concurrently enabled transitions.

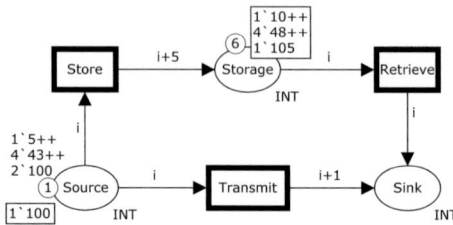

Figure B.2.: Concurrency and conflicts in CPNs.

Steps, Concurrency, and Conflict   Figure B.2 shows a CPN model with three simultaneously enabled transitions. Boldly printed rectangles denote enabled transitions in the depicted CPN model. For the shown marking, the binding of transitions `Store` and `Retrieve`
can fire concurrently (i.e., in parallel) without any interferences. Transition `Store` requires a
single token from place `Source` while transition `Retrieve` requires a single token from place
`Storage`. The pair consisting of a transition and a binding for the variables of the transition
is called a *binding element*. For example, (`Store`, ⟨i=100⟩) is the only possible binding
element for transition `Store`. Transitions `Store` and `Retrieve` can get the required tokens
without competing with each other (cf. the current marking in Figure B.2). In general,
multiple binding elements are concurrently enabled in a given marking if there are enough
tokens on the input places of the considered transitions to simultaneously bind all variables.
However, transitions `Store` and `Transmit` compete for the remaining tokens on place `Source`
and are thus in conflict with each other. Both transitions are enabled in the current state but
only one of them can fire since both require the last token on place `Source`. The resolution
of conflicts is discussed at the end of this section.

A *step* consists of a non-empty and finite multi-set of concurrently enabled binding elements. The effect of firing of a set of concurrently enabled binding elements is the sum
of the effects caused by firing the individual binding elements (interleaving semantics). In
other words, the CPN model reaches the same marking as if the set of binding elements fired
sequentially in arbitrary order. For the marking in Figure B.2, the occurrence of a step with
binding B (see below) always results in markings M_{Storage} and M_{Sink} for places `Storage` and
`Sink` independently of the order of the occurrence of individual transitions:

$$
\begin{aligned}
B = \quad & 1`(\text{Store}, \langle i = 100 \rangle) \; ++  & M_{\text{Storage}} = \quad & 1`105 & M_{\text{Sink}} = \quad & 1`10 \; ++ \\
& 1`(\text{Retrieve}, \langle i = 10 \rangle) \; ++  & & & & 4`48 \; ++ \\
& 4`(\text{Retrieve}, \langle i = 48 \rangle) \; ++  & & & & 1`105 \\
& 1`(\text{Retrieve}, \langle i = 105 \rangle)
\end{aligned}
$$

In general, an *occurrence sequence* describes an execution of a CPN model. It specifies the steps that occur and the intermediate markings that are reached. A marking that is reachable via an occurrence sequence starting in the initial marking is called a *reachable marking*. The existence of a reachable marking with more than one enabled binding element makes the CPN model non-deterministic, i.e., there may exist different occurrence sequences containing different sequences of steps and leading to different reachable markings.

Simulation-based analyses need to select one of the enabled transitions to resolve non-determinism. For CPNs, the simulation randomly chooses among the enabled transitions [Jen98]. Thereby, all transitions are selected with equal probability. Weighting or prioritisation of transitions, like in queueing Petri nets [Bau93, KB06], is not possible for the CPNs introduced by Jensen. Timed CPNs (cf. Section B.4) employ the same policy of choosing among simultaneously enabled transitions, implementing a pre-selection policy [MBB+89], i.e., the transitions are selected before their firing starts.

For CPNs, only the choice between the enabled steps is non-deterministic while the individual steps themselves are deterministic. Once an enabled step has been selected in a given marking, its occurrence always results in a uniquely determined marking. The only exception are random functions discussed in Section B.4. In the next section, we describe hierarchical modelling with CPNs.

B.3. Hierarchical Models

Modellers can structure their CPN model hierarchically into multiple hierarchically related *modules* and *submodules*, also called *subnets* in the context of this thesis. Hierarchy enables modellers to separate different concerns of complex CPN models and use a single module for parts with equal behaviour.

So-called substitution transitions and fusion sets define the hierarchy and communication points for different modules. *Substitution transitions* encapsulate possibly complex behaviour as a single transition. The behaviour of the transition is specified as a separate module with defined input and output places (called input and output ports), which directly relate to the places connected to the substitution transition. *Fusion sets* merge *fusion places* of different modules. Thus, tokens on one fusion place are visible and available for firing on all other fusion places of the same fusion set.

Figure B.3 continues the above example (Figure B.2). Here, the storage of tokens is encapsulated in a separate submodule (Figure B.3(a)) which is now used by two substitution transitions (Store 1 and Store 2 in Figure B.3(b)). Submodules receive tokens from their environment via input ports (places tagged as In, e.g., Source in Figure B.3(a)) and send tokens to their environment via output ports (places tagged as Out, e.g., Sink in Fig-

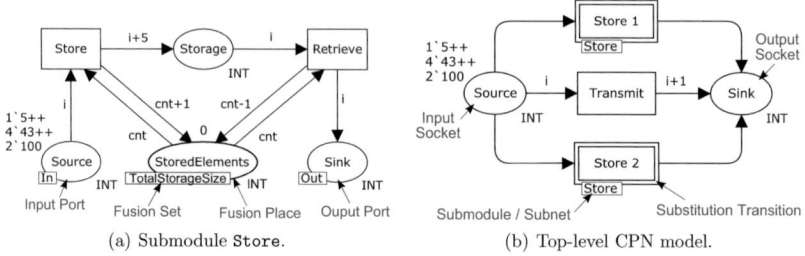

(a) Submodule Store.   (b) Top-level CPN model.

Figure B.3.: Modelling with hierarchical CPNs.

ure B.3(a)). Note that *input/output ports* (tagged as I/O) are also available and support the import and export of tokens. For the example in Figure B.3(a), places Source and Sink constitute the interface for the Store module to exchange tokens with its environment (i.e., other modules). The untagged place Storage is internal to the module and cannot be accessed by other modules.

In Figure B.3(a), Place StoredElements is a *fusion place* and belongs to the *fusion set* TotalStorageSize. Intuitively, all places belonging to the same fusion set can be considered identical. Thus, the marking of a fusion place is identical for all places of the same set in all modules. In the example, the fusion set is used to keep track of the total number of elements of all storages. Therefore, transitions Store and Retrieve increase and decrease the value of the place's token by one.

Figure B.3(b) depicts the higher-level module whose substitution transitions (drawn as double rectangular boxes) are associated with submodule Store. In the CPN notation, the submodule that is associated to a substitution transition is shown as a tag next to the transition. For each substitution transition the ports of the submodule need to be mapped to places of the higher-level module. Analogously to ports, they are called *input, output,* and *input/output sockets*.

The *port assignment* maps the port places of the submodule to the socket places of the substitution transition. After the assignment of a port to a socket, the two places constitute two different views of a single place. Therefore, the port and socket place always share the same marking and hence conceptually become the same place.

In Figure B.3(b), the input and output places of the submodule (Figure B.3(a)) are mapped to places with the same name in the higher-level module for both substitution transitions. Note that both substitution transitions have separate Storage places but share fusion place StoredElements whose tokens thus reflect the total number of elements on the Storage places of both submodules.

Hierarchy allows the decompositions of CPN models in multiple modules that communicate via ports and sockets as well as fusion places. In the next section, we describe the modelling of time in CPNs which is essential for software performance evaluation.

B.4. Time

To include timing aspects into a CPN model, the availability of a token for binding can be deferred by an arbitrary delay. Thus, tokens in timed CPN models can carry a *timestamp* in addition to the token colour. The marking of a place with timed tokens is a timed multi-set which specifies the elements together with their number of appearances and timestamps.

The time value associated with a token (called *timestamp*) is a non-negative integer or real number, from which the CPN Tools only support non-negative integers [JKW07]. The timestamp determines the time at which the token is ready for usage, i.e., the time at which it can be removed from the place by an occurring transition. The tokens on a place carry a timestamp if the colour set of the place is timed (CPN ML keyword `timed`). The distribution of tokens among the places together with their timestamps and the value of the global clock is called a *timed marking*.

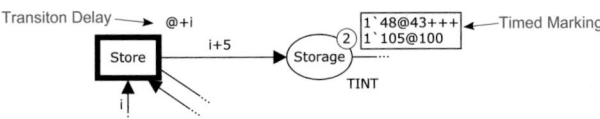

Figure B.4.: Modelling time in CPNs.

Figure B.4 depicts an excerpt of the submodel in Figure B.3(a) augmented with timing information. Transition `Store` now defers the availability of tokens by the current value of their token colour. Therefore, an additional inscription of transition `Store` adds the value (bound to variable `i`) to the current simulation time. The symbol `@` denotes the present value of the global clock of a CPN model, i.e., the current simulation time. The global clock is unique for a CPN model, i.e., in a hierarchical timed CPN model there is a single global clock that is shared among all the modules.

The transition delay in Figure B.4 assigns a timestamp of `@+i` to *all* timed tokens created by transition `Store`. For more fine grained modelling, the timestamps can also be specified for individual tokens at the inscriptions of the transition's output arcs. Instead of the transition delay, the inscription of the arc between transition `Store` and place `Storage` can be changed to `i+5@+i` which – as before – creates a new token on place `Storage` with the timestamp `@+i` but does not affect other tokens created by the transition. Furthermore, arbitrary functions (specified in CPN ML) can determine the timestamp assigned to a token. The functions can be well-known probabilistic distributions, such as Normal, Binomial, Erlang, or Exponential distributions, or can be defined individually. In the latter case, the function can depend on the current marking of the net. For example, the delay can depend on the current number of tokens in a place modelling a load dependent server.

Figure B.4 moreover depicts the current timed marking of place `Storage`. The marking contains two tokens: One with value 48 and timestamp 43 and the other with value 105 and timestamp 100. Thus, all transitions which require a token from place `Storage` cannot be enabled before the global clock reaches 43. Thus, the global clock controls the execution of a timed CPN model. It is similar to event queues found in most simulation engines for discrete-event simulation (such as [LMV02]). The model remains at a given simulation time as long as there are binding elements that are enabled (i.e., have the needed input tokens) and are ready for execution (i.e., the required tokens have timestamps which are less than or equal to the current value of the global clock). When there are no such binding elements, the clock advances to the earliest model time at which binding elements can be executed. Each marking exists in a closed interval of simulation time (which may be a point, i.e., a single moment of time).

Timed CPNs resolve non-determinism with the same policy as plain CPNs. They randomly choose the next binding element from all simultaneously enabled ones, employing a pre-selection policy [MBB+89]. Please see [Jen92] for details.

In the next section, we describe how data collectors can be used to determine the performance metrics of interest.

B.5. Data Collection

The CPN Tools support performance analyses via simulation combined with data collection. This enables performance analysts to conduct a number of simulation runs and collect the performance metrics of interest. They specify by means of *data collector monitors* what data needs to be collected during a simulation experiment. The data can be written in log files for post-processing. Batch simulations help performance analysts to explore the parameter space of a model and conduct multiple simulation runs without user intervention. In the following, we briefly summarise the concepts and possibilities of data collection. For detailed information see [JKW07, cpn].

In general, numerical data can be extracted from binding elements that occur and markings that are reached during a simulation run. CPNs Tools provide some generic data collector but also allow the implementation of user-defined data collector monitors that are specific to a CPN model. For example, the *count transition occurrences monitor* is a generic data collector monitor, which counts the number of times a transition fires during a simulation run. Furthermore, the *marking size monitor* measures the number of tokens on a place during a simulation run. Performance analysts can assign the monitor directly to a transition or place.

Generic data collector monitors require the definition of some *monitoring functions* listed in the following

- The *predicate function* determines when a monitor should collect data from the model, i.e, data is only collected when the function returns true.
- The *observation function* collects numerical data from the model when predicate function returns true.
- The *initialisation function* collects data from the initial marking of the model.
- The *stop function* collects data from the final marking of a simulation.

The data collectors enable performance analysts to determine the performance metrics of interest, such as response time, throughput, and resource utilisation. All data collector monitors can produce log files, statistical reports, and scripts for plotting data values as well as other performance-related output. In the next section, we describe the CPN-patterns employed in the design of the scheduler model in Chapter 3 to Chapter 5.

B.6. CPN Modelling Patterns

Despite their expressive power, CPNs lack some major modelling constructs for software performance evaluation, e.g., queueing places and inhibitor arcs. Mulyar [MvdA05] proposed a set of modelling patterns for CPNs (called *CPN-patterns*) that provide solutions to common problems when modelling with CPNs. In the following, we summarise the patterns relevant for this thesis, namely id matching, id manager, aggregated objects, and basic queues.

Id Matching In CPNs, tokens can represent information about an object, e.g., the state of a process in supply chain management. In many cases, it is desirable to distribute the information among multiple tokens, to change the information while keeping a copy, or to apply multiple modifications to it simultaneously. In such cases, it is mandatory to keep track of the identity of the object whose information is represented by multiple tokens.

The id matching pattern assigns the same identifier to each token holding information about the same object. Multiple tokens can represent data related to the same object. For this purpose, the affected colour sets are extended by an identifier (e.g., an affected colour set T becomes `colset IDxT = product INT * T`). When the information about an object is distributed among multiple tokens (Figure B.5), each token receives the same identifier.

Furthermore, transitions that combine tokens related to the same object have to bind the identifiers of the tokens to the same value.

Id Manager In most cases, the identifiers introduced above have to be unique in order to allow the correct distribution data among tokens and its later merging. Id managers provide the necessary constructs to generate unique identifiers and manage their lifecycle. For the scope of this thesis, only the generation of unique identifiers is important.

Id managers store the next unique identifier on a distinct place (NextID in Figure B.5). Whenever an identifier is requested, transition AssignIdentifier removes the token stored on place NextID, assigns its value to the token requiring a unique identifier, and places a new token with the value id+1 in NextID.

Aggregated Object Sometimes it is necessary to apply changes to or request information about all tokens on a specific place. For example, information about all tokens on a place is necessary for inhibitor arcs and queues described below. Instead of putting tokens on a place individually, the colour set of that place (e.g., T) is changed to a list of tokens (e.g., list T). The considered place then contains a list represented as single token. To access individual tokens, a transition must retrieve and return the whole list. It selects individual tokens using access operators and functions for lists. For example, the expression head::tail assigns the queue's head to variable head and its tail to variable tail. Both variables can be manipulated independently. Since all transitions have to use the list in order to access individual tokens, the Petri net becomes more complex.

Inhibitor Arc An inhibitor arc stops a transition from firing if its input place is not empty. Its realisation is based on the aggregated object pattern, i.e., tokens are not stored directly in a place, but are held within a collection. The inhibitor arc simply tests for the size of the collection. If the collection contains no elements (length list = 0) the transition can be enabled.

Queue In software performance evaluation, queues model the contention for hard- and software resources. In CPNs, the queue pattern models unbounded queues with different queueing policies (also called *scheduling policies* in the context of this thesis). The pattern extends the aggregated object pattern by different queueing policies. The general model is similar for all queueing policies. The place that models the queue holds an ordered list of tokens. The insertion and removal of tokens determines the queueing policy. In the following, we introduce the FCFS (First-Come, First-Served) and priority queueing policies.

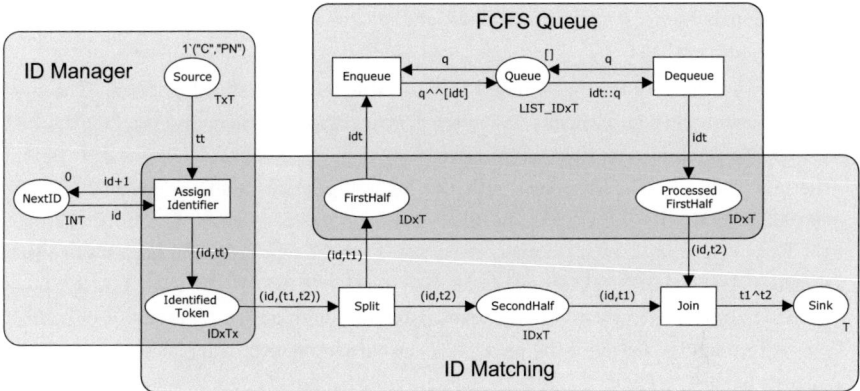

Figure B.5.: Model for different CPN patterns.

The FCFS policy sorts tokens according to their arrival time. For an *FCFS queue*, tokens are appended at the end of the queue and removed from its beginning. Thus, tokens remain in the queue until all tokens that where in the queue at the time of arrival have been removed.

Figure B.5 exemplarily depicts the behaviour of an FCFS queue. The queue stores tokens of type `IDxT` in a list (`LIST_IDxT`). Transition `Enqueue` removes a token (`idt`) from place `FirstHalf` and the list token (`q`, i.e., the queue) from place `Queue`. It appends token `idt` at the end of list `q` and stores the new list in place `Queue`. In CPN ML, `[idt]` denotes a list (`[...]`) with a single element `idt` and statement `q^^[idt]` concatenates the lists `q` and `[idt]`.

Listing B.1: Functions `hasHigherPriority` and `priorityInsert` for priority queues.

```
colset T = INT;                (* Basic colour set of queued tokens *)
colset PT = product T * INT;   (* Adding a priority (INT)            *)
colset LIST_PT = list PT;      (* Colour set for queueing places     *)

fun hasHigherPriority ((t1,p1), (t2, p2)) = (p1 > p2);

fun priorityInsert (element,[]) = [element]
  | priorityInsert (element, head::queue) =
      if hasHigherPriority (element,head)
        then element::head::queue
        else head::(priorityInsert element, queue);
```

If the queue contains at least one element, transition `Dequeue` is enabled. It removes the current queue (`idt::q`) from place `Queue` where `idt` denotes the head and `q` the tail of the queue. Furthermore, it puts the tail back and creates a new token with colour `idt` on place `ProcessedFirstHalf`.

Priority queues order tokens according to an externally defined priority. The priority queue ensures that all elements are ordered with respect to their priority, i.e., the highest priority comes first, the lowest last. Transitions accessing a priority queue always remove the first element, i.e., the token with the highest priority, from the queue. Listing B.1 shows the necessary data types and functions for a priority queue. Colour set `PT` extends the basic colour set `T` by a priority. Collection `List_PT` represents the necessary collection. Function `hasHigherPriority` compares the priority of two `PT` tokens. Finally, function `priorityInsert` directly inserts the token (`element`) into the list if it is empty, or recursively moves through the list until the priority of the current element is larger than the one of the queue's head.

The queue pattern family requires that all transitions insert and remove elements according to the defined policy. Mulyar [MvdA05] proposes further approaches for the modelling of queues. However, all proposed models impose rules for transitions accessing the place. The above variant provides a high flexibility and is thus well-suited for modelling general purpose operating system schedulers.

C. Technological Background

C.1. Benchmark Application

The resource demands specified in the model need to be mapped to actual code that consumes the specified amount of processing time. Therefore, algorithms, like the Fast Fourier Transform or Fibonacci number computations, generates the necessary load. Such algorithms are, for example, used in the SPEC CPU2000 benchmark to measure the performance of a processor [Cor00, Hen00]. The resource demand generator [BDH08] automatically determines fitting input parameters for an algorithm to meet the specified resource demands on a given platform. A calibration identifies the dependency of input parameters and processing time for an algorithm. Its results define the algorithm's input parameters during prototype execution. If, for example, a Fibonacci number generating algorithm needs to approximate a resource demand of 32 ms, then the calibration will determine the amount of Fibonacci numbers to compute during this period, say 253. The prototype uses this value, instead of the specified time, to generate the resource demand of 32 ms. The calibration measures the execution time of an algorithm in the single-threaded case, i.e., its (almost) uninterrupted and undisturbed execution time. During the prototype's execution, the system may process multiple requests concurrently. The measured performance metrics reflect influences of the underlying platform such as resource contention and caching effects. Thus, different load generating algorithms can lead to different performance results when executed concurrently. In the following, we describe the requirements and preconditions of the proposed approach and introduces the calibration as well as the execution of demands in detail. A discussion of open challenges and limitations concludes this appendix.

Calibration Requirements The calibration needs to map specified processing times to input parameters of an algorithm. It must be independent of the actual platform and algorithm, i.e., the calibration must automatically determine the input parameter of an algorithm on a given platform to create the specified resource demands. For example, it may require 43 Fibonacci number computations on one system and 345 on another to generate a demand of 1 ms. In the scenarios considered in this paper, the times taken by the demand generating functions range from one millisecond to several seconds. Furthermore, the framework should support multiple load generating algorithms, since the different behaviour of algorithms (e.g., memory usage) can affect a prototype's performance. Finally, the calibration of an algorithm's input parameters should be fully automated and transparent to the software architect, to achieve a proper applicability of our approach.

Calibration Strategy   In order to fulfil the above requirements, assumptions such as the load of an algorithm is controlled by a single integer value as input parameter, e.g., the amount of Fibonacci numbers generated, must be made. The execution time of each algorithm needs to be minimum for 0 and increases monotonically with the input value. For the Fibonacci number generation, the computation of 0 numbers is (surprisingly) fastest and its execution time increases the more numbers it computes. Except for the need for a monotonically increasing function, we do not make any further assumptions about the dependency of the input parameter's value and the algorithm's execution time. The dependency can be linear, exponential or any other monotonically increasing function.

To efficiently approximate resource demands, we first calibrate an algorithm for a given hard- and software environment. Its input parameters are determined for a set of predefined execution times. The results provide the basis for load generation during a prototype's execution. Since a prototype can issue many arbitrary resource demands, we cannot determine the input parameters for all demands in advance. Instead, we compose requested demands of smaller, previously calibrated ones. In the following, we explain the details of the calibration as well as the resource demand break down.

C.1.1. Determining the Input Value for a Specific Resource Demand

The calibration method iteratively approximates the best input value to reach a specified execution time. Therefore, it implements a variant of the bisection method [BF88], which is a root-finding algorithm.

We want the execution time of an algorithm $exec_{alg}(n)$ with input parameter n to match the specified target execution time t: $exec_{alg}(n) = t$. Thus, we need to solve $exec_{alg}(n) - t = 0$. If we define $f(n) = exec_{alg}(n) - t$, the problem becomes a typical root finding problem with $f(n) = 0$. Figure C.1 illustrates the approximated function $f(n)$ as well as the bisection method. Provided that all implemented algorithms have strictly monotonic behaviour, each generated function has got exactly one root point representing the corresponding iteration parameter to the targeted run time.

To find function f's root, the calibration needs to identify two input values n_{left} and n_{right} that represent the borders of the first interval. The interval must contain the function's root, thus the function must be smaller than zero for the left border $(f(n_{left}) < 0)$ and larger for

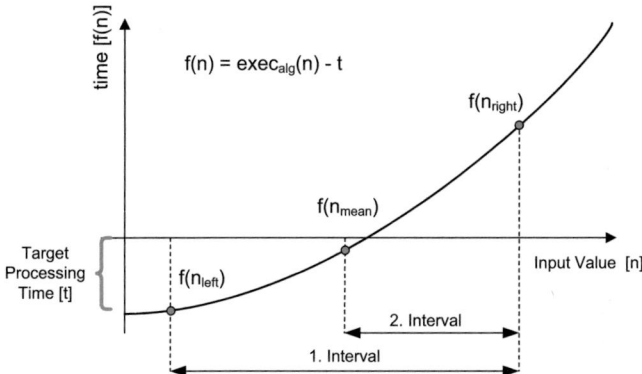

Figure C.1.: Abstract illustration of the bisection method.

the right one ($f(n_{right}) > 0$). For the first, the calibration selects zero ($n_{left} = 0$) as initial value, which corresponds to the smallest possible value of f. To find a value for n_{right} with $f(n_{right}) > 0$, the calibration executes the algorithm with a predefined value. If the result for f is smaller than zero, the calibration doubles the input value and re-executes the algorithm. This continues until a value with $f(n_{right}) > 0$ is found. For the above example, the interval's left border is $n_{left} = 0$. Since the generation of zero Fibonacci numbers consumes no time, the functions value is $f(n_{left}) = -32$. The initial value for the right hand side is $n_{right} = 200$. However, the functions value $f(n_{right}) = -5$ is still below zero. Thus, the calibration doubles the value ($n_{right} = 400$) and determines the new result, e.g., $f(n_{right}) = 48$ which is greater than zero. The initial interval borders are $n_{left} = 0$ and $n_{right} = 400$.

When the borders of the first interval have been determined, the execution of the bisection method starts. It repeatedly halves the interval, determines the execution time of the algorithm for the interval's mean value, and selects the subinterval which contains the function's root. The intervals mean value of the example is $n_{mean} = 200$ with a value of $f(200) = -5$. Thus, the bisection method selects $n'_{left} = n_{mean} = 200$ as left and $n'_{right} = n_{right} = 400$ as right border of the new interval. Figure C.1 illustrates two iteration steps of the bisection method. The approximation terminates as soon as the distance of the interval borders is equal or less than 1 millisecond or a predefined number of iterations is exceeded.

The execution time of an algorithm needs to be determined accurately to enable exact input value calibrations. This requires multiple executions of the algorithm during each iteration of the bisection method. The application of statistical methods removes outliers and achieves stable results over multiple executions. In the next section, we describe how a single resource demand can be mapped to multiple pre-calibrated input values of a load generating algorithm.

C.1.2. Resource Demand Break Down

The bisection method allows us to determine the input value of an algorithm on a specific platform for a certain resource demand. However, the process requires several iterations including multiple executions of the algorithm with different input values. As we want to keep the calibration effort minimum, we focus on a limited number of resource demands whose input parameters are determined during the calibration period. All other resource demands are composed from the predetermined ones.

During the calibration the algorithm's input values for 2^n with $n \in \{0 \ldots 10\}$ milliseconds are determined. The results of the calibration are stored in a table which contains approximated parameters associated with their individual execution times. Using the greedy strategy, an incoming demand is dived into multiple sub-demands of 2^0 ms to 2^{10} ms. To generate the workload of the whole demand, each of the sub-demands is executed sequentially. This allows us to efficiently and automatically approximate different demand types on arbitrary platforms. For example, a demand of 300 ms is approximated by the sub-demands: 256 ms + 32 ms + 8 ms + 4 ms. For each sub-demand the input value of the used algorithm is retrieved from the previous calibration. Executing the algorithm four times with the corresponding input values leads to a total time consumption of 300 ms. The overhead introduced by the break down and multiple executions is much smaller than 1 ms and, hence, can be neglected. This allows an approximation of any demand for any platform and algorithm. Next, we discuss the limitations of this calibration approach.

C.1.3. Discussion

The accuracy of the demand calibration is limited due to disturbances of the underlying platform, like garbage collection or operating system services. During the calibration period, multiple executions of the algorithm in combination with statistical analyses limit the influence of these disturbances. However, these influences can lead to deviations about 6% of requested and actual processing time during the run time of a prototype. Furthermore, it requires to execute the prototype multiple times in order to achieve stable results. The varying execution times are a result of disturbances of the underlying platform and cannot be totally excluded from the resource demand generation. The use of longer calibration runs with more executions of the algorithm can increase accuracy, but cannot totally remove the effect.

On the other hand, it can also be desirable to capture overheads on account of life cycle activities such as garbage collection. An algorithm can, for example, mimic object creations, memory usage, and even trigger stress related effects such as swapping. If the load generating algorithm is chosen in the right way, it will allow software architects to identify the systems load limits and evaluate the effect of memory usage on software performance. However, the amount of memory used cannot be specified within the PCM, but would be defined by the algorithm in use. This allows only vague estimations of the actual memory usage of an application.

The algorithm itself does not model I/O or CPU bursts of a process. The RD-SEFFs of the PCM describe such behavioural aspects of an application, which software architects have to describe explicitly. The following case study demonstrates the accuracy of our approach as well as the influence of the underlying platform and the selected algorithm on performance.

It is often desirable to express the execution time of an internal action in dependency of the system's state. The PCM models such dependencies with stochastic expressions. They can, for example, derive the execution time of an internal action from the number of concurrently running tasks (load dependent server) or from the number of elements in an array. During execution, the performance prototype evaluates the stochastic expressions. The result of the evaluation represents the actual execution time and is passed to the calibrated resource demand, which translates the demand into parameters for the load generating algorithm.

C.2. Workload Generation

The test driver needs to allow a flexible characterisation of workloads (open and closed) and an exact specification of resource demands. It must enable maximum control over the system load, user task behaviour, and task priorities. The actual handling must be comparable for the considered operating systems. To reach this aim, the test driver consists of a load generator and demand servers. Both run in separate operating system processes that communicate via remote message invocation (RMI). The division of the test driver among multiple processes is necessary to assign separate priorities to all involved tasks. For example, the load driver usually recieves a higher priority than the worker tasks. To control task priorities, the *nice* command available in all Unix operating systems is used [SGG05]. Under Windows, its Cygwin implementation [RH] maps the different nice-level to windows priorities. This allows a comparison between the results among different operating systems. The load driver always runs at the highest possible priority avoiding disturbances by the currently executing demand servers. The usage of RMI allows synchronous communication between different processes, but adds additional overhead, e.g., the marshalling and demarshalling of method calls. However, the overhead can be tolerated for the scenarios considered in this thesis (below 3 ms [Bec08]).

C.3. Resource Demand Generation

To evaluate the different influences of processors and operating systems, the demand servers can generate load with different algorithms:

1. Prime number Calculator

2. Fast Fourier Transformation

3. Quicksort (Java Implementation)

These algorithms are common in processor benchmarks such as SPEC CPU2000 [Hen00, Cor00]. The demand servers allow adjusting of the specification of resource demands with milliseconds precision. For each algorithm and execution environment the demand server first calibrates, so that it can translate requested execution times to parameters for the corresponding algorithm (cf. Appendix C.1).

C.4. Experimental Setting

The description of the experimental setup should allow the reproduction of the experiment. It includes a description of the hardware and software environment, the implemented test driver, the measurement method, and a list of possible threads to validity. Furthermore, Appendix C.1 describes the implementation of the benchmark application and discusses how different execution environments influence the measurements. For the experiments, the following hardware and software environments have been used.

Processor:

1. Intel Pentium M, 1.86 GHz, 2 GB RAM

2. Intel Pentium D, 3 GHz, 2 GB RAM

3. AMD Athlon 64 X2 Dual Core Processor 5200+, 2.61 GHz, 2 GB RAM

Operating Systems:

1. Windows XP Professional (SP2)

2. Windows Server 2003 (SP2)

3. Ubuntu 7.10 Desktop Edition (Kernel 2.6.22)

Java Run-Time Environment:

- Java HotSpot(TM) Client VM (build 1.6.0_03-b05, mixed mode, sharing)

List of Figures

List of Tables

Bibliography

[AAB+07]   S. Aalto, U. Ayesta, S. Borst, V. Misra, and R. Nú nez Queija. Beyond Processor Sharing. *ACM SIGMETRICS Performance Evaluation Review*, 34(4):36–43, 2007.

[Aas05]   J. Aas. Understanding the Linux 2.6.8.1 Scheduler. Technical report, Silicon Graphics, Inc. (SGI), 2005.

[AD96]   S. Au and S. Dandamudi. The Impact of Program Structure on the Performance of Scheduling Policies in Multiprocessor Systems. *International Journal of Computers and Their Applications*, 3(1):17–30, April 1996.

[AGM+94]   I. Ahmad, A. Ghafoor, K. Mehrotra, C. Mohan, and S. Ranka. Performance Modeling of Load Balancing Algorithms Using Neural Networks. *Concurrency: Practice Experience*, 6(5):393–409, 1994.

[Apa]   Apache. Apache HTTP Server Project. http://httpd.apache.org. Last retrieved 2008-07-02.

[AS01]   E. Almog and H. Shachnai. Scheduling memory accesses through a shared bus. *Performance Evaluation*, 46(2-3):193–218, 2001.

[Bau93]   F. Bause. "QN + PN = QPN" - Combining Queueing Networks and Petri Nets. Technical report, Fachbereichs Informatik der Universität Dortmund, Germany, 1993.

[BBG97]   M. Bravetti, M. Bernardo, and R. Gorrieri. From EMPA to GSMPA: Allowing for General Distributions. In E. Brinksma and A. Nymeyer, editors, *Proc. of the 5th Int. Workshop on Process Algebras and Performance Modeling (PAPM'97)*, pages 17–33, 1997.

[BC05]   D.P. Bovet and M. Cesati. *Understanding the Linux Kernel*. O'Reilly Media, Inc., 2005.

[BCR94]   V.R. Basili, G. Caldiera, and H.D. Rombach. The Goal Question Metric Approach. *Encyclopedia of Software Engineering*, 1:528–532, 1994.

[BCS06]   M. Bertoli, G. Casale, and G. Serazzi. Java Modelling Tools: an Open
           Source Suite for Queueing Network Modelling andWorkload Analysis. In
           QEST '06: Proceedings of the 3rd international conference on the Quanti-
           tative Evaluation of Systems, pages 119–120, Washington, DC, USA, 2006.
           IEEE Computer Society.

[BCS07]   M. Bertoli, G. Casale, and G. Serazzi. The JMT Simulator for Performance
           Evaluation of Non-Product-Form Queueing Networks. In ANSS '07: Pro-
           ceedings of the 40th Annual Simulation Symposium, pages 3–10, Washington,
           DC, USA, 2007. IEEE Computer Society.

[BD04]   M. Bravetti and P.R. D'Argenio. Tutte le Algebre Insieme: Concepts, Dis-
           cussions and Relations of Stochastic Process Algebras with General Distri-
           butions. In Validation of Stochastic Systems, volume 2925 of Lecture Notes
           in Computer Science, pages 44–88. Springer-Verlag Berlin Heidelberg, 2004.

[BDC02]   M. Bernardo, L. Donatiello, and P. Ciancarini. Stochastic Process Algebra:
           From an Algebraic Formalism to an Architectural Description Language. In
           Performance Evaluation of Complex Systems: Techniques and Tools, volume
           2459 of Lecture Notes in Computer Science, pages 236–260. Springer-Verlag
           Berlin Heidelberg, 2002.

[BDH08]   S. Becker, T. Dencker, and J. Happe. Model-Driven Generation of Per-
           formance Prototypes. In SIPEW 2008: SPEC International Performance
           Evaluation Workshop, volume 5119 of Lecture Notes in Computer Science,
           pages 79–98. Springer-Verlag Berlin Heidelberg, 2008.

[BDHH04]   M.J. Bligh, M. Dobson, D. Hart, and G. Huizenga. Linux on NUMA Systems.
           In Proceedings of the Linux Symposium, volume 1, pages 89–102, 2004.

[Bec08]   S. Becker. Coupled Model Transformations for QoS Enabled Component-
           Based Software Design. Dissertation, University of Oldenburg, Germany,
           January 2008.

[BF88]   R.L. Burden and J.D. Faires. Numerical Analysis. PWS Publishing Co.
           Boston, MA, USA, 1988.

[BGTdM98] G. Bolch, S. Greiner, K. S. Trivedi, and H. de Meer. Queueing Networks
           and Markov Chains: Modeling and Performance Evaluation With Computer
           Science Applications. Wiley & Sons, New York, NY, USA, 1998.

[BH07]   M. Bernardo and J. Hillston, editors. *Formal Methods for Performance Evaluation (7th International School on Formal Methods for the Design of Computer, Communication, and Software Systems, SFM2007)*, volume 4486 of *Lecture Notes in Computer Science*. Springer-Verlag Berlin Heidelberg, May 2007.

[BHK06]   S. Becker, J. Happe, and H. Koziolek. Putting Components into Context: Supporting QoS-Predictions with an explicit Context Model. In R. Reussner, C. Szyperski, and W. Weck, editors, *Proceedings of the 11th International Workshop on Component Oriented Programming (WCOP'06)*, pages 1–6, July 2006.

[BK92]   G. Bolch and M. Kirschnick. PEPSY-QNS – Performance Evaluation and Prediction SYstem for Queueing NetworkS. Technical Report TR-I4-92-21, Universität Erlangen-Nürnberg, Institut für Mathematische Maschinen und Datenverarbeitung IV, 1992.

[BK96]   F. Bause and P. S. Kritzinger. *Stochastic Petri Nets - An Introduction to the Theory*. Vieweg, 1996.

[BKR95]   A. Borshchev, Y. Karpov, and V. Roudakov. COVERS - A Tool for the Design of Real-time Concurrent Systems. In *Proc. 3rd International Conference on Parallel Computing Technologies (PaCT '95)*, pages 219–233. Springer, 1995.

[BKR07]   S. Becker, H. Koziolek, and R. Reussner. Model-based Performance Prediction with the Palladio Component Model. In *Proceedings of the 6th International Workshop on Software and Performance (WOSP2007)*, pages 56–67. SIGSOFT Software Engineering Notes, ACM, New York, NY, USA, February 2007.

[BKR08]   S. Becker, H. Koziolek, and R. Reussner. The Palladio Component Model for Model-Driven Performance Prediction: Extended version. *Journal of Systems and Software*, 2008. In Press, Accepted Manuscript.

[BMdW+04] E. Bondarev, J. Muskens, P. de With, M. Chaudron, and J. Lukkien. Predicting Real-Time Properties of Component Assemblies: A Scenario-Simulation Approach. In *Proc. 30th EUROMICRO Conference (EUROMICRO '04)*, pages 40–47. IEEE Computer Society, 2004.

[BMIS04]   S. Balsamo, A. Di Marco, P. Inverardi, and M. Simeoni. Model-Based Performance Prediction in Software Development: A Survey. *Transactions on Software Engineering*, 30(5):295–310, May 2004.

[Bos02]   S. K. Bose. *An Introduction to Queueing Systems*. Springer-Verlag Berlin
             Heidelberg, 2002.

[BP04]   J.R. Bulpin and I.A. Pratt. Multiprogramming Performance of the Pentium
             4 with Hyper-Threading. In *Proceedings of the Third Annual Workshop on
             Duplicating, Deconstruction and Debunking*, pages 53–62, 2004.

[BP07]   L. Bortolussi and A. Policriti. Stochastic Concurrent Constraint Program-
             ming and Differential Equations. In *Proceedings of the Fifth Workshop on
             Quantitative Aspects of Programming Languages (QAPL 2007*, volume 190
             of *Electronic Notes in Theoretical Computer Science*, pages 27–42. Elsevier,
             2007.

[BSUK07]   E.W. Biersack, B. Schroeder, and G. Urvoy-Keller. Scheduling in Practice.
             ACM SIGMETRICS Performance Evaluation Review, 34(4):21–28, 2007.

[CCF+06]   R. Chanin, M. Correa, P. Fernandes, A. Sales, R. Scheer, and A. Zorzo. An-
             alytical Modeling for Operating System Schedulers on NUMA Systems. In
             *Proceedings of the Second International Workshop on the Practical Applica-
             tion of Stochastic Modeling (PASM 2005)*, volume 151 of *Electronic Notes
             in Theoretical Computer Science*, pages 131–149. Elsevier, 2006.

[CDGH06]   M. Calder, A. Duguid, S. Gilmore, and J. Hillston. Stronger computational
             modelling of signalling pathways using both continuous and discrete-state
             methods. In *Computational Methods in Systems Biology*, volume 3746 of
             Lecture Notes in Computer Science, pages 63–77, 2006.

[CE00]   K. Czarnecki and U. Eisenecker. *Generative Programming: Methods, Tools,
             and Applications*. Addison-Wesley, 2000.

[CGL94]   G. Ciardo, R. German, and Ch. Lindemann. A Characterization of the
             Stochastic Process Underlying a Stochastic Petri Net. *Transactions on Soft-
             ware Engineering*, 20(7):506–515, 1994.

[CMZ02]   E. Cecchet, J. Marguerite, and W. Zwaenepoel. Performance and scalability
             of EJB applications. *SIGPLAN Notices*, 37(11):246–261, 2002.

[Cor00]   Standard Performance Evaluation Corporation. SPEC CPU2000 V1.3.
             http://www.spec.org/cpu/, 2000. Last retrieved 2008-06-10.

[cpn]   CPN Tools. www.daimi.au.dk/CPNTools. Last retrieved 2008-08-20.

[CPR07]   V. Cortellessa, P. Pierini, and D. Rossi. Integrating Software Models and
             Platform Models for Performance Analysis. *Transactions on Software Engi-
             neering*, 33(6):385–401, June 2007.

[Cre05]   M. Creeger. Multicore CPUs for the Masses. *Queue*, 3(7):64–65, 2005.

[CW00]   M. Courtois and M. Woodside. Using regression splines for software performance analysis. In *WOSP '00: Proceedings of the 2nd international workshop on Software and performance*, pages 105–114. ACM, 2000.

[CZS06]   M. Corrêa, A. Zorzo, and R. Scheer. Operating System Multilevel Load Balancing. In *SAC '06: Proceedings of the 2006 ACM Symposium on Applied computing*, pages 1467–1471. ACM, New York, NY, USA, 2006.

[DB78]   P. J. Denning and J. P. Buzen. The Operational Analysis of Queueing Network Models. *ACM Computing Surveys*, 10(3):225–261, 1978.

[Dou02]   B. P. Douglass. *Real-Time Design Patterns*. Object Technology Series. Addison-Wesley Professional, 2002.

[DPE04]   G. Denaro, A. Polini, and W. Emmerich. Early Performance Testing of Distributed Software Applications. *SIGSOFT Software Engineering Notes*, 29(1):94–103, 2004.

[EE00]   J. Engblom and A. Ermedahl. Modeling Complex Flows for Worst-Case Execution Time Analysis. In *In Proceedings of the 21st IEEE Real-Time Systems Symposium (RTSS 2000)*, pages 163–174. IEEE Computer Society, 2000.

[EVW80]   A. Ephremides, P. Varaiya, and J. Walrand. A simple dynamic routing problem. *IEEE Transactions on Automatic Control*, 25(4):690–693, 1980.

[FBH05]   V. Firus, S. Becker, and J. Happe. Parametric Performance Contracts for QML-specified Software Components. In *Proceedings of 2nd International Workshop on Formal Foundations of Embedded Software and Component-Based Software Architectures (FESCA '05)*, pages 64–79, 2005.

[FLM⁺98]   A. Fuggetta, L. Lavazza, S. Morasca, S. Cinti, G. Oldano, and E. Orazi. Applying GQM in an industrial software factory. *ACM Transactions on Software Engineering and Methodology*, 7(4):411–448, 1998.

[FMW⁺07]   G. Franks, P. Maly, M. Woodside, D. Petriu, and A. Hubbard. Layered Queueing Network Solver and Simulator User Manual, May 2007. Last retrieved 2008-01-13.

[FNNS06]   J. Fredriksson, T. Nolte, M. Nolin, and H. Schmidt. Predicting Execution Time for Variable Behaviour Embedded Real-Time Components. In *Proceedings of Workshop on Models and Analysis for Automotive Systems*, December 2006.

[Fra99]   G. Franks. *Performance Analysis of Distributed Server Systems*. PhD thesis, Department of Systems and Computer Engineering, Carleton University, Ottawa, Ontario, Canada, December 1999.

[Fre05]   D. Freedman. *Statistical Models: Theory and Practice*. Cambridge University Press, 2005.

[Fri07]   H. Friedrich. Modellierung nebenläufiger, komponentenbasierter Software-Systeme mit Entwurfsmustern. Masters thesis, Universität Karlsruhe (TH), 2007.

[GL03]   I. Gorton and A. Liu. Performance Evaluation of Alternative Component Architectures for Enterprise JavaBean Applications. *IEEE Internet Computing*, 7(3):18–23, 2003.

[GMS05]   V. Grassi, R. Mirandola, and A. Sabetta. From design to analysis models: a kernel language for performance and reliability analysis of component-based systems. In *Proc. 5th International Workshop on Software and Performance (WOSP '05)*, pages 25–36. ACM, New York, NY, USA, 2005.

[GMS06]   V. Grassi, R. Mirandola, and A. Sabetta. A Model Transformation Approach for the Early Performance and Reliability Analysis of Component-Based Systems. In *Proceedings of CBSE'06*, volume 4063 of *Lecture Notes in Computer Science*, pages 270–284. Springer-Verlag Berlin Heidelberg, 2006.

[GPB+06]   B. Goetz, T. Peierls, J. Bloch, J. Bowbeer, D. Holmes, and D. Lea. *Java: Concurrency in Practice*. Addison-Wesley, 2006.

[GTU91]   A. Gupta, A. Tucker, and S. Urushibara. The Impact of Operating System Scheduling Policies and Synchronization Methods of Performance of Parallel Applications. In *SIGMETRICS '91: Proceedings of the 1991 ACM SIGMETRICS conference on Measurement and modeling of computer systems*, pages 120–132. ACM, New York, NY, USA, 1991.

[Hap05a]   J. Happe. Performance Prediction for Embedded Systems. In *Trustworthy Software Systems*, volume 2, pages 173–196, 2005.

[Hap05b]   J. Happe. Prediction Mean Service Execution Times of Software Components Based on Markov Models. In *Proceedings of the First International Conference on Quality of Software Architectures (QoSA2005)*, number 3712 in Lecture Notes in Computer Science (LNCS), 2005.

[Hap07]   J. Happe. Towards a Model of Fair and Unfair Semaphores in MoDeST. In *Proceedings of the 6th Workshop on Process Algebra and Stochastically Timed Activities*, pages 51–55, 2007.

[HBCM99] M. Harchol-Balter, M. Crovella, and C.D. Murta. On Choosing a Task Assignment Policy for a Distributed Server System. *Journal of Parallel and Distributed Computing*, 59(2):204–228, 1999.

[HBOSWW05] M. Harchol-Balter, T. Osogami, A. Scheller-Wolf, and A. Wierman. Multi-Server Queueing Systems with Multiple Priority Classes. *Queueing Systems: Theory and Applications*, 51(3-4):331–360, 2005.

[HBS+08] M. Hapner, R. Burridge, R. Sharma, J. Fialli, and K. Stout. Java Message Service Specification - Version 1.1. http://java.sun.com/products/jms/, January 2008.

[HBSBA03] M. Harchol-Balter, B. Schroeder, N. Bansal, and M. Agrawal. Size-based scheduling to improve web performance. *ACM Transactions on Computer Systems*, 21(2):207–233, 2003.

[Hen00] John L. Henning. SPEC CPU2000: measuring CPU performance in the new millennium. *IEEE Computer*, 33(7):28–35, 2000.

[HFBR08] J. Happe, H. Friedrich, S. Becker, and R. H. Reussner. A Pattern-Based Performance Completion for Message-Oriented Middleware. In *Proceedings of the 7th International Workshop on Software and Performance (WOSP '08)*, pages 165–176. ACM, 2008.

[HHK02] H. Hermanns, U. Herzog, and J.-P. Katoen. Process Algebra for Performance Evaluation. *Theoretical Computer Science*, 274(1-2):43–87, 2002.

[Hil96] J. Hillston. *A Compositional Approach to Performance Modelling*. Cambridge University Press, 1996.

[Hil05] J. Hillston. Fluid flow approximation of PEPA models. In *Proceedings of the Second International Conference on the Quantitative Evaluation of Systems (QEST'05)*, pages 33–43, Washington, DC, USA, 2005. IEEE Computer Society.

[HKR06] J Happe, H. Koziolek, and R. H. Reussner. Parametric Performance Contracts for Software Components with Concurrent Behaviour. In Frank S. de Boer and Vladimir Mencl, editors, *Proceedings of the 3rd International Workshop on Formal Aspects of Component Software (FACS)*, volume 182 of *Electronic Notes in Theoretical Computer Science*, pages 91–106, 2006.

[HSZT00] C. Hirel, R. A. Sahner, X. Zang, and K. S. Trivedi. Reliability and Performability Modeling Using SHARPE 2000. In *TOOLS '00: Proceedings of the 11th International Conference on Computer Performance Evaluation: Modelling Techniques and Tools*, volume 1786 of *Lecture Notes in Computer Science*, pages 345–349. Springer-Verlag Berlin Heidelberg, 2000.

[HW03]   G. Hohpe and B. Woolf. *Enterprise Integration Patterns: Designing, Build-ing, and Deploying Messaging Solutions.* Addison-Wesley Longman Publish-ing Co., Inc., 2003.

[HZS01]   X. S. Hu, T. Zhou, and E. H.-M. Sha. Estimating probabilistic timing per-formance for real-time embedded systems. *IEEE Trans. Very Large Scale Integr. Syst.*, 9(6):833–844, 2001.

[IBM]   IBM. The Cell project at IBM Research. http://www.research.ibm.com/cell/. Last retrieved 2008-08-16.

[IZG+07]   R. Iyer, L. Zhao, F. Guo, R. Illikkal, S. Makineni, D. Newell, Y. Solihin, L. Hsu, and S. Reinhardt. QoS Policies and Architecture for Cache/Memory in CMP Platforms. *ACM SIGMETRICS Performance Evaluation Review*, 35(1):25–36, 2007.

[Jai91]   R. Jain. *The Art of Computer Systems Performance Analysis : Techniques for Experimental Design, Measurement, Simulation, and Modeling.* Wiley, 1991.

[Jen92]   K. Jensen. *Coloured Petri Nets: Basic Concepts, Analysis Methods, and Practical Use*, volume 1 of *EATCS Monographs on Theoretical Computer Science.* Springer-Verlag Berlin Heidelberg, 1992.

[Jen94]   K. Jensen. An Introduction to the Theoretical Aspects of Coloured Petri Nets. In J.W. de Bakker, W.-P. de Roever, and G. Rozenberg, editors, *A Decade of Concurrency*, volume 803, pages 230–272, 1994.

[Jen98]   K. Jensen. An Introduction to the Practical Use of Coloured Petri Nets. In *Lectures on Petri Nets II: Applications, Advances in Petri Nets, the volumes are based on the Advanced Course on Petri Nets*, pages 237–292, London, UK, 1998. Springer-Verlag Berlin Heidelberg.

[JKW07]   K. Jensen, L. M. Kristensen, and L. Wells. Coloured Petri Nets and CPN Tools for modelling and validation of concurrent systems. *International Jour-nal on Software Tools for Technology Transfer (STTT)*, 9(3):213–254, 2007.

[JLT85]   E.D. Jensen, C.D. Locke, and H. Tokuda. A Time-Driven Scheduling Model for Real-Time Operating Systems. In *Proceedings of the IEEE Real-Time Systems Symposium*, pages 112–122. IEEE Computer Society, 1985.

[KB03]   S. Kounev and A. Buchmann. Performance Modelling of Distributed E-Business Applications using Queuing Petri Nets. In *IEEE International Sym-posium on Performance Analysis of Systems and Software, ISPASS*, 2003.

[KB06]   S. Kouev and A. Buchmann. SimQPN: a tool and methodology for an-
           alyzing queueing Petri net models by means of simulation. *Performance
           Evaluation*, 63(4):364–394, 2006.

[KB07]   M. Kuperberg and S .Becker. Predicting Software Component Performance:
           On the Relevance of Parameters for Benchmarking Bytecode and APIs. In
           R. Reussner, C. Czyperski, and W. Weck, editors, *Proc. 12th International
           Workshop on Component Oriented Programming (WCOP'07)*, July 2007.

[KBH07]   H. Koziolek, S. Becker, and J. Happe. Predicting the Performance of
           Component-based Software Architectures with different Usage Profiles. In
           *Proceedings of the 3rd International Conference on the Quality of Software
           Architectures (QoSA)*, volume 4880 of *Lecture Notes in Computer Science*,
           pages 145–163. 4909, 2007.

[KBHR07]   H. Koziolek, S. Becker, J. Happe, and R. Reussner. *Model-Driven Soft-
           ware Development: Integrating Quality Assurance*, chapter Evaluating Per-
           formance and Reliability of Software Architecture with the Palladio Compo-
           nent Model. IDEA Group Inc., December 2007. To Appear.

[KBHR08]   H. Koziolek, S. Becker, J. Happe, and R. Reussner. Life-Cycle Aware Mod-
           elling of Software Components. In *Proceedings of the 11th International Sym-
           posium on Component-Based Software Engineering (CBSE)*, volume 5282 of
           Lecture Notes in Computer Science, pages 278–285. Springer-Verlag Berlin
           Heidelberg, October 2008.

[KGC+06]   R. Y. Kawasaki, L. A. Guedes, D. L. Cardoso, C. R. L. Frances, G. H. S.
           Carvalho, J. C. W. A. Cost, and N. L. Vijaykumar. A Markovian Perfor-
           mance Model for Resource Allocation Scheduling on GNU/Linux. In *Fron-
           tiers of High Performance Computing and Networking – ISPA 2006 Work-
           shops*, number 4331 in Lecture Notes in Computer Science (LNCS), pages
           844–853, 2006.

[KH05]   H. Koziolek and J. Happe. Performance Metrics for Specific Domains. In
           Dependability Metrics, volume 4909 of *Lecture Notes in Computer Science*,
           pages 239 – 248. Springer-Verlag Berlin Heidelberg, 2005.

[KH06]   H. Koziolek and J. Happe. A QoS Driven Development Process Model for
           Component-Based Software Systems. In Ian Gorton, George T. Heineman,
           Ivica Crnkovic, Heinz W. Schmidt, Judith A. Stafford, Clemens A. Szyperski,
           and Kurt C. Wallnau, editors, *Proceedings of the 9th International Sympo-
           sium on Component-Based Software Engineering (CBSE'06)*, volume 4063 of
           Lecture Notes in Computer Science, pages 336–343. Springer-Verlag Berlin
           Heidelberg, 2006.

[KHB06]   H. Koziolek, J. Happe, and S. Becker. Parameter Dependent Performance
          Specifications of Software Components. In Ch. Hofmeister, I. Crnkovic,
          R. Reussner, and S. Becker, editors, *Quality of Software Architectures, 2nd
          International Conference, QoSA 2006, Västerås, Sweden, June 27 - 29,
          2006, Proceedings*, volume 4214 of *Lecture Notes in Computer Science*, pages
          163–179. Springer-Verlag Berlin Heidelberg, June 2006.

[KN07]   M. Kluge and W. E. Nagel. Analysis of Linux Scheduling with VAMPIR. In
          Proceedings of the 2nd International Conference on Computational Science,
          volume 4488 of *Lecture Notes in Computer Science*, pages 823–830. Springer-
          Verlag Berlin Heidelberg, 2007.

[Kou06]   S. Kounev.   Performance Modeling and Evaluation of Distributed
          Component-Based Systems Using Queueing Petri Nets. *Transactions on
          Software Engineering*, 32(7):486–502, July 2006.

[Koz08a] H. Koziolek. *Parameter Dependencies for Reusable Performance Specifica-
          tions of Software Components*. Dissertation, Universität Oldenburg, 2008.

[Koz08b] Heiko Koziolek. *Dependability Metrics*, volume 4909, chapter Introduction
          to Performance Metrics, pages 199 – 203. Springer-Verlag Berlin Heidelberg,
          2008.

[KST99]   G. Koole, P. Sparaggis, and D. Towsley.   Minimizing response times and
          queue lengths in systems of parallel queues. *Journal of Applied Probability*,
          36(4):1185–1193, 1999.

[Kun91]   T. Kunz. The Influence of Different Workload Descriptions on a Heuristic
          Load Balancing Scheme. *Transactions on Software Engineering*, 17(7):725–
          730, 1991.

[LB05]   P. L'Ecuyer and E. Buist. Simulation in Java with SSJ. In *WSC '05: Pro-
          ceedings of the 37th conference on Winter simulation*, pages 611–620. Winter
          Simulation Conference, 2005.

[Lee06]   E. A. Lee. The Problem with Threads. *IEEE Computer*, 39(5):33–42, May
          2006.

[LFG05]   Y. Liu, A. Fekete, and I. Gorton.   Design-Level Performance Prediction
          of Component-Based Applications.   *Transactions on Software Engineer-
          ing*, 31(11):928–941, 2005. Member-Yan Liu and Member-Alan Fekete and
          Member-Ian Gorton.

[LG05]   Yan Liu and Ian Gorton. Performance Prediction of J2EE Applications Us-
           ing Messaging Protocols. In *Component-Based Software Engineering: 8th
           International Symposium*, volume 3489 of *Lecture Notes in Computer Sci-
           ence*, pages 1–16. Springer-Verlag Berlin Heidelberg, 2005.

[lin]   Linux Kernel Source. `http://www.eu.kernel.org/pub/linux/kernel/v2.`
           `6/linux-2.6.22.19.tar.gz`. Last retrieved 2008-07-28.

[LM99]   Y.T.S. Li and S. Malik. *Performance Analysis of Real-Time Embedded Soft-
           ware*. Kluwer Academic Publishers, 1999.

[LMV02]   P. L'Ecuyer, L. Meliani, and J. Vaucher. SSJ: A Framework for Stochastic
           Simulation in Java. In *Proceedings of the 2002 Winter Simulation Confer-
           ence*, pages 234–242. IEEE Computer Society, 2002.

[LR97]   S. Leonardi and D. Raz. Approximating Total Flow Time on Parallel Ma-
           chines. In *STOC '97: Proceedings of the twenty-ninth annual ACM sympo-
           sium on Theory of computing*, pages 110–119. ACM, New York, NY, USA,
           1997.

[LV90]   S. T. Leutenegger and M. K. Vernon. The performance of multiprogrammed
           multiprocessor scheduling algorithms. In *SIGMETRICS '90: Proceedings of
           the 1990 ACM SIGMETRICS conference on Measurement and modeling of
           computer systems*, pages 226–236. ACM, New York, NY, USA, 1990.

[LZGS84]   E.D. Lazowska, J. Zahorjan, G. S. Graham, and K. C. Sevcik. *Quantitative
           System Performance - Computer System Analysis Using Queueing Network
           Models*. Prentice-Hall, 1984.

[MAD04]   Daniel A. Menasce, Virgilio A.F. Almeida, and Lawrence W. Dowdy. *Per-
           formance by Design - Computer Capacity Planning by Example*. Prentice
           Hall, 2004.

[Maj92]   S. Majumdar. The Performance of Local and Global Scheduling Strategies
           in Multiprogrammed Parallel Systems. In *Eleventh Annual International
           Phoenix Conference on Computers and Communications, Conference Pro-
           ceedings.*, pages 55–62, 1992.

[Mau03]   W. Maurer. *Linux Kernelarchitektur – Konzepte, Strukturen und Algorith-
           men von Kernel 2.6*. Carl Hanser Verlag, 2003.

[MBB+89]   M. A. Marsan, G. Balbo, A. Bobbio, G. Chiola, G. Conte, and A. Cumani.
           The Effect of Execution Policies on the Semantics and Analysis of Stochastic
           Petri Nets. *Transactions on Software Engineering*, 15(7):832–846, 1989.

[MBC+95]   M. A. Marsan, G. Balbo, G. Conte, S. Donatelli, and G. Franceschinis. *Modelling with Generalized Stochastic Petri Nets.* John Wiley & Sons Ltd, 1995.

[MEB88]   S. Majumdar, D. L. Eager, and R. B. Bunt. Scheduling in Multiprogrammed Parallel Systems. *ACM SIGMETRICS Performance Evaluation Review,* 16(1):104–113, 1988.

[MHC02]   R. Monson-Haefel and D.A. Chappell. *Java Message Service.* O'Reilly, 2002.

[MPC04]   R. Le Moigne, O. Pasquier, and J-P. Calvez. A Generic RTOS Model for Real-time Systems Simulation with SystemC. In *Proceedings of the conference on Design, automation and test in Europe (DATE '04),* page 30082, Washington, DC, USA, 2004. IEEE Computer Society.

[MS91]   R. Menich and R. F. Serfozo. Optimality of routing and servicing in dependent parallel processing systems. *Queueing Systems: Theory and Applications,* 9(4):403–418, 1991.

[MTHM97]   R. Milner, M. Tofte, R. Harper, and D. MacQueen. *The Definition of Standard ML.* MIT Press, 1997.

[MvdA05]   N.A. Mulyar and W.M.P. van der Aalst. Patterns in Colored Petri Nets. Technical report, Eindhoven University of Technology, Department of Technology Management, April 2005.

[Nag87]   J. Nagle. On Packet Switches with Infinite Storage. *Transactions on Software Engineering,* 35(4):435–438, 1987.

[OHBSW05]   T. Osogami, M. Harchol-Balter, and A. Scheller-Wolf. Analysis of cycle stealing with switching times and thresholds. *Performance Evaluation,* 61(4):347–369, 2005.

[OHBSWZ04]   T. Osogami, M. Harchol-Balter, A. Scheller-Wolf, and L. Zhang. Exploring threshold-based policies for load sharing. In *Proceedings of 42nd Annual Allerton Conference on Communication, Control and Computing.* University of Illinois, 2004.

[(OM04]   Object Management Group (OMG). UML 2 Superstructure, Final Adopted Specification, 2004. last retrieved 2008-01-13.

[(OM05]   Object Management Group (OMG). UML Profile for Schedulability, Performance and Time. http://www.omg.org/cgi-bin/doc?formal/2005-01-02, 2005. Last retrieved 2008-01-13.

[(OM07a]   Object Management Group (OMG). Meta Object Facility (MOF) 2.0 Query/View/Transformation Specification (ptc/07-07-07), 2007. Last retrieved 2008-01-13.

[(OM07b]   Object Management Group (OMG). UML Profile for Modeling and Analysis
             of Real-Time and Embedded systems (MARTE), Beta 1, 2007. Last retrieved
             2008-01-13.

[(OM07c]   Object Management Group (OMG). Unified Modeling Language: Super-
             structure version 2.1.1, 2007. last retrieved 2008-01-13.

[omn]   OMNeT++ Community Site. `http://www.omnetpp.org`. Last retrieved
             2008-07-28.

[Oso05]   T. Osogami. *Analysis of multi-server systems via dimensionality reduction
             of markov chains*. PhD thesis, Carnegie Mellon University, Pittsburgh, PA,
             USA, 2005.

[PA91]   B. Plateau and K. Atif. Stochastic Automata Network of Modeling Parallel
             Systems. *Transactions on Software Engineering*, 17(10):1093–1108, 1991.

[Pal06]   DFG-Research Group Palladio. PCM Bench. `http://sdqweb.ipd.uka.de/`
             `wiki/Palladio_Component_Model`, 2006. Last retrieved 2008-08-22.

[Pet62]   C.A. Petri. *Kommunikation mit Automaten*. PhD thesis, University Bonn,
             Institut für Instrumentelle Mathematik, 1962.

[PW02]   D.B. Petriu and M. Woodside. Software Performance Models from Sys-
             tem Scenarios in Use Case Maps. In *TOOLS '02: Proceedings of the 12th
             International Conference on Computer Performance Evaluation, Modelling
             Techniques and Tools*, volume 2324 of *Lecture Notes in Computer Science*,
             pages 141 – 158. Springer-Verlag Berlin Heidelberg, 2002.

[RBH+07]   R. Reussner, S. Becker, J. Happe, H. Koziolek, K. Krogmann, and M. Kuper-
             berg. The Palladio Component Model. Technical Report 2007-21, Universität
             Karlsruhe (TH), 2007.

[RH]   Incorporated Red Head. GNU + Cygnus + Windows = Cygwin. `http:`
             `//cygwin.com/`. Last retrieved 2008-07-09.

[RK03]   M. Rawat and A. Kshemkalyani. SWIFT: Scheduling in Web Servers for Fast
             Response Time. In *NCA '03: Proceedings of the Second IEEE International
             Symposium on Network Computing and Applications*, pages 51–58. IEEE
             Computer Society, 2003.

[RL80]   M. Reiser and S. S. Lavenberg. Mean-Value Analysis of Closed Multichain
             Queuing Networks. *Journal of the ACM*, 27(2):313–322, 1980.

[Rod85]   David P. Rodgers. Improvements in multiprocessor system design. *ACM
             SIGARCH Computer Architecture News*, 13(3):225–231, 1985.

[RS95]   J. A. Rolia and K. C. Sevcik. The Method of Layers. *Transactions on
             Software Engineering*, 21(8):689–700, 1995.

[RSSS98]   E. Rosti, G. Serazzi, E. Smirni, and M. S. Squillante. The impact of I/O on
             program behavior and parallel scheduling. In *SIGMETRICS '98/PERFOR-
             MANCE '98: Proceedings of the 1998 ACM SIGMETRICS joint interna-
             tional conference on Measurement and modeling of computer systems*, pages
             56–65. ACM, New York, NY, USA, 1998.

[RUKVB04]   I. A. Rai, G. Urvoy-Keller, M. K. Vernon, and E.W. Biersack. Performance
             analysis of LAS-based scheduling disciplines in a packet switched network. In
             *SIGMETRICS '04/Performance '04: Proceedings of the joint international
             conference on Measurement and modeling of computer systems*, pages 106–
             117. ACM, New York, NY, USA, 2004.

[Rus07]   M. Russinovich.   Inside the Windows Vista Kernel.   TechNet Mag-
             azine, http://technet.microsoft.com/en-us/magazine/cc162494.aspx,
             February 2007.

[SB99]   R. Van Solingen and E. Berghout. *Goal/Question/Metric Method: A Prac-
             tical Guide for Quality Improvement of Software Development*. McGraw-Hill
             Inc., 1999.

[SB01]   R. Van Solingen and E. Berghout. Integrating Goal-Oriented Measurement
             in Industrial Software Engineering: Industrial Experiences with and Ad-
             ditions to the Goal/Question/Metric Method (GQM). In *METRICS '01:
             Proceedings of the 7th International Symposium on Software Metrics*, page
             246, Washington, DC, USA, 2001. IEEE Computer Society.

[Sch68]   L.E. Schrage. A proof of the optimality of the shortest remaining processing
             time discipline. *Operations Research*, 16(3):687–690, 1968.

[Sch84]   P. Schatte. The M/GI/1 Queue as Limit of Closed Queueing Systems. *Op-
             timization*, 15(1):161–165, 1984.

[SG06]   P.K. Saraswat and P. Gupta. Design and Implementation of a Process Sched-
             uler Simulator and an Improved Process Scheduling Algorithm for Multime-
             dia Operating Systems. In *Proceedings of the International Conference on
             Advanced Computing and Communications (ADCOM 2006)*, pages 513–517,
             2006.

[SGG05]   A. Silberschatz, P. Galvin, and G. Gagne. *Operating System Concepts*. Wiley
             & Sons, 7 edition, January 2005.

[SHB02]   B. Schroeder and M. Harchol-Balter. Web servers under overload: How
             scheduling can help. Technical Report CMU-CS-02-143, Carnegie-Mellon
             University, 2002.

[SHB04]   B. Schroeder and M. Harchol-Balter. Evaluation of Task Assignment Policies for Supercomputing Servers: The Case for Load Unbalancing and Fairness. *Cluster Computing*, 7(2):151–161, 2004.

[SKBB07]   K. Sachs, S. Kounev, J. Bacon, and A. Buchmann. Workload Characterization of the SPECjms2007 Benchmark. In *In Proceedings of the 4th European Performance Engineering Workshop*, volume 4748, pages 228–244, 2007.

[SKCB07]   K. Sachs, S. Kounev, M. Carter, and A. Buchmann. Designing a Workload Scenario for Benchmarking Message-Oriented Middleware. In *Proceedings of the 2007 SPEC Benchmark Workshop*, January 2007.

[SKS92]   N. G. Shivaratri, P. Krueger, and M. Singhal. Load Distributing for Locally Distributed Systems. *IEEE Computer*, 25(12):33–44, 1992.

[Smi80]   C.U. Smith. *The Prediction and Evaluation of the Performance of Software from Extended Design Specifications*. PhD thesis, University of Texas at Austin, 1980.

[Smi90]   C. U. Smith. *Performance Engineering of Software Systems*. Addison-Wesley, Reading, MA, USA, 1990.

[Smi02]   C. U. Smith. *Performance Solutions: A Practical Guide To Creating Responsive, Scalable Software*. Addison-Wesley, 2002.

[SPE]   SPEC. SPECjms2007 Benchmark. http://www.spec.org/jms2007/. Last retrieved 2008-08-16.

[Squ07]   M. S. Squillante. Stochastic analysis of multiserver systems. *SIGMETRICS Perfomance Evaluation Review*, 34(4):44–51, 2007.

[SR05]   D. A. Solomon and M. E. Russinovich. *Microsoft Windows Internals : Windows 2000, Windows XP und Windows Server 2003*. Microsoft Press, 2005.

[SWHB06]   B. Schroeder, A. Wierman, and M. Harchol-Balter. Open versus closed: a cautionary tale. In *NSDI'06: Proceedings of the 3rd conference on 3rd Symposium on Networked Systems Design & Implementation*, pages 239–252, Berkeley, CA, USA, 2006. USENIX Association.

[Tan01]   A. S. Tanenbaum. *Modern Operating Systems*. Prentice Hall, 2nd edition, 2001.

[TCM06]   L. A. Torrey, J. Coleman, and B. P. Miller. A comparison of interactivity in the Linux 2.6 scheduler and an MLFQ scheduler. *Software: Practice and Experience*, 37(4):347–364, 2006.

[Tra]   Kernel Trap. Linux: The Completely Fair Scheduler. `http://kerneltrap.org/node/8059`. Last retrieved 2008-08-16.

[TSC92]   D. Towsley, P. D. Sparaggis, and C. G. Cassandras. Optimal routing and buffer allocation for a class of finitecapacity queueing systems. *IEEE Transactions on Automatic Control*, 37(9):1446–1451, 1992.

[VDGD05]   T. Verdickt, B. Dhoedt, F. Gielen, and P. Demeester. Automatic Inclusion of Middleware Performance Attributes into Architectural UML Software Models. *Transactions on Software Engineering*, 31(8):695–771, 2005.

[VS06]   M. Völter and T. Stahl. *Model-Driven Software Development*. Wiley, 2006.

[WBHB03]   A. Wierman, N. Bansal, and M. Harchol-Balter. A note on comparing response times in the M/GI/1/FB and M/GI/1/PS queues. *Operations Research Letters*, 32(1):73 – 76, 2003.

[Wel02]   L. Wells. Performance Analysis Using Coloured Petri Nets. In *MASCOTS '02: Proceedings of the 10th IEEE International Symposium on Modeling, Analysis, and Simulation of Computer and Telecommunications Systems (MASCOTS'02)*, pages 217–221, Washington, DC, USA, 2002. IEEE Computer Society.

[WHB03]   A. Wierman and M. Harchol-Balter. Classifying scheduling policies with respect to unfairness in an M/GI/1. *ACM SIGMETRICS Performance Evaluation Review*, 31(1):238–249, 2003.

[WHBO05]   A. Wierman, M. Harchol-Balter, and T. Osogami. Nearly insensitive bounds on SMART scheduling. *ACM SIGMETRICS Performance Evaluation Review*, 33(1):205–216, 2005.

[Whi83]   W. Whitt. The Queueing Network Analyzer. *Bell System Technical Journal*, 62:2779–2815, 1983.

[Whi86]   W. Whitt. Deciding which queue to join: Some counterexamples. *Operations Research*, 34(1):55–62, 1986.

[Win77]   W. Winston. Optimality of the shortest line discipline. *Journal of Applied Probability*, 14(1):181–189, 1977.

[Wol89]   R.W. Wolff. *Stochastic Modeling and the Theory of Queues*. Prentice Hall, 1989.

[Woo02]   M. Woodside. Tutorial Introduction to Layered Modeling of Software Performance, May 2002. Last retrieved 2008-01-13.

[WPS02]   M. Woodside, D. Petriu, and K. Siddiqui. Performance-related completions for software specifications. In *ICSE '02: Proceedings of the 24th International Conference on Software Engineering*, pages 22–32. ACM, New York, NY, USA, 2002.

[WS03]   L. G. Williams and C. U. Smith. Making the Business Case for Software Performance Engineering. In *Proceedings of CMG*, 2003. Last retrieved 2008-01-13.

[WVCB01]   C. M. Woodside, V. Vetland, M. Courtois, and S. Bayarov. Resource Function Capture for Performance Aspects of Software Components and Sub-Systems. In *Performance Engineering, State of the Art and Current Trends*, volume 2047 of *Lecture Notes in Computer Science*, pages 239–256. Springer-Verlag Berlin Heidelberg, 2001.

[WW04]   X. Wu and M. Woodside. Performance modeling from software components. *SIGSOFT Software Engineering Notes*, 29(1):290–301, 2004.

[YW98]   T.-Y. Yen and W. Wolf. Performance estimation for real-time distributed embedded systems. *IEEE Transactions on Parallel and Distributed Systems*, 9(11):1125–1136, November 1998.

[YWSHB06]   C.-W. Yang, A. Wierman, S. Shakkottai, and M. Harchol-Balter. Tail asymptotics for policies favoring short jobs in a many-flows regime. *ACM SIGMETRICS Performance Evaluation Review*, 34(1):97–108, 2006.

[ZBLG07]   L. Zhu, N.B. Bui, Y. Liu, and I. Gorton. MDABench: Customized Benchmark Generation using MDA. *Journal of Systems and Software*, 80(2):265–282, 2007.

[ZFH01]   A. Zimmermann, J. Freiheit, and G. Hommel. Discrete Time Stochastic Petri Nets for Modeling and Evaluation of Real Time Systems. In *International Parallel and Distributed Processing Symposium*, 2001.